RIGHTS BEYOND BORDERS

Rights beyond Borders

*The Global Community and the Struggle over
Human Rights in China*

ROSEMARY FOOT

OXFORD

UNIVERSITY PRESS

OXFORD
UNIVERSITY PRESS

Great Clarendon Street, Oxford OX2 6DP
Oxford University Press is a department of the University of Oxford.
It furthers the University's objective of excellence in research, scholarship,
and education by publishing worldwide in

Oxford New York

Athens Auckland Bangkok Bogotá Buenos Aires Calcutta
Cape Town Chennai Dar es Salaam Delhi Florence Hong Kong Istanbul
Karachi Kuala Lumpur Madrid Melbourne Mexico City Mumbai
Nairobi Paris São Paulo Singapore Taipei Tokyo Toronto Warsaw

and associated companies in Berlin Ibadan

Oxford is a registered trade mark of Oxford University Press
in the UK and certain other countries

Published in the United States
by Oxford University Press Inc., New York

British Library Cataloguing in Publication Data

Data available

Library of Congress Cataloging-in-Publication Data
Foot, Rosemary, 1948–
Rights beyond borders: the global community and the struggle over
human rights in China / Rosemary Foot.
p. cm.
Includes bibliographical references and index.
1. Human rights. 2. International relations. 3. Human rights—China.
4. China—Foreign relations—1976– I. Title.
K3240.F66 2000 341.4′81—dc21 00–031352
ISBN 0–19–829775–0 (hbk.)
ISBN 0–19–829776–9 (pbk.)

1 3 5 7 9 10 8 6 4 2

Typeset by J&L Composition Ltd, Filey, North Yorkshire
Printed in Great Britain
on acid-free paper by
T.J. International Ltd
Padstow, Cornwall

Dick, Gail, and Tim

Acknowledgements

Writing a book is both a lonely and a collegial process. Those many solitary hours at the computer terminal are balanced by interaction with many inspiring individuals who are generous enough to share their time and their thoughts, as well as to stand ready to ask the tough questions that are sometimes too difficult to face or formulate when working alone. There are many whom I would like to thank in this regard. Elena Jurado proved to be invaluable as a research assistant. Her scholarly contributions and enthusiasm for the project made an enormous difference to its rate of progress. Red Chan kindly helped with the translation of some Chinese materials into English. During my stay at Princeton University, among the graduate students, Phillip C. Saunders and Erica Strecker Downs engaged in an exchange of ideas and relevant research papers. The following either answered my questions, discussed the issues, provided materials, or offered important perspectives: Philippe Van Amersfoort, Philip Baker, George Black, Helen Brooks, Karen B. Brooks, Gregory Chow, Steve Coffee, Danielle Dilley, Adele Dion, John Everard, Richard Falk, Karen Fierke, Per Fischer, Jerry Fowler, Bennett Freeman, Charles Goddard, Guy Goodwin-Gill, Jonathan Hecht, Lord Howe of Aberavon, Jude Howell, Mike Jendrzejczyk, Sidney Jones, Stephanie Kleine-Ahlbrandt, Arlette Laduguie, Beatrice Larouche, Woo Lee, Kerstin Leitner, Tom Malinowski, David Malone, Susan O'Sullivan, Minxin Pei, Nigel Rodley, Tony Saich, Susan Shirk, Markus Schmidt, Sun Shuyun, Jeff Taylor, Caroline Wilson, Sophia Woodman, Rod Wye, and Phoebe Yang. I am grateful to them all. Numerous colleagues and friends in China were also of great help, but I have chosen not to name them.

Marc Williams of the University of New South Wales provided valuable comments on two of the chapters, and a period of respite (together with an opportunity to see Sydney's incomparable millennium firework display) during the last stages of writing. Colleagues and friends at Oxford University have also been generous in discussing aspects of the study at various crucial turning points. Dominic Byatt at Oxford University Press was particularly encouraging when I took the proposal to him, Amanda Watkins efficiently guided the manuscript through the editorial process, and Hilary Walford proved to be keen-eyed and conscientious as a copy editor. Avi Shlaim offered some of his worldly wisdom, which helped me to take some important decisions at an early stage of the project. Ngaire Woods has made suggestions and points that have set me off on new periods of reflection. Karma Nabulsi has played a similar role, and made several useful comments on an extended outline of the argument, one of which proved to be absolutely central to the shaping of the research. Various anonymous reviewers for the Press also commented on this outline argument, offering important perspectives that I might otherwise have overlooked. Adam Roberts made several incisive comments on a central chapter and Tim Kennedy helped to clarify the argument and make it more accessible. Andrew Hurrell is deserving of especial thanks for taking time out of his own busy schedule to cast his sharp eye over the entire manuscript. All those familiar with Andrew and his work will realize how beneficial that has been, although I must remain responsible for all errors and lapses of judgement.

Funding for this project has come from two main sources: the British Academy, which enabled me to make a research trip to China in the late summer of 1999; and the remainder from Oxford University, via the Social Studies Faculty board, and the Cyril Foster and Related Funds. I am grateful to both institutions for their financial support.

I have dedicated this book to Dick and Gail Ullman and Tim Kennedy, all three of whom helped to make the three months spent at the Center of International Studies, Princeton University, in 1997 an exceptionally productive period. I warmly thank the Center, and its Director, Professor Michael Doyle, for inviting me to take part in its Visiting Fellowship programme. To Dick, Gail, and Tim I would like to offer my profound gratitude for providing the warmth of friendship and emotional support so helpful in pushing this project forward.

Rosemary Foot

Oxford,
January 2000

Contents

Abbreviations

ACP	Africa, the Caribbean, and Pacific
ACWF	All-China Women's Federation
ADB	Asian Development Bank
AI	Amnesty International
AID	Agency for International Development
ANU	Australian National University
APEC	Asia Pacific Economic Cooperation
APL	Administrative Procedural Law
ASEAN	Association of South East Asian Nations
ASEM	Asia–Europe Meeting
CASS	Chinese Academy of Social Sciences
CAT	Committee against Torture
CCP	Chinese Communist Party
CCPR	Covenant on Civil and Political Rights
CDP	China Democracy Party
CEDAW	Convention on the Elimination of All Forms of Discrimination against Women
CFSP	Common Foreign and Security Policy
CL	Criminal Law
CPL	Criminal Procedure Law
CRC	Convention on the Rights of the Child
CSCE	Conference on Security and Cooperation in Europe
CTBT	Comprehensive Test Ban Treaty
DRL	Democracy, Human Rights, and Labor
EBRD	European Bank for Reconstruction and Development
EC	European Community
ECOSOC	Economic and Social Council
EPC	European Political Cooperation
EU	European Union
FBIS	*Foreign Broadcast Information Service*
FDI	foreign direct investment
FRG	Federal Republic of Germany
GATT	General Agreement on Tariffs and Trade
GONGO	government organized non-governmental organization
HRIC	Human Rights in China
IAEA	International Atomic Energy Authority
IBRD	International Bank for Reconstruction and Development

ICCPR	International Covenant on Civil and Political Rights
ICESCR	International Covenant on Economic, Social, and Cultural Rights
ICRC	International Committee of the Red Cross
IMF	International Monetary Fund
MFN	Most Favoured Nation
MOU	Memorandum of Understanding
NAPSNET	North East Asia Peace and Security Network
NGO	non-governmental organization
NPC	National People's Congress
NPT	Non-Proliferation Treaty
NQHR	*Netherlands Quarterly of Human Rights*
NSC	National Security Council
OAS	Organization of American States
ODA	Official Development Assistance
PKO	Peacekeeping Operation
PRC	People's Republic of China
RTL	Re-education through Labour
RWI	Raoul Wallenberg Institute
SIDA	Swedish International Development Cooperation Agency
SWB	BBC Monitoring Reports, *Summary of World Broadcasts*
UDHR	Universal Declaration of Human Rights
UNCHR	UN Commission on Human Rights
UNDOF	UN Disengagement Observer Force
UNDP	UN Development Programme
UNGA	UN General Assembly
UNIFIL	UN Interim Force in Lebanon
UNTAC	UN Transitional Authority in Cambodia
UNTSO	UN Truce Supervision Organization
UPI	United Press International
VNO–NCW	Association of Netherlands Businesses–Netherlands Christian Employers' Association
WAD	Working Group on Arbitrary Detention
WTO	World Trade Organization

1

INTRODUCTION

In conversation with a British foreign office official, I asked him whether he could make an interest-based argument to explain his government's attention to China's human rights record in its external relationship with the country. He replied that he could not, except if one looked—uncharacteristically for policy-makers—to the long term, when an improved level of protection might signal Chinese adherence to a set of values more compatible with those operating in the West. In the short term, he thought, regular reference to human rights conditions in China complicated the practice of diplomacy. Yet, he added, the issue could not be avoided, not as a result of ministerial dictat or with reference solely to a recent, more strongly articulated commitment to an ethical foreign policy, but because the issue area had become central in international diplomacy, and particularly so in the case of the global community's relationship with China.[1]

This book accepts that description of present reality, traces how and why that reality has come about, and shows how the normative concern for human rights has influenced the behaviour of key actors within the global system. By key actors, I am referring to selected non-governmental organizations (NGOs), some national governments, and the United Nations' human rights institutions. The latter have been crucial to the elaboration and legitimation of human rights norms, and in providing a platform upon which governmental and NGO criticisms of abuse can be aired; the NGOs themselves have drawn attention to and provided alternative sources of information about norm violation and compliance. The state, however, has played a vital role in carrying the message forward. It is the body that signs the convention and then produces the requisite domestic legislation. Operating externally, the state may create new

---

[1] Discussions in London, Aug. 1999. The public and media uproar surrounding the UK government's attempts to shield President Jiang Zemin from demonstrations during his state visit to Britain in October 1999 confirms both main parts of this statement.

human rights norms, and then utilize the diplomatic tools at its disposal to promote adherence to international standards on the part of other states in the system. Those states that have an active external human rights policy tend to be the developed democracies, with the USA—where China is concerned—often in the van of events. This relates not simply to their relatively greater ability to make such a policy operational, but also to their self-identities as liberal democracies, which creates particular expectations about domestic and foreign policy behaviour.

The decision to focus on China stems in large part from the special problems that it has posed to the operation of the international human rights regime. Beijing's involvement is important to the regime's future credibility and vitality, because of the country's economic, strategic, and demographic weight in global politics. Those same features, however, raise stark dilemmas for those seeking to promote human rights norms: inaction in the face of evidence of China's human rights violations risks increasing cynicism about the regime's impartiality and consistency of application; action, on the other hand, may spark a reaction on China's part that disrupts the notion that we exist in a normatively based international society, undermining claims to universality and the prospects for world order. Nevertheless, dilemmas exist not just for the leading norm entrepreneurs, but also for the Chinese government, which mostly wishes the country to be identified as a 'responsible great power' by those acting as gatekeepers for entry into this club. Active participation in international institutions and treaty regimes can contribute to the award of such status, but, for a government long associated with a Westphalian definition of state sovereignty and strong attachment to state autonomy, participation poses particular challenges.[2] Moreover, adherence to human rights norms has come to be associated with a state's political legitimacy, an attribute that most governments would want to acquire and would acknowledge contributes to the security of the state in both the domestic and the international realms. Yet participation in the rights regime poses particular threats to an authoritarian government because of the domestic political transformation that full adherence to international standards entails.

These dilemmas and their influence on the international regime are at the heart of the analysis presented here. In terms of some of the more specific questions to be considered, I would like to further an understanding of how and why, for example, democratic governments have

---

[2] Helpful to a discussion of China's policies in an interdependent world is Elizabeth Economy and Michel Oksenberg (eds.), *China Joins the World: Progress and Prospects* (New York: Council on Foreign Relations, 1999).

come to be involved in a diplomatic struggle with Beijing over human rights, despite the difficulties that have been created for other policy goals; what has determined their level of involvement with this issue area; and why different types of policies have been promoted in different phases of the relationship. Turning to China, I would like to explain how and why, in October 1998, the Chinese government reached the stage where it felt it necessary to sign the International Covenant on Civil and Political Rights (ICCPR), an especially significant indication of involvement in the international human rights regime because such action not only generates expectations but also imposes wide-ranging obligations on signatories.[3] The covenant has attained considerable legal authority. Its standing and provisions imply that the legitimacy of states rests on fulfilment of the specified requirements, whereas its reporting elements demonstrate that the boundary between the domestic and the international has lost some of its legal salience. China's signature means that many interested parties stand ever more ready to observe and comment on the extent of the country's compliance with this particular human rights covenant, and implies an acceptance on Beijing's part that its understanding of sovereignty has been redefined to incorporate new notions of legitimate authority.

As will be demonstrated in the chapters that follow, China has been drawn steadily into the discourse on human rights and, apart from signature of the ICCPR, has become a member of such core elements as the UN Commission on Human Rights (UNCHR), has signed the International Covenant on Economic, Social, and Cultural Rights (ICESCR), and has signed and ratified the Convention against Torture, the Convention on the Elimination of All Forms of Discrimination against Women (CEDAW), and the Convention on the Rights of the Child (CRC).[4] Beijing's formal participation began soon after the inauguration of its

[3] State parties, after ratification, undertake to respect and to ensure to all individuals within their states the guarantees of protection inherent in the covenant, and to introduce where necessary domestic legislation that will give effect to the rights embodied within it. Such rights include freedom of association, thought, conscience, expression, movement, and religion. States also commit themselves to submit reports to the Human Rights Committee on measures adopted to give effect to such rights one year after accession and thereafter whenever the committee requests them to do so. See Ian Brownlie (ed.), *Basic Documents on Human Rights,* 3rd edn. (Oxford: Oxford University Press, 1992), pt. two, sects. II, III. China signed the International Covenant on Economic, Social, and Cultural Rights (ICESCR) in Oct. 1997, but undoubtedly it is Beijing's violation of the rights contained in the ICCPR that has attracted most attention, especially those connected with matters of due process, the use of torture, religious repression, arbitrary detention, and widespread use of executions. Thus, the struggle over these particular issues will form the major focus of this study.

[4] The State of Ratifications of Major Human Rights Conventions as of 16 June 1997 can be found in *Netherlands Quarterly of Human Rights,* 3 (1997), App. III.

'open-door' economic reform policies first introduced at the end of 1978. Some twenty or so years later, China has not only signed both major human rights covenants, but has hosted visits by the UN High Commissioner for Human Rights, a UN Working Group, and a Special Rapporteur.[5] Over this period, China's discourse in this issue area has shifted from a conception of rights that derived from the Marxist-Leninist roots of the Chinese Communist Party (CCP), to one that is developmentalist in approach but that gives some ground in the direction of the universality and indivisibility of human rights. Moreover, Beijing's participation in the regime signals acceptance that such domestic matters are a legitimate subject of international concern.

Such a spare summary of China's position, however, is not meant to suggest that there has been linear, forward, movement in China's discursive and behavioural practices since the early 1980s: the violent response to and aftermath of the Tiananmen demonstrations seriously interrupted the process, as have changing levels of regime security, together with variations in the level and type of international pressure. Neither will it be claimed that the evolution that has taken place has resulted in truly fundamental changes and has led to a full internalization of international human rights norms. Instead, policy change is sometimes one of form rather than substance and serious obstacles emerge when new ideas and policies come to be implemented. Indeed, as of the time of writing, neither of the two human rights covenants has actually been ratified, and there is widespread expectation that China will enter several reservations before ratification of these two documents. Moreover, for reasons that will be explained more fully later, the global message on human rights has been transmitted in all its complexity and opaqueness: as a result of inherent tensions in the implementation of foreign policies that purport to include a human rights element; variations among governments in levels of commitment to promoting the human rights regime; and the continued questioning—most recently in parts of East Asia—of the universality of human rights. Nevertheless, the transformation of Chinese discourse in this area, its expanded involvement with this issue, and domestic policy reform in the fields of criminal and other related legislation do represent significant and essential steps on the long road to full acceptance of human rights norms, and remain to be explained.

Clearly, domestic factors have served to deepen China's involvement in

---

[5] The Chinese government has stated that it plans to invite the UN Special Rapporteur on Torture to visit, but, as of February 2000, no date has been set. See China, Information Office of the State Council, 'Progress in China's Human Rights Conditions in 1998', BBC Monitoring Reports, *Summary of World Broadcasts (SWB)*, Asia/Pacific, FE/3509 S1/10, 15 Apr. 1999.

human rights questions, and they have also lain behind the inability of the major democratic states to put the issue aside. The work of 'transnational advocacy networks . . . working internationally on an issue, who are bound together by shared values, a common discourse, and dense exchanges of information and services',[6] and that forge links with domestic groups, is also significant in the explanation. The codification of norms in international treaty form similarly helps with the transmission of ideas across borders. As will be argued later, various domestic groups in China have made use of international standards to press their case for particular provisions in new or revised legislation, empowered not only by the Beijing government's decision to participate in the international human rights regime, but also by its recognition of the value of building a domestic 'rule by law'.[7] These developments show the blurring of the domestic and international boundaries. More broadly, they also help to uncover how norms are diffused in the global system, underlining the view of diffusion both as an evolutionary often non-linear process and as an activity promoted through the seemingly discreet policy decisions of significant global actors, such as individuals, governments, international organizations, and transnational and domestic NGOs.[8]

NORMATIVE DIFFUSION

How norms are diffused in the global system, especially for the many that are without well-defined enforcement procedures, is not well understood. In essence, the explanations that exist can be separated in two main ways:

---

[6] Thomas Risse, Stephen C. Ropp, and Kathryn Sikkink (eds.), *The Power of Human Rights: International Norms and Domestic Change* (Cambridge: Cambridge University Press, 1999), 18.

[7] The domestic arena is not covered in this study in anything like the level of detail that it deserves, constrained by my abilities, the difficulties of researching such a topic from inside the country, and my major interest in the global aspects of this process.

[8] The literature on norms and international relations has grown considerably in recent years. I found the following texts to be particularly helpful to this study: Peter J. Katzenstein (ed.), *The Culture of National Security: Norms and Identity in World Politics* (New York: Columbia University Press, 1996); Audie Klotz, *Norms in International Relations: The Struggle against Apartheid* (Ithaca, NY: Cornell University Press, 1995); Martha Finnemore, *National Interests in International Society* (Ithaca, N.Y.: Cornell University Press, 1996); Harold Hongju Koh, 'Why Do Nations Obey International Law?', *Yale Law Journal*, 106 (1997), 2599–659; Andreas Hasenclever, Peter Mayer, and Volker Rittberger, *Theories of International Regimes* (Cambridge: Cambridge University Press, 1997). The recent edited text by Risse *et al.*, *The Power of Human Rights*, has been particularly useful and will be referred to frequently. See also the review essay by Gregory A. Raymond, 'Problems and Prospects in the Study of International Norms', *Mershon International Studies Review*, 41, supp. 2 (Nov. 1997), 205–45.

norms are either seen as being constitutive and deriving from a set of shared understandings, or are defined as regulating behaviour either in the form of constraints or in allowing certain actions. For realists and institutionalists, it is the regulative aspects that are prominent: governments obey norms either because of a fear of punishment by more powerful actors, or because they provide functional benefits and help actors overcome collective action problems. Self-interested behaviour is thus at the root of this explanation, with the assumption that actors will behave in accordance with the rules as long as it is in their material interest to do so.[9] Constructivists, however, take the world of ideas at least as seriously as the material world in their explanations of international reality, and put the emphasis on the constitutive power of norms. This leads actors to ask questions about their role and identity and the appropriateness of different actions with respect to those qualities. In these circumstances, interests are not seen as fixed but can be remade or shaped by social practices that have the capacity to result in shared understandings, shared values, and a new sense of self. Language, ideas, and knowledge, therefore, are closely connected with the establishment and diffusion of norms and can all be seen as helping to constitute an actor's definition of its identity and interests. Thus democratic states, for example, would be expected to promote those values in their foreign policies as both a reflection and a reinforcement of their identities.

I have not found it helpful in this study to draw on one of these analytical approaches to the exclusion of the other, but have concluded that it is more profitable to pay attention to both the power and the symbolic elements in my explanation of behaviour and discourse. Coercive material and verbal sanctions on the part of democratic governments have influenced Chinese discursive practices and its actions at various moments and to lesser or greater degrees. Political distancing, economic, and military sanctions have all been used for a time, and with some effect, especially where the USA is concerned. State-based institutions have also been of value in carrying norms forward, either as vehicles for legitimating verbal condemnation, or as venues for coordinating activity. As most governments recognize, unilateral action carries special burdens because it implies a lack of support by others, casting doubt on the claim of norm violation. Acting alone may also suggest victory for the domestic interest

---

[9] For a recent, determined exposition of the realist case, see Stephen D. Krasner, *Sovereignty: Organized Hypocrisy* (Princeton: Princeton University Press, 1999), Krasner argues that international rules are contradictory, that there is no authority structure to adjudicate among them, and that the powerful will pick and choose among the variety of rules, only adhering to those that best suit their instrumental aims. (p.6). In my study, state reasoning and action seem far more complicated than this implies.

of the sanctioner over global or common interest, especially crucial in an area where claims of norm violation are based on the idea of international standards. Multilateral action, therefore, is a preferred course and is likely to be more helpful to promoting norms consensually rather than coercively. Multilateralism, however, can be a quite demanding form of action. As I shall demonstrate, the UNCHR has been a valuable multilateral body for drawing attention to a country's human rights failings, and has demonstrated the capacity to call violating states to account and effect some positive change in their behaviour. However, the ability to draft and pass resolutions that censure and heighten the level of exposure of such a state depends on the capacity of a majority of member governments of the UNCHR to act in concert. The ability to form a coalition in support of such symbolic sanctions can not only be affected by the persuasiveness of the presumed violator's refutations, or its capacity, sometimes using material resources of its own, to build its own counter-coalition; it can also be influenced by the perceived reliability of the would-be lead sanctioner: an actor's reputation for being able to stay in step with others and the material or moral weight that it can bring to bear against a norm violator.[10]

The competing interests of governments, especially when those they confront are as powerful as China, undermine their willingness to sustain roles as consistent promoters of human rights norms, a level of vacillation that provides openings for others whose identities are intimately and directly bound up with the protection of rights. Human rights NGOs, for example, are major players in the 'rugby scrum' of actors in this issue area,[11] using methods that rest on forms of power different from those the

[10] Lisa L. Martin's work, although it focuses on material rather than symbolic multilateral sanctions, shows why the UNCHR should provide the kind of setting for effective and coordinated actions, but also why it has not always done so. In nearly every case of sanctions, she notes, one state tends to act as the leader, but it needs to establish that it is serious about the sanctioning activity before it can get others to go along. It also needs to establish the level of support likely to be available to it as it weighs the costs and benefits of the proposed activity. Institutional venues, thus, can be important to the success or otherwise of sanctions, because they provide information about the actions others are prepared to take. They also increase the opportunities for bandwagoning behaviour among states, either because states in such institutions would prefer not to be isolated, or because a failure to cooperate in one area can undermine the chances for cooperation in more highly valued ones. See Martin *Coercive Cooperation: Explaining Multilateral Economic Sanctions* (Princeton: Princeton University Press, 1992).

[11] Koh writes of the 'rugby scrum' in 'Why do Nations Obey International Law?', 2631. Koh became the US Assistant Secretary of State for Democracy, Human Rights and Labor in the second Clinton administration. He has predicted a 'day not very far from now when news of gross human rights violations will be posted daily on centralized intergovernmental bulletin boards and in which the foreign ministers of leading powers, leading governmental actors, and NGO leaders will caucus daily by video internet to formulate

state traditionally uses. For some, they have become major challengers to the centrality of the state. As James Rosenau has put it in more general reference to the plethora of actors in the global system, the world at the end of the twentieth century should be understood not so much as a system dominated by states and governments, but as one involving 'congeries of spheres of authority . . . that are subject to considerable flux and not necessarily coterminous with the division of territorial space'.[12] Human rights NGOs in particular have been identified as alternative points of authority in the global system because of their economic, informational, and intellectual resources, which have given them enough clout to assume authority over matters usually within a state's area of competence and responsibility.[13] In this issue area, they are vital in two respects: first, as sources of information, in verifying and evaluating the extent of normative compliance, and in stimulating governments, organizations, and domestic audiences to act against a norm violator; and, secondly, because the density of their networks ensures some degree of global, public exposure, thus heightening the possibility of shaming the non-compliant. To some degree, they have become one of the gatekeepers in determining which governments are worthy of membership in international society and which are not. Their activities partly compensate for the lack of an enforcement mechanism in the human rights area; they can generate costs of a non-material, mainly reputational, kind that may be borne not simply by the violator but also by those governments that have announced their own commitment to the sustenance of the human rights regime, but that might be failing to act with any consistency in support of it.[14]

As noted above, human rights institutions are important to NGOs and

coordinated responses'. He added: 'And, indeed, I believe that this is a way that we ought to try to move.' See 'Promoting Human Rights in the Pursuit of Peace: Assessing 20 Years of US Human Rights Policy', remarks before the US Institute of Peace, Washington, 30 May 1999, Internet edn. pp.7–8.

[12] James N. Rosenau, *Along the Domestic–Foreign Frontier: Exploring Governance in a Turbulent World* (Cambridge: Cambridge University Press, 1997), 39.

[13] Ann Marie Clark, 'Non-Governmental Organizations and their Influence on International Society', *Journal of International Affairs,* 48/2 (Winter 1995), 508.

[14] This is not to suggest that NGO activities should not be subject to careful scrutiny. Andrew Hurrell notes the 'enormous diversity of voices within the NGO movement and the lack of apparent means of mediating between them or evaluating their representational authority'. He also warns that the power relations within transnational civil society itself may be no more equitable than those in the state system, and that the workings of that civil society may indeed serve to reinforce the disparities in the system. See Andrew Hurrell 'Power, Principles and Prudence: Protecting Human Rights in a Deeply Divided World', in Tim Dunne and Nicholas J. Wheeler (eds.), *Human Rights in Global Politics* (Cambridge: Cambridge University Press, 1999), 289–90.

to governments in providing venues for the articulation of a verbal sanctioning policy. But institutions are also significant actors in their own right when it comes to diffusing norms. The annual gatherings of experts and of member governments for human rights meetings raise the profile of the issue area and the level of active diplomacy engaged in by those who suspect their records might come under scrutiny, whether or not their practices actually lead to the formulation of draft condemnatory resolutions. China's concern to win support for its 'no-action' resolution at the UNCHR, and stringent efforts to substitute private debate over its record for the UN public condemnatory route, are a testament to the power of such institutions. Should the UNCHR neglect consideration of the record of a state with a poor level of protection, treaty reporting requirements, and the work and reports of the Special Rapporteurs and Working Groups, remain part of the human rights calendar and produce a further documentary record of the types and levels of abuse.

It is an obvious statement to make, but human rights institutions exist in order to discuss human rights matters and they provide the prime opportunity for member governments and others to engage in rights talk. My research has led me to take this activity and therefore constructivist method seriously in trying to explain evolutionary developments in a normative area that has no direct enforcement mechanisms associated with it. Compliance with human rights norms is voluntary, unless non-compliance can be linked with the denial of benefits in other issue areas. Where that linkage is difficult to establish, we rely on moral persuasion, the power of argument, and the power of shaming in order for these standards to take effect. Other factors in these circumstances of voluntary compliance are also important, such as the domestic salience of the norm, its legitimacy and coherence, and the extent to which it fits with other prevailing and well-established standards;[15] but norms are expressed through language and the process of argumentation and debate can shape what is said subsequently in both domestic and international venues.

---

[15] Thomas Franck points towards the 'compliance pull' of norms that have come into being and operate 'in accordance with generally accepted principles of right process'. See his *The Power of Legitimacy among Nations* (New York: Oxford University Press, 1990), 24. The nature of the supporting normative environment can also affect the levels of compliance. Success in one normative area 'strengthens and legitimates claims in logically and morally related' areas. See Martha Finnemore, 'Constructing Norms of Humanitarian Intervention', in Katzenstein (ed.) *Culture of National Security*, 161. See also Finnemore and Kathryn Sikkink, 'International Norms Dynamics and Political Change', *International Organization*, 52/4 (Autumn 1998); Andrew P. Cortell and James W. Davis, Jr., 'How do International Institutions Matter? The Domestic Impact of International Rules and Norms', *International Studies Quarterly*, 40 (1996), 451–78.

To take this further: there is general acceptance that, whenever feasible, and because of the material and non-material benefits of reputation, predictability, and reciprocity, states prefer to operate in accordance with recognized norms. In order to explain the breach of a rule, therefore, governments often find it necessary to use language strategically, to justify or rationalize such non-compliance. However, at a later stage, that strategic use of language can impose constraints: in these circumstances states may find that they have become so entangled in their justification that the political outcome is removed from the governments' original intention.[16] Moreover, they may often seek to justify their behaviour through reference to other parts of the normative landscape, thereby and possibly inadvertently adding weight to the idea that we operate in a normative community. These speech acts give prominence to values that are shared by other public groups and decision-makers: justification 'is literally an attempt to connect one's actions to standards of justice, or perhaps more generically, to standards of appropriate and acceptable behavior.'[17] This discourse—that is, the process of argument, exposition, and persuasion—among states, international organizations, and individuals has been described as 'the characteristic method by which international regimes seek to induce compliance . . . Persuasion and argument are the principal engines of this process.' However, if an actor remains unwilling to fulfil expectations, 'the possibility of diffuse manifestations of disapproval or pressures from other actors in the regime is present in the background.'[18]

In the absence of direct material costs, disapproval matters only to states that are concerned about reputation, are capable of being shamed, and are sensitive to the exposure of a gap between stated commitment and actual practice. Shaming is an important form of action because it is bound up with state identity, with the idea of belonging to a normative community of states, with civilized behaviour, or with being an insider or outsider.[19] Those insider qualifications have undoubtedly developed, particularly in the period since the 1970s, as Chapter 2 will illustrate in more

---

[16] Karen Fierke, *Changing Games, Changing Strategies: Critical Investigations in Security* (Manchester: Manchester University Press, 1998), 6–7.

[17] Finnemore, 'Constructing Norms', 159

[18] Abram Chayes and Antonia Handler Chayes, *The New Sovereignty: Compliance with International Regulatory Agreements* (Cambridge, Mass.: Harvard University Press, 1995) 25–6.

[19] On the matter of shaming, the importance of recognition, and esteem, see Jon Elster, *The Cement of Society: A Study of Social Order* (Cambridge: Cambridge University Press, 1989); John B. Braithwaite, *Crime, Shame and Reintegration* (Cambridge: Cambridge University Press, 1989); and Axel Honneth, *The Struggle for Recognition: The Moral Grammar of Social Conflicts* (Cambridge: Polity Press, 1995).

detail. This suggests that the rules of sovereignty are by no means fixed: sovereignty cannot be viewed solely as relating to the 'freedom of states to act independently, in their perceived self-interest', or simply as control over territory and those residing within it, but, in the contemporary international system marked by interdependence and a proliferation of international regimes and institutions, it also means being in 'reasonably good standing in the regimes that make up the substance of international life.' It is this 'need to be an accepted member in this complex web of international arrangements' that aids compliance with agreements and norms.[20]

Indeed, since the ending of the cold war, this matter of good standing appears to have been further specified and to have gone beyond adherence to customary rules and regime commitments and has begun to embrace the idea that legitimate sovereignty rests on the practice of democratic governance and humane treatment of one's citizens: that the new international 'standard of civilization' has come to include the acceptance of internationally recognized human rights.[21] Robert G. Herman has argued in reference to the revolutionary change in Soviet foreign policy under Gorbachev and connected with a desire to establish a new 'insider' identity for the former Soviet Union: 'It was becoming clear to a growing number of reformers that the USSR could not take its place among the world's "civilized nations" if it insisted on violating at home and abroad the norms of behavior governing Western democratic regimes' treatment of their own citizens and relations between member states of that community.' Reformers of both a radical and more moderate persuasion wanted the Soviet Union to become a 'normal country', where normality

---

[20] Chayes and Chayes, *The New Sovereignty*, 27. Franck agrees. In *The Power of Legitimacy* he writes that there is 'dramatic evidence that obligations are perceived to arise in the international community as an incident of a state's status as a member of the community' (p.190).

[21] Franck (*Fairness in International Law and Institutions* (Oxford: Oxford University Press, 1995)), emphasizing the democracy aspects of the new standards, writes of a 'newly emerging international law, requiring democratization to validate governance' and that is 'finding its way into codes of regional and global standards and into the practice and jurisprudence of international institutions' (p.85). Jack Donnelly describes such thoughts as being 'serious exaggeration' (and I agree with respect to international institutions). But in reference more specifically to the human rights issue Donnelly also notes that 'human rights represent a progressive late twentieth century expression of the important idea that international legitimacy and full membership in international society must rest in part on standards of just, humane or civilized behaviour'. He goes on, 'despite the continuing split between national and international law embodied in dominant conceptions of sovereignty, the society of states has come to accept that our common humanity makes the way in which any state treats its citizens a legitimate concern of other states, foreign nationals and international society'. See 'Human Rights: A New Sandard of Civilization?', *International Affairs*, 74/1 (Jan. 1998), esp. 21, 18.

was defined partly in political terms as a country that respected individual rights and that had established the rule of law.[22]

This rethinking of the basis for membership in 'civilized' international society has gone on well beyond the former Soviet bloc, and manifests itself in the charters of the Organization of American States (OAS), the Conference on Security and Cooperation in Europe (CSCE), and the Council of Europe, among others. The commitment to democratic principles of governance and the validation of the right to govern on the basis of such principles are particularly prominent features, followed often by a somewhat dangerous assumption that human rights protections will of necessity improve as a result of the introduction of democratic practices.[23] Although the supremacy of that democratic entitlement may be contested elsewhere in the global system, or honoured more in the breach than in the fulfilment, nevertheless, by the mid-1990s, some 130 governments had announced a legal commitment to holding open, multiparty, elections based on a secret ballot and universal franchise. What is more, there has been a move towards international validation of those electoral processes, as governments use international observers to confirm the fairness of the result to undermine the basis for any internal challenge to the authority of the newly elected. Further evidence of this blurring between the domestic and international spheres has come with the additional accessions or ratifications of the ICCPR: as of June 1997, some 138 states

[22] Robert G. Herman, 'Identity, Norms and National Security: The Soviet Foreign Policy Revolution and the End of the Cold War', in Katzenstein (ed.), *Culture of National Security*, 296–7. In the late 1980s, the Soviet Foreign Minister, Eduard Shevardnadze, said much the same thing to an audience of Soviet diplomats: 'The image of a state is its attitude towards its own citizens, respect for their rights and freedoms, and recognition of the sovereignty of the individual' (quoted in Geoffrey Howe, the Rt Hon. Lord Howe of Aberavon, 'Opening Speech', at Amnesty International London Seminar on Human Rights in China, 9 Sept. 1996, 2). The extent to which this desire has been sustained and these norms have 'stuck' with respect to the Russian Federation are in considerable doubt and would take us into the area of consolidation of norms. Consolidation requires both an élite and a broad societal consensus about the validity of the norms, and their successful embedding in legal and institutional regimes. Koh ('Why do Nations Obey International Law?') is particularly helpful on this point.

[23] See Franck, *Fairness*, esp. 85–120. He reports, for example, that the OAS on 5 June 1991 adopted a crucial resolution, which in its preamble states that the 'principles of the OAS Charter "require the political representation of [member] states to be based on effective exercise of representative democracy" and in its operative sections the resolution provides that the Organization's Secretary General shall "call for the immediate convocation of a meeting of the Permanent Council in the event of any occurrences giving rise to the sudden or irregular interruption of the democratic political institutional process or of the legitimate exercise of power by the democratically elected government in any of the Organization's member states" ' (p. 113). On the dangerous assumption that civilian, democratic government has resulted in increased respect for human rights in the Americas, see Hurrell, 'Power, Principles and Prudence', 281.

had acceded and thereby subjected themselves to scrutiny by a Human Rights Committee of eighteen nationals serving in their personal capacities. Some ninety-two states among that 138 had signed the optional protocol that allows individuals to petition against a state party alleged to be violating any provision of the covenant.

Normative diffusion in the human rights area seems, then, to be driven by a combination of factors: powerful states (with the US role being particularly important), NGO pressure, institutions, the new criteria for membership of international society, and the processes of persuasion, argument, and shaming. But it is also important to note that target states are not simply passive, sponge-like, bodies floating downstream in the currents of this environment in an unresisting or uncontested way. The degree to which these elements can shape behaviour varies from state to state, and depends not only on an acceptance that reputation matters, and a capacity to experience shame, but also on such factors as material power, demographic size, degree of openness, and political culture. Robert Keohane and Helen Milner, for example, in their study of the linkages between national economies and the world economy, note the extent to which the impact of the international is mediated at the level of the state: 'Differences in factor endowments, group organization, national institutions and the political strategies of leaders have all helped produce diverse national responses to common international trends.'[24] Other authors, working specifically on human rights, have pointed to 'blocking factors' such as certain forms of popular nationalism, the presence of secessionist movements, threats to territorial integrity, or particular value structures.[25] Resistant governments can either decide to ride out the storm, try to use a competing norm to attack the validity of the one in contention, or explore its lack of specificity to find negotiating leeway. Human rights norms, for example, have been countered often with an appeal to Article 2 (7) of the UN Charter and its emphasis on non-interference in the domestic affairs of states, although increasingly that particular line of argument carries less weight for reasons already outlined connected with the new sovereignty. The current weaknesses of the non-interference argument have meant that those targeted as human rights abusers now more often appeal to the broad-based nature of the human rights regime, and to the continuing universalist/relativist debate, in the hope of countering charges of bad behaviour in one area with evidence of

---

[24] Robert O. Keohane and Helen V. Milner (eds.), *Internationalization and Domestic Politics* (New York: Cambridge University Press, 1996), 14.

[25] Risse, *et al.* (eds.), *The Power of Human Rights*, 260–2.

compliance in another aspect of the regime. An appeal on such a basis may indeed undercut the force of any leverage being exerted to effect change in a human rights record.

THE GLOBAL COMMUNITY AND CHINA

This brief overview of ideas associated with normative diffusion and the role of actors in that process provides the conceptual context for the study that is to come. International human rights norms affect the behaviour of all the actors of interest to this study, and, it is argued, their behaviour in response to those norms helps constitute that environment. Those that I shall identify as most active in the process of promotion, and whose identities are closely or directly bound up with the idea of human rights, have contributed considerably to the deepening of the human rights regime over the period since 1945, a deepening that is the focus of Chapter 2. Of influence too has been the iterative process that the regime has brought into being. China has been a 'latecomer' to the regime, and has responded to a framework largely established before its more active global participation. It entered the UNCHR in 1982, for example, when human rights ideas had already achieved greater salience, a timing that circumscribed Beijing's ability to mount a significant challenge to the codified norms, assuming that it wanted to do so.[26] In later years, however, as it came to understand better the workings of the regime, it was more active and less reactive, able to influence it in ways that will be illustrated in the final two chapters of this study.

   Although China is a latecomer to this and other regimes that make up the substance of contemporary international society, it is, of course, no stranger to the idea of having to satisfy the entry requirements for membership in the international society of states. This historical experience has influenced the nature of its response to current demands and contributed to its *realpolitik* outlook and approach. The early nineteenth century witnessed the breach of the walls that had ensured the separation between China and the West, and the challenge to the Chinese belief that it represented the height of civilization and consequently was the focal point of the universe. The tribute system as a means of dealing with outsiders had reflected this particular understanding, only to be rudely shoved aside by Europeans as they expanded across the globe. China's

---

[26] Risse, *et al.* (ibid. 19–22) make use of the idea of 'world time' and 'norms cascade' in the development of their spiral model of human rights socialization.

inability to put up much resistance led its diplomatic and trading practices in the late nineteenth and early twentieth centuries to reflect those of the dominant European powers. The standard to be satisfied in order for China to gain 'civilized' status, as these countries defined it, involved the protection of the lives and property of foreign nationals; the conduct of diplomatic relations through the institutions of ambassadors and a foreign ministry; and the embrace of international law. Importantly, China's adaptation had consequences for the originators of the diplomatic code, as the government then demonstrated how the criteria could be used against standard-setting states, much as European colonies were to use the originally Western norm of self-determination to lobby for their independence. China, too, used its growing knowledge of international law to develop an argument that the unequal treaties and extraterritoriality imposed upon it by the West after 1842 should be removed. However, even before the removal of these symbols of inequality, the treatment of China began to suggest the country's growing acceptance into international society. The First World War, which marked the start of China's more assertive international diplomacy, and the deliberate casting of its lot with the Allied powers during that conflict, saw China enter into the League of Nations and, with the support of Britain and France, membership of the League Council in 1920, a valued indication of acceptance.[27]

China's membership in international society was not to be in contention again until 1949, with the establishment of the People's Republic (PRC). Beijing's embrace of Marxism-Leninism–Mao Zedong Thought and preference for fraternity with the socialist bloc, together with its direct military clash with UN Command forces during the Korean War between 1950 and 1953, led to its exclusion from most aspects of international society that signified full membership. The government in Beijing remained outside the UN until 1971, the place for China reserved to the alternative seat of government in Taipei, a denial of recognition that struck at the heart of Beijing's claims to legitimate sovereign rule. Beijing was also cut off from bilateral diplomatic relationships with a majority of the world's countries until the 1970s, and from membership of the International Monetary Fund (IMF) and the International Bank

---

[27] Extra territoriality was not to be removed until 1943. For literature that explores the concept of 'standard of civilization' and China's experiences with that, see Gerrit W. Gong, *The Standard of 'Civilization' in International Society* (Oxford: Oxford University Press, 1984); Gong, 'China's Entry into International Society', in Hedley Bull and Adam Watson (eds.), *The Expansion of International Society*, (Oxford: Oxford University, 1984); Yongjin Zhang, *China in the International System, 1918–20: The Middle Kingdom at the Periphery* (Basingstoke: Macmillan 1991).

for Reconstruction and Development (IBRD)—the World Bank—until 1980. Some part of this isolation might have been self-imposed, but other aspects were indeed brought on by external forces,[28] with the USA playing the major role in ensuring the PRC's containment.

The Sino-American *rapprochement* of 1972 marked the initial phase of Beijing's more active international involvement. In the 1970s, China established diplomatic relations with some seventy-two countries, bringing the total to 124 by the end of the decade. Nevertheless, until 1978 the PRC was still recognizably Maoist China, still challenging in certain respects the international status quo. Although it became a member of the UN Security Council in 1971, its passivity was marked, in part because it was learning the rules of the game, but also because it still failed to deem the UN a significant aspect of its foreign policy, or an important independent actor in its own right.[29] Not until Deng Xiaoping had consolidated his position from December 1978 did this begin to change. Vigorously introducing his economic reform agenda, Deng set about reversing China's previous separation from the main currents of international discourse. It marked the start of yet another search to establish China's rightful place in global society, to put behind it that so-called century of humiliation beginning in the 1840s, and become a prosperous, successful, country able to hold up its head proudly. With international assistance on a grand scale, (for example, China became the major recipient of World Bank assistance from the mid-1980s), Deng set out to modernize China in ways never previously tried in the thirty years of socialism. The government also developed an omnidirectional foreign policy, improving ties wherever and whenever it could, especially with its neighbouring countries: the former Soviet Union, India, South East Asian states, among others, were all to experience a Chinese willingness to resolve, or put to one side, issues long in dispute. As well as joining the IMF and the World Bank and applying for GATT membership, Beijing began to take a more active part in other international institutions, including participation in the formerly reviled activity of UN peacekeeping from the early 1980s, and in 1989 seeking membership of the UN Special Committee on Peacekeeping Operations. It also began to sign a number of international conventions: fifteen in the period 1971–6, but

---

[28] For an argument that China was not isolated but was alienated from the international system, see Yongjin Zhang, *China in International Society since 1949: Alienation and Beyond* (Basingstoke: St Antony's/Macmillan, 1998).

[29] Samuel S. Kim, 'China's International Organizational Behaviour', in Thomas W. Robinson and David Shambaugh (eds.), *Chinese Foreign Policy: Theory and Practice* (Oxford: Oxford University Press, 1994), 395, and, more generally for this paragraph, Kim, *China, the United Nations and World Order* (Princeton: Princeton University Press, 1979).

between 1977 and 1987 some 103, including in 1986 the Convention against Torture (although lodging some important reservations) four years after Beijing had become a member of the UNCHR.[30] The reaction of the major states in the global system to China's growing enthusiasm for participation in international society was mostly positive, tempered only by fears that its full inclusion would not coincide with or precede its rise to great power status.

The extent of this fuller participation in international society will be explored in Chapters 3 and 4. Chapter 3 details China's enhanced international engagement after its decision to embark on fundamental economic reform in December 1978. These reforms entangled China in particular international commitments, changed its relationship with the global community, and also resulted in greater external exposure of and knowledge about its state–society relations. Moreover, this coincided with significant developments in the international human rights regime, which further undermined the separation between the domestic and the external and resulted in increased attention to the treatment of individuals and groups within many societies. Chapter 4 will focus more directly on China's encounter with human rights norms in the period 1976 to 1989, and its new explorations of the concept of human rights via membership of the UNCHR. It will also examine the role of the transnational NGO, Amnesty International (AI),[31] the US Congress, together with the more open Chinese discussion of the abuses that took place during the Cultural Revolution of 1966 to 1976, in drawing attention to human rights conditions within the country.

Chapter 5 underlines the dramatic sharpening of that focus as a result of the Tiananmen bloodshed in June 1989. Tiananmen was a critical turning point for the human rights issue: for the Chinese, of course, but also for the global community in its relationship with China, which began to focus particularly on the civil and political rights that were subject to abuse. With the USA taking the lead, material and symbolic sanctions were imposed on Beijing, generating a range of responses from defiance to compromise. From then on, Beijing began to be drawn more

---

[30] For participation in international organizations, see Kim, 'China's International Organizational Behaviour' p.406, table 15.1; for the information on international conventions, see Kim, 'Thinking Globally in Post-Mao China', *Journal of Peace Research*, 27/2 (1990), 193.

[31] Amnesty's first report on China, *Political Imprisonment in the People's Republic of China,* (London, 1978), focused on arbitrary arrest, the use of torture to extract confessions, and long-term detention without trial. These issues, together with particular concern about Tibetans, and the frequent use of executions, have been the main issues of concern to those that have paid attention to China's human rights record, as will become clear in the chapters that follow.

actively—if reluctantly—into the international discourse on rights and into behaviour that signalled its acceptance that outsiders legitimately could comment on conditions inside the country. Chapters 5–8 describe this behaviour, but also pay considerable attention to the evolution in China's language of rights, and the way in which this discursive process shaped what the leadership and others inside China said at later stages of the struggle, both to domestic and to international audiences. This approach has been adopted because of what I have described earlier as the constraining power of language, but also because China is a country where formalized language has long played an important role in helping to constitute the structure of power within the political system. Although control over both avenues and forms of political expression has become more difficult to effect as a result of technological and informational developments, the Party-State still acts, from time to time, to deny access to a wider audience to those who persist in using linguistic formulations deemed incorrect, dangerous, or inappropriate. Thus, close examination of official Chinese political discourse remains a valuable means of gaining insight into the way the core leadership wants policy to be understood and presented. Changes in terminology give insight into policy developments and into the image Chinese leaders want the reader or observer to have of their country.[32] But it is also the case, as argued above, that the language of justification can serve to entangle a state—and China is no exception—in a normative community, and can force it to argue, discuss, and exchange views on the basis of the interpretation of norms, rather than on the validity of the norms themselves.

These chapters are also designed to illustrate that the Chinese government does indeed care about its international image and reputation and thus is capable of being shamed for non-adherence to international standards. Beijing's energetic actions designed to deter the possible passage of condemnatory resolutions at the annual meetings of the UNCHR are one means by which this concern for image can be demonstrated. But particular complexities do arise when considering this matter in reference to China: Beijing's self-identity—that is, the community that matters to it when questions of image arise—was in considerable flux over the last half of the twentieth century, if not for longer than that. Chinese are non-Western, non-white, former victims of Western colonialism and still relatively poor in GNP per capita terms; but they also have the longest continuous political tradition in recorded history, an enviable record of

---

[32] Much insight into this area can be had from reading Michael Schoenhals, *Doing Things with Words in Chinese Politics* (Berkeley and Los Angeles: Institute of East Asian Studies, University of California Center for Chinese Studies, 1992).

cultural achievement through to the eighteenth century, nuclear weapons, membership of the UN Security Council, and the world's largest population. These contradictions have contributed to the fact that Communist China post-1949 has had no durable answer to the questions 'Who are we?' 'What is it that distinguishes us from others?' 'What is important about being Chinese?'[33] Being able to respond reasonably consistently to such questions is important to the security of all states: it helps a state find like-minded others, which may bolster the legitimacy of a regime, and suggest that its domestic and social order can generate the respect and validation of outsiders. It also increases the possibility of working with others in successful pursuit of particular international objectives. Without this durable sense of self, it is difficult for the state in question or its major interlocutors to anticipate future policy stances, thus increasing uncertainty in an already uncertain world. Over the last decade or so, on many occasions we have seen a China that wants to establish the identity of responsible great power. Its constant references to its adherence to and signature of nearly all the major conventions that give current meaning to international life—whether that is the Non-Proliferation Treaty (NPT) or the Comprehensive Test Ban Treaty (CTBT), or the international human rights regime—or its hosting of or participation in all major UN conferences, imply Beijing's acceptance that regime involvement is related to a reputation as a responsible great power. Nevertheless, China also often depicts itself as champion of the developing countries and as the victim of oppressive, hegemonic, forces in the 1990s, much as it had been in its past. It is these developing countries that tend to support Beijing when China resolutions are brought to the vote at the annual UNCHR meeting, suggesting the value of membership in this group. China's sometime identity as a leading member of the developing world also requires an emphasis less on its support of international standards and action, and more on a definition of sovereignty that privileges the domestic realm: that emphasizes territorial control, state autonomy, and non-interference in domestic affairs. Chinese nationalism then is constantly being pitted against its internationalism, and its great power identity against its developing country identity, contributing to our uncertainty about the

---

[33] Lowell Dittmer and Samuel S. Kim (eds.), *China's Quest for National Identity* (Ithaca, N Y: Cornell University Press, 1993), particularly the editors' ch.1 and the chapter by Peter Van Ness, 'China as a Third World State: Foreign Policy and Official National Identity', esp. 198) has proved helpful for this section. See also Lowell Dittmer, 'China's Search for its Place in the World', in Brantly Womack (ed.), *Contemporary Chinese Politics in Historical Perspective* (New York: Cambridge University Press, 1991), and Gilbert Rozman, 'China's Quest for Great Power Identity', *Orbis*, 43/3 (Summer 1999). Rozman argues that the 'notion of China as a great power (*daguo*) has gained a clear-cut victory' over other possible identities (see p. 385).

route it is travelling and the difficulties of understanding its strategic policy goals.

Unsurprisingly, this nationalism and search for community with the like-minded among its neighbours and in parts of the developing world marked China's approach to human rights questions immediately after Tiananmen, leading it to project the global, particularly Western, criticism of these events as part of a wider pattern of division and disharmony between the West and the rest. However, it was not long before China found itself in a position to utilize its great power attributes in order to weaken those divisions between Beijing and the major states in the global community. Its UN Security Council role and potential use of the veto during the Gulf War, its economic resurgence from 1992, and its regional activity in support of the nuclear non-proliferation norm during the high point of the nuclear crisis with North Korea in 1994 assisted that movement over the early 1990s. Nevertheless, China's claims to full entry into the club of responsible great powers remained under challenge, because its main critics—particularly the USA and its Western allies— were unable to overlook entirely China's human rights record in the course of their other dealings with the country.[34]

This inability on the part of the major states to ignore the human rights dimension in relations with Beijing after the Tiananmen bloodshed is the other major focus of this study. The explanation for that continuing, if weakening, concern for China's human rights record rests on three main and related factors. In the period since the 1970s, there has been the explicit introduction of human rights elements into the foreign policies of many states and of regional bodies such as the European Union (EU), although such concerns have had to compete—not often successfully— with other major state interests. Among such governments, the USA has played a leading, if blemished, role, in putting legislation on the books at an early stage (1974), in electing a President who became—whatever Carter's short-term failures in terms of implementation—closely identified with a concern for international human rights, and in developing mechanisms for ensuring that the human rights dimension became embedded in US bureaucratic procedures.[35] Coterminously with these

---

[34] NGOs remained staunch critics throughout, of course, thereby constraining acceptance of China's full membership of international society.

[35] Chinese and other commentators have often argued that the USA has deeper purposes in mind with respect to Beijing: for example, China's peaceful evolution and its embrace of a value system compatible with that operating in the USA; or the utilization of human rights as a weapon designed to undermine or contain China's rising power. Although I would agree that US administrations have sought by various means to draw China into international society and to encourage its adherence to international norms, I see little evidence to suggest that US administrations have assumed either that 'peaceful

individual state decisions were moves at the UN level that reinforced and reflected this changing level of commitment to human rights protections. UNCHR members decided to take more seriously responsibilities for stopping human rights violations wherever they might occur, and not solely, as in the earlier period, in relation to racism and colonialism. Among other matters, this led to an increase in the numbers of UN Special Rapporteurs and Working Groups charged to investigate reported violations in particular countries and of particular kinds, and after 1993 the appointment of a UN High Commissioner for Human Rights. This deepening of international concern about human rights has continued to gather pace: at the end of the 1990s, for example, we saw the establishment of international criminal courts to try those charged with the violation of human rights in Rwanda and Bosnia, a treaty designed to create an International Criminal Court, and the appointment of a UN Secretary General committed to human rights and to promoting the idea that there is nothing in the UN Charter to preclude the recognition that there are 'rights beyond borders'. Finally, and of vital importance to the thickening of this normative structure over this period, there has been the vast increase in the numbers of human rights NGOs. They have played a major role as sources of information to UN bodies, governments, and individuals. As activist organizations, they expose not only the wrong-doing of the human rights violator, but also the failure of the inter-national community to react to evidence of abuse.

For those states that had accepted that their membership in the democratic community of states implied certain obligations, the problems in designing a China policy became threefold: finding the most appropriate means of sustaining a commitment to the human rights regime in the face of competing policy priorities; maintaining a common front with like-minded governments in venues such as the UNCHR, or at meetings of the Group of 7/8; and discovering a way of balancing their commitments to the economic well-being and security of their own domestic con-stituents, while remaining responsive to the demands of domestic and transnational human rights advocates.

The shocking scenes associated with Tiananmen and its immediate aftermath, as Chapter 5 shows, briefly reduced the complexities sur-rounding these three areas: for a time, there was a reasonably common

evolution' is anything other than a complex and long-term project, beyond the life of indi-vidual US administrations, or that China's involvement in the human rights regime will be sufficient to ensure compatability of values, or containment of its power. For a recent Chinese analysis of US intentions, see Zhu Feng, 'Human Rights Problems and Current Sino-American Relations', in Peter Van Ness (ed.), *Debating Human Rights: Critical Essays from the United States and Asia* (London: Routledge, 1999).

front domestically and internationally, sanctions were imposed, and contact with Chinese officials at the highest levels mostly denied. However, governments found these sanctions difficult to sustain as they sought Chinese cooperation within the UN Security Council, and as potentially lucrative economic contracts with an economy returning to double-digit growth rates were dangled before them. The US attempt to maintain the linkage between human rights improvements and China's Most Favoured Nation (MFN) trading status finally foundered in 1994 as a result of astute lobbying by the Chinese government and the US business community. Nevertheless, as Chapter 6 demonstrates, despite the weakening of material human rights sanctions, Western governments could not entirely avoid the burden of their obligations to the international human rights regime. Governments turned their attention to bodies such as the UNCHR and its independent Sub-Commission, institutions that could help to resolve collective action problems by providing information about what others were prepared to countenance in this area of policy. Collective action in these venues might offer something of a shield against possible Chinese economic or political retribution. Their multilateral nature also served to enhance the legitimacy of any criticism of China's record, and, furthermore, seemed to yield some results: despite the UN Commission's inability to do much other than verbally condemn China, the Beijing government fought hard to prevent that formal condemnation, offering some compromises, including promises to sign the international covenants, release selected dissidents, and agree to allow visits to China arranged under UN auspices. However, Beijing also made use of its hard and soft power attributes, using its diplomatic and economic muscle to break down the cover provided by multilateral action and warn governments that they would have to bear material costs for being so bold as to criticize Beijing. China also began to develop its own arguments concerning the nature of human rights, partially aligning itself with the then so-called miracle economies of East Asia in their espousal of the concept of 'Asian Values', and launching attacks on the rights records of its major critics.

Chapters 6 and 7 demonstrate that, between 1992 and 1997, the UN Commission route coexisted with relatively low-key unofficial, sometimes official, bilateral human rights dialogues with China, and the routine raising of human rights cases in bilateral meetings with Chinese leaders as part of a package of state-to-state negotiation that often included strategic and economic questions. However, at the end of this period, and as a result of an intensification of Chinese lobbying, together with Beijing's acceptance that it would finally have to make good on some of the policy promises it had made at earlier stages of the debate, the voting coalition within the UNCHR fell apart. The ostensible argument for the fissure was that the yearly voting ritual had not borne fruit, condemnatory resolutions were regularly being blocked by China's successful use of no-action resolutions, and that this in itself was exposing the weaknesses inherent in UN mechanisms and risked undermining their future effectiveness. It was often argued, too, that China had to be given some credit for certain of the compromises it had made or would make, that the Beijing government had embarked on the long road of legal reform, and that the moment had come for Western states to offer, or step up, their practical assistance with that task.

Thus, private bilateral human rights dialogues, in the spirit of 'consensus' not 'confrontation' as China termed it, won out from 1997. Beijing presented this outcome as a victory, true to some extent because it meant that human rights discussions were far less transparent, and were often to involve foreign ministry officials, who constantly had a range of other issues before them in their negotiations with China, as Chapters 7 and 8 will detail. This move to bilateralism also made it more difficult to shift back to the UN venue, should governments have wished to do so, except under the most exceptional of circumstances. Beijing had largely succeeded in depicting the UNCHR as a confrontational arena, one example among a number that demonstrated China's own impact on the international human rights regime, together with its influence on the discursive practices of its major interlocutors. However, in the course of shifting from the UN forum to the private bilateral dialogue, China had to move beyond promises and actually satisfy certain governmental demands: releasing high-profile dissidents, signing the two UN covenants, allowing the UN Working Group on Arbitrary Detention into the country, and inviting the UN High Commissioner for Human Rights to visit. Moreover, as Chapter 8 shows, once the private dialogues had been substituted for the draft resolution at the UN, there was NGO and other pressure on those engaged in the exchanges to show results, and a heightening of tension over them as China tightened its political controls in 1999, its year of portentous anniversaries.

With respect to the critical USA–China relationship, even though political compromises were forced on both sides in order that the two Jiang–Clinton summits would go ahead in autumn 1997 in the USA, and June 1998 in China, their success or otherwise was almost entirely judged in reference to the human rights aspects of the meetings. A major result of these summits was to prompt the US administration to participate in legal training in China, well behind those such as the Canadian government, the Ford Foundation, or Sweden's Raoul Wallenberg Institute (RWI) in that particular policy area. The message President Clinton tried to promote at these meetings both to the central leadership and to the wider Chinese society was one that reflected the concept of legitimate sovereignty outlined above: if China truly wanted to become and to be recognized as a great power, it needed to have an open society, one that was receptive to new information and ideas; in order to achieve real greatness, it had to find a means of dealing consensually with the unsettling or destabilizing effects of such diverse ideas. For his part, President Jiang Zemin agreed to public debate over human rights, signalling to domestic and international audiences that China had become a fully fledged participant in that discourse.

Global action in response to China's human rights record forms the main focus of the argument that is to come. What I hope to show, and to point up through the deliberate adoption of a chronological approach to the story in Chapters 4 through 8, is a process of diffusion and enmeshment: that actions and reactions at one phase of the struggle have served to constrain and shape the decisions that have come in the next phase, for all actors involved. Where China is concerned, it is important not to overstate this reduction in its ability to take autonomous decisions, but the argument in the ensuing chapters is that Beijing has moved—or been shoved—along a winding and bumpy path that has led to a deepening of its involvement in this issue area. In picking apart those aspects that together describe this process, I focus my attention on four main areas. China's discursive debate has been conducted via bilateral diplomacy, in institutional venues and with domestic groups, and has imposed some constraints on future speech acts and behaviour. Beijing's concern for international image, and membership in the great power club, has led to a recognition that it needs to defend its human rights record, action that has also had discursive and behavioural consequences. The bargaining behaviour in which it has engaged in order to try to ward off pressure has resulted in the Beijing leadership offering short-term concessions, and promises with respect to future action, which has served—inadvertently or not, depending on one's assessment of the objectives of the Chinese leadership—to deepen its ties with the rights regime. Finally, there has been the crucial transnational element, where increased exposure to international rights talk and to the treaty regime has affected domestic debates on law reform and human rights standards. Eventually, this could lead to human rights norms acquiring prescriptive status in the domestic realm and then reaching a stage of being habitually obeyed.[36]

---

[36] Discussions with Andrew Hurrell, and writings by Koh in 'Why do Nations Obey International Law?' and by Risse, *et al.* in *The Power of Human Rights,* have been particularly helpful in thinking this through. Krasner (*Sovereignty*, 31–32) indirectly suggests a neglect on the part of such analysts to matters of implementation in his argument that

Many of the studies of normative diffusion point to the crucial role that individuals or groups within the target society play in ensuring that a norm is taken up, or more broadly disseminated.[37] In the human rights area, reform-minded officials or academic lawyers can appeal to an international norm as a means of furthering their domestic interests in reform and in the drafting of new, human rights-related legislation; and domestic political activists can use their government's signature of international covenants as a means of exposing the contradiction between signature and actual behaviour—as happened with the human rights provisions of the Helsinki Accords. Such activists can also help to ensure that the global community keeps the human rights conditions within their country under review by developing and maintaining links with transnational groups. In addition, previously marginalized domestic groups may be empowered by a government's need to draw upon their expertise in new international negotiating venues, groups that may act as catalysts of change and sources of new thinking.

All of these domestic and transnational features are present in the Chinese case and will be noted throughout and given emphasis in Chapters 3 and 8. Depending on the extent to which such domestic groups maintain their autonomy, they may serve eventually to generate a broader and durable societal consensus behind the idea of human rights protection. That human rights now forms a legitimate subject of study and discussion in China and with other countries cannot be denied or reversed, and has been signalled through the publication, in several languages, of a series of White Papers on the topic, the establishment of study groups, the setting up of an NGO, and the frequent holding of official government-to-government bilateral dialogues on the matter. China has also taken advantage of many schemes offering to help train a cadre of new lawyers and judges, accepted international advice on legal reform, and attempted to publicize the legal changes. Nevertheless, at the end of the twentieth century, despite the many positive developments that have taken place in the areas of increased personal freedom and new or revised laws, the Chinese government does not appear fully to have accepted the prescriptive status of international human rights norms. Neither does its practice represent 'rule-consistent behavior'.[38] This suggests that, despite

international conventions violate Westphalian sovereignty only when they have an impact on domestic authority structures. But in fact these constructivists do consider the domestic level to be crucial.

[37] See e.g. Cortell and Davis, 'How do International Institutions Matter?', 451–78; Kathryn Sikkink, *Ideas and Institutions: Developmentalism in Brazil and Argentina* (Ithaca, NY: Cornell University Press, 1991).

[38] I take these terms from Risse *et al.* (eds.), (*The Power of Human Rights*, 29–30), who define 'prescriptive status' thus: ratification of the respective international human rights

the process of enmeshment outlined above, there are several factors that serve to hold back full internalization of the norms. Some are connected with the inherent weaknesses of the human rights regime, and others with China's own weight in global politics. Both these features affect China's ability to bargain and the types of concessions that have to be offered. Beijing's control over forms of expression—still greater than would be the case in a more pluralist society—also reduces some of the influence of the discursive debate. The leadership's readiness, under certain critical circumstances, to swerve away from policies that show it seeks entrance into international society also limits normative conditioning, as does—finally—its reluctance to embrace fundamental political reform. Human rights norms come into conflict with those in China who believe that the maintenance of CCP control, when under seeming threat, overrides all other considerations, including those of reputation and image, together with the benefits of developing a society based, not on arbitrary use of the rules, but on a true rule of law. As the following chapters show, China is deeply engaged with the international discourse on human rights, but full implementation of the core norms is still to come.

conventions, including the optional protocols; institutionalizing the norms in the constitution and/or domestic law; establishing a domestic human rights complaints mechanism; and consistent discursive practice, supporting the validity of the norms on the part of governments irrespective of the audience. Of course, there may be relatively few governments that fulfil all of these rather demanding criteria: note, in particular, the US failure to ratify the ICESCR and wide use of reservations when ratifying the ICCPR.

PART ONE
The Setting

PART ONE
The Setting

2

The Evolution of the
Global Human Rights Regime

During the 1970s—a time when the Beijing government was becoming more active internationally—the human rights regime reached a major turning point. In 1976 the two international human rights covenants, first introduced in 1966, came into force. A Human Rights Committee, established under the ICCPR and with the remit to consider reports from states that were parties to the covenant, placed an important piece of cement in the great wall of implementation that still awaits completion.[1] Certain democratic states, most notably the USA, but also a number of West European and Scandinavian countries, explicitly introduced human rights concerns into their foreign policies, developments that in the latter cases also affected the external relations of the European Community (EC). NGO capacities in this issue area also expanded rapidly alongside these increased opportunities for lobbying governments newly committed to protecting human rights. UN institutions similarly developed new procedures and mechanisms for monitoring abuses, thus signalling a willingness to take more seriously their responsibilities for stopping violations wherever they might occur.

Matters were not to stand still after these innovations. A further deepening and widening of human rights activity occurred in the post-cold-war era with such decisions as the appointment of a UN High Commissioner for Human Rights, further expansion in the numbers of states claiming democratic status, and the more explicit linking of human rights and democratic governance criteria in the allocation of economic assistance. When the Chinese government began its final debate on whether to sign the two major international covenants, it must have been

---

[1] See Dominic McGoldrick, *The Human Rights Committee: Its Role in the Development of the International Covenant on Civil and Political Rights* (Oxford: Oxford University Press, 1994) for an explanation of its origins and work. It was not until 1986 that ECOSOC directly created a Committee on Economic, Social, and Cultural Rights subordinate to the Council.

influenced by the knowledge that it was joining a group that, as of June 1997, comprised 138 state parties to the ICCPR and 136 to the ICESCR.[2] Neither covenant has any effective coercive means of ensuring implementation of its articles, which partially explains the gap between commitment and practice. However, those states that ratify what are, actually, treaties have given public notice of being bound by their terms, and have accepted the obligation to make periodic reports to UN bodies of measures adopted to give effect to the rights contained within the covenants, a notable expression of the breakdown of the division between the domestic and international realms in this issue area.

The elaboration and deepening of the human rights regime has depended both on factors familiar in the study of international relations and on those that are less often the focus of attention. State interest, the demands of the powerful on the less powerful, and the struggles between East and West and North and South have played their parts; but so too have the processes connected with institutional creation and development, which have prompted the elaboration of norms in this issue area, and resulted in politically and historically contingent social practices becoming more deeply embedded and independent of their origins. Although, as we shall see, there are a number of serious weaknesses associated with the furtherance of human rights protections, China's greater international engagement came at a time when virtually all states were publicly accepting that human rights were a subject of legitimate international concern. Considerable normative convergence had occurred, therefore, if we focus on participatory and rhetorical behaviour in this issue area, even while we take note of the fact that actual levels of protection have frequently fallen far short of the required standards.

BUILDING THE HUMAN RIGHTS REGIME

The fact that it took three decades or more for human rights protections to reach prescriptive status is both surprising if one focuses on the early years of the regime, but more comprehensible if one acknowledges the power political factors that have shaped its development. Crucial too in the explanation is that the embedding of norms is an uncertain, nonlinear process that requires time and a hospitable environment in order

---

[2] See *Netherlands Quarterly of Human Rights,* 3 (1997), app. III, and Rein Mullerson, *Human Rights Diplomacy* (London: Routledge, 1997), 183 n.2. These covenants came into effect after the required thirty-five states had ratified the treaties.

for change to occur. Before 1945, human rights were seldom considered a subject of legitimate concern for states, the division between the domestic and international was virtually unassailable, and the individual had no legal personality when it came to international law. After 1945, that position seemed no longer to be wholly tenable. As the 1948 Universal Declaration of Human Rights (UDHR) suggested near its start, the disregard and contempt for human rights during the Second World War had resulted in acts of such outrageous barbarism that humankind now had no other choice than to rethink its state-based international arrangements. The events that gave rise to the declaration had graphically illustrated the power of the state to abuse its own citizens, which in this instance reached a level sufficient to generate a form of collective moral guilt.

This change, largely initiated by the Holocaust, suggested that, in the genesis of human rights legislation, if not in its subsequent elaboration, the foundations were partly built on changes in belief: on an understanding that some means had to be found for preventing atrocities on such a scale from occurring in the future; on feelings of shame arising from governmental and individual failure to do enough to aid the plight of Jews, Communists, and homosexuals, among others, who met their deaths at the hands of the genocidal Nazis; and on a sense that individuals had to be made responsible for their own actions, whether as murderer or torturer in uniform, or as passive onlooker. The UDHR, a document of thirty articles that embraced both civil and political rights, and economic, social, and cultural rights, was a seminal work. Notwithstanding important developments in the European human rights framework after the Second World War (see below), it together with the UN Charter placed the UN in the engine room when it came to human rights promotion in the early years.[3] Although the Charter offered an uneasy balance between matters to be considered the domestic affairs of states and those that should rightly lead to international concern, it did refer to human rights in its preamble and six of its articles. Article 1 (3), for example, described one of the purposes of the UN to be the promotion and encouragement of 'respect for human rights and for fundamental freedoms for all without distinction as to race, sex, language, or religion'.[4]

---

[3] Tom J. Farer and Felice Gaer, 'The UN and Human Rights: At the End of the Beginning', in Adam Roberts and Benedict Kingsbury (eds.), *United Nations, Divided World* (Oxford: Oxford University Press, 1993), 245. For much additional detail, including the significant role of individuals in pushing the movement forward, see also the work of Paul Gordon Lauren, *The Evolution of International Human Rights: Visions Seen* (Philadelphia: University of Pennsylvannia Press, 1998.

[4] See also Article 55 of the Charter. This needs to be read alongside Article 2 (7) of the Charter, which states: 'Nothing contained in the present Charter shall authorize the United

Article 68 charged the UN's Economic and Social Council (ECOSOC) to set up commissions for the promotion of human rights, bringing into being in 1946 the UNCHR. In December 1948 the UN General Assembly on consecutive days adopted both the Convention on the Prevention and Punishment of the Crime of Genocide and the UDHR.

Despite this early promise, such intensity of activity was not to be sustained. It took some eighteen years before the UN General Assembly introduced the two major human rights covenants that gave force to the range of rights outlined in the UDHR. The Commission on Human Rights, made up of state representatives, together with its principal subsidiary, the nominally independent and expert Sub-Commission on the Prevention of Discrimination and Protection of Minorities, were to prove a disappointment. They carried the main burden when it came to human rights activity, but between 1946 and 1966 the Commission was supine, and not prepared to take action to address complaints regarding violations of human rights.[5] It fell victim to the poisonous cold-war divide in a body that until the early 1960s still favoured the Western world in terms of membership, and to all states' concerns—whatever their ideological position—to prevent any interference in what were still deemed primarily domestic affairs. In the US case, not only the cold warriors, but also the segregationists and advocates of states' rights, helped prevent forward movement,[6] and in the European case their role as colonial powers made them coy about exposing themselves to complaints. The Soviet government's view can be gleaned from its delegate's reaction to the UDHR as it was being presented to the UN General Assembly: it was 'defective primarily because "a number of articles completely ignore the sovereign rights of democratic governments . . . the question of national sovereignty", he maintained, was "a matter of the greatest importance"'.[7] Support for human rights norms had not yet reached prescriptive status,

Nations to intervene in matters which are essentially within the domestic jurisdiction of any state', a statement that Tom Farer and Felice Gaer argued 'offered comfortable shelter for rogue regimes in the early post-war decades' ('The UN and Human Rights', 246).

    [5] At its very first session in 1947 it determined that 'it had no power to take any action in regard to any complaints concerning human rights' (quoted in Farer and Gaer, 'The UN and Human Rights' 247). Farer and Gaer go on to note that ECOSOC 'confirmed the Commission's marvellous self-restraint' and then 'rubbed salt in the self-inflicted wound by deciding that Commission members should not even review the original text of specific complaints by individuals lest, one supposes, the horrors recounted therein should inspire second thoughts about the virtues of moral blindness' (p.247).

    [6] Kathryn Sikkink, 'The Power of Principled Ideas: Human Rights Policies in the United States and Western Europe', in Judith Goldstein and Robert O. Keohane (eds.), *Ideas and Foreign Policy: Beliefs, Institutions, and Political Change* (Ithaca, NY: Cornell University Press, 1993), 145.

    [7] Quoted in Farer and Gaer, 'The UN and Human Rights', 248.

while the principle of state sovereignty, traditionally defined, retained its hold on major states within the global system.

THE RENEWAL OF ACTIVITY

With decolonization and the expansion of developing country representation within the UN, however, significant shifts in voting power within UN bodies helped to breathe more life into the human rights regime. As these states took up UN membership, they pressed for the adoption in 1965 of the International Convention on the Elimination of All Forms of Racial Discrimination (which came into force in 1969). It was their growing numbers that led to the adoption of the two international human rights covenants in 1966. Two procedural innovations of note were also to occur during this period: ECOSOC Resolution 1235 in 1967 authorized the UNCHR to consider human rights violations in particular countries and to engage each year in public debate, the main targets then being Israel in the post-1967 occupied territories and southern Africa; and in 1970 ECOSOC Resolution 1503 mandated the Commission to undertake confidential investigations of complaints wherever there had been a 'consistent pattern of gross and reliably attested violations of human rights and fundamental freedoms'.[8] The aim, primarily promoted by the Soviet bloc and various African states, was to restrict the focus of attention entirely to colonial and dependent territories.[9] However, despite the political rivalry and symbolism that was at the heart of these actions, they promoted forward, tentative, movement on the part of the UN from standard setting to examination of the extent to which those standards were being implemented by states.[10] Incremental advances continued after this. In a body that relied for its influence on public shaming, confidential investigation as foreseen under Resolution 1503 could be seen as undermining those implementation goals. In response to this, from 1978 the Commission began naming countries that had been the subject of 'decisions' even as it continued to withhold the actual details of those decisions.[11]

---

[8] Jack Donnelly, *International Human Rights*, (Boulder, Colo.: Westview Press, 1998), 5. See also Philip Alston, 'The Commission on Human Rights', in Alston (ed.), *The United Nations and Human Rights: A Critical Appraisal* (Oxford: Oxford University Press, 1992), ch. 5.   [9] Farer and Gaer, 'The UN and Human Rights', 274.

[10] Donnelly, *International Human Rights*, 9.

[11] The 1235 and 1503 procedures are extremely complex. Light is shed on these and their deficiencies in Farer and Gaer, 'The UN and Human Rights', esp. 274–86. n.91 Alston ('The Commission on Human Rights', 144–59), also contains a valuable discussion.

Action against Chile in the early 1970s after the military *coup* also heightened the sense that this era represented something of a watershed for the human rights regime. The Chilean case was important because it was the first that involved neither colonialism nor racism, the main focus of attention to that point. Other miscreants that decade, such as Idi Amin of Uganda, Emperor Bokassa of the Central African Republic, and Pol Pot of Cambodia, did not come under the same scrutiny, illustrating the continuing arbitrariness of the UN and the political nature of its Commission. The Chilean case garnered attention, however, because it had involved the overthrow of the socialist government of Salvador Allende, and because Chile had been a member of the Non-Aligned Movement. Leaving these political explanations to one side, its presence on the agenda signalled the larger point—that the UN could use its capacity to try to stop human rights abuses wherever they might occur, provided the political conditions were hospitable to it.[12]

Several further reforms were to occur in the period from the late 1970s. As noted above, from 1978 the UNCHR became more active and open in a number of ways. The more public approach to the 1503 procedure suggested there was a growing acceptance that confidential consideration did not preclude public reference to any given government. The Commission also stepped up its range of fact-finding activities.[13] Meeting sessions were expanded from four to six weeks, and the membership from thirty-two to forty-three (and again with effect from 1992 to fifty-three members). According to Howard Tolley, enlarging the membership in the 1980s brought into the UNCHR new state members who seemed committed to improving the workings of the body. During that period, the Western bloc made up about a quarter of the membership, proportionately larger than its representation in the General Assembly. That fact seems to have galvanized these states, encouraging more frequent meetings of the group and more disciplined voting practices.[14] With the second enlargement in 1992, which added four to Africa, three to Asia, and three to Latin America, the Western grouping lost out proportionately; but there were still other useful organizational changes during this period with agreement that the Commission would meet when an urgent situation arose—provided there was majority support—and that the terms of Special Rapporteurs would be extended from two to three years.[15]

[12] Alston, 'The Commission on Human Rights', 158.   [13] Ibid. 145.

[14] Howard Tolley, Jr., *The U.N. Commission on Human Rights* (Boulder, Colo.: Westview Press, 1987), 101. As will become clear in later chapters, however, since 1998, and with respect to China, there has been evidence of disarray in voting behaviour on the part of the Western group.

[15] Reed Brody, Penny Parker, and David Weissbrodt, 'Major Developments in 1990 at the UN Commission on Human Rights', *Human Rights Quarterly*, 12/4 (1990), 564.

In this new reform environment and with significant prompting from the NGOs, as outlined below, the Commission drafted new standards on torture and religious intolerance. This eventually resulted in the Convention against Torture and Other Cruel, Inhuman, or Degrading Treatment or Punishment, which entered into force in 1987 and required state parties to report to its associated Committee against Torture (CAT) on measures taken to implement the convention. That Committee in turn was empowered to make general comments or recommendations to the state in question. The convention also established procedures for the Committee to consider complaints by individuals against state parties, provided the state adhered to the relevant optional protocol, and to examine complaints by one state party against another under a similar protocol. States that did not opt out of Article 28 of the treaty were also deemed to have permitted the Committee to investigate, on its own initiative, cases in which it had received reliable information that torture was being systematically practised in the territory of a state party to the treaty.[16]

Ratified by 102 states as of June 1997, although with many introducing reservations,[17] this evolutionary process illustrates how human rights legislation that binds large numbers of states can be created as a result of attention to a specific case—in this instance Chile. Moreover, forward movement in this one area clearly had spillover effects in other areas of urgent concern: 1980 saw the appointment of a five-member working group authorized to investigate involuntary disappearances in any country, and it quickly developed urgent action procedures.[18] In 1982, the UNCHR appointed a Special Rapporteur on Summary or Arbitrary Executions, and in 1985 a Special Rapporteur on Torture, who also adopted urgent action responses similar to those used for involuntary disappearances. In 1991 another thematic mechanism was introduced with the establishment of a Working Group on Arbitrary Detention. Abuses in particular countries were not neglected either, as during this period the Commission brought in Special Rapporteurs to deal with specific country allegations. These individual experts, shielded to some degree from the political pressures that came from the mode of operation within

---

[16] Andrew Byrnes, 'The Committee against Torture', in Alston (ed.), *The United Nations and Human Rights*, 523–4; Donnelly, *International Human Rights*, 59–60; Farer and Gaer, 'The UN and Human Rights', 263–4.

[17] At that time, forty-one had opted out of Article 21 on interstate complaints, and thirty-nine out of Article 22, allowing individual communications.

[18] Donnelly (*International Human Rights*, 54–5), reports that in the first decade the group handled over 19,000 cases of disappearance and in roughly one case in ten the whereabouts or fate of the individual was established. The first Special Rapporteur on Torture, Peter Kooijmans of the Netherlands, approached thirty-three governments in his first year.

the Commission, investigated a variety of allegations and then reported their findings directly to the Commission. The logical next development, (although it had first been recommended by Costa Rica in 1965) involved the establishment in 1993 of a UN High Commissioner for Human Rights. As with the Special Rapporteurs, the postholder was expected to deal directly with offending governments, unencumbered by the procedures attached to the Commission's activities.

This thematic approach to abuses, the use of Special Rapporteurs, and the creation of a High Commissioner were designed to raise the status of human rights within the UN structure, to increase the stature of the Commission, and to give it the appearance of a less politicized body. Issues could be projected as global problems, with all countries having the potential to be investigated, not simply ones associated with particular regions or ideological blocs. Philip Alston reminds us, however, that these thematic procedures did emerge from a distinctly political process, as each of the regional groups in the Commission suggested themes that directly targeted adversaries. Importantly, though, such countries were unable to obtain the votes necessary to ensure the disbanding of procedures that might have an impact on their own country once they were in place.[19] This latter point confirms, then, that, since the start of that newly activist phase for the UNCHR, it has not been easy for a particular bloc to capture the work of the Commission, suggesting a growing degree of impartiality for the body. It also suggests that institutions, through a cumulative, incremental process, do have the capacity to take member states beyond what they initially intended when various mechanisms were first established. The fact that intensive lobbying takes place in connection with the work of the Commission reaffirms not solely its political nature but also its authority, given the importance that governments attach to these mechanisms and the outcomes of the UNCHR's deliberations. Moreover, the type of work in which the UNCHR has been engaged since the reform era of the 1970s indicates that the body has moved from standard setting into a period where it has been somewhat effective in responding to violations, and in making recommendations to enhance the level of legal protection for individuals subject to abuse.[20] Writing in 1993, Farer and Gaer claimed that the Commission had a 'capacity for rapid and concrete action that would have been virtually unimaginable twenty years ago'.[21] Tolley notes that, while many states have challenged these new Special Rapporteurs on the merits of cases they have presented to the Commission, crucially they have not ques-

---

[19] Alston, 'The Commission on Human Rights', 175.   [20] Ibid. 197.
[21] Farer and Gaer, 'The UN and Human Rights', 262.

tioned the right of the Commission to authorize such investigations, thereby—perhaps unwittingly—bolstering the particular norm under attack by violators and helping to build up precedent.[22]

The Sub-Commission on the Prevention of Discrimination and Protection of Minorities (in effect a Sub-Commission of Experts of the Commission on Human Rights—a name change that it tried unsuccessfully to introduce in 1984[23]) has also undergone reform and an expansion of its activities as a result of its parent body's decisions. A Commission decision in 1967 authorizing the Sub-Commission to give annual consideration to violations of human rights led it to begin immediate public debate of governmental abuse.[24] The Sub-Commission additionally started to work in private from 1970 under Resolution 1503, referring to the Commission the country situations that merited further scrutiny. By 1985 it had made confidential recommendations on more than thirty countries,[25] and by 1992 around a dozen more.[26] As noted earlier, the Commission from 1978 named the countries subject to its decisions, and from 1984 the Chair started to provide the names of countries that were being kept under consideration and those that had been dropped. Inevitably, this heightening of public exposure led to the increased participation of governmental observers and of NGOs in the plenary debates. In 1977 ten governments intervened in discussions; by 1987 that figure had risen to seventy-two interventions.[27] As had occurred in the parent body, the Sub-Commission too introduced Working Groups and Special Rapporteurs into its proceedings. By the end of its 1992 session, they were at work on a variety of topics, including the fate of indigenous populations, contemporary forms of slavery, and human rights and the environment. Sub-Commission experts introduced secret ballots in 1991 in an attempt to reduce the political pressure on persons whose autonomy had always been compromised to some degree by the fact that they were appointed and reappointed by home governments.[28]

---

[22] Tolley, *The U.N. Commission on Human Rights*, 121.

[23] Asbjorn Eide, 'The Sub-Commission on Prevention of Discrimination and Protection of Minorities', in Alston (ed.) *The United Nations and Human Rights*, 258.

[24] Farer and Gaer report that in 1967 the Commission directed the Sub-Commission to move beyond the problems of minorities and to bring before the Commission 'any situation which it has reasonable cause to believe reveals a consistent pattern of violations . . . [and] to prepare . . . a report containing information on violations of human rights and fundamental freedoms from all available sources' ('The UN and Human Rights', 275).

[25] Tolley, *The U.N. Commission on Human Rights*, 179.

[26] Farer and Gaer ('The UN and Human Rights', 281 n.91) provide a list of countries.

[27] Eide, 'The Sub-Commission', 259, n.207.

[28] Farer and Gaer, 'The UN and Human Rights', 262–3 and n.47.

THE CONTRIBUTION OF
NON-GOVERNMENTAL ORGANIZATIONS

Ignoring for the moment the severe problems the Commission and Sub-Commission have confronted in trying to reduce the incidence of human rights abuse, other features that they share include a shortage of time to undertake sustained discussion of a particular situation or country, and a lack of budgetary resources which affects, for example, their ability to engage in thorough fact-finding missions. This lack, together with specific procedural decisions to permit increased NGO involvement, has provided the opportunity for the NGO to participate in the promotion of human rights at the institutional level, as well as within domestic contexts. Overcoming Soviet complaints in 1969 that NGOs were '"weeds in the field" that desecrated the UN landscape' and that needed to be uprooted, together with the fears of the newly decolonized, which noted that NGO headquarters were largely located in the West,[29] such groups have now become central components of the human rights regime. Although such organizations were hardly new phenomena in world politics, their increased numbers in the 1970s, their greater professionalism, and their ability to operate transnationally began to yield them a special form of power and influence. Between 1950 and 1993 the number of international groups working primarily on human rights was estimated to have increased fivefold, with a doubling between 1983 and 1993. Using technological advances and transnational networks as means to deploy information as quickly and as accurately as possible, they helped significantly to expand the range of countries subject to review.[30]

Amnesty International (AI), for example, from its origins in 1961, built up a staff size and budget that compared favourably with the level of resources that the UN devoted to human rights issues as a whole.[31] By 1977 it had over 150,000 members in more than 100 countries, the US section alone expanding from 3,000 to 50,000 between 1974 and 1976, not unconnected with the Chile episode.[32] Its international research capacity, global reach, and level of expertise in the field, together with a reputation for independence from any one state's point of view, meant that its

[29] William Korey, *NGOs and the Universal Declaration of Human Rights* (New York: St Martin's Press, 1998), 77–8.

[30] Margaret E. Keck and Kathryn Sikkink, *Activists beyond Borders: Advocacy Networks in International Politics* (Ithaca, NY: Cornell University Press, 1998), 10–11.

[31] Ann Marie Clark, 'Strong Principles, Strengthening Practices: Amnesty International and Three Cases of Change in International Human Rights Standards', Ph.D. thesis (Minnesota, 1995), 8.

[32] Korey, *NGOs*, 169; Keck and Sikkink, *Activists beyond Borders*, 90.

opinions started to be sought by governments and by institutions, notably the UNCHR, its Sub-Commission, the Special Rapporteurs, and Working Groups. The award of the Nobel Peace Prize in 1977 enormously increased its visibility and recruitment capacities, and, more importantly, strongly legitimized its human rights work. The UN's thematic rapporteurs were to find it to be particularly helpful to their activities, leading to a relationship that those directly involved have described as 'close'.[33]

There has been no shortage of expert commentators who acknowledge this vital NGO role in the evolution of the human rights regime, including those who display some ambivalence about the NGO place within it.[34] Although grateful for the fact that the NGO informational capacities made it possible for the UN Centre for Human Rights to perform its functions, its Director in 1976, Theo van Boven, also noted that the Centre 'did not have the resources or staff to collect information ourselves, so we were dependent. They did a lot of work which we should do at the UN.'[35] Alston notes: 'one of the most important features of the way in which the human rights regime has evolved is the extent to which NGOs have come to be seen not merely as partners, but as indispensable ones.'[36] Chayes and Chayes agree, arguing that the UN has been virtually completely dependent on the data collected by the NGOs, and that they have performed vital parallel and supplementary functions at almost every stage of the regime's evolution.[37] Various UN human rights bodies make regular use of expert NGO papers; NGO participants have drafted resolutions in collaboration with UN officials and have supplied the bulk of the evidence of violations. Their findings have also been utilized in the reporting mechanisms of the treaty regimes, not always on an official basis, as in the case of the Human Rights Committee, which has allowed members to make informal use of NGO reports as a basis for questioning the accuracy of reports submitted by state parties to the ICCPR.[38] They contribute substantially, therefore, to a system that relies on public exposure to try to tame offenders contributing directly to this shaming process in the UN venue, especially since 1980, when they were first

---

[33] Eide, 'The Sub-Commission', 239.

[34] Andrew Hurrell, for example, has written of the 'enormous diversity of voices within the NGO movement and the lack of apparent means of mediating between them'. Some are 'little more than self-appointed and self-created lobbies, despite their pervasive rhetoric of authenticity.' ('Power, Principles and Prudence', 289).

[35] Keck and Sikkink, *Activists beyond Borders*, 96.

[36] Philip Alston, 'The Committee on Economic, Social and Cultural Rights', in Alston (ed.), *The United Nations and Human Rights*, 501.

[37] Chayes and Chayes, *The New Sovereignty*, 164, 251.

[38] David P. Forsythe, *The Internationalization of Human Rights* (Lexington, Mass.: Lexington Books, 1991), 73.

allowed to name countries directly in their statements before the Commission.[39]

Beyond the provision of information, however, the NGO has also become involved in norm creation. AI, for example, began a one-year, worldwide campaign against torture in 1972, having provided information about Greece under the colonels to the Council of Europe in the late 1960s. With the military *coup* in Chile in September 1973 mentioned above, the environment for norm development in this area became more hospitable. This took the matter beyond the references in Article 5 of the UDHR and Article 7 of the ICCPR. Amnesty produced a 224-page report identifying over sixty countries in which torture was commonplace and generated a million signatures in support of a petition calling upon the UN to outlaw the practice. Having played a large part in helping to draft a declaration on torture, AI seized the chance to press for its formal adoption at the UN General Assembly, which took place with unanimous agreement in December 1975. Yet it took until 1984 before the Convention against Torture was adopted, and a further year before the appointment of a Special Rapporteur in this field,[40] indications that NGO work depended still on state support to bear fruit, as much as the human rights regime had come to rely on the NGO.

Amnesty did not rest here but also contributed to the development of the international norm on disappearances, once again using its connections with formal bodies and with its vast membership base to bring the practice to the attention of governmental and intergovernmental bodies, and to arouse more general public concern. The matter of disappearances was not considered in the UDHR or in the two covenants; thus, in this area, Amnesty helped to extend the concept of human rights. With Chile and Argentina as the two focuses of this campaign, the proposal to establish a Working Group on Disappearances came before the UNCHR in 1980. At first, no government was prepared to make a statement in support. The Chair of the Commission session next turned to the NGOs, and Amnesty made its case, making specific mention of Argentina, Afghanistan, Cambodia, Ethiopia, Nicaragua, and Uganda. Some of those named attempted to deny NGOs the right to criticize any specific government, but the Chair ruled that, while the NGOs were not allowed

[39] Alston, 'The Commission on Human Rights', 202–3.

[40] Clark, 'Strong Principles, Strengthening Practices', 91 ff. Korey, *NGOs*, 170–75. One important feature of the General Assembly declaration was its provision of a definition of torture: 'any act by which severe pain or suffering, whether physical or mental, is intentionally afflicted by or at the instigation of a public official on a person for such purposes as obtaining from him [*sic*] or a third person information or confession, punishing him [*sic*] for an act he [*sic*] has committed or is suspected of having committed or intimidating him [*sic*] or other persons' (quoted in Korey, *NGOs*, 175).

to launch attacks, they could provide information involving particular countries.[41] Once the establishment of the Working Group had been agreed and ECOSOC had ratified this decision, a special meeting with NGOs was set up in order that the new body could learn about their investigatory practices in this issue area. As the director of the UN Human Rights secretariat in Geneva put it, 'we wanted particularly to know what techniques they were using . . . so that we could learn from them'.[42]

The NGO role within the Helsinki process was similarly creative and transforming, demonstrating once again the power of information and of networking. The Helsinki Final Act adopted on 1 August 1975 at the CSCE specifically referred to the ICCPR and the UDHR and endorsed the concept of a right not only to know one's entitlements but also to be able to act upon them. The Soviet government published the whole text of the Helsinki Accords in *Izvestia*, providing a point of leverage for Soviet dissidents and an opportunity for external NGOs to monitor Soviet compliance with its terms. Yuri Orlov, a physicist member of the Armenian Academy of Sciences, formed the Moscow Helsinki Watch Group, a courageous act followed by other similar actions elsewhere in the Soviet bloc, such as Charter 77 in Czechoslovakia, and the Committee of Workers' Defence in Poland. The year 1978 saw the establishment of the US Helsinki Watch, a vital conduit for information to the international media about conditions within the Eastern bloc, a form of protection for the East European monitoring groups, and an important source of moral support for these new bodies. The CSCE review process also provided a venue for NGO collective action and opportunities for the reinforcement of transnational links. By the late 1980s NGOs had rights of access to the meetings, to contact delegates, and to hold their own gatherings in parallel with those of the formal CSCE assemblies.[43]

Governments, of course, had been the initiators of the Helsinki process, even if they had not quite understood where it might end. Moreover, as with the Convention against Torture, in establishing the Working Group on Disappearances, the NGOs active over these issues did rely on

---

[41] Korey, *NGOs*, 252–3. For a riveting examination of the Argentinian military government's attempts to block efforts to have its brutal practices condemned at the UN, see Iain Guest, *Behind the Disappearances: Argentina's Dirty War against Human Rights and the United Nations* (Philadelphia: University of Pennsylvania Press, 1990).

[42] Clark, 'Strong Principles, Strengthening Practices', esp. ch. 4 and p. 170.

[43] Korey, *NGOs*, ch. 10. Human Rights Watch now includes five divisions covering Africa, the Americas, Asia, the Middle East, together with the signatories of the Helsinki Accords. For developments in Eastern Europe, see also Daniel C. Thomas, 'The Helsinki Accords and Political Change in Eastern Europe', in Risse *et al.* (eds.), *The Power of Human Rights*.

the power of sympathetic governments to advance the cause. Nevertheless, a feature of the relationships between certain governments and
NGOs in the late 1970s and 1980s is one of considerable intimacy, with
each providing 'services' to the other when seeking to advance some
particular aspect of the human rights regime. Not coincidentally, NGO
activism and presence increased at the same time as a number of governments in the Western world sought to incorporate a human rights dimension in their foreign policies.

HUMAN RIGHTS AND
THE FOREIGN POLICY OF STATES

Where NGOs relied on the power of information, shaming, and lobbying,
many governments, especially in the developed world, had potentially
more coercive weapons at their disposal should they have wished to influence the human rights practices of other states. This realization was never
more evident than in the USA, and it was changes there in the 1970s that
had a major impact on the normative environment. The resources at
Washington's disposal were manifold, including a comparatively extensive military and economic assistance programme, comprehensive foreign
relations, and significant voting power within international financial institutions. This added up to an impressive, all-round ability potentially to
enforce compliance either through persuasive or directly coercive means,
or through some combination of the two.

The first initiatives in the human rights area came from the US
Congress—action that has been attributed to the burgeoning civil rights
movement, the character and outcome of the Vietnam War, and the
amoral aspects of the Nixon administration's behaviour, whether
expressed through the Watergate break-ins or through its hard realist
approach towards foreign policy.[44] In this respect, there was a comple-
mentarity between the outrage expressed about internal American

---

[44] The Nixon administration, and in particular its Secretary of State from 1973, Henry
Kissinger, was associated with the rejection of human rights considerations in US foreign
policy. As Kissinger put it at his Senate confirmation hearings: 'I believe it is dangerous for
us to make the domestic policy of countries around the world a direct objective of
American foreign policy . . . The protection of basic human rights is a very sensitive aspect
of the domestic jurisdiction of . . . governments' (quoted in Claire Apodaca and Michael
Stohl, 'United States Human Rights Policy and Foreign Assistance Allocations from
Carter to Clinton: Plus ça change, plus c'est la même chose?', Global Studies Program,
Purdue University: Research Papers at www.ippu.purdue.edu, p. 4 (no date and accessed
via Internet, 7 Nov. 1997)).

developments, and the expression of Washington's foreign policy. Congressional reaction to the unsavoury elements of US foreign policy, and to the poor relationship between the executive and legislative branches, prompted Congressional Hearings, chaired by Representative Donald Fraser, which resulted in bureaucratic and legislative changes. A series of 'Sense of Congress' resolutions in 1973 and 1974—later toughened and made mandatory—led to the amendment of the Foreign Assistance Act. It called for the denial of military or economic aid to any government that grossly violated the human rights of its people. Picking up on this mood, possibly for a combination of instrumental and personal reasons, the presidential contender, Jimmy Carter, declared in December 1974 that he had a dream: 'That this country set a standard within the community of nations of courage, compassion, integrity, and dedication to basic human rights and freedoms.'[45] Human rights were clearly entering into the US political discourse at a level of intensity rarely found since the onset of the cold war.

The Harkin[46] Amendment attached to the International Development and Food Assistance Act followed in 1975. It too sought to deny economic aid to those engaging in 'gross violations of internationally recognized human rights . . . unless such assistance will directly benefit the needy people in such country'.[47] Then in 1976 the International Security and Arms Export Control Act emphasized not only the denial of aid to violators, but also the need for the US government to formulate programmes designed to promote human rights. In addition, it was made mandatory for the State Department to file reports on all countries receiving security assistance.

Legislative restraints were also placed on US activity within the international financial institutions. Section 701 of the International Financial Institutions Act of 1977 called on US Executive Directors of these institutions to oppose all financial or technical aid to those countries deemed gross violators of human rights, unless such assistance could be shown to be necessary to supporting basic human needs.[48] These get-out clauses, as will be shown in later chapters, have been subject to wide interpretation,

---

[45] A. Glenn Mower, Jr., *Human Rights and American Foreign Policy* (Westport, Conn.: Greenwood Press, 1987), 15.

[46] Tom Harkin, a one-time congressional staffer, was particularly sensitized to the more unsavoury aspects of US involvement in Vietnam when he discovered the notorious 'tiger cages' in a South Vietnamese prison that had received US assistance (Sikkink, 'The Power of Principled Ideas', 163).

[47] Apodaca and Stohl, 'United States Human Rights Policy and Foreign Assistance Allocations from Carter to Clinton', 3.

[48] Peter R. Baehr, *The Role of Human Rights in Foreign Policy*, 2nd edn. (London: Macmillan, 1996), 87.

if not abuse, but the legislation as a whole has served two of its purposes at least: that of ensuring a check on the human rights situation in particular countries before assistance is given, and a bolstering of the decision to incorporate, to a greater or lesser degree, a human rights dimension into the foreign policy-making process.

The major domestic bureaucratic change of this period came with the creation of the State Department's Bureau of Human Rights and Humanitarian Affairs, obliged to prepare reports on the human rights situation at first in every country that received US security assistance and, later, in all countries that were members of the UN, whether they received US aid or not. The first 'coordinator' for human rights policy was basically marginalized within the department and the reports the State Department produced in the early years were generally regarded as flawed—a function of the Nixon–Kissinger–Ford view that human rights should still be seen as a matter for the domestic jurisdiction of states. The Carter administration, however, somewhat improved matters, bringing in Patricia Derian, who formerly had been active in the US civil rights movement. She had a far higher profile and a much stronger commitment to the project than her predecessor, and the post was upgraded to Assistant Secretary. Her staff of two in 1977 grew to twenty-nine by 1979, and each regional bureau created a full-time human rights officer to work directly with the Human Rights Bureau. Derian appointed Roberta Cohen— formerly executive director of the International League for Human Rights—in early 1978 as her Deputy Assistant Secretary of State, and worked to persuade President Carter to appoint an expert to the UNCHR. In 1980, rather late in the day, the President of the International League for Human Rights, Jerome Shestack, headed the US delegation, and was to play a major role in cajoling and lobbying Commission members, both US aid recipients and allies alike, to support the proposal for a Working Group on Disappearances.[49]

Another innovation during the Carter years was the establishment of a special interagency group, known as the Christopher group (named after Warren Christopher, then the Deputy Secretary of State, who chaired it), designed to help implement the Congressional directives referred to above. It included not only representatives from relevant parties in the State Department, but also officials from Treasury, Defense, Agriculture, Commerce and Labor, the National Security Council (NSC) the Export-Import Bank, and the Agency for International Development (AID). When discussing a loan proposal the Christopher group would draw on State Department and often AI human rights briefing materials as the

[49] Korey, *NGOs*, 188–9, 252–3.

bureaucratic tussle began to decide whether to award the assistance or not.[50] The policy that resulted had the 'unlikely distinction of being both even-handed and inconsistent. It was even-handed in the sense that a country's ability to "escape" the policy did not depend upon the ideological complexion of that country's government', but it did depend on less predictable factors such as the outcome of bureaucratic warfare in the State Department and within international financial institutions, the strength of the domestic lobby on behalf of a particular country, and the degree of aid leverage the administration actually had.[51]

Nevertheless, despite the energy and commitment of Derian and her access to Carter and Christopher, she still had to confront the fact that it was the regional and not the functional bureaux that wielded power in bilateral foreign policy, as had traditionally been the case. This meant that her bureau had to '"kick, scream, and claw" its way into the decision-making process'.[52] And it meant that for those who followed on from her in future administrations, some with less access to top officials, or operating within an environment where it was clear that the President did not wish to give the same priority to human rights, the struggle to remain significant in the policy calculus was even harder. This was to be the case during the Reagan presidency—to China's benefit for one—whose transition team recommended that 'internal policy-making procedures should be structured to ensure that human rights is not in a position to paralyze or unduly delay decisions on which human rights concerns conflict with the vital United States' interests'.[53] The bureau, known in the Carter period as a watch dog, during the Reagan era was described as a team player.[54] The Bush years tended to reflect the approach of his presidential predecessor.

Yet, even during the presidency of the popular Reagan, Congress still showed itself willing to act to constrain the executive branch in the human rights area, rejecting Reagan's first nominee for assistant secretary, Ernest Lefever, because of his known antipathy for introducing human rights considerations into policy-making beyond relations with the Soviet bloc. Reagan marked time for several months before submitting the name of his next nominee, Elliot Abrams. Abrams did make it through the confirmation process, and devoted himself to the task of

[50] Edwin S. Maynard, 'The Bureaucracy and Implementation of US Human Rights Policy', *Human Rights Quarterly*, 11/2 (1989), 209.

[51] John Dumbrell, *The Carter Presidency: A Re-Evaluation* (Manchester: Manchester University Press, 1993), 19.

[52] Maynard, 'The Bureaucracy and Implementation of US Human Rights Policy', 186.

[53] Quoted in Mower, *Human Rights and American Foreign Policy*, 33.

[54] Maynard, 'The Bureaucracy and Implementation of US Human Rights Policy', 186, 193.

producing the required information on human rights, perhaps in part because, as a leaked confidential memorandum of October 1981 to the US Secretary of State put it, a fundamental shift in the administration's human rights policy had become necessary. Without such a shift and a show of consistency in this area, it was argued, other important foreign policy initiatives were likely to be disrupted, an interesting reversal in the more usual argument.[55] Significantly, it was during this period that the US government took the first tentative step to imply there could be a degree of external interest in its own domestic practices when the Senate finally ratified in 1988 the Convention on the Prevention and Punishment of the Crime of Genocide, first adopted by the UN General Assembly in 1948.[56] It was to be several more years, however, before the USA ratified other human rights milestones, such as the ICCPR, the Convention against Torture, and the International Convention on the Elimination of All Forms of Racial Discrimination. Moreover, when ratifying the ICCPR, it issued certain reservations, understandings, and declarations that led the Human Right's Committee to complain that they were intended to 'ensure that the United States has accepted only what is already the law of the United States'.[57] This behaviour undoubtedly compromised US authority, and the effectiveness of this dimension in American foreign policy, although Washington remained a leading norm entrepreneur in the human rights area.

The State Department's obligation to produce the country reports on human rights helped both to promote human rights as a legitimate factor in the making of US foreign policy and, because of the use to which they were put by others, to further the global human rights regime. Although, as noted above, the first reports produced under the Ford and then Carter administrations were deemed inadequate, the criticisms levelled at them by Congress and NGOs in their testimony before Congressional Hearings encouraged improvements. The reporting requirement alone apparently had the effect of altering the practices and norms within the Department of State, to the extent that accurate and unbiased human rights reporting became 'an intrinsically important goal for many key actors'. The public debate that ensued once the reports were submitted to Congress helped to increase, over time, their consistency,

[55] Mower, *Human Rights and American Foreign Policy*, 82–3.

[56] Sikkink, 'The Power of Principled Ideas', 155.

[57] The Human Rights Committee of the ICCPR was also particularly concerned about reservations to Article 6, para. 5, involving the execution of minors, which it believed to be 'incompatible with the object and purposes of the Covenant'. See CCPR/C/79/Add.50 (1995).

accuracy, and comprehensiveness.[58] When some NGOs began to publish their critiques of the reports, these were sent by the bureau to US embassies for use in constructing reports the following year. Embassies and their human rights personnel recognized that, in order to comply with the congressional legislation and to satisfy or even shield from criticism high officials within the State Department, they would have to obtain better quality information. This led them to establish links with local human rights organizations and with opposition groups, thus deepening US understanding of the country in question. Some foreign governments' attempts to avoid embarrassment by sending officials to the State Department before and after the reports had been published suggested these reports were having an effect beyond Washington and the NGO community. It has also been claimed that the threat of public exposure led to actual alterations in human rights behaviour.[59] Many governments have simply resented the publication, but even those that have expressed such resentment have often felt compelled to respond to the charges contained within the report, as we shall see with China in later chapters.

Much of the literature that examines US human rights policy since the Carter era, demonstrates that, in the main, there was no measurable difference between the Carter and Reagan administrations when it came to giving or withholding military aid from governments that abused human rights. It concludes that the human rights policy was *ad hoc*, inconsistent, and even hypocritical, especially under Carter, who was accused of being long on rhetoric and short on action.[60] Yet, it does seem clear that, viewed from a longer-term perspective, the policy gave heart to some of the victimized,[61] led to enduring links between US embassy staffs and parts of the host country human rights community, became embedded in the policy-making process within the Washington bureaucracy, and established a professional commitment within the US State Department to providing reasonably unbiased, accurate information, whatever the particular political beliefs of the US administration in power. US action from the 1970s also reinforced the changes that were taking place at the

[58] Judith Innes de Neufville, 'Human Rights Reporting as a Policy Tool: An Examination of the State Department Country Reports', *Human Rights Quarterly*, 8:4 (1986), 682.

[59] Maynard, 'The Bureaucracy and Implementation of US Human Rights Policy', 231 and n.

[60] A survey of the criticism plus an analysis of Carter's contribution is contained in Dumbrell, *The Carter Presidency*, ch. 7.

[61] As Jacobo Timerman—the Buenos Aires editor imprisoned in Argentina—put it in 1981: 'Those of us who were imprisoned, those of us who are in prison still, will never forget President Carter and his contribution to the battle for human rights' (quoted in Dumbrell, *The Carter Presidency*, 194).

global level, especially those within multilateral institutions, and more broadly heightened international awareness of this issue.

Human rights policies elsewhere in the Western world also suggested that the protection of human rights on a more systematic basis was an idea whose time had come in the 1970s, both at the level of rhetoric and in some cases in policy. Norway and the Netherlands, two of the most active states in this area, both issued extensive White Papers on human rights and foreign policy in 1977 and 1979 respectively, the Dutch paper outlining in considerable detail the dilemmas that all governments faced in attempting to put human rights at the centre of foreign policy.[62] For these countries, development assistance policies from the 1970s also tended to be linked to the protection of rights broadly defined. Both emphasized the need for aid-recipient governments to adopt 'socially just' policies that satisfied basic needs, thus suggesting a commitment rarely found in the USA to the promotion of rights contained within the ICESCR (which the US government had still not ratified by the end of 1999). From the late 1970s, the Dutch tended to balance this concern for social justice with the need for the advancement of civil and political rights within aid-recipient countries, even in the important country (and former colony) of Indonesia, introducing informally from 1977 human rights issues in aid consortium meetings.[63] Such middle-range powers as the Nordic countries, the Netherlands, and Canada have, like the USA, often fallen short of their lofty intentions to incorporate human rights into foreign policy, the policy frequently becoming victim to 'realism's cost-benefit reasoning';[64] nevertheless, where bureaucratic and legal changes have been introduced, governments have been obliged to integrate human rights concerns into the policy-making process, even if those concerns have not always been given priority in the final balancing of factors.

When choosing to work through multilateral institutions—whether the UN, the EU, or the Council of Europe—however, a more sustained approach often proved possible. Multilateralism served to legitimize such actions and provided information about the degree to which individual governments were likely to be isolated or supported in their respective stances.[65] The Netherlands, for example, played an active role in the UN in developing a variety of human rights norms, such as those involving

---

[62] Baehr, *The Role of Human Rights*, 152–3.

[63] Donnelly, *International Human Rights*, 108–9.

[64] David Gillies, *Between Principle and Practice: Human Rights in North–South Relations* (Montreal: McGill-Queen's University Press, 1996), 278.

[65] For further discussion of such ideas focusing on the use of economic sanctions, see Martin, *Coercive Cooperation*.

discrimination against women, persecution for religious beliefs, and the use of torture.[66] Perhaps it had been encouraged to adopt this approach because it had been a prevalent mode of operation among European states, both in terms of external policy and within Western Europe itself. From the very beginning of the European project, there had been a Europe-wide concern with human rights, strongly connected with the experiences of the Second World War. The Council of Europe made respect for human rights and the rule of law a condition of membership. As early as 1950 the European Convention for the Protection of Human Rights and Fundamental Freedoms was available for signature and ratification. Strong monitoring and decision-making powers were granted to the European Human Rights Commission and to the European Court of Human Rights. Between 1953 and 1973 virtually all West European states had accepted that individuals could file complaints and had awarded jurisdiction to the European Court of Human Rights in these matters. The European Human Rights Commission and Court subsequently became very active, receiving thousands of complaints each year.[67]

Having progressed this far with an internal human rights policy,[68] the European Commission of the EC—after 1993 EU—and the Community member states began to develop an external policy in this area, particularly under the remit of European Political Cooperation (EPC). The first major step was the adoption by the Commission, the Council of Ministers, and European Parliament in 1977 of a Joint Declaration on the Protection of Fundamental Freedoms. However, most of the organizational and rhetorical changes were to come in the 1980s. From 1984, for example, a member of the General Secretariat had the task of coordinating the EC's human rights policy, and in 1988 a new directorate within the General Secretariat included a specialist on human rights whose job was to try to enhance intergovernmental cooperation among member states.[69] In July 1986 the Foreign Ministers acting within the framework of the EPC and the Council of Ministers published a declaration on Human Rights and Foreign Policy, a document that was renewed and revised in June 1991.

[66] Baehr, *The Role of Human Rights*, 161.

[67] Sikkink, 'The Power of Principled Ideas', 148–9, 154. Latin America adopted the American Convention on Human Rights in 1969, which is somewhat similar to the European Convention and provides for a commission and a court. The commission, however, has 'broad and vague' powers. The American Convention came into force on 18 July 1978 and the Court of Human Rights was set up in September 1979. By 1991 some twelve states had recognized its jurisdiction. For detail on Latin American developments, see Brownlie (ed.), *Basic Documents on Human Rights*, pt. six.

[68] Note, however, the strong criticism advanced against EU failure to examine its own human rights record in Philip Alston (ed.), *The EU and Human Rights* (Oxford: Oxford University Press, 1999).   [69] Baehr, *The Role of Human Rights*, 109–11.

The Political Committee as the main preparatory organ for the Common Foreign and Security Policy (CFSP) after 1987 had a special working group on human rights. One of its most important roles was to try to ensure cooperation among the EC member states for action in such forums as the UN General Assembly and the UNCHR. From 1986, the Foreign Minister presiding over the Council of Ministers (a rotating six-monthly position) was mandated to send a memorandum on the EC's activities with respect to the promotion of human rights to the European Parliament.[70] The Parliament, in fact, had been active in the human rights field from the beginning of the 1970s, involving itself in 'case work', lending its platform to the victims of abuse, passing resolutions, and issuing Annual Reports. Using its powers under Article 238 of the EEC Treaty and as amended by the Single European Act (1986), agreements between the Community and third states needed the assent of a majority of MEPs, such assent being withheld with respect to Turkey and Israel.[71]

Europe's negotiations with its Lomé partners—sixty-eight African, Caribbean, and Pacific (ACP) states—also began to make oblique references to human rights, although the Lomé III Convention of 1977 put the emphasis on economic, social, and cultural rights and the elimination of apartheid. Lomé IV, signed in December 1989, however, affirmed a commitment by all state parties to all three of the major international human rights documents and to their indivisibility although, significantly, Lomé IV did not include at that stage provisions for the suspension of aid where rights were being violated.[72] The criteria for enlargement of the EC drew attention to the need for new member states to contribute to and not to undermine the EC's identity as a democratic community that protected human rights, the European Council Declaration on Democracy of 1978 making this a condition of entry. Indeed, the idea of members of the European home contributing to this sense of identity goes back much further than this: Greece, for example, was effectively forced to withdraw from the Council of Europe during the period of military rule after the Commission ruled in favour of a joint case filed by Norway, the

---

[70] Baehr, *The Role of Human Rights,* 119.

[71] Andrew Clapham, *Human Rights and the European Community: A Critical Overview* (Baden-Baden: Nomos Verlagsgesellschaft, 1991), 72; Alston, (ed.), *The EU and Human Rights,* 42, and in particular Reinhard Rack and Stefan Lausegger, 'The Role of the European Parliament: Past and Future', in Ibid. ch. 25.

[72] Clapham, *Human Rights and the European Community,* 79–80; and more generally Bruno Simma, Jo Beatrix Aschenbrenner, and Constanze Schulte, 'Human Rights Considerations in the Development Co-operation Activities of the EC', in Alston (ed.), *The EU and Human Rights,* ch. 18.

Netherlands, Denmark, and Sweden that Athens had violated the human rights conditions of the European Convention on Human Rights.[73]

Nevertheless, although this issue area had entered into policy deliberations and the bureaucracy in a way that was not foreseen when the original treaties that formed the basis of the EC were first drawn up, as with that other major norm entrepreneur—the USA—fundamental weaknesses concerning the coordination and prominence of the human rights policy still remained. This implied considerable remaining room for manœuvre on the part of those states with impoverished records of human rights protections, especially for the more powerful among them.

THE POST-COLD-WAR ERA

The ending of the cold war inevitably resulted in the further incorporation of human rights into policy-making and global discourse. As Friedbert Pfluger has written, 'scarcely a multinational conference takes place today without touching on the issue of human rights . . . Scarcely a credit is granted, or foreign aid approved, without a previous check of the human rights situation. Scarcely an infringement of human rights takes place without being greeted by vigorous protests from Amnesty International or even governments.'[74]

The explanation for this further deepening and widening rests not solely on the end to the cold-war divide. It has depended too on longer-term processes, referred to above, connected with the institutionalization of the issue area into governmental and organizational bodies, and the elaboration and specification of new norms that have bolstered other, longer-established ones. The foundational texts have also proven reasonably durable, despite attacks on them, from time to time, as being the product of Western hegemony. However, particular political events after 1989 did contribute substantially to raising the profile of human rights concerns. Although there had been a further democratic wave[75] in Latin America and southern Europe in the 1970s, and among America's Asian allies—notably, South Korea, Taiwan, and the Philippines—in the 1980s, the changes in the Soviet Union and Eastern Europe in the late 1980s and early 1990s had more profound effects on the global human rights regime.

[73] Sikkink, 'The Power of Principled Ideas', 149–50.
[74] Friedbert Pfluger, 'Human Rights Unbound: Carter's Human Rights Policy Reassessed', *Presidential Studies Quarterly*, 19/4 (Fall 1989), 705.
[75] See Samuel P. Huntingdon, *The Third Wave: Democratization in the Late Twentieth Century* (Norman, OK.: University of Oklahoma Press, 1991).

Developments here diminished the need for the West to support unsavoury authoritarian regimes in order better to confront the Soviet communist opponent; they also brought into being a class of states some of which became concerned to find a means of anchoring themselves within the democratic community of states. Hungary, for example, in 1988 became the first East European state to ratify the optional protocol of the ICCPR, the USSR indicating in 1989 that it would also soon become a party to it.[76]

These and the more wide-ranging political developments that saw the end to the East–West ideological divide suggested that there had been some broadening of the consensus on values. The cold-war era had encompassed a struggle to achieve agreement between one group that emphasized individual rights and an opponent that gave priority to the protection of collective rights—a struggle that undermined the claims to universality of values and seriously constrained the notion that there was such a thing as an international society or community. However, the post-cold-war era held out the promise that such claims could at last be made real. These political changes encouraged a widening of the normative agenda, including the argument that human rights had to be more firmly protected, and linked to the promotion of democracy and to economic development through the introduction of good governance criteria when granting assistance.[77] Those dispersing economic assistance, whether the international financial institutions, bodies such as the EU, or individual governments, introduced such criteria more firmly into their deliberations, ignoring the controversies that had previously underlain the argument that there was indeed a link between sustainable development and democratic governance.[78] The EBRD, for example, incorporated in its founding charter the requirement that aid recipients be 'committed to applying the principles of multi-party democracy, pluralism and market economies'. While the World Bank is constrained by its Articles of Agreement from advocating pluralist democracy, its definition of governance comprises such matters as improving accountability, transparency, and the promotion of civil society.[79]

[76] McGoldrick, *The Human Rights Committee*, 17–18.

[77] For a cautionary view about the expansion of this normative agenda, see Hurrell, 'Power, Principles and Prudence'.

[78] This is controversial, because the link is difficult to demonstrate conclusively, and it had been fashionable in the 1960s to argue that the processes associated with economic development could cause the disruption of traditional societies, and this disruption would probably lead to authoritarian rule before the countries emerged prosperous and democratic. See Samuel P. Huntingdon, *Political Order in Changing Societies* (New Haven, Conn.: Yale University Press, 1968).

[79] World Bank, *Governance and Development* (Washington: 1992).

In Europe, the Treaty on European Union, which came into force in November 1993, called for the EU's Common Foreign and Security Policy to aim to 'develop and consolidate democracy and the rule of law, and respect for human rights and fundamental freedoms'. In May 1995 the EU Commission adopted a communication that called for the inclusion of clauses on human rights and democracy in EU agreements with third countries. One example of its use came in 1997 when Mexico tried—unsuccessfully—to negotiate a trade and political cooperation agreement with the EU without the standard human rights clause. The revisions to Lomé IV in 1995 stated that a respect for human rights, democratic principles, and the rule of law was to be viewed as an 'essential element' of EU–ACP cooperation. It also held out the prospect of the suspension of any agreement (Article 366a) in the event of serious violation of any of these essential elements.[80] A similar communication in 1998 defined the requirements more exactly and proposed a number of concrete actions to promote such principles, including legislative, institutional, and administrative reform; human rights education; the strengthening of civil society via an independent media and support for domestic NGOs; and measures to combat corruption. This marked an important shift on the EU's part from an emphasis on sanctions to one of active support for helpful initiatives.[81]

Similarly, such bodies as the OAS stepped up their observation of human rights and democratic practices in member states, especially in the area of election monitoring. On 5 June 1991, OAS Ministers adopted a resolution calling for the immediate convocation of a meeting of the OAS Permanent Council 'in the event of any occurrences giving rise to the sudden or irregular interruption of the democratic political institutional process or of the legitimate exercise of power by the democratically elected government in any of the Organization's member states'.[82] Although it is important not to conflate electoral democracy with human rights protection, the 'irregular interruption of the democratic political institutional process' had frequently led to wide-scale abuses in past instances. In tandem with these developments, individual Latin American

---

[80] Johannes van der Klaauw, 'European Union', Human Rights News in *Netherlands Quarterly of Human Rights*, 13/3 (1995), esp. 276–8. The information on Mexico is contained within *Human Rights Watch World Report 1998*, (New York, 1997), 90.

[81] Johannes van der Klaauw, 'European Union', *Netherlands Quarterly of Human Rights* 16/2 (June 1998), 227–8; Simma *et al.*, 'Human Rights Considerations', 578–82. The publication of the first EU annual human rights report was in 1999: Council of the European Union, *EU Annual Report on Human Rights*, (Brussels, 1 October 1999), 11350/99.

[82] Quoted in Franck, *Fairness*, 113, who also notes that these procedures were invoked for Haiti after the overthrow of the elected Aristede government, and in Peru in April 1992 after the presidential *coup*.

governments, such as Brazil, became more open in acknowledging the poverty of their human rights record, the government of President Fernando Cardoso establishing a National Human Rights Plan, creating a National Secretariat for Human Rights within the Ministry of Justice, and encouraging it to work closely with NGOs to develop joint programmes. Throughout the country, the State Legislative Assemblies formed Human Rights Commissions where they previously did not exist, or strengthened those already in existence.[83]

Multilateral action through the UN Security Council also started to play a major role in advancing the prominence of human rights concerns. The awfulness of events in the Balkans, Iraq, Rwanda, and elsewhere prompted Security Council members, the UN Secretary General, and major NGOs[84] to recognize a connection between gross violations of rights and threats to international peace, even including those, such as China, which were extremely leery of terming such abuses worthy of Article VII action. It has become almost a standard procedure for peace-keeping, peacebuilding, and peace-enforcement operations to include a human rights dimension, whether that is election monitoring, as in such cases as Nicaragua, Cambodia, or Mozambique, or in the broader promotion of human rights norms within the societies experiencing a UN presence.[85] In the case of Cambodia, for example, a UN operation notable among other things for the fact that China dispatched to the country over 400 peacekeepers (a twenty–fold increase over any previous peacekeeping undertaking), the major task of the UN Transitional Authority in Cambodia (UNTAC) operation was to oversee the conduct of free and fair elections. In addition, however, UNTAC was mandated to conduct a human rights education campaign, to encourage early ratification of international human rights instruments, and to investigate allegations of human rights abuses in the country, actions from which the Chinese stood aloof, but which did not prevent their overall participation.[86] In the face of UN Security Council inaction in 1999, NATO engaged in unprecedented military action in Yugoslavia, which depended for its legitimacy on the claim that it was undertaken in support of those whose human rights were being grossly abused.

[83] *Human Rights Watch World Report 1998*, esp. 97.

[84] See, e.g. Boutros Boutros-Ghali, *An Agenda for Peace: Preventive Diplomacy, Peace-making and Peacekeeping* (Report of the Secretary General, 1992); Lawyers' Committee for Human Rights, *In the National Interest: 1996 Quadrennial Report on Human Rights and U.S. Foreign Policy* (New York, 1996), ch. 2; Amnesty International, *Peacekeeping and Human Rights* (London, 1994).

[85] Farer and Gaer, 'The UN and Human Rights', 289–91.

[86] Munro C. Richardson, 'From Warmaker to Peacekeeper: China's Role in the Resolution of the Cambodian Conflict', M.Phil thesis (Oxford, 1996).

Individual governments have also deepened their discursive commitment to human rights, as noted above in the case of Brazil, but also in many other examples. Often these changes have been accompanied by alterations in bureaucratic arrangements that have the potential to push forward the human rights component in foreign policy decisions. The Clinton administration pledged greater attention than in the Bush era and heightened both concern and approval with its call for 'democratic enlargement'. Its reorganization of the Bureau of Human Rights into Democracy, Human Rights and Labor (DRL) served to increase its clout and resources, although it might also have led to an unhelpful conflation of these various areas of activity. The administration has justly been criticized for its failures in the promotion of human rights, and no more strongly than in its relationship with China. Nevertheless, the administration's appointments, the unprecedented access it has afforded human rights NGOs, together with its December 1998 decision to make it the responsibility of all executive departments and agencies to be aware of US international human rights obligations, and to set up an interagency working group on human rights treaties 'for the purpose of providing guidance, oversight, and coordination with respect to questions concerning the adherence to and implementation of human rights obligations and related matters',[87] illustrate the difficulties of avoiding the human rights component in any policy decision. US administrations have to find strong justifications for ignoring human rights concerns and these have to be presented to a variety of sceptical audiences, both domestic and international.

Many of the USA's major Western allies have traversed along a similar route, especially those such as the Nordic countries, the Netherlands, and Canada. Others have lagged somewhat behind for historical and other reasons. In Germany, for example, in October 1991, the Minister for Economic Cooperation and Development announced five criteria for German development cooperation including respect for human rights, participatory democracy, and commitment to the rule of law. No separate human rights section was created, however, and the human rights policy was entrusted to the existing development policy section.[88] Japan too has introduced changes in response to the widening normative agenda at the end of the cold war. In 1989 Japan became the world's largest donor of bilateral foreign aid. Subjected to international criticism that its aid

[87] See US Office of the Press Secretary, White House, Executive Order, 'Implementation of Human Rights Treaties', Dec. 10 1998.

[88] Peter P. Waller, 'Aid and Conditionality: The Case of Germany, with particular reference to Kenya', in Olav Stokke (ed.), *Aid and Political Conditionality* (London: Frank Cass, 1995).

disbursements reflected only its own financial interests, and to domestic calls that it pay more attention to the political complexion of governments it was aiding, the Prime Minister, Toshiki Kaifu, announced in April 1991 four guidelines for an Official Development Assistance (ODA) charter. He stated: 'Full attention should be paid to efforts for promoting democratization and introduction of a market-oriented economy, and the situation regarding the securing of basic human rights and freedoms in the recipient country.'[89] As with other states operating under similar criteria, Japan has attracted serious criticism for failing to live up to these standards in its aid disbursement policies; nevertheless, the rhetorical commitment has opened a political space, as it has elsewhere, for domestic and international groups to mobilize and focus attention on backsliding and to press for changes within the Japanese bureaucracy to help consolidate the new normative commitment.

The strong linkages being made between the idea that those states that protect human rights and fundamental freedoms provide the most propitious conditions for development, including that of human potential, suggest to Donnelly that at the end of the twentieth century we were witnessing the establishment of a new 'standard of civilization'. Governments will be entitled to full membership of international society only to the extent that they observe international human rights standards.[90] Thus, the legitimacy of governments has come to depend not simply on control of territory and peoples and international recognition of that fact, but also on a government's ability to protect some core group of internationally recognized human rights. We have reached a point, Donnelly suggests, where human rights have come subtly to 'shape national and international political spaces and identities by demanding, justifying or delegitimating certain practices'. One-party military rule no longer commands the reluctant acceptance it did in the 1970s, in the same way that colonialism lost its acceptability as state practice much earlier in the twentieth century. We now take more seriously 'the idea that states can be held morally and politically liable at the international level for how they

---

[89] Yasunobu Sato, 'New Directions in Japanese Foreign Policy: Promoting Human Rights and Democracy in Asia–ODA Perspective', in Edward Friedman (ed.), *The Politics of Democratization: Generalizing East Asian Experiences* (Boulder, Colo.: Westview Press, 1994), 116; Hoshino Eiichi, 'Human Rights and Development Aid: Japan after the ODA Charter', in Van Ness (ed.), *Debating Human Rights*. Eiichi concludes that 'the human rights practices of recipient countries are not systematically linked to the allocation of Japanese economic aid', which he attributes mainly to the inability of policy-makers to distinguish between those governments that lack both the human rights infrastructure and the political will for the protection of human rights, from those who lack only the former (see pp. 225–6).   [90] Donnelly, 'Human Rights', 20, 14.

treat their own citizens on their own territory'.[91] Normative development and diffusion have occurred even if convergence with respect to compliance remains severely compromised.

CONCLUSION

The widening and deepening of the human rights idea owes itself to a variety of factors and must include revulsion against genocidal practices during the Second World War, racial discrimination, and the propping-up of repressive regimes in the cold-war era. Important too has been the shifting balance of voting power or bargaining power in UN bodies or state bureaucracies; the changing of legislative and bureaucratic procedures, the consequences of which were only partially realized beforehand and which demonstrate the independent power of institutional arrangements; and a kind of tit-for-tat targeting by adversaries that in the context of fluctuating voting power often served to make less partisan and more global the effects of new initiatives. Formal enforcement mechanisms may be limited, but norms of appropriate behaviour, power-political and bureaucratic processes have pushed the regime forward.

Nevertheless, it is vital to acknowledge for the context of the analysis in this book that there are many mechanisms, both at the state and at institutional levels, that allow the perpetrators of cruelty to avoid being sanctioned. There may be considerable distance between treaty signature and actual ratification, and important exceptions and reservations may be introduced at the time of ratification. Treaty reporting requirements in some cases are relatively infrequent, and lateness or inadequacy in reporting is met with appeals for improved procedural compliance. Those governments that have the capacity to respond to evidence of abuse have several opportunities to back away from a policy they fear might undermine a relationship important to other foreign policy objectives. Consistency of application and the promotion of enforcement in this state-based regime remain serious problems therefore. Indeed, Washington has found it difficult even to agree on a consistent, formal, operational definition of human rights. During the Carter period, his administration finally offered one that stressed 'integrity of the person's rights . . . the right to fulfilment of such vital needs as food, shelter, health care and

---

[91] Ibid. 22, and Donnelly, 'The Social Construction of International Human Rights', in Dunne and Wheeler (eds.). *Human Rights in Global Politics,* 93.

education . . . and civil and political liberties'.[92] But under Reagan, the 'Administration continued to define "human rights" so as to exclude economic rights and to downgrade "integrity of the person"'. [93] The USA, while it is the most prominent of the states proclaiming a commitment to advancing human rights in its external policies, has singularly failed to project itself as the model for others, either as a result of continuing inconsistencies in behaviour, or because of its unwillingness to give priority to international law over domestic legislation. Its recent turn to the promotion of religious freedom for Christians similarly risks a distancing between itself and its major Western and Middle Eastern allies, not to mention the central tenets of the human rights covenants. A past and present record that includes 'genocide against the American Indian population, black slavery, American imperial interventions in the Third World, and the continuing covert and illegal activities of the CIA' renders it a highly flawed participant, even though one should also acknowledge its contribution to the authorship of UN treaties, its provision of a safe haven for large numbers of political dissidents,[94] and deeply embedded freedoms for most of its citizens.

However, there are problems, too, with those US allies that similarly play a prominent role in the human rights regime. A review of EU procedures at the end of the millennium concluded that rhetoric was not being matched by reality, that the 'Union's present approach to human rights tends to be splintered in many directions, lacks the necessary leadership and profile, and is marginalized in policy-making'.[95] The EU's failure to examine on a systematic basis its own continuing problems, especially in the areas of racism and xenophobic practices, undermines its authority to act in this issue area. Those states with the greatest capacities and greatest willingness to contribute to normative diffusion are hardly unblemished as participants, therefore, weakening the message and undercutting the likelihood of implementation of human rights protections. For these and other reasons the competing Westphalian norm of state sovereignty, and its corollary of non-interference, still maintains a hold on many states. This is particularly so among those governments

[92] Dumbrell, *American Foreign Policy: Carter to Clinton* (New York: St Martin's Press, 1997), 18.
[93] Ibid. 86. Dumbrell notes that the US Secretary of State, George Shultz, had 'forcefully to dissuade Reagan from personally inviting [General] Pinochet to Washington' (p. 86).   [94] See Van Ness's Introduction to *Debating Human Rights*, 6.
[95] See 'Leading by Example: A Human Rights Agenda for the European Union for the Year 2000', launched in Vienna, 9–10 Oct. 1998. Annex to Alston (ed.), *The EU and Human Rights*, 921–7, esp. 922.

that have been, perceive themselves to be, and indeed, in certain respects, remain unequal in the international system.

Nevertheless, as we have seen, while concerns regarding inequities in power have constrained the development of the human rights regime, and the democratic states are open to criticism in terms of their external and internal behaviour, they have continued to play the most prominent role on behalf of human rights. That they can perform this role clearly relates to their material capabilities, but active participation is also connected to the normative idea that democratic states should be promoters of human rights protections. The newly democratizing have seen the benefits of this portrayal, as have the consolidated democracies. Thus, despite the weaknesses in the record, since 1945 and in particular since the 1970s there has been a deepening of norms. Increasing numbers of states have moved from debating whether the protection of human rights should be a matter of active international concern, to a discussion of how best to include human rights matters in policies.[96] NGO activity, and institutional, legislative, and bureaucratic innovations when viewed over the longer term, have contributed towards a growing acceptance of the norm that the abuse of certain human rights is wrong, even if various aspects of the regime are still subject to criticism and debate. China, among other states, has played a large part in recent years in ensuring that the politicized nature of the human rights regime continues to receive attention, that the value of the competing norm of state sovereignty continues to be recognized, and that the question of universality of rights, together with the matter of whether we need to assign priorities to particular rights, remains under discussion. At the same time, however, its entry into the debate has come at a time when it has become all but impossible to deny that human rights are legitimately a matter of international concern. Indeed, participation in the discourse itself further legitimates that understanding.

[96] Here I am modifying a point made by Jack Donnelly, who put it as follows: 'In contrast to the 1970s and early 1980s, when debate often focused on whether human rights should be an active foreign policy concern, today the question is usually which rights to emphasize in which particular cases' (*International Human Rights*, 15).

3

The Global Consequences of China's Economic Reforms

It took until the late 1970s before China became directly exposed to the core regimes of the modern international system. Prior to that time, the Communist government in Beijing represented one of the most isolated among states, especially during the period of the Cultural Revolution, 1966–76. At the start of that catastrophic movement, the government recalled all but one of its relatively small number of ambassadors from abroad, and it had few friends among its supposedly primary reference group, the Communist states and parties. No direct air flights linked China's capital to any of the major cities of Asia. Within the UN, the numbers of governments voting against the PRC taking over the seat then held by the Chinese Nationalists rose from forty-seven in 1965, when there had been a tie vote on the issue, to fifty-seven in 1966. This figure reflected a deterioration in China's external relations as chaos on the mainland spilled over into the international sphere.

The PRC was not only politically isolated in the 1960s, it was also militarily insecure. Relations with its former ally, the Soviet Union, were moving towards crisis. In 1966 the Soviets began to transfer some of their best trained forces from Eastern Europe to the Sino-Soviet border. By 1970 some thirty Soviet divisions were in place along its whole length, including those stationed in the Mongolian People's Republic. The Soviet intervention in Czechoslovakia in 1968, the enunciation of the Brezhnev doctrine of limited sovereignty shortly thereafter, the threat of Soviet nuclear attack, and the border clashes in 1969 convinced Chinese leaders that their state was endangered by a 'hegemonic' Soviet Union, a hegemony that was enhanced by the prospects of a reduced US presence in Asia, following Washington's announced withdrawal of its forces from Vietnam. The time was ripe for a more moderate era in Beijing's foreign relations, including the promotion of a *rapprochement* with the USA.[1]

The Ninth Party Congress in April 1969 took the decision to return diplomats to their posts abroad. From 1970 China resumed 'people-to-people' diplomacy on a hectic scale, in 1971 alone issuing invitations to visit to some 200 delegations representing eighty countries. State-to-state relations were also expanded between October 1970 and October 1971, Beijing establishing diplomatic relations with fourteen countries and finally entering the UN. In 1972, the year that President Nixon together with his National Security Adviser, Henry Kissinger, visited China, some twenty-one states established, re-established, or upgraded relations with the PRC, including the UK, Japan, Australia, New Zealand, and the Federal Republic of Germany (FRG).[2] From that time, until the establishment of full diplomatic relations with the USA in January 1979, another seventy-two states (including the USA) formalized ties with China, bringing the total to some 124 countries.[3]

By the time of Mao's death in 1976, therefore, China had expanded at a formal level and to an unprecedented degree its relations with the international society of states. Nevertheless, until Deng Xiaoping consolidated his hold on power in late 1978, the PRC did not undergo fundamental change, and remained committed, as the Party's central mouthpiece, *Renmin Ribao*, put it, to the five 'nevers': 'never permit the use of foreign capital; never run undertakings in concert with foreigners; never accept foreign loans (and by implication) never join the international capitalist IGOs; and never incur domestic nor external debts.'[4] In the 1970s, Beijing remained essentially passive in the UN, failing to join the Group of 77, or to participate in many of the organization's statutory subsidiary bodies, rarely sponsoring a draft resolution, and only using its veto twice. Beijing preferred instead to demonstrate its 'non-hegemonic' behaviour on the Security Council, frequently by not participating in

[1] For discussion of the deterioration in Sino-Soviet relations, see Lowell Dittmer, *Sino-Soviet Normalization and its International Implications, 1945–1990* (Seattle: University of Washington Press, 1992), and, for the *rapprochement* with the USA, Harry Harding, *A Fragile Relationship: The United States and China since 1972* (Washington: Brookings Institution, 1992); Robert S. Ross, *Negotiating Cooperation: The United States and China, 1969–1989* (Stanford, Calif.: Stanford University Press, 1995), and Rosemary Foot, *The Practice of Power: US Relations with China since 1949* (Oxford: Oxford University Press, 1995).

[2] Kim, *China, the United Nations and World Order*, 101–5, and app. A, pp. 511–12.

[3] Harry Harding, 'China's Cooperative Behaviour', in Thomas W. Robinson and David Shambaugh (eds.), *Chinese Foreign Policy: Theory and Practice* (Oxford: Oxford University Press, 1994), 395.

[4] *Renmin Ribao*, 2 Jan.1977, as paraphrased in Samuel S. Kim, 'China's International Organizational Behaviour', in Robinson and Shambaugh (eds.), *Chinese Foreign Policy*, 426–7.

votes at all. It concentrated most of its energy in that body on explaining why it deemed the Soviet Union to be the most dangerous and aggressive state in the international system.

The true change in China's relationship with the outside world is usually dated from December 1978 and the Third Plenum of the Eleventh Central Committee of the Chinese Communist Party. It was at that Plenum that the reformist Chinese leadership, with Deng Xiaoping at the helm, introduced a set of policies that Minxin Pei has described quite simply as 'revolutionary' and as leading to the destruction of 'orthodox communist rule in the country'.[5] China designed the external aspects of its policies, which involved new foreign trade, investment, and borrowing arrangements, the training of Chinese students overseas, and the importation of foreign ideas, to demonstrate that under the guidance of the Communist Party the country could modernize, become strong and united, and hold up its head proudly. The repercussions of these policies in the domestic realm were profound, not solely economically, but also societally and politically. They also were inextricably linked with changes in China's foreign relations outside the strictly economic arena, including improvements in relations with former adversaries, and a more active engagement with international and non-governmental organizations. Although there were few signs that Chinese leaders had altered their essentially *realpolitik* conceptions of international relations, the policies aimed at contributing to the establishment of a peaceful international and regional environment, in order that their country could concentrate on its domestic economic reform agenda. As a result of these decisions, within a few years many aspects of the Maoist legacy were cast aside and China began to be drawn into global society.

The importance of China's participation cannot be overstated, for its non-participation in international regimes inevitably casts doubt on their viability and on the degree of consensus that actually underpins them. China's demographic make-up, its potential and actual environmental, strategic, and economic impact, together with its straddling of 'great-power' and Third World identities, heighten the effects of its behaviour towards the central norms connected with the liberal economic order, nuclear non-proliferation, arms control, and human rights, exposing their weaknesses if it chooses to abjure them and their strengths if it decides to adhere.

The purpose of this chapter is to demonstrate how China's economic reform programme of the 1980s led to an opening of the country to new

---

[5] Minxin Pei, *From Reform to Revolution: The Demise of Communism in China and the Soviet Union* (Cambridge, Mass.: Harvard University Press, 1994), 43–4.

ideas, and to increased interaction with global regimes in all major issue areas. It provides some early sense of the extent to which the global level matters, both in its ability to influence the internal organization of the state, but also in its capacity to shape the image of a particular state held by insiders and outsiders. It is not the intention to discuss in detail at this point the global dialogue with China on human rights, but rather to demonstrate the context of China's participation in this complex web of international regimes that characterize contemporary global society, including that of the human rights regime.

THE RATIONALE FOR REFORM

Mao's death and the subsequent overthrow of the so-called Gang of Four opened opportunities for Beijing's leaders and Chinese everywhere to reflect on the Chairman's period of rule. The economic record was as disturbing as the political.[6] China's rate of economic advance, although quite impressive overall, had been erratic and was punctuated by a famine of major proportions as a result of policies that bore Mao's imprimatur. Beijing had relied on pumping in increasing amounts of capital and labour to sustain high growth rates in the industrial sector. With inadequate agricultural investment, lack of material incentives, and the restrictions imposed by the commune system, grain output in the period between 1953 and 1978 barely kept up with population growth. Living standards stagnated, consumer goods were in short supply, and housing was inadequate, particularly in urban areas. Repeated mass-mobilization campaigns had left the working population ever more enervated and apathetic.

When in the mid to late 1970s increasing numbers of Chinese officials began to make foreign trips, they were shocked by what they witnessed. Although they had anticipated a gap in living standards with Western countries, they were not at all prepared for the obvious successes that Japan and the newly industrializing economies of East Asia had experienced. Here was evidence that the Chinese communities in Taiwan, Singapore, and Hong Kong had done far better than China itself. The long-time rival, Japan, had experienced stupendous growth

---

[6] For this and the following paragraphs I have drawn extensively on Harry Harding, *China's Second Revolution: Reform after Mao* (Washington: Brookings Institution, 1987), Susan L. Shirk, *The Political Logic of Economic Reform in China* (Berkeley and Los Angeles: University of California Press, 1993), and Gordon White, *Riding the Tiger: The Politics of Economic Reform in Post-Mao China* (Basingstoke: Macmillan 1993).

rates, pushing it into the ranks of the advanced economies. These comparisons with the outside world were sobering. China's levels of technological advancement generally lagged ten to twenty years behind world levels and some thirty to forty years in specific areas, a situation that could only worsen with the liberalization of international product and factor markets and the increases in the volume of world trade that were taking place in the 1970s.

Politically, too, the post-Mao leadership was ready to acknowledge that the Cultural Revolution was a 'disaster without precedent in five thousand years of Chinese culture'.[7] On the thirtieth anniversary of the founding of the PRC, the Chinese veteran cadre Ye Jianying described the ten lost years, 1966 to 1976, as 'an appalling catastrophe suffered by all our people'.[8] Manual workers, intellectuals, youth, and officials had all borne pain. Thousands among them were sent or transferred to the countryside, and many officials and professionals were 'struggled against' in public meetings, removed from their jobs, and thrown into prison. Susan Shirk has argued that the 'Cultural Revolution had a genuine traumatic effect on Chinese urban society, compared by some Chinese to the social trauma of fascism in Europe'.[9] The Party, weakened by the attacks on individual members and on its central institutions, was in crisis. Internationally, too, things were not much better. Hostile or wary states surrounded it, and its standing had plummeted from the heady 1950s, when it had respect in the communist bloc and among the newly decolonizing countries. A new basis for its right to rule had to be established, one that would rest on the improvement of living standards for ordinary Chinese, the introduction of rules and decision-making procedures that would provide some confidence that the Maoist era excesses would never occur again, and the reclamation of a right to acknowledgement and equal treatment by other major states in the global system.

The personal experiences of the top leadership reinforced this consensus of aims. Deng Xiaoping, purged twice in the space of a decade, had spent the Cultural Revolution under attack as the number two person in the leadership having taken the capitalist road. Mao and his cohorts thought this warranted two years in solitary confinement and a period under a form of house arrest. His eldest son had been thrown either from an upstairs window or

---

[7] Merle Goldman, 'Human Rights in the People's Republic of China', *Daedalus*, (Fall 1983), 115, quoting *Guangming Ribao*.

[8] Quoted in Peter Van Ness and Satish Raichur, 'Dilemmas of Socialist Development: An Analysis of Strategic Lines in China, 1949–1981', in Bulletin of Concerned Asian Scholars (ed.), *China from Mao to Deng* (Armonk, NY: M. E. Sharpe, 1983), 82.

[9] Shirk, *The Political Logic of Economic Reform*, 13–14. See too White, *Riding the Tiger*, 40–1.

down a flight of stairs because his father was a 'capitalist roader'. Denied medical attention, the attack led to paralysis and confinement to a wheelchair.[10] Hu Yaobang, who became the General Secretary of the CCP from 1980 to 1987 and was a close professional and social colleague of Deng, had suffered in similar ways during those years. He too experienced public humiliation, was forced to do manual labour, and was locked up in a makeshift prison for two and a half years, where he was subject to mental and physical abuse.[11] Hu told Yugoslav journalists in 1980 that he estimated that some 100 million people needed to be rehabilitated as a result of the Cultural Revolution and earlier political campaigns.[12] The coalition in favour of fundamental change was indeed broad.

Initial economic reform efforts were to affect China's peasantry most substantially. The gradual implementation of the household responsibility system and abolition of the communes were an admission that the collectivization of agriculture had not worked and had left many millions in poverty and many more with stagnating incomes. Such changes in policies were undoubtedly popular, but from the perspective of the Party the new opportunities to till one's own land, or to work in the township and village enterprise, engage in trade, or migrate to other, richer parts of the country, were somewhat mixed blessings, since they pointed up that Party membership no longer stood as the sole route to power and certainly not to wealth. It led to a significant loss of Party control in rural areas and an undermining of its authority, leading Deng to advocate in 1980 a more democratic approach to village governance, not because of his belief in the 'merits of a democratic process or system *per se*' but more because elections could help to channel grievances, resolve conflicts, and provide the Party with the kinds of new recruits that could win the confidence of villagers.[13]

Another major group that had to be won over were the intellectuals. With their previously underutilized or denigrated skills, they were recognized as vital to the economic reform effort and to the introduction of

---

[10] David S. G. Goodman, *Deng Xiaoping and the Chinese Revolution: A Political Biography* (London: Routledge, 1994), 77–9.

[11] Merle Goldman, *Sowing the Seeds of Democracy in China: Political Reform in the Deng Xiaoping Era* (Cambridge, Mass.: Harvard University Press, 1994), 26–7.

[12] Andrew J. Nathan, 'Political Rights in Chinese Constitutions', in R. Randle Edwards, Louis Henkin, and Andrew J. Nathan, *Human Rights in Contemporary China* (New York: Columbia University Press, 1986), 106.

[13] Jude Howell, 'Prospects for Village Self-Governance in China', *Journal of Peasant Studies*, 25/3 (Apr.1998), esp. 91. A report of a village election by a member of a Carter Center delegation, which includes the assessment that 'the use of open nominations and secret ballots seems to be on the rise', is available via e-mail from the Foreign Policy Research Institute, Philadelphia (report by James A. Robinson, 'An Election with Chinese Characteristics', 14 Feb. 2000).

professionalism and predictability in all areas of life. The winning-over here related less to economic fixes and more to the creation of a belief that the expression of ideas would no longer result in banishment or worse. As part of this reconciliation effort, the reform leadership tolerated to greater or lesser degrees political debate designed to bind the wounds and close the chapter on earlier eras of oppression. Some of this came through in the 'literature of the wounded', or 'scar' literature—officially sanctioned writings recording the tragic experiences of those caught up in the fanaticism of the Cultural Revolution. Elsewhere, too, there was a loosening and widening of the officially tolerated dialogue on topics that had political resonance. Highly placed intellectuals, or the 'democratic élite' as some analysts have termed them, several of whom were associated with Hu Yaobang, expressed a wide variety of views in official journals, newspapers, and at academic venues. Such views ranged from 'individualism to Western Marxism, from Nietzsche to Freud, from existentialism to Christianity'. In emotionally charged atmospheres they discussed the relative merits of 'new authoritarianism' and democracy, of Chinese culture compared with Western culture, and all was 'tolerated without the imposition of an orthodox view or a conclusive consensus'.[14]

One of the consequences of the market reforms was that the range of media outlets for the expression of these ideas quickly multiplied. Whereas in 1979 the state-owned *Xinhua* book stores controlled some 95 per cent of the retail market, the new collective and private stores raced ahead and by 1988 controlled some two-thirds of it, through their 60,000 privately owned outlets and operation of a supply system. By 1994 it was estimated that China had nearly 600 publishing houses, more than 8,000 periodicals and about 2,100 newspapers, three-quarters of which were non-official. The rapid spread of telecommunications technologies—fax, mobile telephones, and access to the Internet—provided further venues for the dissemination of ideas.[15] Although there were periods of repres-

---

[14] Goldman, *Sowing the Seeds*, 9–10. Stanley Rosen confirms that selected campus surveys revealed that 'almost all students had copies of works by Sartre, Freud, Schopenhauer, Nietzsche, and other Western philosophers', demonstrating that intellectuals had been brought 'into the international marketplace of ideas' ('Dissent and Tolerance in Chinese Society', *Current History*, 87/530 (Sept. 1988), 281).

[15] Pei, *Reform to Revolution*, ch. 5; Goldman, 'Politically-Engaged Intellectuals in the Deng–Jiang Era: A Changing Relationship with the Party-State', *China Quarterly*, 145 (Mar. 1996), 37; Daniel C. Lynch, 'Dilemmas of "Thought Work" in Fin de siècle China', *China Quarterly*, 157 (Mar. 1999), 175. Lynch reports the Chinese Ministry of Public Security's estimate that as many as 620,000 Chinese had access to the internet in 1997, with a rise to 4 million expected by 2000 (p.193). In fact, a survey of Internet use undertaken by the China Internet Network Information Centre in December 1999 reported 8.9 million registered subscribers, 21% of whom were students. See *Far Eastern Economic Review*, 10 Feb. 2000.

sion in the 1980s (and again in the 1990s), such as the 'anti-spiritual pollution' campaign of 1983 and the 'anti-bourgeois liberalization' of early 1987, and various, mostly unsuccessful, attempts were made to regain control over the media, unlike in the past, the attacks were usually made specific in terms of an individual or one piece of writing, and did not encompass a person's entire career or extend to the person's family and colleagues.[16]

Inevitably, the Chinese leadership drew lines beyond which dissent would not be tolerated, and once boundaries had been crossed the Party-State took drastic action. This was especially so where intellectuals had some links with the working class, as with the Li Yizhe movement of 1974–9, or the Democracy Wall Movement of 1978–9. This greater tolerance of one discourse on change compared with another was connected with the level of organization activists or reformers achieved, the extent of radical change being demanded, and the degree to which opinions outran those of the central leadership. The Democracy Wall Movement, which expressed itself through wall posters as well as limited-edition autonomous magazines, and involved disaffected ex-Red Guards, fell foul of the leadership because of its radicalism.[17] Although useful to Hu and Deng in the winter and early spring of 1978–9 for the support it gave to the economic reform agenda, some of the political demands went way beyond those that the democratic élite were promoting at that stage—let alone the Party leadership—and struck at the heart of the Marxist-Leninist one-party system.[18]

TRANSNATIONALISM AND THE ROLE OF IDEAS

This general political loosening, greater access to foreign publications, together with wide-ranging inter-societal contact inevitably influenced the political debate within China in the 1980s, much as had been true after the fall of the Qing dynasty in 1911. Increasingly aware of the failure of the Soviet system, some intellectuals were attracted at first to the

[16] Goldman, 'Politically-Engaged Intellectuals in the Deng–Jiang Era', 37. The Chinese leadership ordered another such attempt to regain control over the media and communications in late 1998, including new regulations imposed on the use of the Internet and governing of social organizations, together with the closure of certain newspapers. See ch. 8 below.

[17] For valuable detail on the operations of the movement, see Wei Jingsheng's interview with *China News Digest*, New York, 4 Jan. 1998.

[18] Goldman, *Sowing the Seeds*, 41–7; and Jonathan Spence, *The Search for Modern China*, (New York: W. W. Norton, 1990), 660–6.

revisions of ideology being undertaken within East and West European socialist parties. Greater access to the writings of Marcuse, Fromm, and the members of the Frankfurt School, together with translations of works by Sartre, Camus, and Kafka, stimulated thinking and writing on alienation, humanism, and existentialism. Later in the decade, enthusiasm was expressed for Gorbachev's policies of openness and reform.

Some in China stepped outside this neo-Marxist framework, calling more explicitly for the development and implementation of civil rights supposedly guaranteed in the Chinese constitution of 1982. They also advocated more specific measures to strengthen the power of the National People's Congress (NPC) as a legislative restraint on the Party-State, a more independent judiciary, and greater press freedom.[19] The world-renowned astrophysicist Fang Lizhi, for example, campaigning for free-thinking in all areas of life, drew his inspiration from the writings of humanist Albert Einstein and the dissident physicist Andrei Sakharov, and his negative examples from the years he had wasted in exile from the scientific community as a result of his rightist label. A regular speaker at conferences abroad in the 1980s and invited to Princeton's Institute for Advanced Study, yet under regular attack at home for his outspokenness and nonconformity, he became the first prominent intellectual to launch a public attack on Marxist-Leninist ideology and to call for participation in policy-making to be based on meritocratic principles. At the Tongji University campus in Shanghai in November 1987 he pointed to the abject failures of all socialist countries since 1945 and declared that the success of the democracies was due to their recognition of the 'basic rights of the people, or human rights', especially freedom from fear of unlawful unrest. Fang began to persuade many members of the democratic élite, although few were willing to be as outspoken as he. In 1988, during the officially sanctioned fortieth anniversary celebrations of the UDHR, where official speakers emphasized the collective rights contained within the document, members of the democratic élite published articles that stressed instead the declaration's guarantees of individual and political rights. The legal scholar Yu Haocheng, for example, went further than most, defining human rights as inalienable, and declaring that the 'practice of using outside interference in one's own internal affairs as an excuse to refuse to discuss human rights conditions in one's own country is no longer credible'. Others outside this élite, but connected with the Democracy Wall Movement of 1978–9, used the occasion of the anniversary to call for Wei Jingsheng's release from imprisonment.[20]

---

[19] Goldman, *Sowing the Seeds*, esp. ch. 1 and pp. 74–5.
[20] These quotations and arguments are drawn from Ibid. 196–8, 268, 288.

Other scholarly discussion outside a Marxist framework drew inspiration from the arguments of the American academic political scientists Samuel Huntingdon and Lucian Pye, and from the direct experiences of the East Asian tigers, especially that of Singapore. Huntingdon's book *Political Order in Changing Societies* was translated into Chinese in 1987 and it attracted the attention of many young intellectuals, some senior reformers in the leadership, and most notably Zhao Ziyang, who took over Hu's post after the latter's forced resignation in 1987. Whereas Hu Yaobang's network had come to believe that democracy was essential for China's development, and that the two conditions were inextricably intertwined, these 'new' or 'neo-authoritarians', as they came to be called, believed in the need for a political transition period during which an enlightened but powerful leader would be strong enough to push through economic reforms and would then guide a politically naïve citizenry, with its growing middle class, along a democratic path. Their primary goal was to avoid the dangerous societal instability that they thought would result from giving power to a largely uneducated populace and in the absence of deeply embedded constitutional and institutional practices.[21] Its importance for the thinking on human rights related to its clear resonance with the developmentalist discourse associated particularly with states such as Singapore.

The neo-authoritarian movement reached its peak in the late 1980s. From January to 4 June 1989, over 250 articles on the topic were published in national and provincial newspapers and journals, and ten symposiums were held in Beijing, Shanghai, Nanjing, and Suzhou.[22] A final major debate between proponents and opponents of neo-authoritarianism took place at the People's University in Beijing in April 1989, just prior to the eruption of protest in Tiananmen Square. The crackdown on the protest after 4 June not surprisingly stifled that conversation, but only for a time, because, over the course of the previous decade, intellectuals and other concerned participants in the debate had gained a level of autonomy unmatched in any other period of relative liberalization since 1949. Where the repression of the Maoist years had weakened their ties to the Party, and their continued persecution in the Deng era—albeit on a lesser scale—had pushed them further along that path, some discovered that market reforms allowed them financial and thus professional autonomy on a scale undreamt of. The reforms in the publishing industry, referred to above, reinforced this new autonomy.

---

[21] Ibid. 275–82; White, *Riding the Tiger*, 249–50; Michael J. Sullivan ('Democracy and Developmentalism: Contending Struggles over Political Change in Dengist China', Ph.D. thesis) (Wisconsin, 1995), provides a detailed discussion of this political debate.

[22] Ibid. 273.

China was becoming, then, a more pluralist society, affecting many beyond the democratic élite.[23]

In 1992, after a period of circumspection and additional controls, some intellectuals took the arguments on political change in China in yet other directions, undoubtedly influenced by the 1989 events and their aftermath, together with the negative effects of the reform process in China that had seen a serious rise in corruption, crime, and an apparent loss of a unifying value system. But they were also influenced by the ending of the cold war: by the overthrow of communist systems throughout Eastern Europe, and then, the final stage in the drama, by the collapse of the Soviet Union itself, politically and economically. Some who reflected on these momentous happenings began to put more stress on 'orderly change directed from above'. This 'neo-conservative viewpoint', as it has been labelled, favoured the promotion of political and social stability via a recapturing of China's cultural tradition, or a reassertion of strong central control. For the neo-Confucianists among them, it was that tradition that could prevent a further moral decline in society and ensure that the dangerous radicalism that China had too frequently experienced would finally be repudiated in favour of orderly processes.[24] This argument gave considerable comfort to the Chinese leadership, except perhaps in its repudiation of the value of the Party's revolutionary past, and in its call to slow the pace of societal upheavals through the imposition of some checks on the import of foreign technology. One area where it could be valuable to the regime, however, was in the human rights field. As China came under increased international criticism after the 4 June bloodshed and repression, the rejuvenation of domestic interest in traditional values, and the belief in their current usefulness for the organization of Chinese society, provided a basis for responding to this external disapprobation. Moreover, it reinforced the leadership's moves to reinvigorate a nationalist spirit, a nationalism that began to unite all intellectual groupings, whether of the neo-Maoist, neo-conservative, or neo-Confucian varieties. The liberal viewpoint struggled to make itself heard once such sentiments had been reignited. Most liberals operated from within the intellectual establishment, but for those brave souls who chose to work outside it, and even to bring into being China's first opposition political party, the China Democracy Party (CDP), their period at liberty proved extremely short lived.

[23] Goldman, 'Politically-Engaged Intellectuals in the Deng–Jiang Era', 50–1.

[24] Feng Chen, 'Order and Stability in Social Transition: Neoconservative Political Thought in Post-1989 China', *China Quarterly*, 151 (Sept. 1997), esp. 594; Merle Goldman, 'Politically-Engaged Intellectuals in the 1990s,' *China Quarterly* Special Issue, 'The People's Republic of China after 50 Years', 159 (Sept. 1999), esp. 702–7.

PARTICIPATION IN INTERNATIONAL REGIMES

Nevertheless, despite leadership attempts to place restraints on certain forms of political organization, Chinese intellectuals remained in close touch with those ideas current among a global intellectual élite. This access was matched by an exposure to more technocratic beliefs, an inevitable consequence of the Party's promise to concentrate on the economic reform agenda, and to deliver a better present and future. In pursuit of this, Deng and his associates realized that China would have finally to overthrow the five 'nevers' of the Maoist era and to associate the country intimately with the global political economy.[25]

The path by which this was achieved is a familiar one and will not be covered in detail here, but it is useful to give some indication of the swiftness and extent of the change. International organizational membership rapidly advanced. In 1980, for example, China joined the previously reviled IMF and World Bank, the Asian Development Bank (ADB) in 1986, and the Asia Pacific Economic Cooperation (APEC) forum in 1991. After Japan, the World Bank quickly became China's most important source of external funding, approving between 1980 and 1989 some $7.4 billion in loans, covering sixty-nine projects primarily in the areas of education, energy, transportation, and agriculture.[26] By the mid-1980s China had not only become the Bank's largest borrower, but had successfully negotiated its first standby credit from the IMF, and had started to raise funds on the Eurodollar bond market.[27] By 1989 Beijing had overtaken New Delhi in becoming the world's largest recipient of official bilateral and multilateral aid, receiving almost $2.2 billion a year.[28] Trade and investment levels raced ahead: foreign trade was to rise from $38.1 billion in 1980, to $69.66 billion in 1985, $111.6 billion in 1989, and $325 billion in 1997, a pace that outstripped world growth levels. Indeed, between 1979 and 1989 China's ranking as a trading nation rose faster than that of any other country.[29] Foreign direct investment also sharply increased, reaching a cumulative total of $44 billion in 1990, about half

---

[25] Even Mao admitted to Henry Kissinger in 1973, 'not without melancholy', that the Chinese would have 'to go to school abroad' (quoted in Kissinger, *Years of Upheaval* (London: Weidenfeld Nicolson, 1982), 69).

[26] Interestingly, while the World Bank wanted to give educational help at the primary-school level, the Chinese leadership wanted to refurbish universities and to provide overseas scholarships. (see *China Development Briefing*, 2, 1, Jan.–Feb. 1998).

[27] Nicholas R. Lardy, *China's Entry into the World Economy: Implications for Northeast Asia and the United States* (London: UPA for the Asia Society, 1987), 4–5.

[28] Samuel S. Kim, 'International Organizations in Chinese Foreign Policy', *Annals of the American Academy of Political and Social Science*, 519 (Jan. 1992),152.

[29] Nicholas R. Lardy, 'Chinese Foreign Trade', *China Quarterly*, 131 (Sept. 1992), 694–5.

of which had actually been utilized at that point.[30] The allure of China's investment market continued even after the Tiananmen upheavals. In 1997 alone, China attracted foreign investment of $45.3 billion, and government reports stated that there were at least 300,000 overseas-financed enterprises in the country.[31] From 1987, the majority of the investment was in manufacturing for export markets. In 1989, foreign-invested enterprises contributed $4 billion in foreign exchange,[32] and foreign-exchange earnings maintained a steady upward curve, reaching $84.3 billion in August 1996 and $140 billion by the end of 1997, the second highest in the world.[33] China changed both its export and its import profile, from exporting predominantly raw materials to selling labour-intensive manufactures, and from importing foodstuffs to buying in industrial products.[34] Over the course of the 1980s its GDP doubled, and it was to double again by the mid-1990s.[35] As Margaret Pearson has noted, it was 'difficult not to be impressed with the speed, magnitude, and depth of China's integration into the global economy during the post-Mao era'.[36]

Revolutionary shifts were also to occur in the security field. In the Maoist era, arms-control negotiations were denounced as efforts to bolster the continuing hegemony of the two superpowers. From the 1980s, however, China began its tentative involvement in the Conference on Disarmament and came under pressure from Third World countries in particular to make a more substantive contribution. By 1996 it had signed some 85–90 per cent of all arms control agreements for which it was eligible, including the NPT in 1992, and the CTBT in 1997, the latter despite its 'junior' status as a nuclear weapons state and military fears that such a ban would freeze this status in place.[37] In October 1997 it became a member of the NPT Exporters Committee (the Zangger committee) 'the first time China [had] joined a multilateral nonproliferation export

[30] Harding, *A Fragile Relationship*, table A-7, 368.
[31] Press Release, Chinese Embassy in London, no. PR9809, 2 Feb. 1998.
[32] Barry Naughton, 'The Foreign Policy Implications of China's Economic Development Strategy', in Robinson and Shambaugh (eds.), *Chinese Foreign Policy*, 55.
[33] Avery Goldstein, 'Great Expectations: Interpreting China's Arrival', *International Security*, 22/3 (Winter 1997–98), 41 n. 13; Press Release, Chinese Embassy in London, no. BB9804, 2 Feb.1998.
[34] Nicholas R. Lardy, *China in the World Economy* (London: Longman, 1994) 31–2.
[35] Goldstein, 'Great Expectations', 40.
[36] Margaret M. Pearson, 'China's Integration into the International Trade and Investment Regime', in Economy and Oksenberg (eds.), *China Joins the World* , 191.
[37] China's disarmament and arms-control policies are discussed in Alastair Iain Johnston, 'Learning versus Adaptation: Explaining Change in Chinese Arms Control Policy in the 1980s and 1990s', *China Journal*, 35 (Jan. 1996); Banning N. Garrett and Bonnie S. Glaser, 'Chinese Perspectives on Nuclear Arms Control', *International Security*, 20/3 (Winter 1995–6); and Michael D. Swaine and Alastair Iain Johnston, 'China and Arms Control Institutions', in Economy and Oksenberg (eds.), *China Joins the World*.

control regime'.[38] The story was much the same with respect to the UN and especially its peacekeeping role.[39] Once again, the initial reason for a more supportive approach to such operations related to the connections China made between a peaceful international environment and the needs of its economic reform process. However, it was also responding to the views of other states. Direct pressure from developing countries for the non-payment of its share of UN Peacekeeping Operations (PKOs) and criticism of Beijing's failure to be involved in an area of UN activity that such states found beneficial contributed to its more positive stance. In January 1982 it started to pay its share of the expenses of the UN Interim Force in Lebanon (UNIFIL) and the UN Disengagement Observer Force (UNDOF) and in 1984 'endorsed almost all the important principles commonly accepted by all other UN member states regarding international peacekeeping'.[40] Later in the decade, it began to explore the possibility of directly involving Chinese personnel, twenty Chinese officers being sent in 1988 to join the UN Truce Supervision Organization (UNTSO) observer group in Beirut, the same year that, after Soviet prompting, it applied for membership in the UN Special Committee. As mentioned in the previous chapter, over 400 Chinese personnel were involved in the UNTAC operation of 1992, two of whom were killed in the course of their duties.[41]

A similar pattern of incorporation occurred in other areas of UN activity. Unwilling at first to become a member of the UNCHR, in 1979 Beijing acquired observer status at Commission meetings, and then in 1982 finally joined that body and its Sub-Commission, together with the Commission on the Status of Women. China participated in drafting such human rights instruments as the Convention against Torture (which it signed in December 1986 and ratified in October 1988), the Convention Relating to the Status of Refugees, and the declaration protecting minority rights. Not surprisingly, it worked actively to ensure the UN General Assembly adopted a Declaration on the Right to Development in 1986. It also moved forward, if with great caution, to voting on human rights situations in particular countries: having previously refused to take part in voting on resolutions concerning Chile, El Salvador, and Guatemala, Beijing abstained on these votes in 1981 and in 1985 voted in favour of a

---

[38] Statement of Robert J. Einhorn, Deputy Assistant Secretary of State for Nonproliferation before the Committee on International Relations, US House of Representatives, 4 Feb. 1998.

[39] A discussion of China's PKO policy is contained in Yongjin Zhang, 'China and UN Peacekeeping: From Condemnation to Participation', *International Peacekeeping*, 3/3 (Autumn 1996), 1–15.   [40] Ibid. 7–8.

[41] Yitzhak Shichor, 'China and the Role of the United Nations in the Middle East', *Asian Survey*, 31/3 (Mar. 1991), 265–6; Zhang, 'China and UN Peacekeeping', 15 n.39.

UNCHR resolution investigating conditions in Chile, although not in El Salvador and Iran. In 1984 it supported the appointment of a Special Rapporteur to investigate the human rights situation in Afghanistan, and demonstrated its willingness to accept the UNCHR procedure of adopting a number of its resolutions without a vote.[42] By early 1997 it had acceded to nine UN human rights conventions, and, as noted previously, at the end of that year and in 1998 signed the crucial two major covenants on human rights.

In a number of cases, the reasons for involvement related not only to the desire to promote the kind of external conditions that would allow for a concentration on domestic economic reform, but also to matters of international prestige. The language used to justify the decision to sign the CTBT, for example, emphasized that

China could not buck this 'great international trend'. There was 'psychological pressure' to join once the other P-5 had joined the negotiations and there was clear support from developing countries. China's signature was consistent with its being a responsible major power, and joining the treaty was part of a 'global atmosphere', such that China would have been isolated had it opposed or sabotaged the treaty.[43]

With respect to the international human rights regime, Chinese leaders constantly referred to their active support and participation within it and—with the USA often as the benchmark—their comparatively good record of accession to some of the covenants, conventions, and protocols.[44]

THE NEW PROFESSIONAL ÉLITES

This concern for international image in the reform era extended to a recognition that full participation in such international regimes required the training of an élite that could promote and protect Chinese interests in such multilateral settings, whether at the official or at the non-governmental or 'track-two' levels. Chinese membership of international NGOs mushroomed particularly dramatically as a result of Beijing's

---

[42] Ann Kent, *Between Freedom and Subsistence: China and Human Rights* (Hong Kong: Oxford University Press, 1995), 103, and *Human Rights in the People's Republic of China: National and International Dimensions* (Canberra: Peace Research Centre, Australian National University (ANU), 1990), 58.

[43] Swaine and Johnston, 'China and Arms Control Institutions', 108.

[44] For a series of such statements, see Andrew J. Nathan, 'China and the International Human Rights Regime', in Economy and Oksenberg (eds.), *China Joins the World*, 137.

greater global activism, with participation in over 1,000 by 1995, making China fourth in Asia behind India, Japan, and South Korea.[45] Even in the crucial security field, new ideas were to be absorbed and exchanged. Chinese participation from the 1980s in arms-control discussions at the official levels required broader involvement at non-governmental levels. This led to the development of regular contacts with the Western arms-control scholarly community, and possibly helped with the Chinese articulation of ideas that supported signature of the NPT, the CTBT, and participation in the Fissile Material Production Cutoff talks.[46] From the government's perspective, then, NGO membership could at times be a double-edged sword, because of an increased societal awareness that state interests and people's interests could in fact be opposed.

The training of this new technocratic élite became a matter of priority. Some of the training came as a welcome result of membership of the major international economic institutions. IMF membership, for example, brought with it regular consultation, training in collection of statistical data, in methodology, and in accounting procedures, together with a full range of lectures, joint seminars, and colloquia.[47] Contacts of these kinds were instrumental in altering the 'perceptions of many Chinese leaders about both the world economy and their own economic performance' within it.[48] Bodies such as the Ford Foundation were early on the scene, from 1979 and at Chinese prompting beginning the funding of direct support for academic and professional exchanges between institutions in China and suitable counterparts in the USA in the fields of economics, law, and international relations.[49] Over time, as a result of these and many similar agreements, thousands of Chinese students and scholars engaged with colleagues overseas, either in degree programmes or in professional meetings, some 75,000 receiving visas to enter the USA alone between 1979 and 1989.[50] Some of the programmes put more emphasis on training inside China itself, such as the work

[45] Ann Kent, 'China, International Organizations and Regimes: The ILO as a Case Study in Organizational Learning', *Pacific Affairs*, 70/4 (Winter 1997–8), 519.

[46] Swaine and Johnston, 'China and Arms Control Institutions', 117.

[47] William R. Feeney, 'China and the Multilateral Economic Institutions', in Samuel S. Kim (ed.), *China and the World: Chinese Foreign Relations in the Post-Cold War Era* (Boulder, Colo.: Westview Press, 1994), 231.

[48] Harold K. Jacobson and Michel Oksenberg, *China's Participation in the IMF, the World Bank, and GATT: Toward a Global Economic Order* (Ann Arbor, Mich.: University of Michigan Press, 1990), 17. Interestingly, there has been an element of reciprocity here: with China as an observer to the GATT in the 1980s, officials in the body have argued that Beijing's participation has helped their work because it has been (up to a point) 'espousing and adhering to their norms' (ibid.126).

[49] See *The Ford Foundation and China*, report no. 488, Jan. 1991, p.7.

[50] Harding, 'China's Cooperative Behaviour', 379.

undertaken in the field of economics by Professor Gregory Chow of Princeton University.[51]

Neither were the law schools to be neglected. This was an urgent requirement, in part because of the Party-State's commitment to reducing the arbitrariness in its behaviour, but also because legal skills were necessary to transform the economy from a planned to a market-based system, especially in areas covering commercial contracts and foreign joint ventures. In the early years of economic reform, many new laws relating to the economic area had to be promulgated—some 250 out of the 300 in all areas that were enacted by 1982.[52]

The task of revitalization in this area was enormous, of course. Lawyers trained during the Chinese Nationalist era had been subject to particularly harsh treatment in a communist political system that perceived law as a tool of class struggle. The profession was all but wiped out in the various political movements in the Maoist era: where China's population grew by 235 million between 1957 and 1980, the number of lawyers stayed the same at 3,000, many of whom were part-time and out of practice.[53]

Initial moves in 1979 were to re-establish the Ministry of Justice and court system and resuscitate the law schools. By 1982 some twenty universities and institutes were offering undergraduate training in law, and an additional 100 colleges offered legal training by correspondence or on a part-time basis. China's goal was to have 50,000 lawyers in place by 1990.[54] In fact, the *China Law Yearbook* reported in 1995 that the number of

---

[51] After visiting China in the summer of 1980 to teach econometrics at the Chinese Academy of Social Sciences in Beijing, and then at six universities in China in 1982, Professor Chow decided it was necessary to write a textbook to explain modern economics, using China as a case study. Following discussion with various Beijing ministries, three summer workshops on microeconomics, macroeconomics, and econometrics were organized between 1984 and 1986. Secretary-General Zhao Ziyang offered his public endorsement of the exercise, signalling the relevance of the study of modern economics to Chinese economic reforms. Subsequent to this, students continued to be taught in China and also in Canadian and US universities (among others). See Gregory C. Chow, *Understanding China's Economy* (Singapore: World Scientific Publisher, 1994).

[52] Kent, *Between Freedom and Subsistence*, 89.

[53] William P. Alford, 'Tasselled Loafers for Barefoot Lawyers: Transformation and Tension in the World of Chinese Legal Workers', in Stanley B. Lubman (ed.), *China's Legal Reforms*, (Oxford: Oxford University Press, 1996), 27. In 1988, only 3% of those working in the courts, procuratorates, and in judicial administration had received legal training at the college level, and 43% had no legal training whatsoever. See Anders Mellbourn and Marina Svensson, *Swedish Human Rights Training in China: An Assessment*, report prepared for the Swedish International Development Cooperation Agency, Feb. 1999, p.11. An interesting Chinese perspective on the traditional and Maoist legal cultures is contained in Xin Chunying, *Chinese Legal System and Current Legal Reform* [in Chinese and in English] (Konrad–Adenauer–Stiftung [KAS] Occasional Papers, Beijing Fa Lu Chubanshe, 1999). [54] Spence, *Search for Modern China*, 705–8.

trained lawyers was close to 100,000,[55] and likely to rise to some 150,000 by the end of the century. China organized its first bar examination in 1986, and, by 1994, 400,000 people had taken it with a pass rate of just under 20 per cent.[56] Constitutional reform accompanied these changes, the 1982 revised constitution being presented as a 'decisive break with the recent past', with the placing of rights near the beginning of the text designed to underscore this.[57] But many other notable pieces of legislation were passed in these two decades, including the country's first Criminal Procedure Law (CPL), adopted 1 July 1979 and revised in significant ways in 1996, and laws on prisons, judges, police, procurators, and lawyers. The leadership also passed legislation expanding political rights, such as the Election Law for the NPC and the Local People's Congresses.[58]

China also designated international law as one of the priority areas and in September 1979 thirty undergraduates were admitted to Beijing University as majors in the field, 'the first such comprehensive program in China's history'. While only thirteen articles on international law were published in China in 1979, that number had risen to 110 by 1984. In 1981 came the production of a definitive textbook, which shaped the development of the field. Another first for Communist China was the election of a Stanford University-trained Chinese delegate, Ni Zhengyu, to the International Court of Justice at the Hague, where he was reported to have performed 'dedicated work'.[59]

The leadership realized that outsiders would be needed to help with such a rapid programme of expansion in the legal realm. Hong Kong was an attractive and notable source of expertise and from 1987 at least three different law schools in China began the study of Hong Kong law as a specialty and translation of Hong Kong laws into Chinese. Hong Kong also became engaged, with the British Overseas Development

---

[55] Lawyers' Committee for Human Rights, *Opening to Reform? An Analysis of China's Revised Criminal Procedure Law* (New York, Oct. 1996), 9.

[56] Lawyers' Committee for Human Rights, *Lawyers in China: Obstacles to Independence and the Defense of Rights* (New York: Mar. 1998), 39. The format of the examination is largely similar to that of other countries.

[57] Nathan, 'Political Rights in Chinese Constitutions', 124; Kent, *Between Freedom and Subsistence*, p.85. Although the 1982 constitution did contain elements of political reform, including a clearer separation of roles between State and Party and greater independence for NPC deputies, other articles put in peril the various civil freedoms that ostensibly were guaranteed (ibid.). The constitution was revised again in 1999 to encompass the provision that the PRC 'shall be governed according to law'. See Chapter 8 below.

[58] The fate of the CPL is discussed in some detail in Lawyers' Committee for Human Rights, *Opening to Reform?* 2 ff. Kent (*Between Freedom and Subsistence*, 90) provides a fuller list of new laws. For an analysis of some of these new laws, see the excellent reports by the Lawyers' Committee, *Opening to Reform?* and *Lawyers in China*, and Xin, *Chinese Legal System*.   [59] Spence, *Search for Modern China*, 709–10.

Administration and the University of London, in a programme of training for young lawyers that involved four months at the School of Orien-
tal and African Studies, three months in barristers' chambers in the
Temple and Lincoln's Inn Fields, and then the final two months in Hong
Kong working in the private sector before returning to China.[60] Other
funding bodies and governments followed suit, the Ford Foundation aiding a programme of legal educational exchanges between Chinese and US
institutions from 1983, and in 1989 funding opportunities for members of
China's Legislative Affairs Commission of the NPC to send study missions abroad, invite foreign experts to China, and to obtain foreign legal
materials to aid in the drafting of such key codes as the administrative,
press and media, copyright and publishing laws, and so on. From 1989
Ford became involved in the training of the judiciary, which also provided for contacts with counterparts overseas.[61]

These kinds of exchanges showed that the experiences of legal experts
and bodies overseas were proving useful in the promulgation of new laws.
But there were other reasons promoting the study of international legal
standards, including China's signature of various international conventions, foreign criticism of China's failure to live up to such international
standards, and the references made by domestic legal reformers to them
as a means of bolstering support for their own reform agenda. For example, China as a signatory of the CRC signed onto the principle (Article
40, 2 (b, i)) that all those charged with a criminal offence were to be presumed innocent until proven guilty. Prominent legal academics in China
lobbied hard on the basis of this commitment for China explicitly to
incorporate this principle into its revised CPL. China's legal scholars were
also calling for the abolition of 'shelter and investigation', an administrative measure under which the police had been allowed to hold onto suspects without any prior approval from the procuratorate. Alongside this
domestic criticism, these and other aspects of China's CPL came under
the international spotlight which apparently contributed to the decisions
to introduce amendments.[62] Indeed, these transnational linkages have led
some to conclude that

---

[60] Daniel R. Fung, 'Hong Kong: China's Guide to the 21st Century: The Sherpa Paradigm', paper given at Asian Studies Centre conference, St Antony's College, Oxford, May
1998, pp.33–5. Daniel Fung is Solicitor-General of the Hong Kong Special Administrative
Region.   [61] *The Ford Foundation and China*,12–13.
[62] A Public Security Official in the Ministry cited international controversy as one reason for removal of shelter and investigation. See Lawyers' Committee for Human Rights,
Opening to Reform?, esp. 80 n.305. NPC Vice-Chairman Wang Hanbin was also quoted in
the Chinese press as contending that the revisions to the CPL would help to refute 'some
Western countries' smears and slanders' against China in the human rights field (see p. 11
n. 35). A fuller discussion of the CPL will come in Chapters 7 and 8.

the amount of time and energy spent on studying foreign legal systems and international standards and visiting other countries as part of the legislative process, as well as the frequency with which advocates of a particular position point to similar practices in other countries, indicate that China and the drafters of its laws do see themselves as part of the international community and are receptive to foreign ideas and assistance.[63]

Such an optimistic assessment, however, should not be allowed to obscure the vastly difficult problems of implementation that often serve to stymie the impact of these attempts at legal reform. The vastness of the effort required, the low level of legal awareness, together with the low regard in which the legal profession is still held, contribute significantly to the difficulty. But more significant is the Party's continuing control over the macro-political and economic environment, which sets constraints on the levels of legal autonomy. These matters will be taken up again later. What we can conclude, perhaps, at this point is that China's reference to international legal standards in its reform efforts, together with its signature of particular international conventions and covenants, have provided points of leverage for both internal and external critics, especially given Beijing's concern with international image. However, as later chapters will demonstrate, when political opposition has shown signs of becoming better organized, threatening the power of the Party-State, then concern with image or legal provisions have been overridden.

CONCLUSION

The China of the 1990s was undoubtedly markedly different from that of the Maoist era. As a global actor, the country became more engaged, had greater opportunities to express its viewpoint on international matters, and found itself in a position to help to underpin or undercut some of the central norms of the global system. Clearly, its statements and level of participation in a number of areas that it once repudiated promoted the idea of China no longer as a 'system challenger' but broadly as a 'system maintainer'.[64]

China embarked on its open-door policies for reasons connected with both state and regime security, but many of the consequences were unknowable in advance. The Communist Party wanted to find a new basis

[63] Lawyers' Committee for Human Rights, *Lawyers in China*, 107.

[64] These terms have been used in a number of Samuel Kim's works, including those cited above.

of legitimacy, and economic reforms leading to an increase in levels of development and a rise in international status were important to renewing that right to rule. It also wanted to mobilize talented Chinese who once had been overlooked or worse. Once the decision to engage internationally had been taken, this contributed to a greater pluralism within Chinese society, and to the establishment, particularly in the major cities, of a populace better informed about and more often in direct contact with the world beyond, and more reflective about the impact that conditions inside the country were having on individuals and groups. Greater global interaction in the economic, security, educational, legal, and political fields diminished the capacity of the state to impose barriers between the domestic and foreign spheres, marking a significant break between the Mao and Deng eras. Of all the regimes with which it began to be involved, however, the human rights regime—more robust from the 1970s—represented a particular kind of challenge to the authoritarian Party-State. The following chapters will explore how China has dealt with that challenge and chart the kinds of constraints imposed by global forces in an issue area Beijing had once seen as being entirely within the domestic purview of states.

PART TWO

The Process

4

The Generating of Attention, 1976–1989

Over this period of the Chinese leadership's exposure to the human rights regime, it received decidedly mixed signals about the levels of compliance required, suggesting certain trends but no clear conclusions about the strength of the obligations that would be incurred through participation. First, despite the deepening of global concern about human rights, governments would often treat with leniency or understanding certain states with records that deserved close scrutiny, such as China. This was acutely obvious in the case of the Carter administration, because of the President's self-identification with the human rights issue and as a result of his decision to offer succour to Soviet dissidents but not to their equivalents in China. Secondly, and pulling gently in the opposite direction, the power of various sub-national and transnational groups to generate global attention to human rights abuses inside China was growing, indicating to the Chinese government that its international political environment in this issue area was capable of undergoing significant change. Moreover, the forms of domestic unrest towards the end of the 1980s, together with the nature of the internal debate about the future of China's political system, demonstrated the indivisibility of the external and internal spheres and that actors in both domains could work together to promote similar objectives. Even to a Chinese leadership that predominantly viewed the world through a realist lens, it was becoming evident that the global system was made up of actors other than states, the most powerful of which would have some ability to determine which issues and events would warrant attention and judgement. Towards the end of the 1980s, therefore, Beijing had discovered that, while greater global involvement could bring rich rewards, it could also reduce a government's ability to maintain control over both domestic and external realms.

Information about the abuse of human rights in China became available in a halting fashion over this period from 1976 to 1989. The inconsistency in the global response was built upon a number of separate strands of reasoning and argument, and, as yet, there was little to bond these strands together. The dominant reaction among governments was to offer understanding and suggest caution where Beijing was concerned. The tacit anti-Soviet alliance between China and the Western states that had been so notable a feature since the early 1970s shielded China from too close a governmental scrutiny. But it was more than just strategic interest that explained this sympathy: the socio-economic changes inside China seemed so striking and potentially so promising that many global actors who under other circumstances might well have been expected to take a lead remained watchful and passive. Beijing's more cooperative stance in a number of major policy arenas, including the UN, the international financial institutions, and disarmament negotiations, was sufficiently novel for relatively minor actions to evoke praise rather than blame. The external behaviour and public statements of the Chinese authorities themselves also evinced a willingness to explore even the difficult issue area of human rights and to expand their conception of such rights. Beijing's participation in human rights bodies and signature of some of the international conventions, notably the one against torture, suggested a growing responsiveness to global human rights norms and the realization that full participation in the international community required adherence to certain minimal rules of behaviour. On the whole, therefore, global actors viewed China as a fragile plant that needed to be nurtured if it were to become more deeply embedded into the central norms of the international system. And, since China had been especially isolated from international discourse during the Maoist era, there was much to be done in all fields—economic, political, social, and strategic. For some in the global community, China's attitude towards human rights was simply one important area among a number of other significant areas.

CATALYSTS IN THE MID TO LATE 1970s

I argued in Chapter 2 that the human rights regime had undergone a deepening and widening in the 1970s as a result of changes in UN human rights institutions, the growth in numbers of NGOs, and the rhetorical focus on human rights in the Carter era. These developments were as yet having only minimal effects on attitudes towards China: academics and others interested in China were aware of abuses suffered during the Cultural Revolution and in earlier political campaigns, such as the 1957 Anti-Rightist Movement, and some university study groups in North America and Europe did write articles and send the occasional telegram to those who could have generated a political debate. But such groups did not actively seek roles as lobbyists nor to define themselves as professional lobbying organizations.[1] However, as the Cultural Revolution drew to a close in China between 1974 and 1976, the Chinese themselves reminded those willing to listen that those ten lost years represented a period of despotism without parallel in China's modern history. Chinese officials spoke of the millions that had suffered and that needed to be rehabilitated; and young, disillusioned Red Guards tried to explain how such a catastrophe had come to pass. The Li Yizhe group in Guangzhou in 1974 produced a lengthy wall poster attacking the Communist Party for having produced a new élite that abused its power and suppressed the democratic rights of the people. Protests in Tiananmen Square in April 1976, which turned ugly when public security officials tried to remove wreaths commemorating the recently deceased Premier, Zhou Enlai, were indicative of the resentment at the termination of the mourning period for Zhou, but more broadly of the anger at the chaos that the Cultural Revolution and the Gang of Four leadership had wrought.

With better sources of information about these forms of dissent, those writing on China began to turn their attention more directly to the political abuse of power inside the country. Prompted by these protests and the arrest of the Li Yizhe group, Susan Shirk, the US academic and China specialist, for example, published an article in 1977 in the prominent American journal *Foreign Policy*. In it she warned presciently of the strong possibility that dissent would grow in China, arising out of the disillusionment felt by the Red Guard generation, and she used a relatively extensive discussion of the Li Yizhe wall poster, as a means of explaining the roots of discontent among younger, educated Chinese.[2]

The mid-1970s also marked the start of international NGO interest in China. AI's resources had begun to increase substantially by this time, the

---

[1] Roberta Cohen, in her major article on this topic (which will be drawn on extensively in the following pages), mentions two US organizations: The Chinese Human Rights Society, formed in 1975, and The Society for the Protection of East Asians' Human Rights, established in 1977, with James Seymour as its President. She notes too the activity of French sinologists, who also took a lead in drawing attention to human rights violations in China (Cohen, 'People's Republic of China: the Human Rights Exception', *Human Rights Quarterly*, 9/4 (1987), 469–70). Ms Cohen's own important role is similarly worth recording: among a number of major posts in the human rights field, she was a Deputy Assistant Secretary of State for Human Rights between 1980 and 1981 during the Carter administration, and honorary secretary 1985–6 to the Parliamentary Human Rights Group, founded in 1976 as an independent forum in the UK Parliament for the defence of international human rights.

[2] Susan L. Shirk, 'Human Rights: What about China?', *Foreign Policy*, 29, (Winter 1977–8), 109–27. Shirk became the Deputy Assistant Secretary of State for East Asian and Pacific Affairs, US Department of State, during the second Clinton administration.

US section alone growing from 3,000 to 50,000 members between 1974 and 1976.[3] Amnesty had been concerned about the relative international neglect of human rights conditions in China, especially when compared with other Asian countries such as South Korea, South Vietnam, and Taiwan. Beyond Asia there was a growing emphasis on Eastern Europe, which arose from the Helsinki process. Thus, in 1976 it announced the beginnings of a research programme on the PRC. For an organization whose reputation would stand or fall by the quality of its information and its maintenance of an unbiased approach to investigation, a major concern was to pool and verify information from as many sources as possible. At that time it relied on academics, journalists, contacts in Hong Kong, Westerners formerly imprisoned in the country, and the Chinese official and international media. It also wrote to the Chinese government for information: in 1977, for example, enquiring about the fate of those arrested after the April 1976 demonstrations. Having built up case details on a number of individuals, it began to adopt Chinese prisoners of conscience. That research programme, started in 1976 and culminating in 1978 in Amnesty's first major report on China, absorbed in 1977 about one quarter of its research time devoted to Asia—a mark of the importance attached to the decision and the scale of the task involved.[4] Thus, there was a crucial link during this period between those Chinese whose actions served to bring their grievances to international attention, the open-door policy, which allowed greater access to outsiders and the world's press, an international climate more attentive to human rights matters, and a determined international NGO, such as Amnesty, concerned about the lack of global balance in the reporting of human rights abuses and ready to use the occasion of the 1976 demonstrations to focus attention on China.

The 1978 report concentrated on most major issues of concern to Amnesty, including arbitrary arrest, the use of torture to gain confessions, and the long-term detention of suspects without trial. It also attempted an early evaluation of the civil and political rights contained within the new 1978 constitution. Subsequently, in its annual reports, it kept tabs on the constitutional and legal developments that came in the

---

[3] *Amnesty International Report 1977* (London, 1977), 174–9. On AI resources: in 1970 the international budget was £28,000 and the international secretariat employed only nineteen people. By 2000 its budget rivalled that of the UN's in the human rights field. See *Amnesty International Report 1980* (London, 1980), 6, and Keck and Sikkink, *Activists beyond Borders*, 90.

[4] Interview at Amnesty offices in London, 26 May 1999; *Amnesty International Report 1977*, and Cohen, 'Human Rights Exception', 505. Amnesty's first report on China was called *Political Imprisonment in the People's Republic of China* (London, 1978). It was the first on China by any NGO.

wake of China's modernization policies, and also published further major studies on issues of particular concern: in 1984 a report on prisoners of conscience and the death penalty in China; in 1987 (and designed to appear just after China's signature of the Convention against Torture) one on the abuse and ill-treatment of prisoners; and in January 1989 another on the country's use of the death penalty.[5] This unfavourable publicity had an impact in China, as we shall see in the final section of this chapter. One more localized but revealing effect of Amnesty's focus on China can be gleaned from the Chinese publication *Propaganda Trends*. This publication referred to the 'flaws and imperfections' in an article that had appeared in the *Yangcheng Evening News* on 18 January 1983 and that described 'in detail the entire process of Wang Zhong's execution'. According to *Propaganda Trends*, the newspaper 'should not have reported certain uncivilized acts performed by the judicial organs in the process of administering justice', the main reason appearing to be because, 'in recent years, through various channels, Amnesty International has called on us to abolish the death penalty and has made a lot of publicity about how inhumane, et cetera et cetera, it is of us to retain the death penalty'. It went on: 'The report . . . mentioned here easily gives those who oppose us internationally an opportunity to cook up excuses for doing so. Hence, we hope all media units will pay attention and under no circumstances include concrete descriptions of executions in propaganda reports dealing with death sentences.' This was hardly the response that Amnesty would have desired, but it was an early indication that the Chinese authorities were concerned about such criticism and the country's international image.[6]

Improved foreign access to Tibet provided a global audience with information about unrest in that region. As growing numbers of visitors and journalists were allowed into the area, especially towards the end of the 1970s, and publicized their findings, this energized Tibetans abroad, internationalized the Tibetan struggle, and prompted Amnesty to take up the cases of those arrested for political or religious reasons.[7] A Tibetan lobby became active, eventually leading to the setting-up of groups in London, at the UN in New York and in Washington. At this point, however, neither Amnesty nor the Tibet lobby was to receive much support. The most the Carter administration could be prodded into was praise for China's willingness to admit the abuses of the past and an expression of

[5] A useful list is contained in Kent, *Between Freedom and Subsistence,* 155–7.

[6] 'Avoid Giving Amnesty International Pretexts', trans. in Micheal Schoenhals (guest ed.), 'Selections from Propaganda Trends: Organ of the CCP Central Propaganda Department', *Chinese Law and Government* (Winter 1991–2), 51.

[7] Cohen, 'Human Rights Exception', 508–9.

hope that all Chinese would have a better future.[8] In addition, it was not until the mid to late 1980s that other NGOs, such as Asia Watch (later called Human Rights Watch/Asia), the Lawyers' Committee for Human Rights, and the Committee to Protect Journalists, among others, would turn their attention to China.[9]

EXPLAINING GOVERNMENTAL PASSIVITY

That democratic governmental responses were not stronger at this juncture owes much to this fact of the Chinese willingness to admit past wrongs and the indications Beijing gave that it would work to ensure the adoption of a legal framework that would provide some of the necessary protections. In November 1978 the Party termed the 1976 Tiananmen demonstration a 'revolutionary' and not a 'reactionary' movement, a significant determination for those caught up in the event. It was clear, too, that most Chinese intellectuals, so often the target of previous mass campaigns, were now to be given better protection, since they were deemed vital to the success of China's modernization efforts.[10] International restraint also related to the continuing difficulties of acquiring hard evidence about conditions inside this vast country. A 1978 report prepared by the US Congressional Reference Service for a Subcommittee of the House Committee on International Relations stressed in its pages devoted to China the difficulties of accurate assessment and the conflicting nature of the conclusions reached by those allowed access in the 1970s. It also sought to provide a balanced picture, commending China, as Shirk had done in her article, for improvements the PRC authorities had introduced after 1949 in the areas of public health, education, and rural development.[11] Very often the demographic weight of China crowded out other images associated with the abuse of the individual, or

[8] Cohen, 'Human Rights Exception', 450. As James Mann has put it, certainly China was less repressive in 1979 than it had been during the Cultural Revolution, but the Carter administration never 'attempted to explain away the Soviet Union's policies of the 1970s by saying that they were better than during the worst days under Stalin's terror' (*About Face: A History of America's Curious Relationship with China, from Nixon to Clinton* (New York: Alfred Knopf, 1999),101).

[9] Andrew J. Nathan and Robert S. Ross, *The Great Wall and the Empty Fortress: China's Search for Security* (New York: W. W. Norton, 1997), 185. Between 1983 and 1993 the number of international human rights NGOs doubled (from 79 to 168). See Keck and Sikkink, *Activists beyond Borders*, 90 and, 11 table 1.

[10] Goldman, 'Human Rights, 119.

[11] US House of Representatives, *Human Rights Conditions in Selected Countries and the U.S. Response*, prepared for the Subcommittee on International Organizations, by

of particular classes of individuals. Most who contemplated China's demography, its past history, and future needs felt restrained in offering either criticism or advice. Carter's frequent references to the fact that China contained one quarter of the world's population seemed indicative of his belief that it was essential to maintain a friendly relationship with a country whose actions, oppositional or supportive, could be so consequential.[12] In other contexts, those millions seemed menacing, almost dispensable to the Chinese, but an immigration time bomb for other countries. When Deng and Carter discussed in Washington in January 1979 the matter of MFN status for the PRC and the emigration requirements associated with the Jackson–Vanik amendment, Deng stated: 'If you want me to release ten million Chinese to come to the United States, I'd be glad to do so.' Carter's memoirs added: 'And, of course, everyone laughed,' but undoubtedly somewhat uneasily.[13]

While these factors certainly played their part, there were, of course, more immediate, political reasons for acting with restraint. As noted earlier, China was at last emerging from its previous isolation. It was understood that Chinese participation in such global institutions as the World Bank or other of the UN's specialized agencies could bolster the legitimacy of such organizations and contribute to a belief that the values on which they were built were indeed universal, or at least relatively uncontested. More particularly, the Carter administration was keen to ensure as smooth a transition as possible in the normalization of its relations with the PRC, recognizing that, with critical issues such as the status of Taiwan still unresolved, the basis of the relationship remained fragile. The legacy of the previous two decades' unproductive policy with respect to the PRC, which had led the USA to lose the support of its major Western allies, weighed heavily on the post-Nixon administrations. Then, of course, there was the Soviet factor. Of major significance in shaping US policy was the belief that the national interest, as most Carter administration officials defined it, required a normalized relationship with China because of the leverage it would provide Washington over its and China's major strategic enemy, the Soviet Union.[14] Why jeopardize a

Congressional Research Service (Washington: US Government Printing Office, 1978), 184–95; Shirk, 'Human Rights',126.

[12] See USA, *Public Papers of the President*, Jimmy Carter, vol. 1, (Washington: Government Printing Office 1980–1) for examples.

[13] Jimmy Carter, *Keeping Faith: Memoirs of a President* (London: Collins, 1982), 209. The Jackson–Vanik amendment to the 1974 Trade Act prohibits MFN status being allocated to those non-market countries that restrict their citizens' right to emigrate. It was originally introduced in connection with the former Soviet Union, given its restrictions on Jewish emigration.

[14] As James Mann pithily puts it, under Carter and Brzezinski, the 'special Washington

policy that had taken so long to bring to fruition and that promised much in terms of improved regional and global security and stability? Even the combative head of the State Department's Human Rights Bureau indicated a willingness to mark time, stating in December 1978, 'It is our view that you can't really get very far if you are not talking to people.'[15]

Thus, during Deng Xiaoping's visit to the USA in 1979, although Carter did raise his concerns about religious freedom, the possible censoring of American students chosen to study in China and Chinese in the USA, and his worries about the restrictions likely to be imposed on travel in China for US journalists, he did so in sessions that Carter himself described as the least formal, almost light-hearted parts of the programme.[16] This was not the moment when Carter would be prepared to heed the words of a Chinese dissident who, in an open letter to the President, published in an unofficial Chinese journal on 1 January 1979—the day that diplomatic relations were formally established—asked him to pay attention to China's human rights situation.[17] Neither was much said or done when the Chinese government in the spring of 1979 decided to crack down on the Democracy Wall Movement, and later in the year, after a six-hour trial, to sentence its central figure, Wei Jingsheng, to fifteen years imprisonment. That sentence led the State Department to issue a mild rebuke: the USA was 'surprised and disappointed' at its severity. Subsequent arrests that year evinced no further protests even of this degree of mildness, convincing Deng Xiaoping, for one, that there were few international repercussions from the locking-up of such dissidents. As Deng put it in 1987: 'Look at Wei Jingsheng . . . We put him behind bars, and the democracy movement died. We haven't released him, but that did not raise much of an international uproar.'[18]

WASHINGTON'S LEADING ROLE: US BUREAUCRATIC RIVALRY AND INSTITUTIONAL CONSTRAINT, 1979–1987

Once diplomatic relations were established between China and the USA, however, a number of associated legal requirements ensured an intensification of the debate among bureaux within the State Department and

view of China—that it was not so much a country as a military strategy—reached its apogee'. (*About Face*, 97).

[15] Patricia Derian, quoted in Cohen, 'Human Rights Exception', 475.
[16] Carter, *Keeping Faith*, 207, 209.
[17] Goldman, 'Human Rights', 137. The letter appeared in *Enlightenment*, 3, 1 Jan. 1979.
[18] Cohen, 'Human Rights Exception', 477, 450; Mann, *About Face*, 102–3.

between the Congressional and Executive branches of government. In 1980 the State Department submitted a human rights report on China. Although it remained concerned about the quality of the information available to it, the final version of the report reflected the Beijing embassy's candid criticisms rather than points that bolstered Carter's desire for good relations. It focused on China's large prison system, the ongoing political trials, and the extensive surveillance apparatus available to the state authorities.[19] Roberta Cohen has argued that this information 'certainly influenced the Carter administration's decision not to sell police equipment to the PRC, which turned into the State Department's most acrimonious dispute over human rights in China'. That dispute pitted the Human Rights Bureau against the East Asian and Economic bureaux, the latter of which were concerned about the overall damage to the relationship that might result from the denial of such equipment. In this instance, however, the inter-agency 'Christopher group' decided to ban its sale, given the denial of such items to other Asian countries on human rights grounds, and because it was impossible to make a national security argument to justify trade in such equipment.[20]

The year 1980 also witnessed the first Congressional Hearings on China's human rights situation. These Hearings were again the occasion of a major dispute between the East Asian and Human Rights bureaux, Derian throwing off her previous restraint and reporting the continued existence in the PRC of 'entrenched patterns of harassment, arbitrary arrest and harsh punishment without fair trial for political dissent'.[21] Her vigorous statements were as vigorously rebutted by those in the East Asian Bureau who, rather than concentrating on the problems that remained, pointed to the more positive trends in the country, indicating, among other things, the lessening of the constraints that had taken place on the expression of dissenting views. The 1980 *Country Report* on human rights published in 1981 reflected a similar set of dichotomies: on the one hand, it noted that the legal system had been revitalized, but that the Party still played an interventionist role in vital aspects of trials and sentencing. It reported that there had been a widening of the political debate in the NPC and in the press, but only provided certain core values were not challenged.[22] These alternative ways of framing the problem in China—a worrying current situation versus a more promising future, or the glass half empty versus the glass half full—were to form central

---

[19] US Department of State, *Country Reports on Human Rights Practices for 1979* (Washington: Government Printing Office, 1980); Cohen, 'Human Rights Exception', 479.
    [20] Ibid.   [21] Ibid. 477.
    [22] US Department of State, *Country Reports on Human Rights Practices for 1980*, (Washington: Government Printing Office, 1981), esp. 573–5.

features of the debate in many fora, among academic China specialists, in human rights NGOs, in Congress as well as within administrations from Carter to Clinton.

As noted in Chapter 2, the Reagan administration came into office in 1981 with the intention of concentrating its attention in the human rights field on those allegedly sponsoring terrorism. It also intended to fight a new cold war with Moscow. Reagan had little doubt that it was the Soviet Union that was the 'greatest violator of human rights in all the world',[23] leading him to refuse to support UN action condemning Chile, for example, and even to contemplate inviting General Pinochet to the White House.[24] John Holdridge, Reagan's Assistant Secretary of State for East Asian Affairs, described China before Congress as a 'friendly, developing country',[25] and indeed in May 1983 the administration undertook a further liberalization in its technology transfer policy with respect to China, declaring it a 'friendly non-allied country' and thus having the same status in the technology transfer area as the USA's West European allies.[26]

Nevertheless, despite a significant deepening of ties between the USA and China in the areas of trade, nuclear cooperation, and technical, cultural, and scientific exchange over the course of the two Reagan administrations, neither the Human Rights Bureau, nor Congress, nor the citizens of China would remain entirely quiescent. Even at this end of the political spectrum and in an administration that contained many wedded to *realpolitik*, the human rights issue continued to rear its head. Reinforcing this was the publication in the USA of much new popular literature on China in the early 1980s, several books billed as 'exposés' of the real and unpalatable 'truth' about the country.[27] The Human Rights Bureau, under new management in 1981, may have suffered a loss of credibility, but it too tried its hand at contesting an ADB loan to China on human rights grounds (although it was overruled).[28] The most contentious bureaucratic issue involved the Chinese tennis star, Hu Na, who requested political asylum in 1982. The request took eight months to resolve, with the China desk at first wanting her denied such status, and the Human Rights Bureau fighting to give it to her. The Bureau's case rested on legal and moral arguments, but it also made the political point

---

[23] Reagan is quoted in Ross, *Negotiating Cooperation*, 169.

[24] Henning Boekle, 'Western States, the UN Commission on Human Rights, and the "1235 Procedure": The "Question of Bias" Revisited', *Netherlands Quarterly of Human Rights*, 13/4 (1995), 385; Dumbrell, *American Foreign Policy*, 86.

[25] Cohen, 'Human Rights Exception', 480.

[26] Lardy, *China's Entry into the World Economy*, 4–5.

[27] A useful review of four such books, by Canadian, British, and American authors, has been written by Beverley Hooper and published in *the Australian Journal of Chinese Affairs*, 10 (1983), 157–68.   [28] Cohen, 'Human Rights Exception', 481.

that extended publicity over the asylum matter would ensure an attack on the President from domestic conservative circles. The East Asian Bureau suggested alternative means of dealing with the problem, such as renewing her immigrant visa at regular intervals, or offering the prospect of a life in Taiwan. Eventually, but with some obvious reluctance at the highest levels of State, asylum was offered—not a pattern that was sustained, however, in a number of future cases.[29]

The development of economic and military ties between Washington and Beijing had the effect of expanding the basis of the relationship, but it also entailed a provision under US law that human rights considerations had to be an integral part of the policy decisions in these areas. In June 1984 China formally became eligible for the US Foreign Military Sales Program, which meant it could buy US weaponry and obtain government financing for such purchases. These developments prompted Congressional Hearings. Those held in October 1985 featured, among others testifying, Professor Andrew Nathan, who represented the views of AI mainly by presenting the results of Amnesty's recent reports on China. James Lilley, then Deputy Assistant Secretary of State for East Asian and Pacific Affairs, represented the views of the State Department. Lilley argued that, although there remained serious human rights problems in China, progress had also taken place, and his administration had determined that China was not a country that was 'engaging in a consistent pattern of gross violations of internationally recognized human rights', significant wording because, if this particular phrasing could not be applied to the country, Beijing would not be subject to the denials contained within the congressional legislation of the 1970s.

The debate on arms sales was already heavily skewed in Lilley's favour, as members of Congress focused on their singular concerns rather than the overall picture. The main purpose of the Hearings seemed to be to lambast China for its population-control policies.[30] Congressman Chris Smith, a pro-life activist, who regularly trawled for information about forced abortions from the Chinese press, dominated the questioning. The upshot of the 1985 Hearings was to terminate funding for the UN Fund for population activities, but the administration's broader policy of developing ties with China was not seriously threatened. A steady stream of arguments, some of which would return to haunt later US administrations, carried the day: the situation in China was improving, especially when compared with the era of the Cultural Revolution; China had a

---

[29] Ross, *Negotiating Cooperation*, 228–9; Cohen, 'Human Rights Exception', 485.

[30] Or 'obscene population control experiment', as the House had put it in a resolution in 1984 passed 289 to 130.

different value system from the USA and thus had to be held to different standards; and—in a direct appeal to those primarily concerned about Moscow—China was a major player in an anti-Soviet containment strategy that was the centrepiece of administration foreign policy efforts.

Competing objectives also clouded the human rights issue in other Western governments' policies towards China. The Australian Foreign Minister, Bill Hayden, noted in November 1983 that the growing importance of the China relationship was a two-edged sword: the more important it became, the more would become known about the absence of individual rights within the country. However, he predicted that his country would not approach the question 'antagonistically or in a moralizing way', adding the familiar sympathy for the 'magnitude of China's tasks of economic and political management'.[31] With respect to West European governments, inevitably, perhaps, much of the attention of these states was directed to the Helsinki process and the close monitoring of Soviet and East European compliance with the human rights provisions contained in the Helsinki Final Act. The French government did have some success in its direct representations to the Chinese government, in 1978 on behalf of the three activists implicated in the Li Yizhe wall poster, and then again in 1981 when the artist Li Shuang, the fiancée of a French diplomat, was arrested because of her association with a foreigner and her work as an independent artist;[32] but there were few other such approaches. In the absence of any sustained, general, criticism, Chinese leaders must have taken comfort from the overall governmental tendency to treat the country as unique, deserving of special treatment, especially in the light of its presumed different set of values and the demographic problems with which it grappled.

Britain, of course, was almost entirely absorbed in the 1980s in its negotiations with China over the retrocession of Hong Kong, a process that it approached with extreme circumspection. This caution stemmed from a belief that the best means of guaranteeing Hong Kong's future

[31] The Australian Foreign Minister's statement can be found in *the Australian Journal of Chinese Affairs*, 11 (Jan. 1984). See too in the same issue the speech by Professor Geoffrey Blainey of Melbourne University and then Chairman of the Australia–China Council, a semi-governmental body designed to help develop relations with the PRC in the cultural field. Speaking in a private capacity he stated: 'we employ a double vision in looking at Russia and China. At present we close our eyes to the suppression of civil liberties and to the iron hand of authority in China whereas we denounce similar events within the Soviet Union. The day will come when many Australians . . . will be outspoken about events which they at present ignore in China'(p. 101).

[32] Cohen, 'Human Rights Exception', 531. The EC began to adopt an external human rights policy only in the mid to late 1980s; thus, institutionally, it was not yet in a position to attempt to formulate a collective view among member states. See Chapter 2 above.

freedoms was to ensure a productive working relationship with the Chinese negotiators, not anger them with criticisms of policy in China itself. This approach, in fact, was typical of the way the British had dealt with Beijing over many decades, and was inevitably to be reinforced with the surfacing of the Hong Kong issue. When Hua Guofeng visited Britain in 1979 and a group of Chinese appealed to Prime Minister Thatcher to raise the case of Wei Jingsheng with the Communist leader, the appeal was ignored. (In fact, she said she never received the appeal letter.) Similarly, when Hu Yaobang came in 1986, despite Amnesty briefings on ten political prisoners, Thatcher informed the organization subsequently that she had spoken only in generalities with Hu over the matter, asking him to take note that Britain considered important 'the current development of legally-enshrined rights in China'.[33]

Western governments were also circumspect in their dealings with China in the UN framework. As noted in Chapter 2, in the late 1970s and early 1980s, and in the wake of the resolution against Chile, the UNCHR began to highlight human rights concerns under both its 1235 and 1503 procedures in a larger number of countries and from a more extensive geographical spectrum. At its March meetings in 1986 and 1989 the UNCHR criticized Chinese actions in Tibet, but these did not represent the formal start of systematic attention.[34] The Netherlands government had shown itself to be particularly active in initiating Commission resolutions, especially from 1981, and it also played a prominent role with regard to Chile from 1975. It brought forth no complaints against China's record, however. The USA during the Reagan era, on the other hand, gathered a certain amount of notoriety by its failure to support resolutions citing severe abuse in both Chile and Guatemala, even in the latter case when four states from the Western group were among the initiators of the relevant resolution. It was a notoriety that was to grow worse in 1987 and 1988, when Washington began what has been described as a campaign against Cuba culminating in 'unfoundedly exaggerated allegations against Havana'.[35] Given its apparent determination to use the UNCHR for overwhelmingly political ends during this period, it is not surprising that it raised few questions about the conduct of its strategic ally, China.

Such circumspection with respect to China at first marked the UN behaviour of NGOs.[36] The PRC had been excluded from taking up its seat

[33] Cohen, 'Human Rights Exception',485, 488.

[34] Ann Kent, *China, the United Nations, and Human Rights: The Limits of Compliance* (Philadelphia: University of Pennsylvania Press, 1999), 46.

[35] Boekle, 'Western States', 385, 389 including n. 71.

[36] Cohen, 'Human Rights Exception', 490.

in the UN for so long, and that matter of exclusion had become over the years so contentious, that, once Beijing did enter the organization, country representatives and NGOs appeared prepared to give it space to adjust. Chinese representatives also remained quite passive throughout the 1970s, adopting at best a 'championship' rather than a 'leadership' role.[37] Amnesty sought a dialogue with China's UN representatives only from the mid-1970s, possibly realizing that Chinese officials needed to undergo a period of training and learning, or more probably because that was the time when this international NGO began its serious concentration of effort on the PRC. Despite past UN General Assembly attention to conditions in Tibet in 1959, 1961, and 1965, neither Tibet nor the rest of China was the focus of attention until the mid-1980s.[38]

Nevertheless, as noted in earlier chapters, China did become an observer at the UNCHR from 1979, joined it in 1982, and two years later entered its Sub-Commission. In 1986 China signed the Convention against Torture, although, importantly, on ratification in 1988 it chose to opt out under Article 28 of the provision that allowed the Committee to undertake a confidential inquiry into evidence of the systematic use of torture. It also became active in formulating the right to development. This greater level of involvement with human rights questions seemed to persuade the NGOs that China's period of adjustment was now drawing to a close and Amnesty in 1985 submitted information on executions in China to the Special Rapporteur on Summary and Arbitrary Executions. The Rapporteur's report was coy about referring to China by name but did refer to it indirectly as a country with a large number of executions 'for a wide range of criminal offences normally not punishable by death'.[39] His annual report in 1988, was more direct, however, listing China along with another twenty-six governments as being asked to reply to his communications about alleged arbitrary executions. In 1988, the Special Rapporteur on Torture described in his annual report the forty-two cases of torture investigated under urgent action procedures. Once again, China was named as one of those that was subject to investigation.[40]

---

[37] This passivity is a major theme in Kim, *China, the United Nations and World Order*. See also Samuel S. Kim, 'Behavioural Dimensions of Chinese Multilateral Diplomacy', *China Quarterly*, 72 (Dec. 1977), and 'Whither Post-Mao Chinese Global Policy?', *International Organization*, 35/3 (Summer 1981).

[38] Cohen, 'Human Rights Exception', 490. In the 1986 and 1989 sessions of the UNCHR, China was criticized over the abuse of human rights in Tibet. However, co-sponsors of a Tibet resolution at the August 1988 session of the UN Sub-Commission were induced to withdraw it as a result of successful lobbying on China's part. See Kent, *China, the United Nations, and Human Rights*, 46.

[39] Cohen, 'Human Rights Exception', 538.

[40] John Tessitore and Susan Woolfson (eds.), *Issues before the 43rd General Assembly of the United Nations*, (Lexington, Mass.: Lexington Books, 1988), 135, 140–1.

Thus, over the course of the 1980s, China's greater openness to out-siders, its increased international visibility, together with the extension of the human rights framework into areas where China appeared particu-larly vulnerable, began to influence the discursive position of the UN, if not yet especially those of the major states in the global system. Never-theless, even here, at least where the USA was concerned, the bureaucratic innovations introduced by the US Congress in the early 1970s and con-solidated under Carter did make some difference. Despite Reagan admin-istration attempts to ensure that the strategic rationale for good relations with China was not upset by attention to human rights issues, the annual mandated human rights reports extended their coverage of China from fifteen pages in 1985 to twenty-one in 1988, not dissimilar from the amount of attention accorded the Soviet Union, (fifteen and twenty-three). The critiques of the 1987 and 1988 reports, undertaken by Human Rights Watch and the Lawyers' Committee for Human Rights and high-lighting the China section, obviously served further to increase the atten-tion on Beijing.[41] As we have seen, the Human Rights Bureau, despite particular unreceptiveness at the highest levels of the executive branch in the 1980s, did go in to bat over some issues, and Congress through its var-ious Hearings indicated an increasingly restive attitude.

The signals to China were decidedly mixed, however, with a US response that was fragmented and indicating the difficulties of inserting in a sustained manner human rights aspects into policy formulation. Other Western Governments were as yet not prepared to focus much attention on human rights during the Deng era. Overall, such govern-ments still favoured the strategic rationale for good relations with Beijing, and tended to treat such bodies as the UNCHR largely as a venue for pro-moting particular political causes, which as yet did not include China. The sympathy for China's new course and the difficulties it faced was pal-pable, encouraging the Beijing leadership to continue its well-honed skills for dealing with domestic dissent.

THE SHARPENING OF ATTENTION: 1987–1989

Despite this basis to the Western relationship with China, US congres-sional restiveness and NGO criticism were to accelerate between 1987 and

---

[41] David Zweig, 'Sino-American Relations and Human Rights: June 4 and the Chang-ing Nature of a Bilateral Relationship' in William T. Tow (ed.), *Building Sino-American Relations: An Analysis for the 1990s*, (New York: Paragon House, 1991), 64.

1989 as a result of a series of disturbances in Tibet from late September 1987 through to early March 1989. In a number of instances this resulted in the direct firing on demonstrators, and finally the establishment of martial law on 7 March 1989. The coincidence of these events with the improvements in Soviet–American and Sino-Soviet relations, representing the thawing in crucial features of the cold war, helped to loosen the constraints that the security rationale had imposed on Western criticism of China.

However, importantly, China still received the kind of sympathetic treatment referred to above based on the scale of the economic reforms taking place and the problems it faced. Western press coverage was generally understanding, even in reference to developments in Tibet. Certainly the Tibetan cause was taken up vigorously in the editorial and other pages of numerous Western newspapers and magazines, but commentary was constrained by the stated fear that the major beneficiaries of the unrest in Tibet might well be those conservative officials in Beijing striving to put a brake on the economic reform efforts.[42] The ousting of China's liberal General Secretary of the CCP in January 1987, Hu Yaobang, must have awakened these fears.

Nevertheless, those Western political figures particularly concerned about developments in Tibet did voice their concerns and took action to demonstrate their belief that Chinese behaviour in Tibet was unacceptable. The European Parliament invited the Dalai Lama to speak before it in June 1988, Lord David Ennals, the co-chair of the UK all-party group of 'Parliamentarians for Tibet' returned from a visit in April 1988 and spoke out against the poverty and brutality that he had witnessed, the US State Department also sent a Deputy Assistant Secretary that month to raise US concerns, and Canberra sent its Foreign Minister in July.[43] To coincide with the higher profile of the Tibet issue and of the Dalai Lama himself, Human Rights Watch/Asia published two reports in 1988, one of which elicited a sharp official Chinese comment questioning its accuracy and the sources used.[44]

The unrest in Tibet also generated US congressional action. In September 1987 Congressman Tom Lantos, with the assistance of the

[42] See e.g. Nicolas Kristof in the *International Herald Tribune*, 7 Oct. 1987, Jasper Becker, *Guardian*, 8 Mar. 1988, and editorial in the *Daily Telegraph*, 5 Apr. 1988.

[43] See numerous press reports, e.g., *Independent*, 11 Apr. 1988, *International Herald Tribune*, 19 Apr. 1988, *Financial Times*, 20 July 1988, *Independent*, 29 July 1988. The Parliamentary Human Rights group published a report in April 1988 by William Ledger, entitled 'The Chinese and Human Rights in Tibet', timed to coincide with the Dalai Lama's visit to London. The Australian Foreign Minister credited the release of fifty-two prisoners to his interventions on the topics of religious freedom and human rights.

[44] Chinese reactions are recorded in *International Herald Tribune*, 13 Feb. 1988.

Congressional Human Rights Caucus, brought the Dalai Lama to Washington, during which visit Lantos made certain that he was accorded some of the treatment that would be appropriate for a head of state. The Dalai Lama presented a five-point peace plan, which received the support of a number of Congresspersons, twenty-six of whom wrote to China's leader, Zhao Ziyang, requesting that he give consideration to the ideas outlined in the plan.[45] With the October governmental crackdown, and the detention of two Americans in Tibet, the Senate passed a resolution 98 to 0 condemning China's action, and conditioning the supply of further weapons and high-technology exports to China on presidential confirmation that Beijing was 'acting in good faith and in a timely manner to resolve human rights issues in Tibet'. It also called upon Reagan to arrange a meeting with the Dalai Lama. Later, in an amendment to the Foreign Relations Authorization Act of December 1987, Congress determined that PRC treatment of Tibet should be made 'an important factor' in Sino-American relations.[46] When the State Department responded with the familiar refrain that attention should be paid to the great advances that China had made in its political and economic reform programme and that the Chinese government had the right to ensure stability within a territory that was a recognized part of China, this response 'triggered strong congressional and media attacks on administration policy'.[47] The State Department had to admit in October 1987 that it had not reacted firmly enough to the deteriorating situation in the province, hence the visit by J. Stapleton Roy in April 1988. But, when Roy suggested that his department understood and accepted the differences between US and Chinese cultural values and political systems and told the Senate that it was inevitable that China would give priority to social discipline over political reform, the gulf between the executive and legislative branches seemed to grow wider still.[48] Given this general executive branch attitude, when Reagan met the Chinese Foreign Minister, Wu Xueqian, in March 1988, not surprisingly he failed to raise the issue of Tibet, despite an appeal that he should do so by the Dalai Lama, Human Rights Watch,

---

[45] Zweig, 'Sino-American Relations', 88 n. 17; *Keesing's: Record of World Events* (London: Longmans), 34 (1988), 35717.

[46] Zweig, 'Sino-American Relations', 62; Karube Keiko, 'The Influence of Human Rights on International Politics: A Case Study of US Relations with the People's Republic of China, 1977–1992', Ph.D. thesis (Virginia, 1995), 254; *Keesing's*, 35717.

[47] Robert S. Ross, 'The Bush Administration and China: The Development of a Post-Cold War China Policy', in Tow (ed.), *Building Sino-American Relations*, 19; Zweig, 'Sino-American Relations', 62. The State Department Report of 1 Oct. 1987 was called 'Special Report on the Treatment of Minorities in China'.

[48] *International Herald Tribune*, 19 Oct. 1987, and 19 Apr. 1988; Keiko, 'The Influence of Human Rights', 254.

and a *New York Times* editorial that urged him to remind the Foreign
Minister that 'for Americans, human rights are as much a part of our foreign policy as economics'.[49] What a part of the Senate wanted, especially
those members who returned from a visit to Tibet in late 1988, was rather
more consistency on the part of the executive branch: it should be 'as
forceful in deploring China's human rights violations in Tibet as it has in
rightfully criticizing Soviet treatment of Jews and political dissenters'.[50]

This lack of executive branch sensitivity to the growing congressional
concerns over China's human rights policy showed all the signs of being
continued during the Bush presidency. The Bush administration contained many of those who had honed their geo-strategic outlooks during
the Nixon–Kissinger era, a time when human rights and foreign policy
were seen almost as oxymorons. Bush had been the US representative in
China in 1974 and 1975 and then Director of the CIA before becoming
Reagan's Vice-President. He considered himself as having specialist
knowledge of China and certainly he remained convinced of the country's continuing global and regional importance. Bush's National Security
Adviser, Brent Scowcroft, and the Deputy Secretary of State, Lawrence
Eagleburger, made up the coterie of those most closely engaged in formulating China policy and both previously had worked closely with
Kissinger. They too regarded China as a state of strategic importance to
the USA and had little sympathy with the idea of making its human
rights policy a matter of major concern.

Nevertheless, it was against the background of the Tibet disturbances,
and the international attention that had been generated in the wake of the
official criticism of Fang Lizhi, one of the three main targets of the 1987
campaign against bourgeois liberalization, that the US embassy in
Beijing advocated issuing him and other political activists with an invitation to President Bush's banquet in the capital in February 1989. This
would be a way for Bush to express his support for China's democracy
movement without having to raise human rights questions directly with
Chinese leaders. Since the USA was the host on this occasion, and it was
to be a large gathering, US embassy officials believed that the Chinese
leadership would not raise any serious objections. In this, they were to be
proved wrong, as Chinese police moved in to prevent Fang from attending the dinner. Fang's treatment became the main feature of the news
reports of Bush's trip, and when the President's mild response to this
interference became known in Washington, Bush was roundly criticized

[49] Keiko, 'The Influence of Human Rights', 261. Robert S. Ross, 'National Security,
Human Rights, and Domestic Politics: The Bush Administration and China', in Kenneth
Oye, Robert J. Lieber, and Donald Rothchild (eds.), *Eagle in a New World: American Grand
Strategy in the Post-Cold War Era*, (New York: Harper Collins, 1992), 286.   [50] Ibid.

for it and for having failed to raise human rights issues in his pre-banquet meeting with Zhao Ziyang. The President's statement that his administration preferred to apply pressure to countries privately rather than publicly did not serve to placate his opponents.[51] Thus, on the eve of the momentous student-led demonstrations in Tiananmen Square, the Bush administration was in a vulnerable position with regard to its China policy, unreceptive to the obvious indications that there were now quite serious divisions in Washington between the executive and legislative branches, and that élite opinion, as represented in the main media outlets, was now far more attentive to the question of repression in China. The domestic consensus that had more or less been held together while the Soviet Union represented the USA's major strategic enemy was no longer in place.

CHINA'S RESPONSE

Chapter 3 illustrated how free-ranging the domestic intellectual debate on human rights had become in China over the course of the 1980s, with calls for the protection of civil rights, legislative restraint on the Party-State, an independent judiciary, and greater press freedom. China's official international discourse on human rights during these years, however, put the emphasis on engagement with its external interlocutors rather than exploration of the concepts. That official discourse had four main components: it admitted past wrongs, noted current weaknesses, and sometimes attacked its critics for interference in its domestic affairs or for slandering the country. In addition, however, it began to respond to the charges levelled against it and tried to project itself as playing a constructive global role through its support of international human rights instruments. Domestic legal and constitutional reform also helped to bolster the argument that the Chinese leadership was coming to recognize that the rule of law was indispensable to its reform efforts and essential to the projection of an image as a civilized great power.

There were somewhat weak precedents for China's move to project itself as a supporter of human rights, even during the Maoist period; but, unlike in the Deng era, self-examination and self-criticism had not been a strong Chinese suit then, leaders preferring instead to comment

---

[51] Ibid., 292. The story of this invitation to Fang and the Bush administration's subsequent attempt to blame Winston Lord and the Embassy in Beijing for failure to flag that such an invitation might lead to trouble is told well in Mann, *About Face*, 175–83.

frequently on human rights violations in other countries. As might have been expected, from the 1950s Beijing attacked the South African regime for its policy of racial discrimination, and supported America's African-American community in its struggle for civil and political rights. With the onset of the Sino-Soviet conflict, it accused the Soviet government of oppressing its national minorities, and women. The Thai government was attacked in 1958 for discriminating against its overseas Chinese, in the course of which Bangkok had 'violated fundamental, internationally accepted human rights'. The Palestinians were supported in their 'just struggle to win their national rights and recover their homeland'.[52] This emphasis on group rights in the Maoist era did not preclude some attention being paid to the violations of the civil rights of individuals. The American Occupation forces in Japan were criticized in 1950 for proscribing the activities of the Japanese Communist Party, thereby violating 'freedom of speech and of thought as well as respect for fundamental human rights'. Soviet citizens critical of governmental policies, Beijing appeared shocked to report, were 'watched, followed, summoned, and even arrested, imprisoned or diagnosed as "mentally ill" and sent to "mental hospitals".'[53] In 1977 it criticized the Soviets again for imprisoning and exiling its political dissidents, and even gave its support to democracy advocates in Taiwan.[54] Much as with governments elsewhere, therefore, Chinese leaders would use whatever seemed applicable at different times within the human rights code to attack their adversaries, with considerable disregard for the possible consequences for their own situation or fear of being labelled hypocritical.

What was novel about the post-Mao era was the apparent willingness to admit that the Communist Party leadership had also erred during its recent past, and especially in the area of civil rights. Even in an official treatment of human rights produced in November 1979, Mao's designated successor, Lin Biao, and the Gang of Four were criticized for trampling upon the legal system and encroaching on the rights of Chinese citizens.[55] Hu Yaobang put it more concretely, informing Yugoslav journalists that about one-tenth of the Chinese population would have to be rehabilitated if the effects of the Cultural Revolution and earlier mass

---

[52] Nathan and Ross, *The Great Wall*, 179–80.   [53] Ibid. 180.
[54] Kent, *Human Rights in the People's Republic of China*, 58.
[55] 'Notes on the Human Rights Question', *Beijing Review*, 45, 9 Nov. 1979, 20. This article, while it emphasized human rights as bourgeois rights, also introduced a developmentalist discourse, arguing that, as the economic and cultural levels of the population rose, citizens' rights to freedom and democracy could also be more fully realized. Of course, the focus on Lin Biao and the Gang of Four provided the author with a vehicle to criticize individuals and not the political system that had facilitated their rise to power.

campaigns were to be overturned.[56] The President of China's Supreme Court acknowledged that large numbers of Chinese had been wrongfully imprisoned. Deng Xiaoping, during a speech to Party cadres on 16 January 1980, reported: 'According to incomplete statistics, 2,900,000 people have now been rehabilitated, and many more have been rehabilitated whose cases were not put on file or tried.' He also informed the media that a million deaths had occurred during the Cultural Revolution.[57] In his conversations with President Carter in January 1979, he stated that 'the Chinese were struggling to make changes in their system of justice because there was no uniformity of punishment for serious crimes . . . He said that China favored the unification of any divided families, was not censoring the press, and had recently been permitting substantial freedom of speech and expression.' Deng added, however, that in China 'these liberties had to be approached very cautiously'.[58]

Statements acknowledging continuing problems in the country occasionally matched these admissions of past abuses. During the period of China's signature and ratification of the Convention against Torture, for example, a member of the Supreme Procuratorate acknowledged in an interview in November 1986 that the use of torture and other 'unhealthy practices' was carried out by the police, although he claimed only in 'isolated' regions. He also promised that police who used torture would be re-educated and in 'very severe cases' punished. The point was to ensure they carried out the law 'in a civilized fashion'. A year earlier, China's interior minister, Ruan Chongwu, had admitted that 'a minority of officers are arrogant in their work, corrupt, and resort to torture during interrogations'.[59] After China's NPC had actually ratified the convention in 1988, a member of China's UN delegation stated that this action indicated 'the wish and determination of the Chinese government to resolutely oppose torture and other inhuman treatment or punishment'. She also noted, however, that the road ahead was likely to be a rocky one, adding 'as a vast country with a large population, China still has much to do with regard to the prohibition of torture and other inhuman treatment or punishment'.[60] That year, officials of the Supreme Procuratorate were quoted in the English language newspaper, *China Daily*, as calling for more open trials, and for the new Criminal Law to be fully implemented

---

[56] Nathan, 'Political Rights in Chinese Constitutions', 106.

[57] *Amnesty International Report 1979* (London 1979), 87 and *Amnesty International Report 1980*, 193; Cohen, 'Human Rights Exception', 448.

[58] Carter, *Keeping Faith*, 207. Within three months the Democracy Wall activists would be arrested and imprisoned.

[59] *Foreign Broadcast Information Service* (FBIS), Daily Report, China (hereafter Chi-) 86–229, 28 Nov. 1986.   [60] *FBIS*-Chi-88-220, 15 Nov. 1988.

in all areas of the country. The article, in reporting a sixfold increase in the numbers of cases involving human rights violations as compared to a similar period in the previous year, was trying both to express the size of the problem and to convince the reader—presumably, especially the foreign one—of the increased vigour with which the investigatory mechanisms were being applied.[61]

Chinese officials' greater willingness to speak and write about past and present human rights violations in their country carried with it, as we have seen above, the danger that international criticism would increase rather than diminish. Any behaviour that seemed to indicate that these new-found intentions to provide better legal protections and to root out abuse were being ignored or transgressed would more likely be highlighted and attacked. China's 1983 anti-crime campaign, which resulted in a steep increase in executions, led AI to send a letter to China's President in October appealing for its cessation. Acknowledging receipt of the letter, a Chinese Foreign Ministry spokesman described the use of the death penalty as a 'normal measure and routine work' designed to maintain public order.[62] After AI had published its report in September 1984 on prisoners of conscience and the death penalty in China, in November a spokesperson from the Ministry of Public Security held a press conference for foreign and home journalists at which he felt obliged to justify the use of executions and to produce statistics to demonstrate that their extensive use had resulted in a significant drop in the level of crime.[63] More privately, however, as noted earlier, the publication *Propaganda Trends* admonished a daily newspaper for giving Amnesty ammunition in its graphic description of the execution of a convicted criminal.

As noted above, Beijing had started to be more open about the problem of the use of torture in China at the time of its signature of the convention, and also because in March 1987 Amnesty sent a memorandum to the Chinese government suggesting certain ways of introducing safeguards against the resort to such means. Later in the year, AI published its report, *China: Torture and Ill-Treatment of Prisoners*. In response to this, Chinese officials started to display some irritation with Amnesty, a spokesperson for the Beijing Public Security Bureau describing the 1987 report as 'without the least factual basis' and 'purely malicious slander and fabrication'.[64] At a press conference, a Chinese Foreign Ministry spokesperson when asked about the report argued that the 'Chinese Government has always objected to the use of torture and strictly forbids

[61] *FBIS*-Chi-88-159, 17 Aug. 1988.   [62] *FBIS*-Chi-83-214, 3 Nov. 1983.
[63] *Amnesty International Report 1985* (London, 1985), 206.
[64] *FBIS*-Chi-87-174, 9 Sept. 1987.

the extortion of confessions by compulsion'. What his government seemed particularly to object to about the report was less its substance, however, and more that Amnesty had made use of China's own reporting of the violations that had occurred. It was on the basis of these news items that Amnesty had taken 'advantage . . . to vilify China', he claimed.[65] Human Rights Watch/Asia's reports on Tibet were similarly attacked, a Chinese Embassy official describing them as inaccurate and based on 'questionable' sources.[66] The notion that others—organizations or governments—had a right to expose and criticize Chinese practice, rather than continue simply to applaud it for a willingness to acknowledge and start to deal with abuse—was still difficult to accept.

It was equally or even more difficult to accept the criticisms that emanated from Washington, mainly from the US Congress. Commenting on a wide-ranging resolution passed by the House Foreign Affairs Committee urging China to improve civil rights, including the guarantee of a free press, religious belief, assembly, and travel, a *Renmin Ribao* commentary described such resolutions as 'arrogant interference in China's internal affairs', and it threatened to start exposing some of the weaknesses in civil rights protection in the USA. Nevertheless, it also took time to explain the improvements that had occurred in China over recent years and reaffirmed its determination to improve the legal system 'so that the people's rights of democracy and freedom will be truly protected by law'.[67]

The Chinese government reacted similarly when the US State Department and Congress, among others, began to focus on the problems in Tibet, particularly after the demonstrations in the autumn of 1987. House and Senate resolutions and amendments adopted in the years between 1987 and 1989 brought forth three kinds of responses: accusations that Congress was trying to break up the Chinese state and was offering support to Tibetan 'separatists' (hence it was interfering in 'China's internal affairs' and encroaching upon its 'sovereignty and territorial integrity'); and that it had failed to note that the Chinese authorities had done much to improve the lot of a people previously living as feudal serfs.[68] Beijing also refused to accept the description of the forceful crackdown on the demonstrators as a violation of their human

---

[65] *FBIS*-Chi-87-180, 17 Sept. 1987. Amnesty's researchers had made good use of Chinese statements and of China's legal journals. China's academic lawyers had been focusing on various weaknesses in China's legal system throughout the reformist 1980s. For further detail, see Timothy Gelatt, 'Law Reform in the PRC after June 4,' *Journal of Chinese Law*, 3 (1989).   [66] *International Herald Tribune*, 13 Feb. 1988.

[67] *FBIS*-Chi-86-149, 4 Aug. 1986.

[68] See e.g. *FBIS*-Chi-87-196, 9 Oct. 1987; Chi-88-095, 17 May 1988; *Beijing Review*, 10–16 Apr. 1989.

rights, and tried to recast it as a necessary response to social disorder. As a Chinese spokesperson was quoted as saying in response to a reporter's question about the European Parliament's Tibet resolution, passed after martial law had been declared in Lhasa on 7 March, the 'Lhasa riot [was] not a human rights issue, but only an attempt by a few separatists to provoke riots to split up the country. The riots undermined public order, damaged property and killed people.'[69] In a response to a US House of Representatives' resolution in May 1989, the Foreign Affairs Committee of the Chinese NPC repeated these sentiments: the House resolution was gross interference, was slanderous, and distorted facts. The imposition of martial law was not a human rights matter, but was a Chinese move to 'safeguard the unity of the country . . . to maintain public order, guard the sanctity of the law, and to ensure the safety of life and property of the Tibetan people, especially the Lhasa residents'.[70]

These forms of indirect dialogue between certain international actors and China, during which the Chinese leadership attempted to find an alternative legal and normative justification for its behaviour, as well as Beijing's growing sensitivity to international criticism, encouraged a developmentalist turn in China's official human rights rhetoric. At first, this seemed to be because officialdom could marry such an approach with the Marxian notion of economic base determining the political super-structure.[71] However, later on, although the dominant refrain continued to be that the global community needed to pay attention to gross violations of human rights resulting from racism, colonialism, invasion, or occupation,[72] other arguments started to be advanced that would later serve to open up the Chinese conception and discussion of rights. As early as 1982, and in reference to the introduction of China's revised constitution that year, a major article in *Beijing Review* acknowledged that the rights guaranteed in that constitution were 'first subject to its social system and then to its economic, cultural, and other objective conditions'. It added: 'Therefore, in a developing socialist country like ours,

---

[69] *Beijing Review*, 10–16 Apr. 1989, 18. See also the article by She Duanzhi, 'Human Rights Abuse or Prejudice?', ibid. 18–19. In response to the US Department of State 1987 *Country Report*, China's Foreign Ministry spokesperson said: 'The improper comments on China's internal matters made by the U.S. State Department in its human rights report constitute an open interference in China's internal affairs'. (*FBIS*-Chi-88-030, 16 Feb. 1988).   [70] *FBIS*-Chi-89-098, 23 May 1989.

[71] A good example of this is the article in *Beijing Review*, 9 Nov. 1979, referred to above.

[72] Therefore, Beijing frequently condemned in the 1980s the Soviet occupation of Afghanistan, the Vietnamese in Cambodia, apartheid in South Africa, and Israel's denial of the Palestinian right to self-determination. See, e.g. *FBIS*-Chi-84-037, 23 Feb. 1984; Chi-85-055, 21 Mar. 1985; Chi-85-100, 23 May 1985; Chi-88-239, 13 Dec. 1988.

full implementation of the citizens' rights will take time.'[73] Five years later, a *Beijing Review* article made a similar argument, but made more of the claim of positive change: there had been 'consistent improvements in human rights' in the PRC, and 'building the socialist legal system ha[d] put it on the right track towards greater civil liberties'.[74]

Such arguments became more complex to handle as the Chinese government was drawn into the work of the UNCHR and after it had ratified (by 1988) some seven international human rights instruments, including the Convention against Torture.[75] As noted earlier, having started as an observer in 1979, in 1982 China joined the UNCHR and later its Sub-Commission of supposedly independent legal experts. It moved gradually on the questions of human rights violations in Chile, El Salvador, and Guatemala, changing its position from a refusal to participate in the vote to an abstention. It finally voted in support of a UNCHR resolution requesting an investigation of the situation in Chile in 1985, and in 1986 voted for a UN General Assembly resolution entitled 'The Situation of Human Rights and Fundamental Freedoms in Guatemala'. In 1984 it supported the appointment of a Special Rapporteur to investigate the human rights situation in Afghanistan, and generally accepted the practice of consensus voting in the UNCHR even when such resolutions clearly involved matters connected with civil and political rights.[76] As a result of such participation, a number of Chinese statements suggested that Beijing deserved to be commended for its active role in the international human rights movement, and it started to draw attention to the fact that it had signed more international conventions than Washington, the latter holding back, it noted, because some of their clauses were seen to 'run counter to America's laws'.[77] US behaviour, therefore, signalled to Beijing that there was considerable room for manœuvre within the international human rights regime, that reservations could be used to ensure the primacy of certain domestic interests,

---

[73] *Beijing Review*, 26 July 1982, 22.

[74] *Beijing Review*, 9 Feb. 1987, 23–4. An article in *Gongren Ribao* still written within a Marxist framework stated 'that the development and guaranteeing of human rights, which is a product of human civilization, is also a gradual process . . . We cannot hope to settle the human rights issue in a day'. (*FBIS*-Chi-87-178, 15 Sept. 1987).

[75] A list of those ratified as of Feb. 1987 is included in *Beijing Review*, 9 Feb. 1987, 24.

[76] Kent (*Human Rights in the People's Republic of China, 58*) lists these as including decisions and resolutions on human rights in Burma and Chile and also such others as the 'Right of Freedom of Opinion and Expression', 'Human Rights in the Administration of Justice', 'Independence and Impartiality of the Judiciary, Jurors and Assessors and the Independence of Lawyers', 'Administrative Detention without Charge or Trial', and 'Political Prisoners', among other similar resolutions and decisions.

[77] *Beijing Review*, 10–16 Apr. 1989.

and that there was a weakness at the core of US congressional criticism of China's record.

In a surprising and consequential move, in 1988 the Chinese authorities decided to organize a week-long celebration of the fortieth anniversary of the UDHR. A *Renmin Ribao* editorial, in trying to explain why the 1948 declaration was worth celebrating, found itself in something of a tangle, arguing the orthodox line that, while (for example) racial segregation, genocide, the slave trade, and terrorism should be condemned internationally, most other matters related to domestic affairs and should not come under the international spotlight. It also stressed that rights and freedoms could not be enjoyed by a people subject to colonial exploitation, or unable to develop its own natural resources or national economy. On the other hand, the editorial also argued that collective rights could not be stressed at the expense of individual rights, that such individual rights constituted 'the basis for practising democratic politics', and that 'the more complete and perfect the democratic and legal systems . . . the more actively people will involve themselves in governmental and public affairs, and this is conducive to the country's prosperity', an argument that Deng had used in 1980 when advocating a more democratic approach to village governance. Here, the Party newspaper seemed to be in conversation with members of China's democratic élite, who were emphasizing in their publications the UDHR's guarantees of individual civil and political rights. The editorial demonstrated a similar desire to provide a bridge between the official line and the arguments of domestic reformers when it noted that, while a citizen's fundamental rights and obligations differed according to the social, economic, and political conditions in each country, and that one country could not impose its own standards upon another, yet 'internationally-accepted standards should be respected when a country enacts laws to this end'.[78]

It was a complex argument that appeared to be trying to appeal to various constituencies, but also gently to be pushing in the direction of greater attention to individual rights and international standards. Two additional statements of particular note were a *Beijing Review* article that reminded readers that civil as well as cultural and social rights—such as 'the right to life, personal freedom and security, equality before the law, the freedom of religious belief, protection of the rights of minorities, the right to work, social security . . . provided for in international instruments'—were contained within the Chinese constitution.[79] Another *Xinhua* statement reported the views of a professor of international law at

[78] *FBIS*-Chi-88-234, 6 Dec. 1988.
[79] *Beijing Review* article in *FBIS*-Chi-88-234, 6 Dec. 1988.

the Chinese Academy of Social Sciences, who noted that China's constitution and laws now basically reflected those articles contained within the
UDHR, and that, although China's legal system was 'still imperfect and
a lot of people in China lack a sense of law . . . the human rights situation would be further improved with the improvement of the legal system'.[80] Thus, the fortieth anniversary of the UDHR seemed to bring out
the argument first that, since China had enacted laws based on international instruments, the international community had the right to expect it
to comply with those laws, but secondly, and somewhat in contradiction
with this first statement, that China—at its level of development, including its level of social development—could not yet be held to the same
standards as more advanced countries. Nevertheless, China, it suggested,
was seeking to reach those standards, and moreover was now in a much
better position to understand them as a result of its increased participation in the human rights regime. Such participation, clearly, was beginning to expose China to new experiences and to the need to take policy
positions on delicate international questions, and requiring it to engage—
still predominantly indirectly—in a human rights discourse with its critics and peers.

CONCLUSION

In the 1970s the Carter presidency and legislative changes in the US Congress and within UN institutions provided an environment that heightened general sensitivity to human rights abuses wherever they might be
occurring. Where China was concerned, in the pre-Tiananmen period, it
was the NGO (particularly AI), the US Human Rights Bureau, parts of
the US Congress, and, towards the very end of the period, the UN,
through its Commission and various thematic mechanisms, that were to
be the most influential external forces in drawing attention to China's
record. These, together with debate among China's intellectual élites,
proved important in prompting changes in the country's discursive practices. As yet, other governments did not play a major role and neither was
the US executive branch amenable to putting its newly established relationship in presumed jeopardy by paying special attention to this delicate
area: indeed, if there was to be any discussion with Beijing about this
issue at all, then Washington preferred private to public diplomacy.
    US strategic objectives with respect to the Soviet Union largely

---

[80] *FBIS*-Chi-88-235, 7 Dec. 1988.

explained the executive branch's stand, together with the scale and potential of the country's economic reforms. However, other arguments were
also important and keenly felt: China needed to be given time to improve
its legal system and behaviour; in addition, Americans had to accept that
there might well be cultural reasons why China would attend first to
social stability and then to the matter of civil and political rights. Some
media and governmental commentators also made the point that the
power of reformers relative to conservatives within the central leadership
would be undercut if support was offered to protesters, and that the problems that the Chinese leadership faced were both huge and unique, and
thus deserving of some sympathy. China after all was engaged in fundamental reform in all strategic areas. These kinds of arguments suited a
Chinese leadership experimenting somewhat gingerly with reform in the
legal, economic, and political fields.

However, this tacit argument for inaction was difficult to sustain.
China's greater openness, as we have seen, provided new sources of official and unofficial information about conditions and attitudes within the
country. This, together with AI's sense that there had been an unwarranted neglect of China's human rights situation, played an important
role in first stimulating focused reporting. Once diplomatic relations had
been established between the USA and China, this had implications for
human rights policies. The China section of the State Department's
human rights report became subject to scrutiny each year, and part of the
public record, the bestowing of MFN status or the enactment of military
sales legislation, led to China's rights record forming a part of the decision-making process, and economic assistance to China via the ADB or
indirectly through the UN's programme on population control required a
human rights dimension to be taken into account. Even if human rights
concerns were deemed to be in competition with other US interests, and
in many instances ran a poor second to them, these concerns often had to
form a part of the foreign policy calculus, whatever the political complexion of the administration in Washington. In the UN context, too,
once China had begun to play a more prominent role in its work, had
signed a number of major international human rights conventions, and as
the organization itself began to adopt more elaborate mechanisms for
investigating state behaviour, then China started to appear in the list of
countries that warranted attention.

What the Chinese leadership learned from this interaction and behaviour was undoubtedly somewhat contradictory. With regard to the USA,
there were clear signs that by the end of the decade there had been some
breakdown in the policy consensus that had accorded China protection
from harsh criticism over its human rights failures. However, it was also

the case that the continuing cold war provided Beijing with leverage, and that congressional criticism was issue-specific and not broad-based. Moreover, there was evidence of some weakness in US support for universal human rights standards, given the different emphases in the various *Country Reports,* and the varying levels of praise or blame for China's record emanating from different parts of the US bureaucracy. Finally, certain kinds of political dissidents in China, like the scholar Fang Lizhi, would attract attention and support if treated harshly, but other, less well-known activists, like Wei Jingsheng, apparently could be treated with impunity. Overall, therefore, Beijing understood that its international image with respect to the issue was not in serious jeopardy; neither was it required to strike any significant strategic bargains in this area to reduce external criticism. Enhanced levels of discursive engagement and international legal commitment, domestic legal reform, and an increased willingness to atone for the violations that had occurred during Mao's last ten years seemed to satisfy many outsiders at this stage.

However, it should also have become clear to Beijing that human rights considerations had become embedded in Washington's political structures and would continue to play some role in the USA's future relationship with China. Similar policies were in the offing or deepening in many other countries with which China had developed a relationship. It was also plain, too, that NGOs were going to persist in their investigatory and informational roles, and that, because of their increased capabilities and access to policy arenas, they would continue to pressure UN institutions and governments to act to fulfil their legislative commitments. China's experience, too, was that, if a country projected itself as one that was supportive of the human rights framework, as shown for example, by celebrating the UDHR, then some commentators would demand explanation for behaviour that appeared incongruent with the terms of that framework. This required new forms of justification from the Chinese leadership, when, for example, it responded harshly to the demonstrations in Tibet. In this case it called upon an alternative powerful international norm—the protection of territorial integrity—in order to reframe the nature of the Tibetan protests and to justify its particular response to the unrest.

Overall, the 1980s were a period of relative domestic calm for China, especially when compared with the immediately prior Cultural Revolution era. In these circumstances, spurred by domestic discussions and external signals, the Beijing leadership determined that it would project itself internationally as a state that was not fundamentally opposed to the human rights regime, but one that was still in the process of perfecting its legal system and engaged in changing the attitudes and behaviour not only of those required to implement it, but also those living under it. Legal developments over the course of the 1980s could be used to bolster these claims, as could indirect debate with its major external critics. It was only with the Tiananmen crisis that this debate was catapulted onto an entirely new plane, exposing the shallowness of the domestic societal consensus over both the pace of reform and its circumscribed nature.

5

Tiananmen and its Aftermath, June 1989–November 1991

The Chinese government's authorization of the use of deadly force on 4 June 1989 against peaceful demonstrators accomplished in one stroke what unrest in Tibet, earlier student demonstrations, the arrests of political activists, and reports of torture had failed to achieve: global attention became sharply focused on human rights violations in China. The steady growth of activism in this issue area and the multiplication of information channels, including, as in this case, live television broadcasts, guaranteed such attention, where once such abuses probably would have gone unrecorded. Some twenty years earlier, in October 1968, for example, the Mexican military had fired into a student demonstration killing between 300 and 500 people but it had attracted muted international attention, even though within ten days the country was to play host to the Olympic Games.[1] In this case the Mexican government was able to control most of the information about the killings and there were few independent sources able to challenge its version of events. By 1989 we were in a different communications era and such secrecy was no longer possible.

In the early weeks and months of this human rights crisis, Western and Japanese governmental responses were reasonably well coordinated, aided by the unequivocal nature of the evidence of abuse, US leadership, and significantly timed and already scheduled meetings of the G7 in July and of the UN Sub-Commission in August. Multilateral sanctions of both a symbolic and material kind were imposed on China and hurt it economically, politically, and in terms of its international image. This propelled China along a path that began with denial and the countering of the human rights norm with that of state sovereignty and non-interference, but from early 1990 resulted in some tactical concessions.

---

[1] Keck and Sikkink, *Activists beyond Borders*, pp. viii–ix.

Later still, its behaviour—if only occasionally its rhetoric—indicated some softening of its strict definition of state sovereignty.[2]

However, despite this initial coordinated set of responses mainly among major democratic states, there were several signs that multilateral accord would prove difficult to sustain. The Bush administration, even as it set about imposing sanctions, indicated a desire to normalize relations with the Chinese government as speedily as possible, comforting Beijing with evidence that not all governments wanted human rights issues entirely to override all other areas in their relations with the PRC. In other capitals, US administration actions similarly cast doubt on the credibility of its commitment to sanctions, and governments less convinced of the value of the policy, such as the Japanese, sought opportunities to exploit such indeterminacy. More significantly, though, an unexpected international event—the Gulf crisis—which posed a new and potentially more devastating challenge to global norms concerning use of force, territorial integrity, as well as human rights, given the war aims of the Iraqi government, provided Beijing with crucial diplomatic leverage. As a member of the UN Security Council, China's cooperation was needed and in consequence many of the sanctions that had been imposed melted away. Nevertheless, the stain of Tiananmen proved more resistant to removal, complicating to this day China's relations with liberal democratic governments whose identities are connected with a respect for human rights. The 4 June events also ensured the regular attention of NGOs, reinvigorated by the presence of new recruits of Chinese origin, and of the UN human rights regime as its bodies and Special Rapporteurs continued to garner information on widespread human rights abuses within the country.

EARLY INTERNATIONAL RESPONSES

Millions around the world, and particularly the American public, were deluged with shocking evidence of the officially sanctioned violence. In preparation for the state visit of President Gorbachev to Beijing in May 1989, major US television networks had already begun to reinforce their Beijing bureaux. But with the massing of students in Tiananmen Square

---

[2] In this sense, therefore, Chinese behaviour fits recognizably within the early stages of the 'spiral model' of human rights change detailed in Risse *et al.* (eds.), *The Power of Human Rights*, esp. chs. 1, 8.

from 15 April as a result of the death of the reformist former Party Secretary, Hu Yaobang, even more from the media were sent to cover developments. They were not to regret that decision. The crowds gathered, several participants started hunger strikes, Zhao Ziyang, the Chinese leader most sympathetic to their demands, was dismissed on 17 May, and martial law declared on 20 May. New technology such as minicameras and direct satellite links permitted vivid, live coverage to be broadcast to the USA, hour by hour if deemed sufficiently newsworthy. This led to a substantial increase in the number of reports on China over this period.[3]

The media, much like global activists, ' "frame" issues to make them comprehensible to target audiences'.[4] In this instance, from Sunday, 4 June, the China story became one of pro-democracy protesters being brutally suppressed by a leadership that was dominated by the inflexible and unreconstructed, willing to sustain their positions of power at seemingly any cost. As tensions had grown over the May–June period, numbers watching in the USA had risen steadily, apparently more than 75 per cent of Americans 'following the story closely or very closely'.[5] Not surprisingly, therefore, there were immediate demands that the Bush administration register its horror in some tangible form. That Sunday, a group of US officials from various bureaux—experts on China, human rights, international law, and international finance—met to consider courses of action. Interestingly, the US Assistant Secretary of State for human rights, Richard Schifter, who to this point had not paid much attention to China, at last more fully fulfilled the functions of his bureaucratic role: he outlined a number of provisions in US domestic law that either mandated or permitted the President to take action against China, including opposition to lending by the international financial institutions. Although this latter aspect of the sanctions policy was not made public until action could be coordinated with Japan and the Western allies,[6] the administration did go ahead on 5 June with the bilateral suspension of all sales of weapons and of exchanges between military leaders.[7] On 20 June, after further discussions with US allies, the administration decided to expand

---

[3] The three commercial networks broadcast some 600 reports between January and June 1989 compared with less than fifty for the whole of 1988. At the height of the tension, between mid-April and mid-June China took up nearly 25% of the network evening news programmes and was the lead story on more than half of the broadcasts. Harding, *A Fragile Relationship*, 240.   [4] Keck and Sikkink, *Activists beyond Borders*, 2.

[5] Harding, *A Fragile Relationship*, 240.   [6] Mann, *About Face*, 195–7.

[7] These measures included a ban on the $550 million project 'Peace Pearl' designed to upgrade the avionics for China's F-8 fighters, on four artillery-locating radar systems worth $62.5 million, and on a programme to upgrade ammunition production facilities. Jingdong Yuan, 'Sanctions, Domestic Politics, and U.S. China Policy', *Issues and Studies*, 33/10 (Oct. 1997), 95.

the sanctions and, among other steps, banned all exchanges with the Chinese government above the level of assistant secretary, halted the implementation of the Sino-American agreement on nuclear cooperation, and instructed its representatives at the World Bank and ADB to postpone consideration of new loans to China. NGOs kept up the pressure, Human Rights Watch/Asia in an open letter calling for an even tougher response, such as the recall of the US ambassador and the revoking of China's MFN trading status. The US Congress at the end of June, supported by human rights groups, Chinese studying in the USA, and large parts of the press, for its part sought to codify and broaden these sanctions, introducing a conditional element in its legislation that required either that the President certify before the lifting of such measures that China had made 'progress on a program of political reform' or that he would waive sanctions only for reasons of 'national security'. That Bill passed in the House 418 to 0 votes. However, the President was reluctant to have his hands tied quite so tightly in the foreign policy field and, working with the Senate, substituted a phrase that made clear the President could lift sanctions if it was in the 'national interest', a much broader waiver authority than that offered in the House Bill.[8]

The USA's major allies had been proceeding in a similar fashion, the EC on 27 June 1989 announcing joint sanctions against the Beijing government. As intended, these mirrored those the Bush administration had imposed, including a ban on high-level ministerial visits and on sales of military equipment, the suspension of government-guaranteed loans, and the issuing of a highly condemnatory statement. EC members also extended visas for some 10,000 Chinese students who wished to extend their periods of stay abroad. The French government went further than most in giving political asylum to a number of those who had been prominent in the democracy movement. It attracted Beijing's particular ire when it gave such dissidents a special place in the bicentenary parade on Bastille Day.[9] Britain and Portugal, because of their ongoing negotiations over the future retrocession of Hong Kong and Macao, were exempted from the ban on high-level ministerial visits, although Britain did postpone the next scheduled meeting of the Joint Liaison Group. Despite London's special status with regard to contacts, Tiananmen affected British policy towards China and Hong Kong in other significant ways. In order to respond to the over one million Hong Kong Chinese who had taken to the streets to express their mood of anger and dismay

[8] Harding, *A Fragile Relationship*, 230–4; Richard Bush, 'The Role of Congress in Shaping Washington's China Policy', *Heritage Foundation Reports*, 9 July 1991.

[9] David Shambaugh, 'China and Europe', *Annals of the American Academy of Political and Social Science* (Jan. 1992), 110.

after the killings, and to give them some confidence in their future, Governor David Wilson condemned the bloodshed, campaigned in London to extend the right of abode to larger numbers of Hong Kong British passport-holders, made preparations to introduce a bill of rights, and pressed on with plans for a new airport. Already complex and difficult negotiations took on a new edge—especially with the appointment of the more openly combative Christopher Patten in 1992—impossible to smooth over until well after the formal handover of Hong Kong had taken place on 1 July 1997.[10]

The Japanese government also stayed in step with the Western group. Most significantly, it terminated the negotiations with China on the Third Yen Loan package worth 810 billion yen (at a minimum $US6 billion), despite an obvious reluctance unequivocally to condemn China's actions or isolate the country. One assessment of the economic cost to China has estimated that commitments of new bilateral foreign assistance declined from $3.4 billion in 1988 to $1.5 billion in 1989 and $0.7 billion in 1990 and that, on the basis of a 20 per cent annual increase in aid commitments, Tiananmen cost China some $11 billion in bilateral aid over four years.[11] David Zweig records that 'by July 1989, the G-7 had frozen $10 billion in aid and loans from the World Bank and Japan as well as another $780 million in World Bank loans slated for the end of June'.[12] Such coordinated action among Western countries and Japan was important if the condemnations and sanctions were to have any chance of making a material impact on Beijing and undoubtedly these economic measures did hurt the Chinese economy, in broad terms China experiencing a two-year decline in its credit rating, foreign investment, exports, and tourist visits.[13] The statement that came out of the G7 meeting in Paris in mid-July calling for Beijing to create the internal conditions that would avoid its further isolation was important because, although it contained no new sanctions, it publicly confirmed that all the major industrialized states believed the Chinese leaders had gone well beyond the bounds of an acceptable response to the civil disorder that had rocked the capital city.

Also significant among the multilateral responses were those made through various UN offices. Shortly after the Tianamen Square killings, the UN Secretary General called for the 'utmost restraint' by the Chinese

---

[10] Sino-British negotiations over the handover of Hong Kong are covered succinctly in Michael B. Yahuda, *Hong Kong: China's Challenge* (London: Routledge, 1997), and Steve Y.-S. Tsang, *Hong Kong: Appointment with China* (London: Tauris, 1997).

[11] Donnelly, *International Human Rights*, 120.

[12] Zweig, 'Sino-American Relations', 75.

[13] Nathan and Ross, *The Great Wall*, 187.

government and on 6 June the UN's Special Rapporteur on Summary
and Arbitrary Executions, whose 1989 report had already pointed to
unlawful Chinese killings in Tibet, also appealed to the government to
curb its excesses. During the same period some 1,263 employees from the
UN Secretariat, including Chinese representatives, sent an open letter to
the UN Secretary General asking for a special session of the UNCHR,
impossible to arrange because there were as yet no such urgent action
procedures.[14] On 19 June, the International Confederation of Free Trade
Unions sent a complaint to the International Labour Organization alleging violations of union rights. AI issued statements that framed the
Tiananmen crackdown to correspond with UN human rights terminology, describing the killings of peaceful demonstrators as 'extrajudicial
executions'. The International League for Human Rights reached the
judgement that, even if the Chinese government had rightly determined
that the circumstances within the country represented a time of national
emergency, Beijing had violated certain rights that were non-derogable
under international law.[15]

In this highly charged atmosphere, the UN Sub-Commission met in
August for its annual meeting. With the spotlight clearly to be on China,
and in response to NGO urging, Agenda item 6—'Question of the Violation of Human Rights and Fundamental Freedoms'—was moved forward for early consideration. From the beginning of the debate, the
NGOs applied a coordinated strategy, agreeing that the representative
from the International Commission of Jurists would deliver the closing
speech on behalf of them all.[16] The International League for Human
Rights did much of the legwork: according to its then Director, Felice
Gaer, it prepared a detailed 101-page report on Tiananmen, engaged in
extensive lobbying of Sub-Commission members, and assisted Chinese
students and others presenting eye-witness testimony. Gaer worked
closely with Jerome Shestack, the former US ambassador to the UNCHR
and President of the League, utilizing his contacts with Sub-Commission
members.[17]

Li Lu, a student on the wanted list, gave his dramatic version of events,
leading a member of China's observer delegation at the Sub-Commission
to walk out of the room, later to return to describe Li as a 'criminal'. The
French expert, Louis Joinet, voiced a strong objection to this language,
arguing that, while Li might be deemed a criminal inside China, it was not

---

[14] John Tessitore and Susan Woolfson (eds.), *Issues before the 44ᵗʰ General Assembly of
the United Nations* (Lexington, Mass: Lexington Books, 1989), 158.

[15] Kent, *Between Freedom and Subsistence*, 187–8.

[16] Details of his speech are contained in Kent, 'China and the International Human
Rights Regime', 16.   [17] Korey, *NGOs*, 158.

possible under international law for China to impose its laws outside its own territory.[18] Chinese tactics to undermine support for the draft condemnatory resolution included pressuring the ambassadors in Beijing from the countries whose experts were represented on the Sub-Commission, and informing others that bilateral economic relations would inevitably be damaged. Some participants reported an 'unprecedented Chinese invasion' during which 'there appeared no way in which a member of the Sub-Commission in need of a tea-break could escape the diplomatic offensive'; others that they had seen a senior Chinese diplomat in the coffee bar 'summoning the 26 delegates one by one to lecture them to the need to consider their country's friendship with China'.[19] China's methods were to prove counter-productive and led the Sub-Commission to hold its first ever secret ballot. Admittedly, its members voted on a mildly-worded resolution, but China wanted no resolution at all. It read:

The Sub-Commission . . . Concerned about the events which took place recently in China and about their consequences in the field of human rights, 1. Requests the Secretary-General to transmit to the Commission on Human Rights information provided by the Government of China and by other reliable sources; 2. Makes an appeal for clemency, in particular in favor of persons deprived of their liberty as a result of the above-mentioned events.

It passed fifteen votes to nine on 31 August, with the six Western members being joined by four or five Latin Americans and some African and Asian experts.[20]

Despite the mildness of the wording, there was no doubting its significance as the first ever resolution to criticize a permanent member of the UN Security Council for its human rights violations. For a body that relies on public shaming as a means of attempting to change governmental behaviour, this was a critical moment. As Chinese actions demonstrated, the Beijing government was prepared to make extensive efforts to prevent a resolution that severely undercut the legitimacy of its version of events. Neither could it stop important procedural innovations being introduced at that meeting including the use of the secret ballot, and legal agreement to expand the right of governments to speak on any matter of concern and not simply on those of concern to one's own state. The secret

---

[18] Kent, 'China and the International Human Rights Regime', 12.

[19] Bard-Anders Andreassen and Theresa Swinehart, *Human Rights in Developing Countries: 1990 Yearbook* (Kehl: N. P. Engel Publisher, 1991), 107; *FBIS*-Chi-89-169, 1 Sept. 1989.

[20] The text of the resolution is in Kent, 'China and the International Human Rights Regime', 14–15. Much useful detail on this session is in Kent, *China, the United Nations, and Human Rights*, 56–60.

ballot seemed a valuable new means of undermining the capacity of powerful states to manipulate other countries' voting decisions and might be
important for the future. Also important was the coordinated strategy
adopted by a wide range of the NGOs. The speeches of their leading
spokespersons, together with the public debate that Sub-Commission
members had with Chinese experts and observers, described in more
detail in the later sections of this chapter, were useful reminders of the
obligations that states shouldered as a result of commitments made in the
area of human rights.[21]

China's behaviour continued to be subject to UN scrutiny in the coming months, in some instances as required by the ongoing process of
reporting, in others as a result of the Tiananmen crackdown. The report
of the Special Rapporteur on Torture, Peter Kooijmans, was distributed
as a UN document in December 1989, outlining the urgent appeals he
had sent to the Chinese government concerning the treatment of those
arrested during the first week of June 1989 in Beijing and those detained
over a longer period in Tibet.[22] The CAT, in receipt of China's own report
submitted on 1 December as part of the reporting requirements imposed
on all signatories of the Convention, deemed it inadequate, and required
Beijing to submit supplementary information.[23] The UN Special Rapporteur on Summary or Arbitrary Executions regularly requested information from China regarding executions in Tibet and on the killings
associated with the events of 4 June. The UN Working Group on
Enforced or Involuntary Disappearances reported in 1990 to the Commission on twenty-four cases of disappearance that had occurred in 1988,
none of which had been explained by the Beijing authorities.[24] The Chinese record was being assailed from all sides.

Of greatest moment, however, and in part because of the publicity that
it generated, the UNCHR began in spring 1990 consideration of the Sub-
Commission's China resolution. As instructed in that resolution, the UN
Secretary General submitted his report, a full thirty-three pages outlining
human rights violations in China and utilizing information provided by

---

[21] More welcome to Beijing was the decision also to allow a government the right to
respond to a Sub-Commission vote. Robin M. Maher and David Weissbrodt, 'The 41st Session of the UN Sub-Commission on the Prevention of Discrimination and Protection of
Minorities', *Human Rights Quarterly*, 12/2, (1990), esp. 291–306; Kent, 'China and the
International Human Rights Regime', esp. 10–18.

[22] UN ECOSOC, E/CN.4/1990/17, 18 Dec. 1989.

[23] This request for an additional report was an unusual one and Chinese representatives
were said to have been 'visibly upset by the Committee members' reaction' to its first, inadequate, eleven-page report. For further, illuminating detail on the fate of this document, see
Kent, *China, the United Nations, and Human Rights*, 93–100.

[24] Andreassen and Swinehart, *Human Rights in Developing Countries*, 120.

AI, the International League for Human Rights, and the International Committee of Health Professionals. With Australia playing a leading role, and Tokyo offering counsel, it was thought that a mild resolution, co-sponsored by the seventeen Western member countries together with Japan, had a good chance of being passed. In draft, it took note of the Sub-Commission debate and the Secretary General's report, welcomed China's release of some 573 prisoners detained after 4 June, and called for the transmission of additional information to the Commission's next session.[25] However, a fierce Chinese rebuttal, together with Western failure to lobby effectively, and a vote a day earlier than expected, led Pakistan's 'no-action' resolution to pass narrowly, 17–15–11, Beijing gaining the support of the former Soviet Union, the Ukraine, Pakistan, Cuba, Somalia, Iraq, Cyprus, Yugoslavia, Sri Lanka, India, Bangladesh, and five African states. Yet, there was little room for Chinese complacency, for, despite this outcome, Hungary and Bulgaria had voted with the Western bloc, highlighting the possible future fragility of Moscow's and Kiev's support; the African countries were split, many abstaining and one country (Swaziland) voting against; and several Latin American countries, such as Argentina, Brazil, Colombia, Mexico, Peru, and Venezuela, also decided to abstain.[26]

The failure of the resolution to pass owed much to politics and little or nothing to the Chinese argument that the government had been acting in June 1989 to prevent, as it put it, 'a handful of people from violating the law'.[27] As an indication of the extent to which Beijing abhorred being the subject of a UN condemnatory resolution, China sent a forty-person delegation to the Commission meeting, and, as noted earlier, its members had to apply much pressure to garner that slim majority, threatening various economic and political consequences should governments not support the 'no-action' motion. China's Foreign Minister also arrived in Geneva, ostensibly on another matter—yet another indication of how important it had become to China to counter even such mildly worded criticism from a UN body. A further major indication of the temper of the times, and of how out of step China's interpretation of sovereignty

---

[25] John Tessitore and Susan Woolfson (eds.), *Issues before the 45th General Assembly of the United Nations* (Lexington, Mass,: Lexington Books, 1990), 153.

[26] Ibid. 153–4; Kent, 'China and the International Human Rights Regime', 20–1. China's explanation of its actions around 4 June is contained in E/CN.4/1990/SR.40 (meeting held 26 Feb.). Ambassador Fan Guoxiang's discussion of the relationship between state sovereignty and human rights is in E/CN.4/1990/SR.50 (meeting held on 5 Mar. 1990). In his view: 'In international law, sovereignty was the most important attribute of a State, with the result that the realization and protection of human rights could not exclude the principle of sovereignty' (p.8).

[27] Statement quoted in Kent, 'China and the International Human Rights Regime', 20.

then appeared, came with the rejection at the end of the Commission's session of a Cuban resolution—probably prompted by China—to invoke Article 2 (7) of the UN Charter in support of the principle of non-intervention in the area of human rights.[28] According to one scholar of this period, this defeat, together with the narrowness of the margin of success on Pakistan's no-action motion, was pivotal and probably forced China to give up its attempts to persuade others that human rights were not a legitimate subject for international scrutiny.[29]

For a large part of the first year after Tiananmen, therefore, the message to Beijing from various parts of the global community was reasonably clear, if hardly deafening. Furthermore, especially where the UN was concerned, the expectation was that the focus would continue to remain on China, especially since the next meeting of the Sub-Commission, in August 1990, would be taking up the question of Tibet. In many respects, Tiananmen appeared to have changed the landscape for the long-term future, because large-scale human rights violations in China could not be denied even by the relatively few who were sympathetic to Beijing's argument that it had needed to restore order on 4 June, and that stability was more important than freedom of expression. Moreover, there was more of a willingness to acknowledge that human rights violations had been prevalent over a long period. Where previous US State Department reports on China's human rights record, for example, had put considerable weight on the improvements that were in train, the 1990 report, which was highly critical of Chinese actions, noted that, despite various guarantees in the Chinese Constitution, and previous reports of improvements in a variety of areas, all such guarantees had always been qualified by reference to the interests of the state. This report suggested, therefore, that violations were endemic in the system.[30] This harsher language led the New York-based Lawyers' Committee for Human Rights to express its considerable satisfaction with the State

---

[28] Tessitore and Woolfson (eds.), *Issues before the 45th General Assembly*, 154; Brody, *et al.* 'Major Developments in 1990', 569; Kent, 'China and the International Human Rights Regime', 21.

[29] Kent, *China, the United Nations, and Human Rights*, 62, although China's first White Paper on Human Rights produced in Oct. 1991 renewed the arguments on state sovereignty and non-interference (see final section of this chapter).

[30] US Department of State, *Country Reports on Human Rights Practices for 1989* (Washington: Government Printing Office, 1990). To give some examples from that report: 'China's judiciary is not independent but is controlled by the CCP . . . . Due process rights are stipulated under the Constitution but are often ignored in practice . . . Those arrested for crimes of counterrevolution frequently are tried in secret and family members are not informed of the charges or details of the case. Credible reports suggest that even years after the conviction and imprisonment of a person considered a dissident, family members still do not know the details of the alleged crime' (pp. 806–7).

Department report, describing the section on China as a 'model for all country reports'.[31]

THE SHIFTING OF PRIORITIES

At this stage, the unacceptability of China's behaviour had been made plain, but this message was not without its ambiguities, and was to become more opaque as the months went by. As noted above, the intention had been at the August 1990 session of the UN Sub-Commission to introduce a resolution on Tibet; however, this was dropped in exchange for China's agreement not to oppose a resolution on Iraq. Moreover, the body came under criticism from some members of the Commission, who queried its right to adopt resolutions on human rights violations in particular countries. Ironically, the US and Chinese Commission members were on similar ground here, the former complaining that the Sub-Commission was behaving like the parent body itself, a Chinese delegate objecting to its tendency to become politicized, to give too much space to the NGOs, and to allow the procedural introduction of the secret ballot.[32] Major states, then, remained vigilant against any loss of power to this expert, supposedly more autonomous, non-state-based body. However, the main reason for inaction on the part of the Sub-Commission related to the Gulf War and China's obligatory role as a Security Council member, which prompted governments to weigh their concerns about human rights violations in China against other major foreign policy objectives.

The problem of competing foreign policy objectives with respect to Beijing had always been present, of course, a function of that country's great power potential as well as the particular beliefs of officials in major states, especially those in US administrations. The Bush administration contained many who had worked with Nixon and Kissinger at the time of the Sino-American *rapprochement*. From the start of the Tiananmen crisis, these officials had indicated in various ways their concern not to alienate or isolate a country as important as China. Shortly after the late June vote in the House to impose additional sanctions, Bush had sent his National Security Adviser, Brent Scowcroft, and his Deputy Secretary of State, Lawrence Eagleburger, to Beijing on

---

[31] *FBIS*-Sov-90-149, 2 Aug. 1990.

[32] Reed Brody, Maureen Convery, and David Weissbrodt, 'The 42nd Session of the Sub-Commission on Prevention of Discrimination and Protection of Minorities', *Human Rights Quarterly*, 13/2 (1991), 261, 274, n. 65; Kent, *China, the United Nations, and Human Rights*, 63.

the weekend of 1 and 2 July to convey the message that if the Chinese leaders valued good relations (as Washington obviously did) then they would have to stop the wave of arrests, imprisonments and executions that were taking place. Clearly, the Chinese regime did not yet feel secure enough to stop the crackdown, placing Bush in a dilemma. His only choice, he believed, was to authorize his officials to act unilaterally to prevent a further deterioration in bilateral relations. Neither were other high-level contacts entirely ruled out: in late July, for example, the US Secretary of State, James Baker, requested a private meeting during the Paris conference on Cambodia with the Chinese Foreign Minister, Qian Qichen. Later in September Baker met him again, this time in New York, to convey a similar message that improved US–Chinese relations required Beijing to take certain steps. Other gestures also conveying a desire not to isolate China completely included the issuing of preliminary licences to permit the Hughes Aircraft company to exchange information on the Chinese launching of US-manufactured satellites, discussions between US and Chinese officials on China's admission to the GATT, and permission for Chinese technicians to return to work on the upgrading of the F-8 fighter aircraft. Designated 'Friends of China', the former President, Richard Nixon, and his Secretary of State, Henry Kissinger, also visited the country in October and November, both telling Chinese leaders of the extent to which Tiananmen had undercut Beijing's support in the USA. For his part, Deng Xiaoping used them to convey a partially conciliatory message that, provided Bush made the first step to improve relations, he would find China ready to reciprocate.[33]

Domestic critics in both countries attacked these efforts to sustain the bilateral relationship even in this circumscribed form. Groups such as Human Rights Watch lobbied hard in Washington, testifying repeatedly to Congress about a variety of human rights abuses in China and issuing a series of reports focusing on those detained for political activities. To boost the reliability and sources of information on China, this NGO opened an office in Hong Kong in late October 1990, the destination of a number of Chinese dissidents. Shifting the focus away somewhat from intellectuals and students and towards the plight of Chinese workers who had suffered particularly egregious punishment after 4 June, this NGO began to publicize the case of Han Dongfang, a founding member of the Beijing Autonomous Workers' Federation. The decision to label him China's 'Lech Walesa' assisted the organization's efforts to enlist the help of colleagues in Helsinki Watch and to have Solidarity pay attention to

[33] Mann, *About Face*, 217–18; Ross, 'National Security', 296–8.

his plight.[34] It was an effective way of making a relatively unknown individual such as Han more real to this NGO's target audiences.

Many in the US Congress found the information provided by the human rights organizations vital to the promotion of their legislation. This helped to cement ties between these two kinds of administration critics, risking the perception that some campaigning groups were becoming too much the arm of one branch of the government, despite their obvious need to remain impartial on home territory. In late 1989 and early 1990, the House and Senate turned to consider two issues about which various domestic groups had expressed concern: the fate of Chinese students in the USA and the renewal of MFN status for Chinese trade. Congresswoman Nancy Pelosi's Bill designed to allow Chinese students to remain in the USA gathered swift momentum from the autumn of 1989. Approached first by her Chinese constituents, Pelosi's staff used previous contacts with immigration lawyers, who had worked on the issue of Central American refugees, to draft the necessary legislation. Chinese students in touch with these developments effectively lobbied Pelosi's office and were told to contact their own members of Congress. The Bill swiftly garnered 250 co-sponsors and was passed by clear majorities in the House and Senate. Bush chose to use his pocket veto, and then compounded the anger this action generated by sending Eagleburger and Scowcroft on a second trip to Beijing, revealing over the same period the existence of the previous, secret, July meetings in the Chinese capital. After Christmas, the House voted to overturn the President's veto, and only after the administration's extensive lobbying was it possible for the President to prevent a repeat of this action in the Senate.[35]

Scowcroft's and Eagleburger's December visit was designed to convey to Beijing the steps necessary to dilute congressional anger against it, anger which they said could well impede the retention of MFN status for China when it came up for renewal in June 1990. Scowcroft himself aggravated that hostility when he permitted himself to be photographed toasting his Chinese hosts, reportedly saying that 'negative forces' in both countries had sought to 'redirect or frustrate our cooperation'.[36] This statement reinforced the sense that the executive branch did not take the human rights aspect of policy as seriously as its congressional critics. Some reciprocal easing of tensions did take place in January, possibly as a result of the visit: Washington announced it would no longer oppose all World Bank loans to China, supporting those that attended to the basic

---

[34] *Human Rights Watch World Report 1991* (New York, 1990), 299.
[35] Zweig, 'Sino-American Relations', 76–8.
[36] Harding, *A Fragile Relationship*, 257.

needs of the Chinese people, and on 10 January Beijing lifted martial law and on the 18th released some 573 prisoners who had taken part in the Tiananmen demonstrations. But the uneasy compromise forged in Beijing between those urging the leadership to be flexible and those stressing the need to retain strict political controls in China precluded the leadership from making other major gestures—such as the release of Fang Lizhi and his wife from the American embassy.[37] Indeed, on balance, the argument was probably won in Beijing at that stage by those who argued that the Scowcroft visit had demonstrated that China did in fact retain strategic leverage in Washington even as the cold war was ending and that it needed to do very little to ensure the normalization of Sino-American relations.[38] As Bush had stated at a press conference in early January 1990: 'Some people think the best way to make changes for human rights in China is isolation: don't talk to them, try to punish them by excommunication. I don't feel that way.'[39]

However, the debate over MFN renewal showed that even congressional anger with the Bush administration had its limits. This sent a similarly contradictory message to the leaders in Beijing. Many of those in Congress who had staunchly supported sanctions in the area of military sales and high-level exchanges baulked when it came to damaging overall US–China trade relations. Testimony from American wheat exporters, toy manufacturers, and a persuasive brief from the US–China Business Council magnified their concerns.[40] Others pointed to the damage that would be wrought on the Hong Kong economy if MFN were to be revoked, and still others argued that denial of MFN would disproportionately hurt America's natural allies in China, the economic reformers. Chinese students resident in the USA were also divided over the matter. Nevertheless, vocal and powerful critics of retaining the MFN status remained. The Chinese leadership, perhaps realizing that the President had used up much political capital during the Pelosi episode, and that renewing MFN was still going to be difficult to bring off, offered some help of its own, releasing an additional 211 prisoners, agreeing to purchase $4 billion of Boeing aircraft, together with quantities of US wheat, and at the end of June at last allowing Fang Lizhi to leave the US embassy. Finally, at the year's end, Bush's policy of MFN renewal had not been challenged but the terms of the debate inside and outside Con-

---

[37] The Fang Lizhi episode is covered well in Mann, *About Face*, 237–40, who argues that 'Fang was effectively ransomed in exchange for a resumption of international loans to China' (p. 240).

[38] This argument is outlined persuasively in Harding, *A Fragile Relationship*, 255–6.

[39] President Bush, quoted in *Human Rights Watch World Report 1990*, 288.

[40] Zweig, 'Sino-American Relations', 81–2.

gress over that autumnal period indicated that conditional renewal was likely to be the form in the years to come as trade and human rights questions became firmly entwined.

If US signals to China reinforced the sense that there existed real struggle within the country over policy priorities, Japan's government made plain that its sanctions were not designed to last long. This weakened the belief that the concept of an international society and agreement on international norms in this issue area rested on secure foundations. There was a range of reasons for Tokyo's distinctive stance, and not simply those more obvious ones connected with the desire to shore up its economic interests in the country. Japan's past history of relations with China, its abhorrent wartime policies, its sense of belonging not only to the developed West but also to Asia, and sympathy for China's concern to maintain stability made it reluctant to condemn Beijing as forthrightly as it might have done. Thus, although, as noted earlier, the Tokyo government decided to suspend negotiations on the Third Yen Loans package and agreed to support the sanctions outlined at the G7 summit in July 1989, its most oft-quoted remarks concerned its worries that China would be unduly isolated. In support of this, Tokyo tended to match each of Bush's most conciliatory gestures, even to go beyond them, as when a Foreign Ministry official went to the Chinese embassy in Tokyo to explain why his government had associated itself with the G7 sanctions policy statement of July 1989.[41] Between August and December 1989 Tokyo's policy seemed designed to send subtle signals that it wished to retain informal and unofficial contacts as a prelude to the full normalization of relations at an early date. This prompted Deng Xiaoping in September 1989 to state to a former Japanese Foreign Minister that he had detected 'some difference' between Tokyo and Washington.[42] Like the US Secretary of State, Japan's Foreign Minister used the occasion of the Cambodian peace conference to have discussions with Qian Qichen. On 7 August Tokyo decided to offer China $1 million in emergency aid for flood relief. By mid-August 1989 it was reported that about 80 per cent of the thirty-three Japanese firms with offices in Beijing were in full operation again and that the freeze on current aid projects had been lifted.[43] Restrictions on travel to Beijing were formally removed in late September, the same month that fifteen members of the Japanese Diet, led by former

---

[41] K. V. Kesavan, 'Japan and the Tiananmen Square Incident: Aspects of the Bilateral Relationship', *Asian Survey*, 30/7 (July 1990), 674.

[42] Quoted in Harding, *A Fragile Relationship*, 263.

[43] David Arase, 'Japan's Foreign Policy and Asian Democratization', in Friedman (ed.), *The Politics of Democratization*, 90.

Foreign Minister Masayoshi Ito, conferred in Beijing with the new
post-Tiananmen leadership of Li Peng and Jiang Zemin, as well as with
Deng Xiaoping.[44]

Japanese ministers and visitors stressed that two conditions needed
to be fulfilled in order for full normalization of relations to occur: martial law had to be lifted in Beijing and Fang Lizhi allowed to leave the
US embassy. When the former was announced on 10 January and
prompted by the earlier US decision to send a high-level diplomatic
mission to Beijing in December 1989, Japan swiftly breached the wall
on diplomatic contact. It invited Zou Jiahua, head of the State Planning Commission, and Li Tieying, chair of the State Education Commission, to visit, following this in April 1990 with a restoration of
contacts at the vice-ministerial level.[45] At the same time, the Director
of Japan's economic cooperation bureau visited Beijing to restart negotiations for the Third Yen Loans.[46] Fang Lizhi's release on 25 June 1990
was neatly timed to occur just prior to the Houston G7 summit,
shortly after which Japan announced its formal decision to renew negotiations on the yen loans package. As a Foreign Ministry official
explained, Japan believed that it was not right to isolate China; what
the Japanese government wanted to see was 'China reintegrated or
returned to normal relations with the international community'.[47]
Much to Tokyo's satisfaction, Bush gave his support for the relaxation
of Japan's aid embargo and the G7 also announced its agreement to
World Bank lending that promoted economic reforms or environmental protection, suggesting widespread acceptance that China's gestures
should trigger a positive response. With Tokyo's normalization of relations all but complete in mid-1990, it seemed that little political cost
would be borne if Japan took other major, symbolic, steps ahead of
its Western allies: thus, in August 1991 Prime Minister Kaifu visited
Beijing, nevertheless exacting some *quid pro quo* from China in drawing forth its commitment 'in principle'—on the anniversary of the
dropping of the atomic bombs on Japan—to the signing of the nuclear
NPT.[48]

[44] Yuko Kato, 'Determinants of Japanese Responses to Tiananmen: June 1989 to
August 1991', M.Phil thesis (Oxford,1992), 15–16.

[45] Harding, *A Fragile Relationship,* 264.

[46] Kato, 'Determinants of Japanese Responses', 20.

[47] Quoted in Harding, *A Fragile Relationship*, 264. ASEAN leaders said much the same
thing, cautioning their Western dialogue partners not to close the door on China. See
Chen Jie, 'Human Rights: ASEAN's New Importance to China', *Pacific Review*, 6/3
(1993), esp. 229.

[48] John F. Copper, 'Peking's Post-Tienanmen Foreign Policy: The Human Rights Factor', *Issues and Studies*, 30/10 (Oct. 1994), 62.

EC members also tended to shadow the behaviour of the Bush administration, suggesting that a sanctions policy without the USA was deemed virtually useless. The Community used its various summits—for example, at the end of June 1989, in January 1990, and again in October 1990—to signal important stages in policy. The joint sanctions that it had imposed in the wake of Tiananmen held reasonably well until the early to middle part of 1990. A week after the Chinese government had lifted martial law in Beijing, the EC12 welcomed the move, while expressing continuing concern over the fate of students imprisoned or being hunted down. Individual states within the EC then began to break away from the coordinated approach. In February, France offered China new loans and authorized its export credit guarantee body to cover the China risk. Italy made the same move that month, to be followed by the FRG in April, although Bonn still took such decisions on a case-by-case basis.[49] After the Houston summit in the summer of 1990 a number of other sanctions began to be lifted and various opportunities were sought—at the meeting of the UN General Assembly in September and October, for example— to hold talks with China's Foreign Minister.[50] The EC summit in Luxembourg on 22 October 1990 provided an opportunity to try to tie these strands together again, with the EC12 formally deciding to retain the ban, as had the USA, on military sales and military contacts. Further breaches in the common foreign policy were still to come, however, as Spain became the first EC country after Tiananmen to send its Foreign Minister to Beijing.[51]

In these first months after 4 June, therefore, there were cracks in the material and symbolic aspects of the governmental sanctions policy, partly in response to relatively minor Chinese concessions, but also because the US executive branch was not seen to be fully behind that policy. As Lisa Martin's work on multilateral economic sanctions has shown, in nearly all such cases, one state acts as leader and this state needs to establish a firm commitment to the sanctions policy in order to ensure more widespread cooperation. Coordinated policy is always difficult to sustain in the absence of institutionalized venues where the leading sanctioner can signal its firm commitment, and link cooperation on this one issue to longer-term interests in the benefits of institutionalized agreement.[52] These cracks were almost inevitably likely to widen in this case

[49] See such reports in *Le Monde*, 23 Mar. 1991, *Financial Times*, 7 Feb. 1990, *International Herald Tribune*, 28 Feb. 1990, and *FBIS*-WEU-90-069, 10 Apr. 1990.

[50] *FBIS*-WEU-90-188, 27 Sept. 1990.

[51] The Spanish foreign minister's visit took place in late Nov. 1990. *FBIS*-WEU-90-205, 23 Oct. 1990; *International Herald Tribune*, 23 Nov. 1990.

[52] See Martin, *Coercive Cooperation*.

because of China's perceived importance to global and regional order, a perception sharpened still further in the light of unexpected developments in the Gulf during which the leading sanctioning states began to identify China less as the human rights violator and more in terms of its great power role as a UN Security Council member, capable of wielding its veto.

THE IMPACT OF THE GULF WAR

The UN Sub-Commission's trade in August 1990 of the Tibet for the Iraq issue and the October 1990 turning point in EC policy reflected the widespread argument at governmental levels that, as a Permanent Member of the UN Security Council, China needed to be induced to support the West's Iraqi policy, and later on that it even deserved to be rewarded for not obstructing it. Many commentators attributed the relaxation in various Western governmental policies, especially in the economic field, to Beijing's cooperative attitude, although, as noted above, the economic sanctions policy was already beginning to soften before the Gulf crisis. Shortly after Saddam Hussein had raised the stakes, the US administration signalled to Beijing how important its role potentially could be: not only did American diplomats stationed in Beijing and Shanghai hint that this conflict represented an opportunity for Beijing to improve relations with the USA, but the administration also sent Assistant Secretary of State Richard Solomon to the Chinese capital, the highest ranking official since the Scowcroft–Eagleburger visit in December 1989.[53] The US Secretary of State, James Baker, also met his Chinese counterpart yet again, this time in Cairo on 6 November to discuss the crisis, although Baker did apparently raise in private the subject of China's human rights record.[54]

Over the course of the Gulf episode, China voted for all ten UN resolutions that imposed political, military, and economic sanctions against Iraq, and eventually abstained on Resolution 678, which permitted the use of armed force to compel an Iraqi withdrawal from Kuwait. Resolution 678 provided China with most of its bargaining leverage, as the country's leaders hinted to Secretary of State Baker that all three voting outcomes—an affirmative vote, a veto, or an

---

[53] Ding Xinghao, 'Managing Sino-American Relations in a Changing World', *Asian Survey*, 31/12 (Dec. 1991), 1160; Harding, *A Fragile Relationship*, 271.
[54] *Human Rights Watch World Report 1991*, 295.

abstention—were still possible. To rule out the veto, the US adminis-tration agreed that China's Foreign Minister would be received in Washington after the Security Council had met, and that an affirmative vote would be rewarded with a meeting between Bush and Qian.[55] The build-up to this vote, and the eventual Chinese abstention (i.e. not an affirmative vote), which, as Harry Harding suggests, was a highly likely outcome anyway,[56] seems to have attracted undue levels of reward, including, most importantly of all from China's perspective, the meet-ing with Bush at the White House. Coming alongside other benefits, such as the resumption of Tokyo's development aid programme to China, the release of some $240 million under the Third Yen Loans package, and World Bank lending of $275 million, China must have been pleased with its diplomatic work. And more was to come: after the Security Council vote, the Bank extended its first 'non-basic-needs' loan to Beijing since the Tiananmen killings,[57] West European govern-ments such as Germany unlocked their aid packages, making new loans available for 1991. France signed a credit agreement worth FF1.31 billion[58] and over the same period concluded various high-pro-file commercial deals.

THE FATE OF THE HUMAN RIGHTS REGIME

What was left, then, in late 1990 and early 1991 to ensure that Tiananmen was not entirely removed as a constraint on China's relations with major parts of the international community and that the global human rights regime retained some credibility with reformers both inside China and in the outside world? On the surface, at least, matters looked bad for that regime, for in February and March 1991, the time when the UN

[55] Harding, *A Fragile Relationship*, 272.

[56] Harding argues convincingly that the 'most plausible option for Peking was to abstain from the vote . . . Given China's reservations about employing military power against Iraq, and its recollection that the precedent for such action by the United Nations had been directed against China during the Korean War, it was difficult for Peking to vote in favor of the American-sponsored resolution. And yet, it was equally difficult for China to oppose it, especially if it were the only permanent member of the Security Council to do so. A veto would defy world opinion and enrage the United States. Once the Soviet Union indicated that it would vote in favor of military force against Iraq, therefore, a Chinese abstention was virtually assured' (Ibid. 271–2).

[57] J. Mohan Malik, 'Peking's Response to the Gulf Crisis', *Issues and Studies*, 27/9 (Sept. 1991), 115–17.

[58] *FBIS*-WEU-90-242, 17 and 24 Dec. 1990. Commercial deals were concluded, for example, with Citroen and Volkswagen in Nov. 1990.

Commission met in Geneva, China was in the midst of its trials of the democracy activists arrested after the Tiananmen demonstrations, yet no resolution on China was introduced at that meeting.[59] China was, however, the focus of attention in the less-politicized areas of UN machinery. The Special Rapporteur on Summary and Arbitrary Executions referred to China in his 1991 report; the CAT (as noted earlier) called on China to provide a supplementary report and recorded that it was concerned about 'use of evidence obtained by torture, the organization of the judiciary and its lack of independence, poor conditions of detention, limits on detainees' contacts with family, and the role of medical personnel in establishing the fact of torture'. The Special Rapporteur on Torture also named China in his 1991 report as having been the subject of an urgent communication.[60]

In addition, despite having come under criticism from members of its parent body, the UN Sub-Commission returned to consider the Tibet question in August 1991. (NGOs were in fact responsible for this, having reached an informal arrangement whereby the Tibet resolution would alternate with a broader one on China, in order that the Tibet question received a fair and detailed hearing.)[61] In a strongly worded resolution, which passed 9–7–4, the Sub-Commission expressed concern at the 'continuing reports of violations of fundamental human rights and freedoms which threaten the distinct cultural, religious and national identity of the Tibetan people'. It also called on the Beijing government fully to 'respect the fundamental rights and freedoms of the Tibetan people'. The significance of this resolution rested on the fact of its criticism of long-standing Chinese policy, unlike the Tiananmen resolution, which was a response to a single dramatic and shocking event. Also of significance was the fact that the Chinese attending the Sub-Commission meeting once again lobbied hard to prevent its passage, but in the event were unable to prevent the slim majority in its favour.[62]

NGOs also were not to be deflected from their cause and kept up the barrage of information and pressure on governments to live up to their formal commitments. In response to the EC's adoption in June 1991 of a declaration on human rights, implying the future development of a more consistent and coherent policy in this field, Amnesty submitted several reports to the Commission and the Parliament on conditions in China.

[59] John Tessitore and Susan Woolfson, *Issues before the 46th General Assembly of the United Nations* (Lexington, Mass: Lexington Books, 1991), 198. China was still mentioned at the Commission meeting during the general discussion on human rights violations.
[60] Ibid. 180–1.   [61] Interview with NGO adviser in London, Feb. 1999.
[62] Karen Reierson and David Weissbrodt, 'The Forty-Third Session of the UN Sub-Commission on Prevention of Discrimination and Protection of Minorities: The Sub-Commission under Scrutiny', *Human Rights Quarterly*, 14/2 (1992), 246–7; Kent, *China, the United Nations, and Human Rights*, 63–4.

Human Rights Watch/Asia announced a decision to devote more time and resources to its programme on China and Tibet than on any of the other countries of concern to it in Asia. It began a major campaign in 1991 focusing on forced labour in Chinese prisons and the export of products made under prison conditions, passing on the information gathered to the US Customs Service.[63] The timing of that NGO's revelation of these conditions coincided neatly with the consideration in the USA of the MFN question. Prison labour was an angle on human rights that had the capacity to appeal to a wider constituency in the USA because of its connections with unfair trade, the fact that such exports violated US domestic law, and that it could be projected as relating to 'slave labour', which evoked memories of Japanese and German policies during the Second World War. The stopping of forced labour became one of the provisions in the House of Representatives' 1991 MFN Bill. This prompted Bush to promise uncommitted Senators, when it was their turn to vote on the issue, that the State Department would try to negotiate a memorandum of understanding with Beijing that would establish procedures for the prompt investigation of allegations that certain exports had been produced by prison labour.[64]

The congressional and executive branches' battles over the retention of MFN status in 1991 also illustrated the capacity of human rights considerations still to impose some constraints on US–China relations. In May 1991 President Bush announced that he wished to renew that status without conditions. However, conditional renewal was the mark of bills introduced in the House and the Senate that year. The strongest among them (sponsored by Nancy Pelosi and George Mitchell) called for renewal in 1992 only provided that, among other demands, China had

- accounted for citizens detained, accused, or sentenced because of pro-democracy protests;
- released political prisoners taken from the pro-democracy protests;
- adhered to the Joint Declaration on Hong Kong . . .
- stopped jamming Voice of America broadcasts; and
- made 'significant' progress in (1) ending the harassment of Chinese citizens in the United States, (2) granting access for humanitarian and human rights groups to prisoners, trials, and detention centers, and (3) taking action to stop human rights violations.[65]

---

[63] *Human Rights Watch World Report 1992* (New York, 1991), 394–5.

[64] Ibid. 386, 392. In fact, the memo was not agreed to in principle until Nov., and did not include greater international or US access to prison workshops.

[65] Robert F. Drinan and Teresa T. Kuo, 'The 1991 Battle for Human Rights in China', *Human Rights Quarterly* 14/1 (1992), 31.

Mitchell's Bill contained the additional provision that continuing MFN status also depended on the restriction of the transfer of missiles to Syria, Iran, and Pakistan, suggesting that there were other issues perhaps of equal or even greater salience and concern to some members of the Senate. The House Bill passed by a majority large enough to ensure the overturning of any subsequent presidential veto (313–112); thus, the Bush administration's attention focused on the Senate, requiring the President to establish a means of appealing to those Senators harbouring doubts about the wisdom of using the MFN weapon in this way. He argued for separation of human rights from trade questions and promised instead a raft of measures designed directly to address concerns in the commercial fields. Over the course of the spring, Bush had sent other signals designed to placate his domestic critics and to warn the Chinese government—meeting with the Dalai Lama (the first such contact with any US President), and denying the export of certain high-technology products.[66]

The outcome of the vote in the Senate demonstrated the difficulties of trying to attach human rights conditions to trade matters. While Senator Mitchell's Bill did attain its majority, this was still twelve votes short of the number required to override a presidential veto. Crucial to this outcome were the votes of seven Democrats from states that sold large quantities of agricultural products to China, who had been additionally influenced by substantial lobbying from the National Association of Wheat Growers. Such lobbying raised questions about the relationship between the governed and the governors in democratic societies and the dilemmas that can be posed by constituents who ask whether their economic interests should not be given priority over the needs of foreigners. Others involved in the lobbying effort included US and Hong Kong companies with high economic stakes in China, both of which could develop an appealing argument about the need to maintain economic stability in Hong Kong in the lead up to 1997. Intense efforts by the Bush administration involved frequent White House meetings with congressional members, and twice-weekly legislative strategy discussions. More unusually, the Chinese government itself entered the lobbying arena, hiring the US public relations firm Hill and

---

[66] In detail Bush stated that he had '(1) directed the US Trade Representative to investigate China for illegal trade practices under the Special 301 provisions of the Trade Act for failing to protect US intellectual property rights, (2) called for strict enforcement of US textile agreements with China, (3) asked the Customs Service to investigate charges that China is exporting prison-made goods to the United States, and (4) pledged to support Taiwan's application to the GATT'. See Drinan and Kuo, 'The 1991 Battle for Human Rights in China', 34, and Harding, *A Fragile Relationship*, 280.

Knowlton to represent its interests. Pitted against this formidable line-up were the human rights groups, labour organizations, and overseas Chinese students.[67]

If the Bush administration insisted on separating MFN from human rights, what did it envisage as a human rights policy? Its main elements involved the beginnings of a dialogue with Chinese leaders over human rights conditions in the country. In December 1990 Richard Schifter, the US Assistant Secretary of State for Human Rights and Humanitarian Affairs, held discussions with a range of Chinese officials from the courts and the public security bureau. Schifter presented a list of some 150 political prisoners on whom he sought information, including such well-known activists as Chen Ziming, Wang Juntao, and Wei Jingsheng. He also asked that US embassy personnel be allowed to send observers to political trials and requested, unsuccessfully, that he be invited to visit a jail.[68] In subsequent months, his office worked with human rights groups to expand the list of political detainees to over 800, passing this quietly to the Chinese in June 1991. In November that year, Secretary of State Baker on the first US high-level official visit to Beijing took up the matter of this expanded list, receiving some accounting from the Chinese of the 800 prisoners. But there were, of course, other items on his agenda, such as China's trade practices and the sale of missiles and nuclear technology in the Middle East, raising anew questions of how best to establish priorities and measure progress in the bilateral relationship.

It was difficult to project Baker's trip overall as productive, however, China's obduracy perhaps being explained by its belief that the US administration saw its main adversary as Congress and an active NGO lobby rather than China itself. Two dissidents were prevented from meeting members of Baker's delegation, the Chinese refused to allow US or international access to prison factories, and Deng declined to see Baker to accept a letter from President Bush that appealed to him to use his influence to heal the rift between America and China. This forced Baker to read the letter aloud during a final meeting with Chinese foreign ministry officials in order to get his government's message across. China did offer to abide by the Missile Technology Control Regime, but only if the USA would lift its sanctions on computer and satellite sales to China. Baker also affirmed—much to Beijing's satisfaction—that Taiwan would not be allowed to enter the GATT before China was admitted.[69]

---

[67] Drinan and Kuo, 'The 1991 Battle for Human Rights in China', 34–7.

[68] *Human Rights Watch World Report 1991*, 296–7.

[69] *Los Angeles Times*, 16 and 24 Nov. 1991. Baker did meet with Premier Li Peng, however, during which he referred to the Tiananmen massacre as a 'tragedy'. But this conciliatory phrasing cut little ice with the hard-line Li, who replied: 'The actions in Tiananmen

Numerous other US allies attempted a similar approach with the Chinese. The French Foreign Minister, Roland Dumas, on a trip to China in April 1991 and with a similarly crowded agenda, had tried to offset the impact of such high-level contact with leaders in Beijing with a statement that ties would become fully normalized only after imprisoned dissidents had been pardoned and there was evidence that human rights were being respected.[70] China was also induced to invite a French human rights delegation to visit the country. That delegation's subsequent report, produced in October 1991, proved quite hard-hitting commenting on the lack of judicial independence, the underestimation by the Chinese authorities of the numbers of those imprisoned, and the pervasiveness of the extra-legal process of administrative detention, one that had possibly ensnared between two million and four million people.[71]

China also issued an invitation to an Australian human rights delegation. Canberra's objective in sending such a group, according to the Australian Foreign Minister, Gareth Evans, was to reinforce the argument that human rights questions were not simply internal matters, but could legitimately be subject to international scrutiny.[72] But the visit came about as Australian and Chinese diplomats were considering ways to improve relations between the two governments, suggesting that a bargain was at the heart of it. The delegation's subsequent report, much like the French one, criticized China's judicial practices, and stated that the indictment of those suspected of committing 'counter-revolutionary crimes' infringed those rights guaranteed in the UDHR. Its fiercest criticisms were directed at the infringement of rights in Tibet, rights that it noted were compromised in all areas, including religious freedom, access to education, and freedom of movement. Importantly, however, the report also welcomed the legal reforms that had been introduced in the country, thus contributing to an atmosphere that would allow for a continuing exchange of views and visits.[73] And indeed a second Australian delegation was sent in late 1992, bringing the total to five countries at that point that had mounted such efforts, including, alongside Australia and France, Austria, Britain, and Switzerland.

Square were a good thing. We do not regard them as a tragedy' in light of lessons learned from the political upheaval in what was now the former Soviet Union. See Mann, *About Face*, 250–3, for further details of Baker's trip and the Li quotation.

[70] *FBIS*-Chi-91-088, 7 May 1991; WEU-91-200, 16 Oct. 1991.

[71] Kent, *Between Freedom and Subsistence* 218–19. The names of members of the French delegation are detailed in *FBIS*-Chi-91-198, 11 Oct. 1991.

[72] *International Herald Tribune*, 13 July 1991.

[73] Kent, *Between Freedom and Subsistence*, 218; Kent, *China, the United Nations, and Human Rights*, 160.

By late 1991, therefore, the promotion of human rights protections in China rested on a somewhat *ad hoc* mix of measures: the continuing work of the UN and its Special Rapporteurs and reporting requirements, an active NGO movement, forceful advocacy in the US Congress and European Parliament, and a series of uncoordinated meetings between governmental officials and their Chinese counterparts during which human rights matters competed with other parts of a complicated foreign policy agenda. Despite this lack of a clear strategy, however, the Chinese government had at the end of this period been induced to accept visits by both official and expert delegations, indicating a grudging receptiveness to the idea that human rights conditions inside China could legitimately be subject to international scrutiny.

THE EVOLUTION IN CHINA'S RESPONSE

The outcome of a domestic factional struggle over how to interpret and react to the actions of the global community—and especially those of Washington—and the passage of time without major crisis sufficient to allow the leadership in Beijing to regain its composure, inevitably affected the Chinese response to external developments in the two years after the Tiananmen massacre.[74] The specific elements in the Chinese strategy involved a mix of insisting rhetorically on the overriding quality of the Westphalian norm of state sovereignty and non-interference, offering limited concessions at well-timed moments, and using its political, strategic, and economic weight to create policy dilemmas for its interlocutors. Its discursive practices changed significantly when it decided to take to the offensive and promote its own view of human rights through the publication of a White Paper in October 1991, and to upgrade its attacks on the human rights records of its major critics. The latter two features were connected with an unfolding strategy to promote the idea of a 'dialogue' on human rights between equal, sovereign, states, which reinforced its argument that mutual governmental agreement to these forms of discussions did not undercut its particular definition of sovereignty.

Two lines of argument quickly emerged in Beijing in response to the imposition of sanctions after Tiananmen. So-called conservatives advocated punishing those countries that had developed a sanctions policy, an act that would be doubly beneficial because it would reduce China's contact with the global community thereby cutting opportunities for 'foreign

---

[74] Harding (*A Fragile Relationship*, 235–7) records the main parameters of this debate.

interference' in China's internal affairs. This grouping argued that the West, with the USA at its head, had long been adopting a 'peaceful-evolution' strategy towards China, one designed to subvert the socialist system. Imposing sanctions was simply another method of weakening the Beijing government.

Others among the leadership acknowledged that demonstrators did indeed desire to see the downfall of China's communist regime and that there had been Western interference in internal affairs, but did not extend the argument to encompass a firm strategic link between these political activists and the West. As Deng stated in a public speech on 9 June: 'If we had not stopped them, they would have brought about our collapse.' Shortly after Jiang Zemin's appointment as Party Secretary, he described the events leading up to Tiananmen as a 'counterrevolutionary rebellion aimed at opposing the leadership of the Communist Party of China and overthrowing the socialist system'.[75] An article in the English-language *Beijing Review* in November 1989 was particularly uncompromising, describing the 'counter-revolutionary rebellion in Beijing' as an attempt to 'overthrow the leadership of the Chinese Communist Party and subvert the government of the socialist People's Republic of China'. Focusing explicitly on the question of rights, it went on to argue that there were no universal and abstract human rights, that different concepts of rights were evident in the way particular countries drafted their laws, and that internationally defined rights could not override domestic laws (quoting Britain's Lord Denning in support of this). Finally, it turned to the USA and, while noting that the US Congress had still not ratified the two international covenants, it finished by accusing Washington of 'gross interference in another country's internal affairs'. As the article put it:

A certain country has used its embassy to provide shelter for a criminal wanted by the host country, intervening in the host's normal judicial activities; allowed wanted criminals to conduct activities aimed at subverting another government; discussed the internal affairs of another country in its own Congress and imposed economic sanctions on that country just because they share different values; and even set as a precondition for improving bilateral relations the lifting of martial law.[76]

Events in Eastern Europe compounded Beijing's sense of insecurity that autumn and winter. That same *Beijing Review* article quoted above had made the unfortunate choice of singling out for approval the Soviet Union and Romania as having constitutions with provisions regarding public ownership similar to China's own. However, Moscow under Gorbachev

[75] Both statements are quoted in Copper, 'Peking's Post-Tienanmen Foreign Policy', 53.
[76] *Beijing Review,* 6–12 Nov. 1989, 14–16.

was set on its path of radical political reform, and December saw the execution of the Romanian President, Nicolae Ceausescu, an event so shocking to the Beijing leadership that it placed army and police units on alert and further tightened political controls.[77] Chinese leaders tried to reduce this growing sense of isolation by establishing diplomatic relations with Singapore, Indonesia, and Saudi Arabia in 1989 and 1990, and increasing contacts with Third World leaders, especially those that would visit swiftly after the Tiananmen events, affirm that the crackdown was China's 'internal affair', and that it was 'up to the Chinese people to choose their own road and future'.[78] Indeed, two-way visits between Chinese and ASEAN leaders in 1990 have been described as 'record-breaking . . . not only in their frequency but also in the ranking of the visiting leaders'.[79]

However, more moderate appraisals of the post-Tiananmen position were also available from those Chinese who counselled patience, suggested minimal concessions, and pointed out that neither developing countries nor the Soviet bloc represented viable alternative partners for a China set on sustaining high economic growth rates. Particularly at the turn of the year and into the early spring of 1990, Chinese leaders sought advice from research institutes in Beijing and Shanghai, and from the foreign policy establishment on how best to stabilize the key relationship that had been damaged as a result of Tiananmen—that with Washington. These advisers recommended moves such as allowing Fang Lizhi to leave the US embassy in Beijing for asylum outside China, releasing more of those detained after 4 June, and searching for ways to demonstrate China's continuing political, economic, and strategic importance to the USA and its allies, points that were discussed at a series of high-level meetings in the spring of 1990 and at one presided over by Jiang Zemin in June.[80]

All of these suggested actions were in fact carried out from the start of 1990. Beijing saw the lifting of martial law on 10 January, leading to the easing of the US administration's objection to World Bank loans. In 1990 and 1991, China released three batches of prisoners detained at the time of Tiananmen, and lifted martial law in Tibet in May 1990, probably all timed to coincide with various phases of the MFN debate. China's leadership let Fang and his wife leave the US embassy also at a time calculated to have an impact on the MFN issue, agreed to purchase

---

[77] Ross, 'National Security', 302.
[78] This statement was made by G. N. Azad, General Secretary of the Indian National Congress, during his meeting with Jiang Zemin in Beijing in July 1989. See *Beijing Review*, 17–23 July 1989.   [79] Chen Jie, 'Human Rights', 228.
[80] Harding, *A Fragile Relationship*, 262–3, 434 n. 26. For example, such reports were submitted by the Institute of American Studies at the Chinese Academy of Social Sciences and by the Shanghai Institute of International Studies.

up to seventy-two aeroplanes from Boeing, and made the first of two purchases of US wheat in June 1990 for similar purposes.[81] Beijing also used other means of bringing home to the USA its regional and global importance, not only during the Gulf War, but also in discussions concerning such global norms as non-proliferation of weapons of mass destruction, and during negotiations concerning Cambodia and North Korea. In direct reference to Washington's human rights policy, China began from the spring of 1991 to adopt a more assertive strategy, China's Foreign Minister (much as the November 1989 *Beijing Review* article had done) pointing to Washington's hypocritical stance in its refusal to ratify the major human rights conventions on the grounds that they came into conflict with domestic law. *Renmin Ribao* then pushed the argument much further, accusing the USA of violating certain key rights and carrying out policies of apartheid, racial discrimination, torture, and sex discrimination.[82] As noted above, China's concessions at the time of MFN renewal did make a difference to the MFN outcome, and undoubtedly influenced China to continue with such tactics in subsequent years. The satisfaction that must have been derived from criticizing the US record, particularly its failure to ratify the key human rights conventions was also to prove irresistible, becoming central to the discourse in the years to come.

One of China's biggest challenges was to find a means of preventing an unfavourable voting outcome at the annual meetings of the UN's human rights bodies, or better still to shift attention away from the country's record entirely. Tactics here often lacked subtlety: Beijing tried to reduce the power such organizations could have largely arising from their multiple memberships by targeting individual ambassadors or representatives from particular countries. As noted earlier, during the 1989 meeting of the Sub-Commission, which brought forth a mildly worded resolution expressing concern at developments in China, Beijing's representatives outside the conference room threatened diplomats with trade and aid sanctions against their country. This prompted the employment of the secret ballot—an unwelcome consequence, from China's perspective, of its own heavy-handed tactics.[83]

---

[81] Ross, 'National Security', 306.

[82] Copper, 'Peking's Post-Tienanmen Foreign Policy', 66.

[83] The *Manila Chronicle* reported that the Chinese embassy in Manila filed a diplomatic protest over the condemnatory statement made by the independent expert from the Philippines, Mary Concepcion Bautista. The Foreign Affairs department in Manila passed that protest onto Bautista, who pointedly responded that she had participated in the meeting in her personal capacity, and that the Sub-Commission was an independent body whose main concern was human rights. See *FBIS*-EAS-89-174, 11 Sept. 1989.

China lobbied hard again at the meeting of the UN Commission in 1990, as noted earlier, sending a huge diplomatic delegation to pressure participants, indirectly backed up by China's Foreign Minister, who went to Geneva to give a press conference, ostensibly on another matter. It was reported that one African diplomat was visited in his hotel by 'ten Chinese trying to explain to him how best to vote in order to avoid unnecessary complications in his country's relations with China'. Several ambassadors in Beijing were summoned to the Foreign Ministry and Chinese ministers visited a number of African countries. Such tactics had an impact. Although at the 1989 Sub-Commission meeting delegates had expressed 'unusual agreement' about the extent of the repression after Tiananmen, and did not accept China's depiction of events, nevertheless by the spring of 1990 a number of Commission members had been swayed in support of Beijing for politico-economic reasons: ' "They are our friends," "They send us economic aid," or "They are bringing political pressure on our government." '[84]

This unsophisticated approach outside the meeting room was matched by a similar one inside it. The Chinese expert and the country's observer delegates to the 1989 Sub-Commission made four main interventions. Three forms of reactions were implicit in Chinese statements and followed a familiar pattern for recalcitrant governments: the literal denial (nothing happened), the interpretive denial (what happened should be seen as something else), and the implicatory denial (what happened was justified).[85] One Chinese with observer status claimed that the Beijing authorities had to take action to end the disturbances in order to 'safeguard the human rights and fundamental freedoms of the vast majority of the Chinese people', that there had not been 'a single person . . . killed by the army or run over by military vehicles', and that such actions designed to restore order were in fact 'a domestic affair of the State concerned alone and no foreign country or international organization had a right to intervene on any pretext whatsoever'. This final claim drew a sharp retort from the Algerian expert, who argued: 'On the principle of non-interference, no State could claim any longer to be a special preserve, and the concept had gradually given way to that of international interest in the field of human rights.' China's expert on the Sub-Commission, Tian Jin, unwisely referred to Article 2 (7) of the UN

[84] Andreassen and Swinehart, *Human Rights in Developing Countries*, 107; Kent, 'China and the International Human Rights Regime', 19; Tessitore and Woolfson, *Issues before the 45th General Assembly*, 154.

[85] Stanley Cohen describes these as predictable responses on the part of perpetrator governments: see his 'Government Responses to Human Rights Reports: Claims, Denials, and Counterclaims', *Human Rights Quarterly*, 18/3 (1996), 517–43.

Charter.[86] This prompted a vigorous response from the French expert, Louis Joinet, who reminded Tian of those provisions in the Charter, especially Article 55, which in fact called for 'universal respect for, and observance of, human rights and fundamental freedoms', concluding that, if the Sub-Commission were to go along with Tian in advocating the principle of non-interference in the sphere of human rights, it might as well shut up shop. NGO representative Niall McDermot continued the defence of the human rights regime, pointing to the Sub-Commission's and Commission's responsibilities in this area, and reminding China of the obligations it had accepted under treaties it had signed. Moreover, in a reminder of the way in which governments can become caught in their own moral rhetoric and behaviour, McDermot stated that China's own past actions had given legitimacy to 'the right of the international community to scrutinise the human rights performance of other countries'. China, he noted, had 'voted in favour of resolutions that had sent human rights investigators to countries such as Afghanistan, South Africa and Chile and had joined in consensus resolutions in respect of conditions in other parts of the world'. However, at this stage, Chinese representatives remained reluctant to drop their argument stressing state sovereignty and non-interference; hence, when the Sub-Commission passed its mildly worded resolution, the Chinese representative harshly responded: 'The Chinese Government categorically rejects this resolution. It is null and void and has no binding force on China whatsoever.'[87]

At the 1990 Commission meeting, Chinese delegates adopted a slightly different tactic and picked up a part of the McDermot theme, noting their country's support for and willingness to abide by the UN Charter in its respect and protection of human rights and fundamental freedoms and emphasizing their government's active involvement in UN human rights work.[88] However, in a report on the failed outcome of the resolution, China showed itself to be unreconciled still to the consequences of participation in an international human rights regime. It described that unsuccessful resolution as a 'move . . . designed [to] provide a forum for those with ulterior motives to continue their slandering of China in order to interfere in China's internal affairs'.[89] It had used similar language in reaction to the US State Department's yearly human rights report a month earlier, claiming it to be 'based on rumors and lies' and accusing

---

[86] Article 2 (7) reads: 'Nothing contained in the present Charter shall authorize the United Nations to intervene in matters which are essentially within the domestic jurisdiction of any state.'

[87] Quoted in Kent, 'China and the International Human Rights Regime', 12–16.

[88] Ibid. 20.   [89] *FBIS*-Chi-90-045, 7 Mar. 1990.

the US government of 'flagrantly interfer[ing] in the internal affairs of China and seriously encroach[ing] upon China's sovereignty'.[90] Indeed, Chinese statements attempted to undermine the prestige of the UN human rights bodies through this usage of terminology designed to demonstrate how major states had been manipulating such meetings for political ends, criticizing countries that attempted to 'peddle ideology . . . in the name of human rights' and governments that used 'human rights to practise power politics, [and] interfere in other countries' internal affairs'.[91] When the Tibet resolution was passed at the 1991 meeting of the Sub-Commission, Chinese delegates refused to accept it as a genuine expression of concern about human rights practices in that area. They similarly described that resolution as 'null and void' and as having 'no binding force' on their country, characterizing it as a cynical attempt to foment disorder and to split Tibet from China.[92]

Such a response to global demands in the human rights area suggested the power of traditional domestic modes of thought that were resistant to the argument that external actors had a legitimate right to comment on and react to events in China itself. Other Chinese behaviour suggested, however, that interacting with the global community on human rights issues was forcing a deeper appraisal of what it meant to be a participant in such a regime, and at least persuaded the Chinese leadership to recognize that the issue of human rights could not be wished away. On the contrary, officials would need to have coherent answers ready when they were called upon to defend their country's record or when criticisms were voiced. Human rights law had not previously been regarded as a suitable subject for teaching or research in China, but in April 1990 the People's University in Beijing hosted a conference on the theory of human rights, and the capital was the host site also in April of the fourteenth Conference on the 'Law of the World', Tian Jin giving a speech entitled 'A Look at the Relationship between Human Rights, National Sovereignty, International Peace and Development'. More such gatherings were to come: in June, the Legal Research Institute of the Chinese Academy of Social Sciences held a conference on the theory of human rights, which later led to the establishment of a Human Rights Research Unit within the Academy. In September, the Research Centre for Social Science Development under the State Education Commission held its conference on the topic, additionally symbolizing the official authorization of scholarly discussion of human rights. Such events led to the publication of a large number of

[90] *FBIS*-Chi-90-036, 22 Feb. 1990.
[91] Copper, 'Peking's Post-Tienanmen Foreign Policy', 55.
[92] Kent, 'China and the International Human Rights Regime', 24.

works on the topic: a Chinese bibliography published in 1992, for example, contained a list of 296 articles on human rights in major newspapers and journals between 1979 and 1992, with some 50 per cent of them appearing in 1991.[93] The conferences offered a number of different perspectives, although at this stage they focused on the philosophical bases of particular positions rather than paying close attention to the specifics of human rights treatment in China.[94] Continuing into 1991, and as somewhat freer debates began to take place, four major themes emerged: 'the question of class and human rights; the relationship between individual and collective rights; the importance of social and economic rights versus political rights; and the question of international protection of human rights and state sovereignty.'[95]

Tian Jin's 1990 speech was of particular interest, in part because of his role as China's 'independent expert' at the UN Sub-Commission, but also because of the obvious desire that his ideas reach a wider international audience: hence its publication in the English-language weekly *Beijing Review*. It had three main themes. The first emphasized the historically contingent nature of rights: ' to insist on uniformity will amount to imposing a specific political system, ideology or perspective of human rights on other countries.' What there was in the way of common international standards related, he said, to opposition to 'racism, colonialism, gross violations of human rights caused by foreign occupation and aggression'. His second argument was that governments had the main responsibility for protecting human rights and that the principle of non-interference was still applicable in this domain except in areas relating to genocide or apartheid: 'To contend that human rights supercedes national sovereignty is not only without foundation in international law, but also reveals the ulterior motives of a few countries.' Finally, Tian argued for redirecting attention towards peace and development, and especially towards the latter, as a precondition for the protection of collective human rights, noting particularly that the connections between human rights and development were not receiving the attention they deserved. Probably in an attempt to circumscribe the nature of the discussion among legal circles in China, Tian argued that the 'major task before the legal professionals of various countries' was to develop international law in the area of the right to development as a basic human right.[96]

[93] Kent, *China, the United Nations, and Human Rights*, 149–50.

[94] Philip Baker, 'China: Human Rights and the Law', *Pacific Review* 6/3 (1993), 246–7; Zhou Wei, 'The Study of Human Rights in the People's Republic of China', in James T. H. Tang (ed.), *Human Rights and International Relations in the Asia–Pacific Region* (London: Pinter, 1995), 83.   [95] Ibid. 88.

[96] *Beijing Review*, 28 May–3 June 1990.

The sobering experience of activity within the UN Commission and Sub-Commission culminated in a Chinese decision to formulate an authoritative statement in the form of a White Paper on human rights. Scholarly activity was designed to feed into that process and by April 1991, at a conference organized by the Law Faculty of People's University, the right to subsistence had become well established as one of the main lines of scholarly argument.[97] By June 1991, all of the major themes that were to appear in the White Paper had been thoroughly aired at scholarly venues. The White Paper finally emerged in the autumn, a Chinese version in October and the English version in November, later to appear also in French, German, Japanese, and Spanish translations.[98] Described in one Chinese publication as an offensive weapon with which 'to fight with hostile foreign forces and . . . to educate our cadres, masses, and, in particular, our young people at home' and in another as aiding 'the international community understand the human rights situation as it is in China, [and] educating the Chinese people to see clearly western human rights advocators' lies', it received star billing in the official party newspaper, *Renmin Ribao*, and was quickly followed by a reference booklet, edited by the *Hongqi (Red Flag)* press, designed to be used as a study guide for a nationally organized campaign.[99] It was a signal indication, if there had been any doubt, of the power of international criticism to force a formalized response. The objectives behind its publication showed clearly the transnational aspects of the human rights debate.

[97] Kent, *China, the United Nations, and Human Rights*, 152. However, such a bald summary hardly conveys the relative richness of this debate. For a fuller discussion, see pp. 148–55. For example, an article by Zhang Wenxian, referred to in Kent, p. 153, was especially notable for its challenge to the idea that precedence should be given to economic and social rights. It also cast doubt on the claim that Marx viewed economic, social, and cultural rights as the basis of civil and political rights. See also Ronald C. Keith, *China's Struggle for the Rule of Law* (New York: St Martin's Press, 1994), esp. 60–69.

[98] The English version — China, Information Office of the State Council, *Human Rights in China* (Beijing: Foreign Languages Press, 1991) — comprises a preface and ten sections and was described by Li Peng as 'the basis of our response'. He went on: 'while assuming the defensive, we must be ready to launch offensives as well. The white paper serves as an offensive' (quoted in *FBIS*-Chi-92-141, 22 July 1992). Zhu Muzhi's commentary on the White Paper is in *Beijing Review*, 11–17 Nov. 1991. Zhu was then director of the Information Office of the State Council. He later became head of China's first human rights 'NGO'. I bought my copy of the White Paper in a tourist hotel's bookshop in Beijing.

[99] See *FBIS*-Chi-92-141, 22 July 1992; Zhou, 'The Study of Human Rights', 88. Its aims with respect to young Chinese do not seem to have been realized: as James D. Seymour records, 'this illiberal tract met with opposition from Chinese at home and abroad', Beijing university students putting up a critical poster and dissidents abroad dismissing it as 'all lies' (Seymour, 'Human Rights in Chinese Foreign Relations', in Kim (ed.) *China and the World: Chinese Foreign Relations in the Post-Cold War Era*, 210 and n. 33, 223).

The opening preface and subsequent chapters of that White Paper confirmed that a major reason behind its publication was to respond to that external criticism. The preface noted the commitment of the Chinese government and people to the safeguarding and improvement of their human rights situation, and the respect in which the various declarations and conventions adopted by the UN were held. But it also argued that the 'evolution of the situation in regard to human rights is circumscribed by the historical, social, economic and cultural conditions of various nations, and involves a process of historical development'. Foreshadowing an argument that was to achieve much greater prominence over the course of the 1990s, it stated that, 'owing to tremendous differences in historical background, social system, cultural tradition and economic development, countries differ in their understanding and practice of human rights'. This relativist argument linked with a developmentalist one also admitted that, while China had achieved much in the field of human rights, there was 'still much room for improvement.' It went on: 'It remains a long-term historical task for the Chinese people and government to continue to promote human rights and strive for the noble goal of full implementation of human rights as required by China's socialism.'

The next section of the White Paper began with China's familiar exposition of the massive crimes committed by Western and Japanese imperialists from the time of the Opium War until the founding of the PRC in 1949. From that time when the Chinese people had 'stood up as masters of their own country', they had won 'for the first time . . . real human dignity and the respect of the world', together with 'the basic guarantee for their life and security'. However, the basic right of subsistence, which the White Paper described as the most important of all human rights, had been tackled urgently only under the leadership of the CCP which still regarded that right as an 'issue of paramount importance in China today'.[100] It outlined in highly exaggerated form the Party's substantial achievements since 1949 in all areas covered by the two international human rights covenants, and closed with a statement of support for the efforts of the UN in promoting 'universal respect for human rights and

---

[100] In an important elaboration of this point, Kent (*China, the United Nations, and Human Rights*, 157) argues that the Chinese term *shengcun quan,* which can mean both threats to physical security as well as rights to subsistence, was used in such a way in the White Paper as to ignore that former element, concentrating solely on economic and social rights. However, interestingly, an article by Yu Quanyu, published as a defence of the White Paper, in the light of the Western world's criticism of the priority it had given to subsistence rights, defined subsistence in a far broader way and in terms that made it compatible with the UDHR. Yu wrote: 'The Universal Declaration of Human Rights describes

fundamental freedoms', noting China's active participation in UN work in this area. However, much as Tian had done a year and half earlier, it maintained that 'priority should be given to the safeguarding of the right of the people of the developing countries to subsistence and development, thus creating the necessary conditions for people all over the world to enjoy various human rights'.

Indeed, the continuities with Tian's arguments elaborated in spring 1990 were quite striking: the emphasis on the collective rights of the whole Chinese people; on subsistence and development as priorities within the human rights area; on the role of national governments in promoting their citizens' human rights, emphasizing yet again state sovereignty as the overarching norm and as reflected in Article 2 (7) of the UN Charter: 'the argument that the principle of non-interference in internal affairs does not apply to the issue of human rights is, in essence, a demand that sovereign states give up their state sovereignty in the field of human rights, a demand that is contrary to international law.' The publication of the White Paper seemed to suggest, then, that, although external pressure had persuaded the Chinese leadership that it needed to explain more fully its position on human rights, the interaction with governments, institutions, and activists in the period after the 4 June killings had not led to an acceptance of the argument that individuals could be the subject of international law.

CONCLUSION

Although there was no fundamental shift at the official level in China's perspective on human rights, the impact of Tiananmen on China's external relations was undeniably severe and it was induced to make some concessions in response to criticism of its human rights abuses. The country was damaged economically and psychologically and the great power status that it craved seemed further out of reach. It was, after all, the first permanent member of the UN Security Council ever to have its human

human rights as "everyone has the right to life, liberty and the security of person". It also puts the right to life in order of first priority. "The right to life" and "security of person" referred to here all belong to the same idea as the right to subsistence. The term "liberty" mentioned here has a broad connotation. "Personal freedom from encroachment" is part of the freedom right. Our concept of the right to subsistence also includes "personal freedom from encroachment"' (*Beijing Review*, 6–12 Jan. 1992, 12). The article also appeared in *Renmin Ribao*, 26 Nov. 1991, which suggests a desire to promote the argument internally as well as externally.

rights behaviour condemned in a resolution, and, judging by its behaviour at the UN Commission, this criticism by a UN body stung Chinese leaders, illustrating the power of universal institutions. For a time, the Western states and Japan imposed economic and political sanctions, isolating China to a degree not experienced since the late 1960s. Neither was it proving easy for Beijing to persuade others to define state sovereignty in ways that excluded international involvement in this issue area. With this realization came Beijing's difficult decision to sanction internal study of the concept of human rights and to produce a White Paper on the topic for internal and external use. China thus set off a domestic debate that would inevitably expand, with consequences difficult to chart in a country that now had many more avenues for the expression of ideas and dissemination of information.

However, China's experience of interacting with the global human rights regime also demonstrated anew the complexities of sustaining the human rights aspect in foreign policy. The normative signals from the UN bodies were reasonably clear in confirming that the Chinese leadership had undertaken actions deserving of condemnation and that it could not legitimately project the norm of state sovereignty and non-interference as being in direct conflict with human rights obligations. But individual governments within the industrialized world sent a more mixed message, especially as other international issues began to assume greater prominence. Some evinced sympathy for China's claim that it needed to restore order; others saw rights as matters that could, or had to be, traded either to satisfy domestic constituents for reasons of economic gain, or for reasons of international and national security. The Chinese leadership quickly realized that it could use its weight within the global system to defy certain of the international demands and explore these underlying weaknesses in the global human rights regime—hence well-timed purchases of Boeing aircraft, or veiled threats of using its veto in defiance of majority interests in the UN Security Council.

Yet, despite China's relative power, the leadership also recognized the necessity for compromise and that its major democratic interlocutors—for all their vacillation, whatever their political leanings, or how realist they were in their approaches to foreign policy—would retain some human rights element in those policies. Legislative requirements, NGO vigilance, the separation of powers in the USA, and policies that reflected the values associated with democratic states would help to ensure that. Post-Tiananmen Chinese exiles would also reinforce this environment as many became committed to the human rights movement, provided access to additional information sources, or set up new NGOs. China engaged in overt bargaining with its major international critics in order to reduce its level of isolation. But production of the White Paper, its reception of human rights delegations, and the sending of its own delegations to other countries represented Beijing's acceptance that it could not avoid engagement in some level of direct global debate over human rights. In internal documents and statements, Chinese leaders described this move as a shift from a defensive to an offensive strategy, undertaken as much for domestic as for external reasons. Offensive strategies, however, if anything require deeper engagement. This resulted in China's entry after 1991 into new phases of the argument, together with a more active search for the like-minded beyond those it had come to count on, or could induce to provide support, within such bodies as the UNCHR.

6

The Shift to Multilateral Venues,
1992–1995

The first eighteen months after the Tiananmen bloodshed marked the height of global criticism of China's human rights record. Public opinion and international and domestic NGOs prompted governments to act within UN channels, to toughen bilateral policies, and to form coalitions of the like-minded. UN Special Rapporteurs fulfilled their mandates, as did the UN Sub-Commission and its parent body, the UNCHR. Either through the imposition of diplomatic and economic sanctions, or through public condemnation, they all performed roles as reasonably stern 'teachers of norms' for this period.[1] In response, the Chinese leadership moved through the phases of intense repression of political activists, and the argument that international action represented unwarranted interference in its internal affairs, to a time of tactical concessions and limited engagement in the discourse on human rights, marked most obviously by the publication of the White Paper in October 1991.

The years 1992 to 1995, however, quickly gave some indication of the difficulties that would be faced by those who wished to move China beyond tactical concessions towards genuine acceptance of the validity of some of the core human rights norms. Major Western states, together with Japan, continued to reduce the bilateral pressure, for economic and strategic reasons. China's recapturing of its high economic growth rates from 1992 enhanced its ability to pose policy dilemmas for those interested in competing in the China market, as well as for far weaker countries, poised to benefit from China's own economic dealings with them. The Beijing leadership, concerned about threats to the Party-State, uneasy that the global focus on oppression in Tibet might give a boost to the forces of independence there and beyond, and fearful that informed

---

[1] See Risse *et al.* (eds.), *The Power of Human Rights*, 271, and Martha Finnemore, 'International Organizations as Teachers of Norms: The United Nations Educational, Scientific, and Cultural Organization and Science Policy', *International Organization*, 47/4 (1993).

Chinese might react unpredictably towards a Beijing government that was plainly on the defensive with respect to its international interlocutors, decided to renew its efforts to regain the initiative. The 1991 White Paper had been a major first stage in that strategy. It provided Chinese officials and scholars, required to respond in the international arena to human rights criticisms with an authoritative text upon which to draw. Beijing went further, however, in trying to link up with other governments in East Asia in the exploitation of a common dislike of Western triumphalism, sometimes expressed through the imposition of institutionally based economic conditions for lending in this post-cold-war, unipolar, world. This growing coincidence of interest between China and countries such as Indonesia, Malaysia, and Singapore bolstered Beijing's belief that it had regained some degree of control over this policy area, implied that the human rights regime was broad enough to encompass a variety of views, and suggested that this diversity of viewpoint could usefully be framed as a North–South or an Asia–West division. The Chinese leadership thus began to launch more extensive, direct attacks on Western countries, particularly on the USA, and on the major international NGOs.

Nevertheless, the relative density of the human rights regime ensured that some constraints still operated on China's international diplomacy, requiring Beijing to respond both verbally and diplomatically at key moments in the human rights calendar. As the major states' sanctions policies weakened—especially with the US retreat on the MFN issue in 1994—governments tended to make greater use of such multilateral institutions as the UN Commission and Sub-Commission. This route could help to shield them from Chinese economic retribution, and also provide the democracies with a response to NGO critics who pointed to a serious disjuncture between rhetorical and legislative commitment to human rights and their actual behaviour. Moreover, with the breakdown of the former Soviet voting bloc in the Commission, there was greater chance of passing a resolution critical of China's record. In addition, the Special Rapporteurs and Working Groups that operated under the remit of the UNCHR had formal procedures less subject to political manipulation than individual governments, and reporting schedules that ensured continued attention to conditions within China.

THE USES OF THE 1991 WHITE PAPER

As noted in the previous chapter, the publication of the White Paper sparked numerous officially sponsored discussion meetings on human rights inside China. Conservative forces in particular viewed the debates, and the White Paper itself, as contributions to the task of explaining to young Chinese why their country's priorities differed from those of people in the West, and as a way of dealing with international criticism of China's record. As Li Peng is reported to have remarked on the White Paper's release, it was a combative response to those 'Western hostile forces' who were attacking China. Articles appearing after the White Paper's publication frequently drew on Deng Xiaoping's 1985 statement in order further to boost the legitimacy of its central argument. As Deng had put it: 'What are human rights? Are human rights for the majority or for the minority, or for the people of the whole country? So-called 'human rights' as understood in the Western world and human rights we talk about are two different things. There are different viewpoints regarding this matter'.[2] With the official sanction for Chinese scholars 'to throw themselves into the battle' against the West and thereby undermine its strategy of 'peaceful evolution', the central propaganda department organized the speedy publication of some nine books on various aspects of human rights, many of which sought to pit their interpretations of Western thinking on rights against the supposed viewpoints of socialist or Third World states.[3] White Papers were obviously thought of as useful ways of signalling latest leadership thinking on the topic: thus, in the following years, further such publications appeared, for example, on criminal reform, religious freedom, and in December 1995 an important follow-up to the 1991 more general document called 'Progress of Human Rights in China'.[4]

The main arguments in the first White Paper, with its emphases on rights to subsistence and development, appeared regularly but not always consistently in official speeches in the years immediately following its publication. China also undertook a more sustained attack on the USA, pointing to its unwarranted targeting of China's human rights record and to the weaknesses in the USA's own record of protection. Beijing justified the focus on the USA by reference to Washington's leading role in spearheading the criticism of China, by its ability to line up other Western countries, together with Japan, and because of the centrality of human rights to what was termed its 'peaceful evolution strategy'.[5] Washington's policy was criticized for its arbitrariness, selectivity, and double standards. Articles pointed out, for example, that Washington had delayed its

---

[2] *FBIS*-Chi-91-232, 3 Dec. 1991; and Chi-91-218, 12 Nov. 1991.

[3] FBIS-Chi-92-121, 23 June 1992.

[4] By 1995, according to a *Beijing Review* report, some 100 academic works and about a 1,000 academic papers, together with several volumes of translation, had been published. *Beijing Review*, 4–10 Mar. 1996, 20.   [5] *FBIS*-Chi-92-141, 22 July 1992.

own signature of the international covenants on grounds that were not dissimilar to China's own reasons for wariness, that it had failed to condemn Israel for violating human rights in the occupied territories, and that conditions within the USA were sufficiently dire that Washington ought to have scrutinized its own record before commenting on that of other countries.[6] One of Beijing's most forthright statements occurred in February 1992 at the UN Commission. There it described the USA as a country where police brutality, crime, and racial discrimination were rife. Its criticisms of China were proof that the USA 'was simply attempting to divert the international community from the situation in [its] own country'.[7] Washington was also regularly accused of sustaining a 'cold-war mentality' in the post-cold-war world, an allegation that Beijing also made against such NGOs as Human Rights Watch/Asia and AI. These attacks on the NGOs, and the bracketing of them with the USA, represented an attempt to cast aspersions on their political neutrality.[8]

RELATIVISM VERSUS UNIVERSALISM

During the early 1990s, Chinese criticisms of US society, its articulation of a human rights position that encompassed subsistence and development, together with the demand that developed states be more sensitive to the diversity of viewpoints on what constituted human rights, fitted well with the attitudes of governments elsewhere in its region, particularly the positions taken by Singapore, Malaysia, and Indonesia. Since the ending of the cold war, after President Bush's enunciation of his idea of a 'New World Order', and the Clinton administration's espousal of the goal of 'democratic enlargement', such South-East Asian governments had been accusing the USA and other Western governments of trying to impose their versions of democracy and human rights on the world. Of particular concern were the various moves both bilaterally and multilaterally to make development aid conditional on a good human rights and governance record. As noted in Chapter 2, in 1991 and 1992, the EC and Japan, for example,

---

[6] *FBIS*-Chi-92-121, 23 June 1992.
[7] E/CN.4/1992/SR.38, 21 Feb. 1992 and SR.36, 20 Feb. 1992.
[8] *FBIS*-Chi-94-036, 23 Feb. 1995. As the Chinese delegate to the UN Commission stated, 'Amnesty International and Human Rights Watch have not changed their mentality since the Cold War . . . How can they assess the human rights situation in China without prejudice?'

introduced new criteria for their development assistance, and in 1990 the US AID announced that its aid decisions would take account of a government's progress towards democracy. Other international financial institutions, such as the World Bank, although its terms of agreement forbade its open advocacy of democracy, also introduced 'good-governance' criteria for borrower countries, including encouragement for the development of a civil society.

Weaker states, whether potential targets of such conditionality or not, yet still smarting from their colonial pasts, were not likely to remain quiescent. In June 1991, for example, the Malaysian Permanent Representative to the United Nations, Razali Ismail, criticized the incorporation of Charles Humana's freedom index in the 1991 version of the UN Development Programme (UNDP) report, an index that he said ignored 'freedoms which are fundamental to the very survival and dignity of every single human being', such as freedom from hunger and disease.[9] He went on: 'Why are these freedoms not given as much weight as something as misplaced and out of context as homosexuality used as an indicator?' Chinese officials launched almost identical attacks, also demanding that the UNDP 'fully take into consideration the member states' tremendous differences in development level, cultural traditions and social system' and not impose a minority's values and standards on others.[10] President Yang Shangkun's visit to Malaysia in January 1992 turned into an occasion where he and Prime Minister Mahathir Mohamad could underline their joint belief that their peoples' values differed from those of Westerners, that social and political stability, and the rights of subsistence and development, were the most important rights for their countries to safeguard.[11] Senior Minister Lee Kuan Yew in a speech in November 1992 agreed with these relativist sentiments: 'one cannot ignore the history, culture and background of a society. Societies have developed separately for thousands of years at different speeds and in different ways. Their ideals and their norms are different. American or European standards of the late 20th century cannot be universal.'[12] South-East Asian officials supported China's argument that the USA was in no position to point the finger at others: American society, it was averred, suffered from delinquency, unwanted pregnancies, the breakdown of family life, high crime

---

[9] Razali Ismail's speech at the 38th Session of the governing session of the UN Development Programme, 11 June 1991, quoted in Aki Okubo, 'The 'Asian Values' Debate in Singapore and Malaysia: Motives for Challenging Universal Human Rights in the 1990s', M.Litt thesis (Oxford, 1998), 18.   [10] *FBIS*-Chi-92-029, 12 Feb. 1992.

[11] For further details, see Chen 'Human Rights', 235.

[12] Quoted in Okubo, 'Asian Values', 16.

rates, and a disrespect for those in authority.[13] Asian values, on the other hand, combined respect for authority, and the rights of the community over those of the individual.

This growing coincidence of belief about the dangers of Western triumphalism and of a post-cold-war era in which a hegemonic USA appeared to operate under few constraints reinforced Chinese moves away from arguments that explored the dichotomies between Marxist and bourgeois conceptions of rights and towards arguments that stressed cultural and historical relativism and the priorities of developmental states. China had found a constituency of support not from among its Marxist neighbours, such as Vietnam, but from among the 'soft authoritarians' of South East Asia. The Singapore model, indeed, was particularly attractive to China because it was developed by Chinese who seemed to have found the key to economic success.[14] The stress that Singaporean officials placed on the need for social and political stability as the means to material prosperity matched the line of argument that Chinese officials wished to promote both domestically and internationally. Moreover, the discovery of this sympathetic constituency could not have come at a better time as far as China was concerned, because it helped its recovery from diplomatic isolation in the immediate aftermath of Tiananmen, and provided it with a potential base of political support at the forthcoming UN World Conference on Human Rights, to be held in Vienna in June 1993.

Regional preparatory meetings preceded this major world conference, the Asian one held in Bangkok between 29 March and 2 April. In the run-up to the Bangkok conference, China elaborated on the position it would be taking in March and presumably also at Vienna in June. Official speeches indicated the extent to which China's leaders wished to highlight the compatibility of their position with those of their South-East Asian neighbours. As early as February 1992, Chinese officials were arguing that an individual country should be allowed to determine the measures necessary to protect the human rights of its people 'in the light of its history, tradition and level of economic development'. It was also important, China believed, that an exploration of the relationship between development and human rights be undertaken at Vienna, for experience and history had shown that in most developing countries, including in China, human rights could best be achieved in conditions of 'social progress, social stability' and where there was economic advancement.

---

[13] See e.g. Kishore Mahbubani, 'The Dangers of Decadence: What the Rest can Teach the West', *Foreign Affairs*, 72/4 (1993).
[14] Chen, 'Human Rights', esp. 230–3.

The resolution of 'problems of food, housing, employment, education and health care' were the most pressing matters.[15] At the end of the year, Beijing's ambassador to the United Nations made available an even more authoritative statement of his government's likely position at Vienna. Ambassador Li first called on delegates to ensure the world conference reflected 'reality in the field of international human rights activities' and stressed the necessity to pay special attention to the concerns of developing countries, which made up the overwhelming majority of the world's population. Priority, he stated, needed to be given to the gross violations of human rights that arose from racism, apartheid, colonialism, and foreign aggression, the right to development should be reaffirmed as an inalienable human right, the indivisibility and interdependency of human rights should be emphasized, and the principles of state sovereignty, mutual respect, and equal exchange should be acknowledged. He also repeated the new emphases in the official position: that improvements in human rights conditions should be allowed to emerge progressively, 'in line with [a country's] own values . . . social environment and cultural tradition . . . Such practice as imposing on others one or a few countries' political systems, economic mode and values, including their human rights concept must be rejected,' he added.[16]

At Bangkok itself, the head of the Chinese delegation, Ambassador Jin Yongjian, made further attempts to bridge any remaining divide between Beijing's 1991 position and that of its regional neighbours: 'the hard-working, brave and intelligent Asian people have cultivated the splendid cultural tradition of respecting the rights of the state, society, family and individual. This culture has played an important role in maintaining stability of the state and society and promoting steady development of the economy and society.'[17] This language showed up in the preamble of the Bangkok official declaration and in some of its articles together with thoughts China had articulated in earlier statements—respect for national sovereignty, the right to development as an inalienable human right, and the arguments about non-selectivity and indivisibility. Although the final declaration might not have given all of these features the priority that China believed they deserved, Beijing could live with the consensus reached, especially since in its subsequently most oft-quoted paragraph the Bangkok gathering recognized that, 'while human rights are universal in nature, they must be considered in the context of a dynamic and evolving process of international norm-setting, bearing in

---

[15] E/CN.4/1992/SR.38, 14 Feb. 1992.
[16] Speech at the Third Committee of the 47th Session of the UN General Assembly. *Beijing Review*, 21–7 Dec. 1992.   [17] *Beijing Review*, 19–25 Apr. 1993.

mind the significance of national and regional particularities and various historical, cultural and religious backgrounds'.[18]

Chinese delegates thus went to Vienna surrounded by those who were reasonably close to its position on human rights (only Japan and Cyprus of the Asian group had submitted reservations to the Bangkok declaration) and determined that the World Conference would not ignore the work of the regional meetings.[19] Accordingly, at Vienna, China's Vice Foreign Minister, Liu Huaqiu, reiterated arguments about state sovereignty and relativism. A later Chinese report on the conference attempted to emphasize the coincidence of interest with Asian neighbours and the developing world, quoting at length the statement of Singapore's Minister for Foreign Affairs, Wong Kan Seng, who had also argued at the World Conference that the global community could not 'ignore the differences in history, culture and background of different societies. They have developed separately for thousands of years, in different ways and with different experiences. Their ideals and norms differ.'[20] Despite Japan's demurral at Bangkok and strong stand at Vienna in favour of universalism and against the notion that international involvement with human rights represented an interference in internal affairs, China undoubtedly did not take this too seriously. Tokyo on more than one occasion signalled that it could be flexible in its interpretations of human rights when in direct contact with Chinese officials, describing China as 'half-right' in September 1992 in laying stress on the argument that the most fundamental human rights were food and shelter, and in March 1994, less than a year after Vienna, stating that it was not sensible for Western countries to try to impose their political values on other countries.[21]

---

[18] *Beijing Review*, 31 May–6 June 1993. China was far less happy with Bangkok's institutional recommendations, including support for national and regional human rights bodies, the promotion of dialogue between governments and NGOs, and strengthening the UN Centre for Human Rights. See Kent, *China, the United Nations, and Human Rights* for an extensive discussion of China's positions in the run-up to Vienna, esp.161–9.

[19] As the head of the Chinese delegation to the Fourth Session of the Preparatory Committee for the World Conference, Ambassador Jin Yongjian, put it on 21 Apr.: 'Any endeavor to draft a final document for the World Conference without taking into due consideration the three regional declarations of Asia, Africa and Latin America is not in conformity with the spirit of UNGA resolution and is, therefore, unrealistic and unpractical' (*Beijing Review*, 31 May–6 June 1993). China did not get its way at Vienna, however, as later sections of this chapter will show.

[20] See the *Beijing Review* report on Vienna, 5–11 July 1993, Tang (ed.), *Human Rights*, app. III, 'Statements by Representatives of Asian Governments at the Vienna World Conference on Human Rights', esp. 213–17.

[21] See *FBIS*-EAS-92-173, 4 Sept. 1992, and EAS-94-054, 21 Mar. 1994. Compare this with the Japanese government's statement at Vienna, in Tang (ed.), *Human Rights*, app. III, pp. 217–19.

THE ECONOMIC WEIGHT OF CHINA

If China, then, had found a congenial reference group and was deriving strength from an 'Asian-values' debate that created doubts in some quarters about the validity of Western attacks upon China's record, its economic recovery from 1992 deepened the policy dilemmas facing its prime critics, over and above those that had been revealed in the eighteen months after Tiananmen. A significant boost to economic reform had come with Deng Xiaoping's visit to southern China during the Chinese New Year in 1992, during which he described this economic motor for the Chinese economy as a model for the rest of the country. This political signal that the economic reforms were once more in the ascendant in China reassured outsiders and those inside the country who were committed to the reform process. Economic growth rates, which had dipped alarmingly between 1989 and 1991, took off once again, reaching 12.8 per cent in 1992 and 13 per cent in 1993. Where foreign direct investment (FDI) had fallen 43 per cent in the last quarter of 1989 in comparison with the same period in 1988, it rose steadily from 1992, making China the second largest recipient of FDI in the world.[22] In May 1993 the IMF announced that, based on purchasing power parity calculations, China's economy was four times bigger than previously estimated, and that the size of its economy placed it behind only the USA and Japan. Two-way trade levels also grew steadily, by 1995 totalling $280.9 billion, making China the world's eleventh largest trading nation.[23]

China's increased involvement in the world economy, and its own economic growth projections, could not fail to have a policy impact. For democratic governments concerned about electoral popularity, it raised sharply the question of who such rulers primarily represented: should the possible improved prosperity of one's own people be bought at the expense of the core human rights of those overseas?[24] Beijing thought it

[22] Contracted foreign investment for 1992 reached $14.6 billion, and for 1993 $18 billion. Jude Howell, *China Opens its Doors* (Hemel Hempstead: Harvester/Wheatsheaf, 1993), 91; Christopher Findlay and Andrew Watson, 'Economic Growth and Trade Dependency in China', in David S. G. Goodman and Gerald Segal (eds.), *China Rising: Nationalism and Interdependence* (London: Routledge, 1997), 113.

[23] David M. Lampton, 'China Policy in Clinton's First Year', in James R. Lilley and Wendell L. Willkie II (eds.), *Beyond MFN: Trade with China and American Interests* (Washington: American Enterprise Institute, 1994), 29; Findlay and Watson, 'Economic Growth', 108.

[24] Some Americans had a clear sense of priorities when US jobs and prosperity were pitted against other policy goals of a longer-term and more-generalized nature. For example, Michael Armstrong, the Chief Executive Officer of Hughes Aircraft, argued in November 1993 in reference to sanctions imposed on the sales of satellites : 'It escapes me what effect our laying off 4,000 to 5,000 more people in California and shifting this export business to Europe has on the Chinese. I know it doesn't affect missile technology transfer, but I do know it affects American jobs, American families, American business and the American satellite technology base' (quoted in Mann, *About Face*, 287).

could shape the answer to that dilemma in most if not all of such countries. In June 1992 China sent its biggest ever buying mission to Europe,
with Germany as a particular target.[25] Sino-German economic relations
deepened quickly, with Bonn emerging as China's leading trading partner
in Europe. Chancellor Kohl and a huge entourage visited in November
1993[26] and signed contracts worth DM7 billion. Fortunately, from
China's perspective, news of these contracts appeared on the front page
of the Seattle newspapers as President Clinton, Treasury Secretary
Bentsen, Commerce Secretary Brown, and the head of the National
Economic Council, Rubin, arrived in that west-coast city for the first
APEC summit.[27] Kohl, obviously delighted with the reception he received
in China, described the agreements as 'a start . . . not the end of the line'.
He went on, 'seen in these terms, it will naturally have enormous repercussions for Germany as an export nation. Next to the Japanese, we are
the world champions in exporting.'[28] Japan itself did its best not to be left
behind, awarding China more bilateral aid than any other country, sending the Emperor on an unprecedented visit to Beijing in October 1992,
and starting the Fourth Yen Loan negotiations in October 1994, apparently unconstrained by the four principles of ODA outlined two years
earlier.

The French government also set out to regain its share of the China
market, damaged after its initial policies in response to Tiananmen and
further still after it had decided to sell sixty Mirage 2000–5 bombers to
Taiwan.[29] In April 1994 Prime Minister Édouard Balladur visited Beijing,
receiving promises that French industry would soon be awarded contracts
for the development of power stations, telecommunications, high-speed
trains, and sales of wheat.[30] In July, the French Minister for Foreign
Trade followed up Balladur's essentially political visit with one that obviously stressed the economic, given the accompanying party of some 125
business people. Following President Jiang Zemin's return visit in
September, France and China signed trade agreements worth $2.5 billion.[31]
In response to NGO and media calls to justify this *rapprochement* and the

---

[25] *International Herald Tribune*, 20 June 1992.
[26] Kohl was accompanied by four ministers and forty senior managers (described somewhat unfortunately by Hamburg TV as the 'largest German expedition to China since
Count Waldersee ordered the crushing of the uprising of the boxers in 1900'). *FBIS*-WEU-
93-223, 22 Nov. 1993.   [27] Mann, *About Face*, 293.
[28] *FBIS*-WEU-93-223, 22 Nov. 1993.
[29] *FBIS*-WEU-94-015, 24 Jan. 1994. During a thirty-minute meeting between Foreign
Minister Qian Qichen and President Mitterrand in Paris in Jan. 1994, Qian reportedly gave
French businesses something to savour. He said: China 'is a market with strong potential
for foreign businesses, particularly French ones, which are welcome'.
[30] *FBIS*-WEU-94-069, 11 Apr. 1994.
[31] *Human Rights Watch World Report 1995* (New York, 1994), 148.

priority now being given to the economic relationship, French officials made two kinds of arguments: one based on China's economic, demographic, political, and strategic weight, and the other on the claim that the USA had not maintained its sanctions. As Foreign Minister Alain Juppé put it in April 1994, Washington had still not refused China MFN trading status and had in fact 'already closed the Tienanmen Square chapter'.[32] In his view, other Western countries were simply losing out to the Americans and Japanese. Why should France stand alone, he asked? It was a classic example of the weakness of sanctions in the absence of regular, institutionalized contact to maintain cooperation. The French government made the convenient assumption that it was a follower, and hence in danger of being left behind, rather than a leading participant in the creation of a sanctions policy.

Despite Juppé's remarks, at that point the MFN debate in Washington was still alive and the Tiananmen chapter had not quite closed. This was due to an active NGO and congressional interest in ensuring there was at least some exposure of the issues at stake each time that China's MFN trading status came up for renewal, and a result of an earlier Clinton commitment to give greater prominence to human rights concerns.[33] As noted earlier, the Bush administration in 1991 broadly had argued for the separation of human rights from trade questions, promising instead measures that would come down hard on China when it operated against US commercial interests, and attempting to institutionalize a bilateral human rights dialogue. The Bush presidency continued this approach into 1992: for example, threatening China with high tariffs on selected exports if it did not sign a market access agreement by October, and finally signing a Memorandum of Understanding (MOU) with Beijing in August on the prevention of prison labour exports that included provisions for on-site inspection. With respect to the 'dialogue' on human rights, Washington and Beijing held high-level discussions in January and March, only for these to be cut off in October after Bush decided to sell Taiwan F–16 jet fighter aircraft.

Congress, however, continued with its efforts to sustain the linkage between trade and other Chinese policies that evoked concern, and twice introduced bills in 1992 to link MFN status to improvements in China's

---

[32] *FBIS*-WEU-94-068, 8 Apr. 1994. 'Tienanmen' spelling as in original.

[33] One concrete change that his administration did introduce, for example, was an instruction to American embassies for each section to contribute information and to corroborate reports of human rights violations, an attempt further to ingrain this dimension of policy into the bureaucracy. See US Department of State, *Country Reports on Human Rights Practices for 1993*, (Washington: US Government Printing Office, 1994), overview section.

record on human rights, market access, and nuclear proliferation issues, the second Bill in the summer of 1992 a more refined version of the March legislation. Modelled on a proposal first outlined by Human Rights Watch, that later Bill threatened the loss of preferential tariffs on state-owned as opposed to privatized industries unless specific human rights improvements took place.[34] The assumption was that this diminished the risk of harming those enterprises that contributed to the liberalization of China. This Bill, with its more selective targeting, won support in both the House and Senate but still did not garner enough votes in the Senate to override President Bush's September 1992 veto. However, Clinton would later review this idea of selected sanctions as a possible source of compromise in the MFN debate.

Presidential candidate Clinton chose to target Bush's China policy to demonstrate the incumbent President's supposed indifference to supporting democracy around the world: 'there is no more striking example of President Bush's indifference to democracy than his policy towards China.'[35] He also presumed that a link had to be made between trading status and human rights. However, in the following months, Clinton's position underwent some modification regarding the conditions to be imposed on Beijing. By September he was supporting the thrust of the modified Bill that had called for removing MFN trading status only from state-owned enterprises. Once assured of his election victory, he shifted slightly again, his remarks after meeting Bush and congressional leaders betraying a greater understanding of the complexity of the arguments on this question: 'We have a big stake in not isolating China, in seeing that China continues to develop a market economy. But we also have to insist, I believe, on progress in human rights and human decency.'[36] Nevertheless, despite this air of ambiguity, the expectations were that some conditions for the extension of MFN status would be introduced, but this time the President, rather than Congress, would take the lead. The administration thus set up an inter-agency working group at the end of January with the task of presenting policy options. By the spring, senior officials within the Clinton administration, such as US Trade Representative Mickey Kantor, Secretary of State Warren Christopher, and the Assistant Secretary of State for East Asia and Pacific Affairs, Winston Lord, all implied in public statements that renewal of MFN would be conditional

---

[34] *Human Rights Watch World Report 1993* (New York, 1992), 165; Diane F. Orentlicher and Timothy A. Gelatt, 'Public Law, Private Actors: The Impact of Human Rights on Business Investors in China', *Journal of International Law and Business*, (Fall 1993), 100.

[35] Clinton on the campaign trail, quoted in Lampton, 'Clinton's First Year', 10.

[36] Clinton on 19 Nov. 1992, quoted in Lampton, 'Clinton's First Year', 14.

on progress in human rights. But a consensus also developed within the administration that the President, while trying to establish greater unity with Congress, had to regain the initiative from the legislative branch in this area of policy: hence the growing preference for a presidential executive order rather than congressional legislation.

Representative Pelosi and Senator Mitchell, in cooperative mode, held off introducing their bills in the two houses of Congress until 21 April, after Lord's confirmation hearings in the Senate. Their legislation reflected the aims of the 1992 bills, including specific targeting of state-owned enterprises if China failed by 1994 to release political dissidents and those imprisoned for religious beliefs, did not allow unrestricted emigration, or proved unwilling or unable to comply with the MOU on prison labour exports. In congruence with these sentiments, the 28 May executive order conditioned 1994 MFN renewal on seven criteria, two of which related to the pre-existing requirements of US law regarding emigration and prison labour exports, and five of which required China to demonstrate 'overall, significant progress' in such areas as humane treatment of prisoners, the release of non-violent political dissidents, and those held for the expression of their religious beliefs.[37]

Economic factors did, of course, play a large role in Clinton's backing-away from absolute revocation of China's trading privileges in 1993: the growing economic weight of China—or more pertinently its future potential—referred to above was undeniable. As a mark of their earnestness on this issue, in mid-May 1993 more than 300 business firms and associations publicly urged Clinton to renew MFN unconditionally, six major corporations writing separately to the President drawing his attention to projected exports to China in excess of $105 billion between 1993 and 2010.[38] The Chinese themselves pointedly emphasized the economic argument in their discussions and dealings, one senior official informing David Lampton of the National Committee on US–China Relations in April 1993 that China would soon be one of the biggest buyers of aircraft, and these could be Boeing (one in six aircraft produced in fact was then being sold to China), that there were rich opportunities for cooperation in the fields of oil and natural gas exploration, that China's demand for automobiles was 'growing rapidly', and that the telecommunications market was ripe for exploitation. In case the message was not already crystal clear, he added: 'If you . . . come into the market too late, it will

---

[37] David M. Lampton, 'America's China Policy in the Age of the Finance Minister: Clinton Ends Linkage', *China Quarterly*, 139 (Sept. 1994), 602.
[38] Lampton, 'Clinton's First Year', 154 n. 24, 19.

be occupied by others. The Chinese market is a big cake. Come early and you get a big piece.'[39]

It was an argument that was to play strongly the following year, too, exposing the problems that were built into a formula that required China to demonstrate an indeterminate 'overall, significant progress' in specific areas of human rights. Fearing that the outcome of the 1994 determination would go against its interests, the business lobby stepped up its campaigning. Some 800 representatives of large and small businesses, trade associations, and farming and consumer groups wrote to Clinton arguing that a failure to renew MFN would jeopardize more than 180,000 high-wage American jobs. Californian companies—a key state for Clinton in the 1996 re-election campaign—were especially vocal, claiming that $1.7 billion worth of exports and 35,000 jobs depended on MFN renewal. Moreover, European allies, especially Germany, seemed poised to benefit economically, human rights groups had moved away from total revocation of MFN, the Chinese dissident community in the USA was split on the sagacity of the policy, and friends of America, such as Hong Kong and Taiwan, would suffer as a result of revocation because of their economic interdependence with the mainland economy. As in 1993, in 1994 too China did its best to bring home the economic message. In January, Vice Foreign Minister Liu Huaqiu bluntly told Robert Rubin that former supporters of the USA's human rights policy such as France, Germany, and Canada were now lapping up the contracts; in mid-April China sent a trade mission to the USA with another huge shopping list, shortly after Balladur of France had been on his fence-mending expedition to Beijing.[40] France may have blamed the USA for breaking ranks; but the Chinese leaders seemed to be telling Americans that their NATO partners were, in fact, the ones that had pulled the rug from under Washington's policy.

For the US administration, China's strategic role was also important, more so than for its European allies because of Washington's central position in formulating or sustaining global and regional security policies and the EU's continuing failure to develop a more autonomous, common, European defence outlook. Both Washington and Beijing played key roles in the North Korean nuclear crisis, for example, especially in the difficult years of 1993 and 1994, which served to highlight the strategic dimension in their bilateral relationship. In the spring of 1994, the USA and North Korea moved frighteningly close to all-out war, the US

[39] Ibid. 22. Indeed, Chinese officials did make numerous major purchases throughout the USA in 1993, spending on jetliners, cars, and oil exploration equipment, concluding a major deal with AT&T, and offering to buy US steel. Orentlicher and Gelatt, 'Public Law, Private Actors', 103.

[40] Mann, *About Face*, 296; Lampton, 'America's China Policy', 605, 613.

Secretary of Defense, together with the Chairman of the Joint Chiefs of Staff, summoning in mid-May 'every active four-star general and admiral in the U.S. military, including several brought from commands across the world, to a Pentagon conference room'. According to an officer on the Defense Department's Joint Staff, it was 'a real meeting of real war fighters to decide how they were going to fight a war' with North Korea.[41] Alongside this, Washington developed a programme for increasingly tough sanctions in response to North Korea's refusal to cooperate with the International Atomic Energy Authority (IAEA). The administration saw China as the next most important participant in the sanctions policy and wanted its help in bringing home the message to Pyongyang. Although publicly Beijing consistently opposed sanctions, Chinese diplomats in Pyongyang and Beijing informed the North Koreans in June that 'the strength of international opinion was such that China might not be able to veto them'. Beijing urged Pyongyang to retreat from its uncompromising stance on IAEA inspections, 'or face drastic consequences without Chinese protection', a warning that apparently had considerable impact.[42] This moment became an important turning point in the nuclear crisis, although it was certainly not the end of it. As in the 1991 Gulf War, China had been blessed with excellent timing and could demonstrate yet again the leverage membership of the UN Security Council and its position in Asia gave it on international issues of major concern to the USA.[43]

These political and economic signals from Washington, together with its impressive economic growth figures, emboldened China and convinced it that it had to do very little in 1994 to fulfil the terms of the 1993 US executive order. When the US Secretary of State visited China in March 1994 to discuss human rights questions, it was in the knowledge that the Chinese police had detained a dozen dissidents just prior to his arrival, including those of particular concern to the USA such as Wei Jingsheng and Wang Dan.[44] Christopher's visit also coincided with a meeting of China's NPC, a time therefore when political compromise with overseas visitors was even less likely. The Secretary of State's visit was portrayed in major parts of the media as a public relations disaster, Clinton allegedly and somewhat disingenuously asking in apparent exasperation: 'What

---

[41] Don Oberdorfer, *The Two Koreas: A Contemporary History*, (Reading, Mass.: Addison-Wesley, 1997), 315 and esp. chp. 13.   [42] Ibid. 320–21.

[43] Such activity must have given especial resonance to the arguments advanced at a meeting arranged by the Council on Foreign Relations in March 1994 during which Carter's Secretary of State, Cyrus Vance, argued that the USA needed to focus on the 'overall strategic relationship with China' and not focus solely on one aspect of those ties in such a way as to damage 'cooperation across the board' (Lampton, 'America's China Policy',608).

[44] Wei had met openly and publicly with John Shattuck just prior to Christopher's visit and had been arrested again shortly after that.

the hell is Chris doing there now?'[45] Despite China's public rebuff of Christopher, the movement towards removal of the linkage between trade and human rights issues continued, much as the Chinese had suspected would happen. On 26 May 1994, Clinton announced the unconditional renewal of MFN trading status for Beijing, while making it clear in his statement that the Chinese had not made 'overall significant progress' in the areas outlined in the 1993 executive order. In the view of his administration, that linkage between MFN trading status and human rights was no longer constructive: 'we have reached the end of the usefulness of that policy, and it is time to take a new path toward the achievement of our constant objectives. We need to place our relationship into a larger and more productive framework.'[46] For Human Rights Watch, and notwithstanding the French government's argument that the USA had ended the 'Tiananmen chapter' even before this statement, the collapse of the linkage policy was a signal disappointment. That NGO stated that it removed the 'last vestige of meaningful pressure on China from the international community', because others among China's trading partners 'had long since given priority to expanding economic ties'.[47] In subsequent years, although MFN status would continue to be debated in Congress, there were never enough votes to re-establish the link in any meaningful way.

THE ROOTEDNESS OF HUMAN RIGHTS POLICY

Whether or not that May 1994 decision marked the finish of meaningful international pressure, we can agree that it represented the end of a highly public and contentious dimension to the USA's human rights policy. Nevertheless, as Andrew Nathan has argued, human rights remained a 'structural weakness for China's diplomacy' and a component part of many governments' policies towards China.[48] Clinton's May 1994 statement, in which he explained his 'more productive framework', also promised 'more contacts . . . more trade . . . more international cooperation' together with 'more intense and constant dialogue on human rights issues'. Human rights activists inevitably saw this statement as being too vague. It may well have been projected in Beijing as a victory for

---

[45] Lampton, 'America's China Policy', 610.   [46] Ibid. 603.
[47] Quoted in Ming Wan, 'Human Rights and Sino-US Relations: Policies and Changing Realities', *Pacific Review*, 10/2 (1997), 243.
[48] Andrew Nathan, 'Human Rights in Chinese Foreign Policy', *China Quarterly*, 139 (Sept. 1994), 643.

American pragmatism in the face of unworkable policies.[49] As was clear from Chinese statements regarding the size of its market, and its timed releases of dissidents, the leadership continued to believe that, at least in terms of bilateral relations, human rights concerns were wholly political matters that could be bargained away for other more powerful interests. Yet, although there were many signals that illustrated the contingent nature of human rights questions for Western and other governments, neither these governments nor the Chinese authorities could entirely ignore this aspect of the relationship. Evidence of widespread abuse continued to filter through to governments and NGOs kept up a barrage of reports as well as pressure. Moreover, perceived difficulties in addressing the matter may well have toughened policy in other seemingly unrelated or less closely related areas: in the US case, in the negotiations for protection for intellectual property and for market access, and in the relationship with Taiwan; in the UK case, in the decision to put in place a Hong Kong governor ready to confront Beijing on the issue of the democratization of the territory.[50] It may well also explain why in Europe as well as in the USA governments accorded the Dalai Lama increased political access.

With China having stated publicly that it would welcome a human rights dialogue with other countries, this laid it open to pressure to make good on this claim. In consequence, an 'endless procession of VIP visitors' from 1991 came to Beijing making 'public representations on human rights, including the French Prime Minister, the Japanese Prime Minister, two Australian parliamentary delegations, several U.S. Congressional delegations, an EC delegation, the Polish Foreign Minister, a Canadian parliamentary delegation, [and] a delegation of EC ambassadors visiting Tibet'.[51] The US Assistant Secretary dealing with human rights, John Shattuck, also was given permission to visit Tibet for a week in October 1993, in exchange for a meeting between Presidents Jiang Zemin and Clinton at the November APEC gathering.[52] However, despite the bargain that may have been at the root of that November meeting in Seattle, a 'vivid [human rights] discussion', according to White House reports, took up nearly a half of the ninety minutes that the two were together.[53]

---

[49] Suggested to David Lampton while in Beijing. See 'America's China Policy', 613.

[50] See Nathan, 'Human Rights', 638.

[51] Ibid. 637. Premier Li Peng had stated at the UN Security Council summit in January 1992: 'China values human rights and stands ready to engage in discussion and cooperation with other countries on an equal footing on the questions of human rights' (quoted in ibid. 641).

[52] The visit took place between 10 and 17 Oct. 1993. *Human Rights Watch World Report 1994*, (New York, 1993), 157, reports the Sino-American political bargain that was struck.

[53] *Washington Post*, 20 Nov. 1993. According to a Chinese report of the meeting, President Jiang told Clinton: 'There are nearly 1000 nationalities and approximately 200

As noted earlier, Shattuck conducted another round of discussions in Beijing in February 1994, hardly a success from Washington's perspective, since Wei Jingsheng was picked up and imprisoned again shortly after his meeting with the US official. In fact, treatment of Wei demonstrated the extent to which such individuals had become agents of barter, but not always to Beijing's benefit. Wei had been released from custody in September 1993, just days before the International Olympic Committee was to vote on the site for the year 2000 Olympic Games, and his release was widely interpreted as being related to that vote. Judging from the extensive publicity accorded this application in Beijing in 1993, the leadership had been confident that its bid would be successful. However, in July, the US House of Representatives passed a resolution declaring that China's human rights record made it ineligible to act as host, and in August sixty Senators, led by Senator Bill Bradley, wrote to the International Olympic Committee arguing that awarding China the Games would 'confer upon China's leaders a stamp of approval . . . they clearly do not deserve'. The European Parliament passed a similar resolution on 15 September,[54] and shortly afterwards Britain's Foreign Secretary, Douglas Hurd, also spoke out against China's bid. Releasing Wei was never likely to be enough to dent the impact of this international campaign, and served merely to underline the arbitrariness of Chinese legal processes.

Once Beijing had agreed to receive various human rights delegations, any influence that it might have had over the reports that finally emerged depended on its willingness to receive future delegations, which in some cases served to tone down the language. But even this toning-down could not be guaranteed, especially since these early delegations contained those with expertise in international human rights law. The seven-person delegation of the former UK Foreign Secretary, Lord Geoffrey Howe, for example, included the academic and chief legal adviser to AI, Nigel Rodley. (In 1993 Rodley became the UN's Special Rapporteur on Torture.) The delegation spent only one week in China in December 1992, but its candid report, produced in June 1993, demonstrated that it had made the

nations on earth, with a great variety of cultural traditions and lifestyles, making the world rich and colorful. This fact is also reflected in human rights concepts. In the developed countries of Europe and the Americas and in the developing countries of the East, there are also differences in the concept of human rights owing to varying cultural traditions, ways of life, and stages of development.' Jiang went on to expound his interpretations of Chinese ancient philosophy and the positions of Locke and Spinoza. See *FBIS*-Chi-94-031, 15 Feb. 1994. Despite the formulaic nature of this encounter, however, once the direct discussion on rights had been started, it was more probable that the topic would be taken further when the two met in the future.

[54] *Human Rights Watch World Report 1994*, 156. The unsuccessful Olympic bid rankles the leadership and some Chinese to this day .

best possible use of its limited time there. The delegation reported that it had 'met some of the authors of harrowing accounts of brutality and violence' and commented that there was 'a powerfully strong case for China to answer'. While it welcomed Chinese 'improvements in economic and environmental standards for the country's enormous population', this did 'not relieve the Chinese leadership from the legal and moral obligation to adopt and enforce reforms . . . If anything they emphasise the irrelevance to the needs of China today of the old fashioned Stalinist rhetoric which attacks universally accepted principles of human rights law as products of "bourgeois legal theory".'[55] Similarly, during the various trade missions referred to above, where the signature of economic deals was obviously paramount, domestic interest groups, international human rights NGOs, together with the requirements of domestic legislation, prompted often reluctant government leaders to raise human rights concerns. Despite steady developments in Sino-German economic relations, Chancellor Kohl was pressed to hand over lists of political detainees on whom his government wanted information each time he met with a high-level Chinese official. During return visits to Germany, the Foreign Minister Qian Qichen, and then the Premier, Li Peng, were met by waves of political protests, leading Li Peng to cut out a part of his German tour in 1994.[56]

Although China publicly interpreted the Bangkok and even the Vienna human rights conferences as vindicating its relativist arguments, the final outcomes for China showed both the lack of domestic consensus with regard to the human rights debate within individual regional states, and China's relative isolation at the international conference. The Asian NGOs represented at the Bangkok meeting bluntly stated that the official declaration, quoted earlier, reflected 'the continued attempt by many governments of the region to avoid their human rights obligations, to put the state before the people, and to avoid acknowledging their obligations to account for their failures in the promotion and protection of human rights'.[57] The NGO declaration stated: 'universal human rights standards are rooted in many cultures. We affirm the basis of universality of human

[55] Senior members of this delegation have confirmed in interviews in Feb. and Mar. 1999 that China's invitation came as a result of pressure from Prime Minister John Major, who had been forced to visit Beijing in Sept. 1991 to overcome political obstacles that had arisen over the construction of Hong Kong's new airport. The report is entitled: *Visit to China by the Delegation led by Lord Howe of Aberavon* (London: HMSO, 1993), pp. v, 8. This final phrase is an indication that, although China's rhetoric had changed in international venues, it had not among officials with less exposure to the outside world.

[56] *Financial Times*, 9 July 1994; *FBIS*-WEU-92-048, 11 Mar. 1992.

[57] *Japan Economic Newswire*, 2 Apr. 1993. According to James Tang, the Asian NGOs were perceived as the best-organized group at Vienna, and were the second largest after the Western Europeans. See conclusion to Tang (ed.), *Human Rights*, 195.

rights which afford protection to all of humanity . . . While advocating cultural pluralism, those cultural practices which derogate from universally accepted human rights . . . must not be tolerated'.[58] Responding to the argument that human rights represented an attack on state sovereignty, the NGO statement turned that argument on its head, claiming that it was precisely the universal nature of such values and concerns that would act to protect sovereignty.[59]

Adverse media comment on Chinese officials' behaviour at the Vienna conference in June similarly revealed the weaknesses in China's diplomatic position. China was portrayed as taking a lead role in the move to exclude full NGO participation in the conference. Its own NGO, established in 1993, presumably as a direct result of the planned international conferences, and chaired by a former head of the Party's Propaganda Department, Zhu Muzhi, lacked credibility and was derided as a GONGO—a government organized non-governmental organization.[60] Beijing also sparred with the Austrian government over its invitation to the Dalai Lama to speak, alongside other recipients of the Nobel Peace prize, at the opening ceremony of the conference. (The invitation was eventually withdrawn, although the Tibetan leader did manage to speak outside the AI tent.)[61] Chinese statements at Vienna also represented something of a regression to an earlier era and stressed the UN role in eliminating 'colonialism, racism, apartheid and massive and gross violations of human rights as a result of foreign invasion and occupation'. More expectedly, China focused on the right to development and subsistence as priorities, reiterated that human rights were 'closely associated with specific social, political and economic conditions and the specific history, culture and values of a particular country', and argued that these differences would inevitably result in a 'different understanding and practice of human rights.'[62] However, the final declaration at Vienna

[58] A/CONF.157/ASRM/4, para. 1, quoted in Okubo 'Asian Values', 97.

[59] *Human Rights Watch World Report 1994*, 139.

[60] The leader of this delegation at Vienna was Li Yuanchao of the Chinese Communist Youth League. It also contained Li Baodong, who was listed as a research fellow, but had been a diplomat at China's embassy in Washington. Subsequently, he has played a prominent official role in the bilateral governmental human rights dialogues and has represented China at the UNCHR. See Kent, *China, the United Nations, and Human Rights*, 175. Li Baodong's treatment of Xiao Qiang of the New York-based NGO, Human Rights in China, when Xiao Qiang argued that the prized tickets for seats in the main conference hall should go to genuine NGOs, is described at ibid. 176.

[61] Linda Gail Arrigo, 'Notes from the Field: A View of the United Nations Conference on Human Rights, Vienna, June 1993', *Terra Viva*, no. 7, 18 June 1993, 71. China's NGO was booed when it asserted that a unanimous NGO resolution to invite the Dalai Lama was unacceptable. See Kent, *China, the United Nations, and Human Rights*, 174.

[62] See Liu's speech in Tang (ed.), *Human Rights*, app. III, pp. 213–17.

addressed these points directly and decided differently: 'While the significance of national and regional particularities and various historical, cultural and religious backgrounds must be borne in mind, it is the duty of
States, regardless of their political, economic and cultural systems, to
promote and protect all human rights and fundamental freedoms.'[63] On
the specific matter of the right to subsistence and development as a
priority, the declaration stated: 'While development facilitates the enjoyment of all human rights, the lack of development may not be invoked to
justify the abridgement of internationally recognized human rights.'[64] In
recognition of its relative isolation on these issues, its negative and obviously upsetting press coverage, and the poor reception of its treatment of
the NGOs, Beijing decided to drop its objections to the draft of general
principles of human rights, while continuing to hold to its reservations
regarding international enforcement mechanisms, such as the establishment of a UN High Commissioner for Human Rights. It also went on
record in support of giving 'equal emphasis' to civil, political, economic,
social, and cultural rights and the right to development.[65]

Beijing's hosting of the UN's Fourth World Conference on Women in
1995 was a similarly mixed experience for the Chinese authorities, as it
became embroiled in controversial themes involving Tibet, female infan-
ticide, and family planning. With some 30,000 NGO participants in atten-
dance, together with the full panoply of official delegates, the
organizational problems were anything but easy. But the Chinese decision
at the last minute to switch the venue of the NGO forum to a town some
distance from the official site once again betrayed its fear of the unofficial, less well-orchestrated aspects of international conferences. Thus, in
the absence of a change in approach to NGO activities and some movement in its behaviour in respect of human rights, its experiences at this
and the Vienna conferences must have brought home to the leadership the
constraints on the country's ability to play either a high-level role or to act
as host state for such prestigious events. It would also have to forgo the
media benefits that would otherwise be derived from its activism in this
issue area.[66] Internationalism had its price, therefore, in its exposure of

[63] Quoted in *Netherlands Quarterly of Human Rights*, Human Rights News, UN, pt. 3
(1993), 295.   [64] Ibid. 298.
[65] Arrigo, 'Notes from the Field', 71; Kent, *China, the United Nations, and Human
Rights*, 179–81. China complained more than once about its treatment in the world's press.
[66] Jude Howell discusses the positive impact that the hosting of such an event, especially
the hosting of the NGO forum, had on the All-China Women's Federation (ACWF). She
argues that 'through participating in preparatory committee meetings abroad ACWF
cadres have gained experience in international affairs to an extent unprecedented in the history of the organisation and unrivalled by other mass organisations . . . the ACWF now
enjoys a vast network of international contacts, has experience of both operating at

Chinese to alternative viewpoints, and to media, NGO, and governmental criticisms. There was indeed a diversity of viewpoints in evidence at such gatherings, but China could neither guarantee that others would follow its lead nor that it could exact any retribution if others spoke out against Beijing's positions at these forums. Moreover, operating through multilateral bodies that worked to provide consensual outcomes enhanced the legitimacy of the positions reached, reducing the weight of Chinese charges of selectivity, discrimination, or targeting.

THE UN COMMISSION ON HUMAN RIGHTS

The support for universalism expressed at Vienna, together with the removal of most bilateral sanctions operating against China, influenced governments to give greater prominence to multilateral mechanisms for registering disapproval of Beijing's human rights record. An approach to the problem either through the UN and its Specialized Agencies, or in the case of European states through EU mechanisms that had started to strengthen after 1992 with the introduction of the CFSP under the Maastricht provisions, obviously had its attractions. Apart from the broader benefits of multilateral cooperation, alluded to above, the UN Commission and its Sub-Commission seemed a more attractive route than in the past. This was so, despite the increase in the Commission's membership from forty-three to fifty-three states in 1992, many of which came from the developing world (a constituency presumed likely to support China). Optimism rested on the fact that the ending of the cold war meant a fracturing of the Soviet voting bloc, and a rise in the number of states more committed to democratic principles. Thus, the possibilities for overturning the Chinese 'no-action' motion seemed to have been enhanced from the early 1990s. The actual experience, however, was inevitably more complicated than that.

As noted in Chapter 5, in August 1991 the UN Sub-Commission had passed 9–7–4 a strongly worded resolution on Tibet, expressing concern at the 'continuing reports of violations of fundamental human rights and freedoms which threaten the distinct cultural, religious, and national identity of the Tibetan people'. The resolution also called on the UN

governmental and non-governmental levels and has a much better understanding of the workings of the UN. Furthermore, in hosting the NGO Forum the ACWF has entered the vocabulary of non-governmental women's networks, despite the fact that its credentials as an NGO are ambiguous' (Howell, 'Post-Beijing Reflections: Creating Ripples but not Waves in China', *Women's Studies International Forum*, 20/2 (1997), 241).

Secretary General to transmit to the Commission at its next meeting in early spring 1992 information on the situation in Tibet. This he duly did in the form of a seventy-one-page note containing information from the Chinese government, from the Tibetan lobby, and also from twelve NGOs.[67] The EC, in an apparently new-found zeal for common action, seized on the Tibet issue and sponsored a resolution based on a draft that the Tibet lobby had previously circulated. However, utilization of this draft made the resolution politically problematic because of its association with a separatist movement. An apparent failure on the part of European governments to coordinate with its natural allies further compromised this action, with the USA, Japan, and Australia being particularly exercised over the matter.[68] From Washington's perspective, a resolution that showed strong reliance on the Tibetan lobby and that was entitled 'The Situation in Tibet' was seen to conflict with its 'one-China' policy; thus, the head of its Delegation pressed for a general China resolution instead. After 'acrimonious exchanges within the Western group', a compromise was finally reached with a resolution entitled 'The Situation in China/Tibet', and a broadening of the language in the original preamble to include reference to China more generally.[69] But the doubtful genesis of the resolution had done its damage. When the delegate from Portugal, Gomes, introduced the resolution on behalf of its sponsors, the Chinese delegate, Fan Guoxiang, immediately targeted it as something that was 'not based on genuine concern for human rights, but was in open support of a handful of Tibetan separatists in exile abroad who sought to split Tibet from China'. He also claimed that the revised draft resolution was the 'same as the earlier version which had been circulated in the Commission by Tibetan separatists masquerading as representatives of non-governmental organizations'. Others who spoke after Fan, such as Kamal from Pakistan, Roa Kouri from Cuba, and Masri from Syria, all made reference to an alleged attack on the principles of sovereignty and territorial integrity, prompting the US and Portuguese delegates to affirm that no challenge was being launched to the territorial unity of China. When Pakistan introduced its no-action resolution on China's behalf, it passed easily, 27–15–10, with all African states either voting in favour or abstaining, and most Latin American states, apart from Costa Rica, also abstaining.[70]

---

[67] E/CN.4/1992/37, 21 Feb. 1992.

[68] Joe W. Chip Pitts III and David Weissbrodt, 'Major Developments at the UN Commission on Human Rights in 1992', *Human Rights Quarterly*, 15/1 (1993), 137–42; Kent, 'China and the International Human Rights Regime', 25–6.   [69] Ibid. 26.

[70] E/CN.4/1992/SR 54/Add.1, 4 Mar. 1992. Apparently, a majority of African states had arrived in Geneva with instructions not to support a resolution directed at China. Kent,

Chinese news reports presented the outcome of the resolution as a victory for the developing countries with which China shared 'the same destiny' and held the same views, and as a triumph over the attempts of the 'big and rich countries' to dismember the 'small and poor countries'. Moreover, it stated, such action was against a world trend 'calling for all countries, no matter how big or small, to be equal'.[71] Nevertheless, despite this apparent solidarity among the developing world, it was presumably of some comfort for the Western governments that the Czech and Slovak Federal Republic, Hungary, and the Russian Federation had voted with them against the no-action resolution. Thus, the EU was prepared to act again at the next meeting of the Commission, in February–March 1993. There, the EU12, led by Denmark, and with the support of Costa Rica and Japan, introduced another draft resolution whose main purpose was 'to express serious concern regarding the human rights situation as described in a number of reports placed before the Commission'. The Danish delegate went on to assert that 'fundamental freedoms were severely restricted, including freedom of expression, religion, assembly, association, as well as the right to a fair trial. The administration of justice in China did not meet international standards in certain important respects. People were detained without trial for long periods, the death penalty was arbitrarily applied, and there was no independent judiciary.'[72] It was quite a litany, one that the Chinese delegate had tried to refute before the introduction of the resolution, stating that China had 'made great efforts in recent years to build up its legal system', and quoting a former UN Secretary General speaking in Hong Kong in 1992 who had said that 'there was not enough evidence to maintain that there had been large numbers of human rights violations in China, that China had been successful in realizing the most fundamental of human rights, namely, solving the country's problem of food and shelter, and that the human rights record of China had been far better than that of many other countries'. A few days later, he averred that political reforms were

China, the United Nations, and Human Rights, 65. However, despite China's success, it did feel compelled to respond in additional ways, China's Information Office of the State Council publishing in Sept. 1992 its first White Paper on Tibet, entitled *Historic Sovereignty and the Human Rights Situation in Tibet* (Beijing: Foreign Languages Press) in order directly to rebut its critics. The voting outcome reinforces the findings of Risse, Ropp, and Sikkink, who conclude on the basis of several case studies that the presence of forces threatening the territorial integrity or internal cohesion of the state act as 'blocking factors' in the promotion of the human rights regime domestically. See Risse, *et al.* (eds.), *The Power of Human Rights*, 260–1. Although these authors are thinking about such factors in the context of the state that is particularly affected by the presence of such threatening forces, it seems clear that governments that can relate to these factors are also affected.

[71] *FBIS*-Chi-92-047, 10 Mar. 1992.   [72] E/CN.4/1993/SR.66, 16 Mar. 1993.

accompanying those in the economic area.[73] However, during the discussion of the draft resolution and China's move to prevent debate through the no-action device, the British delegate referred to the reports of the thematic rapporteurs, which he stated gave 'clear, incontrovertible evidence of a disregard to human rights in a number of areas'. The Russian Federation's delegate argued that the international community was entitled to express its concerns about human rights violations in China without laying itself open to the charge that it was interfering in its internal affairs, and that, although he had taken note of the positive changes that had been happening in China, he was concerned too about reports of human rights abuse. The roll-call vote on China's no-action motion produced the result twenty-two in favour, seventeen, against with twelve abstentions.[74]

With an eye on the Vienna conference and its developing and Asian country allies, China publicly interpreted the introduction of the condemnatory resolution as a Western attempt to scupper its right to development: 'Instead of wishing to see a prosperous and strong China in which the people can enjoy a happy life, they want to do everything possible to set up roadblocks on China's course of development.' A *Xinhua* report of proceedings reminded its readers that the world was a 'diverse one' and that countries with different social systems, historical and cultural traditions, and levels of development would naturally have different concepts of human rights.[75] However, in its attempt to cast this as an issue that had split Western countries from the developing world, China failed to point out that its margin of victory was smaller on this occasion, that three states that had voted in favour of the no-action device in 1992 had on this occasion abstained, that two new countries to the Commission, Bulgaria and Poland, had voted against, together with the Czech Republic, Romania, and the Russian Federation as former members of the Soviet bloc, and that newcomer South Korea had chosen to abstain.[76]

In the light of this reduced margin of victory, NGOs prepared for the next meeting of the Sub-Commission—where the Tibet issue was due to be raised again—with renewed optimism. That optimism was to be misplaced, however. Participants in the session reported it as 'one of the most politicized in the memory of long-time NGO participants' purportedly relating to structural changes in the global system, and the perception that only China was left to act as a bulwark against US hegemony. More directly probably the outcome was also a result of intense political

[73] E/CN.4/1993/SR.45, 1 Mar. 1993, and E/CN.4/1993/SR.53, 4 Mar. 1993.
[74] E/CN.4/1993/SR.66, 10 Mar. 1993.   [75] *FBIS*-Chi-93-047, 12 Mar. 1993.
[76] See details of roll-call vote in E/CN.4/1993/SR.66, 10 Mar. 1993, and discussion in Kent 'China and the International Human Rights Regime', 29.

lobbying on the part of Chinese officials, which led to a political row involving the British and other Sub-Commission experts. Fateful too was that the Tibet issue had become closely associated with the matter of territorial integrity. The poisoned atmosphere led to a large margin of support for the no-action motion on Tibet, even though it was voted on in secret. It passed 17–6–2, contributing to general dismay among the NGOs, an early closure of the proceedings, and a failure to produce a final report.[77] The following year the Sub-Commission decided to remove itself as far as possible from political pressures and not to discuss country situations that were already being dealt with by the Commission.

With the Sub-Commission damaged by this exercise, the focus shifted to its parent body, which once more had before it a draft resolution on the situation in China. This time China introduced its own procedural no-action motion, where surprisingly perhaps the vote in favour of it again shifted slightly against Beijing. Prior to the vote, the Chinese delegate had described China as a 'democratic country where the rule of law was respected', and as one that had played a constructive role within the UN in the human rights area. Thus, the real motives for attacking China, he alleged, were either—as in the case of the Tibet issue—to dismember it, or to force it from a development path that it had freely chosen.[78] Perhaps in order to undercut China's attempts to ally itself with the poor and weak in the developing world, and its bid to evoke memories of colonial mis-rule, the British and American delegates argued that the Commission should not avoid the issue of human rights in the PRC simply because China was a big and powerful country with a strong trading position.[79] The EU spokesperson, while welcoming the release of some political activists and the willingness of China to receive foreign human rights delegations, appealed to China to grant a general amnesty to all those who had demonstrated peacefully on 4 June. In a reference to China's own argument that it had a good record of support for international human rights law, he called on Beijing to guarantee respect for human rights in accordance with international standards, and to strengthen its commitment to the human rights regime by acceding to the two international covenants on human rights.[80] The no-action vote passed 20–16–17, the majority one less than in the preceding year. It would have been closer still if the Polish Foreign Minister had not been persuaded by

---

[77] A fuller discussion of this session is in ibid. 29–40.
[78] E/CN.4/1994/SR.60, 7 Mar. 1994, and E/CN.4/1994/SR.50, 2 Mar. 1994.
[79] E/CN.4/1994/SR.65, 9 Mar. 1994.   [80] E/CN.4/1994/SR.51/Add.1, 2 Mar. 1994.

his Chinese counterpart to change his country's vote at the last minute, and if Poland had not persuaded Romania to do likewise.[81]

The closeness of this vote, combined with the Clinton administration's decision to remove the tie between MFN trading status and human rights conditions in China, led the 1995 meeting of the UN Commission to be deemed a crucial one. The USA lobbied well in advance in support of a resolution condemning China's record. For example, the Geneva resolution was a part of the agenda of National Security Adviser Anthony Lake when he went in December 1994 to Ethiopia, Gabon, and Zimbabwe. The head of the US delegation to Geneva, Geraldine Ferraro, was in touch with a number of Latin American states.[82] The administration also began consulting with its likely co-sponsors—Japan and the EU —early in the cycle. China for its part continued its strenuous lobbying efforts, apparently warning EU member states that there would be severe consequences for EU–China trade if it supported the resolution. Premier Li Peng wrote to his Polish counterpart promising support for a Polish seat in the UN Security Council. Other reports suggested that the Chinese had circulated a memorandum to all developing countries represented on the Commission threatening to cut off aid if they failed to support China's no-action motion. One graphic illustration of both sides' determination to win came on the evening of the vote on the no-action resolution:

Chinese and American diplomats faced one another directly outside a telephone booth occupied by an [*sic*] Representative who had called his capital to clarify his voting instructions. Reportedly, a senior American official had telephoned that country's President after word surfaced that its vote was changing to support 'no action.' Both the Chinese and the American diplomats were determined to escort that Representative back to the session.[83]

---

[81] The details of the roll-call vote are in E/CN.4/1994/SR.65, 9 March 1994 and the background regarding the Polish and Romanian position in Kent, 'China and the International Human Rights Regime', 41. China had apparently agreed to support Poland's bid to gain one of the non-permanent Security Council seats, a mark of recognition that obviously meant more to Warsaw than its newly acquired status of a democratic state. See Human Rights Watch, *Chinese Diplomacy, Western Hypocrisy and the UN Human Rights Commission* (New York, Mar. 1997), 10. A Foreign Ministry representative later claimed before the Polish parliament that the vote was the result of a junior official's mistake, suggesting that Polish politicians were divided over which identity—UN Security Council member or supporter of human rights values—was more important to the country.

[82] Human Rights Watch, *Chinese Diplomacy, Western Hyprocrisy*, 4. Human Rights Watch had been very active, too, lobbying the European Commission in Brussels to join the USA, and writing to some twenty-five members of the UNCHR urging that a resolution be introduced. Korey, *NGOs*, 355.

[83] Richard Dicker (from Human Rights Watch/Asia), 'The Prospects for Effective Human Rights Monitoring: China, a Case Study', paper presented at a UN 50th Anniversary Conference on 'The Rise of East Asia and the UN', co-sponsored by the ROK

The resolution, introduced by France and co-sponsored by the USA, the EU, Japan, and the Dominican Republic, expressed 'concern at continuing reports of violations of human rights and fundamental freedoms in China'. In reply, the Chinese delegate pointed to the great strides China had made in the previous ten years in developing its legal system and promoting democracy, and it criticized the sponsors who had not 'baulked at using coercion to obtain support for the draft resolution'. He appealed blatantly and directly for support from elsewhere in the developing world, arguing that the resolution was designed to halt China's economic development and was 'targeted . . . at the developing countries as a whole'. He then introduced the no-action motion, which for the first time resulted in a tied vote, 22–22–9, which therefore meant it was defeated. This time, Poland and Romania voted against, as did Bulgaria, the Russian Federation, a number of Latin American states, and also the Philippines. US efforts in Africa had been to no avail, as all three states visited by Lake voted with China.[84] The outcome meant that, at last, there would be consideration of the substance of a resolution on human rights conditions in China.

The resolution's introduction, as the first item on the agenda the following morning, was a curiously low-key affair. With only the USA and China speaking to it, it was defeated by one vote: 21–20–12, with Russia unexpectedly voting against. The Russian foreign ministry, commenting on journalists' questions as to the purpose of the Russian Foreign Minister's visit to China, which coincided with this meeting of the UN Commission, described it as being to 'create favorable conditions' for a third summit between the Russian and Chinese leaders. Other Russian media reports, referring directly to Moscow's vote against the resolution, took the Russian foreign ministry to task for choosing expediency over principle, and suggested that at the root of the no vote was a concern about the parallels that might be drawn between Chinese actions in Tibet and Russia's war in Chechnya.[85] This slim victory nevertheless did not prevent Chinese officials from portraying the defeat of the substantive resolution as a triumph, nor their repeating that the motion had been targeted not

Committee for the 50th Anniversary of the UN and the International Institute for Strategic Studies, London, held in Seoul, 12–14 June 1995, 7–8. One interviewee stated that the senior American official was in fact Vice-President Al Gore (interview in London, Feb. 1999). See also for information on Poland, Human Rights Watch, *Chinese Diplomacy, Western Hypocrisy*, 10.

[84] Poland had come under media pressure for its action in the 1994 vote; the Philippines, which had voted with China in 1992 and came back on the Commission in 1995, voted against no action, probably because of the dispute that flared up with China over the ownership of Mischief Reef in the South China sea. For full details of the voting, see E/CN.4/1995/SR.59/Add.1, 7 Mar. 1995.   [85] *FBIS*-Sov-95-049, 14 Mar. 1995.

just at China but at all developing countries. To demonstrate 'power politics in action', a subsequent *Xinhua* report criticized the co-sponsors of the resolution, and particularly Washington, for 'vigorous' lobbying and attempting to 'coerce some member states of the Human Rights Commission'. It accused the West of trying to impose its own conception of human rights on others, and called for dialogue and cooperation rather than confrontation.[86] The Chinese government then decided to suspend all governmental bilateral human rights dialogues for the rest of the year.

   Despite the defeat of the moderately phrased China resolution, this represented a disturbing outcome as far as the Chinese were concerned, as its subsequent behaviour indicated. Its intense lobbying had not prevented it from coming under the spotlight. Indeed, Egypt and Ethiopia, which had voted with it on the 'no-action' resolution, but then recorded an abstention on the substantive resolution, argued that equal treatment for all implied that China could not use its claimed developing country status to prevent debate. Other governments were influenced by the fact that those such as Nigeria, Russia, and the USA had also faced critical resolutions in the past, but had not resorted to the no-action device,[87] further questioning China's claim of special status. China's use of this procedural method also demonstrated the intensity of its dislike of being the subject of a substantive resolution, underlining yet again a concern with international image.

CHINA AND THE THEMATIC MECHANISMS

As noted in Chapter 2, from the early 1980s the UN had created Special Rapporteurs and various Working Groups whose remits concerned investigations into such matters as torture, summary or arbitrary execution, enforced or involuntary disappearances, and arbitrary detention. These groups and individuals, whose reports, more than those provided by the media or NGOs, had developed 'a unique credibility', were slowly developing an authority to suggest implementation measures in their particular areas of concern. Moreover, they were accomplishing this with the reluctant acquiescence of governments.[88] Beijing, of course, was among the most reluctant—for example, joining Malaysia, Syria, Nigeria, and India in taking a strong stand in 1994 against a resolution that allowed the Special Rapporteur on Torture (now Nigel Rodley) to recommend

---

[86] *FBIS*-Chi-95-047, 10 Mar. 1995.   [87] Dicker, 'The Prospects', 9–10.
[88] Ibid. 11.

that the Centre for Human Rights provide advisory services to offending governments. China's grounds were that it denied the 'essential criterion', as Zhang Yishan put it, that such services could be offered only at the express request of sovereign states.[89] That year, Beijing's representative also launched an appeal to rationalize the Commission's agenda, and to cut back on the number of Special Rapporteurs because of problems of duplication, a lack of coordination, and their drain on the financial resources of the UN. China also complained that rapporteurs on civil and political rights made up the largest number to the neglect of economic, social, and cultural rights, and recommended that the Commission should appoint rapporteurs on the basis of equitable geographical distribution, an obvious attack on the professionalism and neutrality of these individuals.[90]

The year 1995 was significant not just for the vote on the substantive resolution at the UNCHR but also as the first that material critical of China featured in every Special Rapporteur's and Working Group's report.[91] Over several previous years, the Special Rapporteur on Torture, then Peter Kooijmans, had been recording in his annual reports the various urgent appeals he had made to the government of China, especially on behalf of those involved in the Tiananmen protests or in demonstrations in Tibet. In response to his 1992 report and his letter to Beijing in September 1992, the government noted that its constitution forbade torture, had laid down penalties for those who disregarded the law in this area, and had given compensation to those who were found to have had their rights violated. In addition it described the accusation that torture was 'routine' in China as being entirely unfounded, and argued that the cases detailing severe abuse were 'nothing but fictitious and malicious rumours'.[92] In 1993 the new Special Rapporteur, Nigel Rodley, produced a hard-hitting report on China in which he wrote of the 'persistence of an extensive problem of torture and severe ill-treatment of prisoners in various parts of China, despite the existence of legal provisions aimed at repressing it'.[93] Again in 1995 he noted he had continued to receive information indicating that the use of torture in China's penal institutions was 'occurring with frequency', and was 'particularly pervasive' in Tibet. He also sent to the Chinese government several urgent appeals, a number of which elicited a response,[94] and requested that he be invited to visit the

[89] E/CN.4/1994/SR.42, 25 Feb. 1994.   [90] E/CN.4/1994/SR.38, 24 Feb. 1994.
[91] Dicker, 'The Prospects', 16.
[92] The report of the Special Rapporteur is in E/CN.4/1993/26, 15 Dec. 1992.
[93] E/CN.4/1994/31, 6 Jan. 1994. The Special Rapporteur had passed on in 1993 four urgent appeals and details on thirty-four individual cases to the Chinese government.
[94] E/CN.4/1996/35/Add.1, 16 Jan. 1996. Amnesty was also active on this issue at this time. Shortly after the issuance of China's second periodic report to the CAT in 1995, it

country. Once again, China emphasized that, since acceding to the Convention against Torture in 1988 it had introduced legislation strictly prohibiting abuse, and had tried to strengthen its monitoring mechanisms in order to prevent torture. It also suggested, however, that Rodley and others had better understand that improvements here were going to take some considerable time: for torture to be 'eliminated permanently, all forces in society had to be mobilized and the competence of legal officials improved'.[95]

This reference to the need to train China's legal officials had also been raised explicitly in another Special Rapporteur's report, that dealing with discrimination based on religious belief. Again, China had featured regularly in this rapporteur's annual reports, and he had indicated a willingness to visit China if invited. A visit, in fact, did take place between 19 and 29 November 1994, the first visit to the country by any Special Rapporteur, and another indication that in some instances the Chinese government could modify its stricter versions of state sovereignty, especially if its hosting of the visit helped its case at subsequent meetings of the UNCHR. The report of the visit listed those he met, the legislation currently in force, and the special concerns he had raised. Recommendations submitted, couched in the most delicate language that could be mustered, included amendments to the constitution to underpin a guarantee of respect for religious freedom, the extension of that right to members of the Communist Party, and a governmental lead in bringing about new modes of behaviour and a new culture of religious tolerance among prison authorities, and in the society at large. To that end he also stressed 'the importance of giving State officials and judges adequate human rights training, especially on the subject of religious freedom', and suggested that the technical and advisory services of the Centre for Human Rights might be helpful in this area.[96]

The pressure on China to allow such rapporteurs to visit was relentless in this period. The Special Rapporteur's reports on Extrajudicial, Summary, and Arbitrary Executions had been bitingly critical of China,

commented that basic safeguards to prevent abuse—such as 'early and regular access to lawyers'—were still absent, and that the investigation and prosecution of cases of torture were 'arbitrary and inconsistent'. See Amnesty International, 'Torture and Ill-Treatment: Comments on China's Second Periodic Report to the UN Committee against Torture', ASA 17/51/96, Apr. 1996. Beijing, in the spring of 1999, suggested it would soon issue an invitation to the Special Rapporteur to visit.

[95] E/CN.4/1994/SR.28 17 Feb. 1994. Bodies such as the Ford Foundation, for example, had long been helping with the financing of such legal training. Starting in 1989, it gave support to the Chinese Training Centre for Senior Judges, the Centre receiving $730,000 between 1990 and 1996. See *The Ford Foundation and China*, Report no. 488, (Jan. 1991), 11 and *Ford Foundation Annual Reports* produced 1990–96.

[96] E/CN.4/1995/91, 22 Dec. 1994.

despite his request to be offered the opportunity to visit the country. In 1992, while praising Beijing for its willingness to provide replies to his various communications, he noted that there were 'remarkable contradictions between the general denials contained in the replies of the Government of China concerning those allegations, and the precise and detailed allegations he had received from credible non-governmental sources'. He also noted with concern 'the large number and broad range of offences subject to capital punishment': some thirty-four under the 1979 Penal Code, and then many more under subsequent decisions of the Standing Committee of the NPC.[97] His 1995 report noted the serious shortcomings in legal representation and review of cases before application of the death penalty, dismay at the increased number of executions, including those which 'reportedly took place before the Fourth World Conference on Women', and serious alarm about reports that executed prisoners were 'being used as a source of supply of body organs for medical transplantation'. He concluded by recording that Beijing had not yet replied to his requests submitted each year from 1992 to 1995 to visit the country.[98]

Beijing was particularly agitated by the activities of the Working Group on Arbitrary Detention, in part because of the decisions it reached on China, but also because it took the 'lead in developing methodology for effective implementation' of its recommendations.[99] China had been a focus of attention for the Working Group in 1993 and 1994 when it considered the cases of a number of Catholics and Protestants who had been sentenced under China's Re-education through Labour (RTL) provisions.[100] Having reviewed the cases, the Group declared the 'deprivation of freedom [as being] inherently arbitrary in character', in violation of the UDHR and of the ICCPR. This meant that a whole category of imprisonment in China had been declared inherently arbitrary. The Working Group also submitted its decisions in December 1993 in the cases of two of the best-known political dissidents, Chen Ziming and Wang Juntao, who had been brought to trial with another thirty such activists in early 1991 on charges of 'counter-revolution' and had received harsh, thirteen-year sentences. NGOs and legal specialists focused on the various dubious aspects of these trials including their speed, the limited opportunity afforded to prepare a defence, and the

---

[97] E/CN.4/1993/46, 23 Dec. 1992.
[98] E/CN.4/1996/4, 25 Jan. 1996.   [99] Dicker, 'The Prospects', 12.
[100] Under this scheme, individuals can be sentenced without trial and solely on the basis of a police administrative hearing for terms of up to three years. Chinese official sources stated that some 230,000 were in detention under this provision in 1998 and that some 2.5 million had been so detained over the previous forty years. Factsheet from Chinese Embassy, London, 9 Feb. 1998.

refusal of the defendants' right to appoint his or her own legal adviser.[101]
Here again the Working Group declared the detention of Wang and Chen
arbitrary and in violation of the UDHR and ICCPR. It called on the
Chinese government to take steps to remedy the situation and to bring its
practices into line with international standards. Prior to the issuance of
both its decisions, the Group had requested information from the Chinese
authorities and then passed on the replies to the original complainants
for comment. The effect of this was to put the 'burden of proof on the
government to disprove the allegations', thereby setting a normative
standard that provided the opportunity to press for particular changes.[102]

China's response to these decisions was harsh and vitriolic. Its alternate
delegate at the UN Commission meeting in March, Zhang Yishan,
claimed that the Working Group had gone beyond its mandate, had
'politicized the issues', and had filled its report 'with examples of the type
of selectivity and double standard that had been rampant during the
cold-war era'. He railed against its temerity in declaring the legislation of
certain states invalid, and avowed that it had no right to review and evaluate the 'political institutions of sovereign states', or to declare institutions such as 'people's courts' and 'supreme courts of State security' as
neither independent nor impartial. Ominously, in response to the Working Group's expressed desire to visit China, Zhang warned that a 'lack of
goodwill and impartiality on its part towards his country and its disregard for his government's explanations made it difficult to envisage a visit
in an atmosphere of cooperation'.[103]

Thus, in terms of UN action, 1995 was not a good year for the Chinese
government. Bilateral governmental pressures might have reduced, but
Beijing had been the subject of a substantive resolution at the UN Commission, had featured in all thematic reports, and was under pressure to
allow Special Rapporteurs and the various Working Groups to visit the
country. Already the Special Rapporteur on Religious Intolerance had
been in China, a visit that Beijing subsequently used to illustrate its support for UN human rights activities.[104] But that Special Rapporteur had
called on the Beijing authorities to be more proactive in training its officials and educating its citizenry as to the true meaning of tolerance.
China's response at the 1995 meeting of the UN Commission had veered
between recording its efforts at legal reform and its model behaviour as a
member of the UN human rights regime, and hitting out at the Commis-

[101] Kent, *Between Freedom and Subsistence*, 204. Chen's and Wang's association with
the deposed leader, Zhao Ziyang, has been said to account for the length of their
sentences.   [102] Dicker, 'The Prospects', 13–14.
[103] E/CN.4/1995/SR.27, 16 Feb. 1995, and see report in *FBIS*-Chi-95-034, 21 Feb. 1995.
[104] E/CN.4/1995/SR.21, 13 Feb. 1995.

sion and its various thematic mechanisms. At the 1995 session, Zhang called for 'comprehensive reform' of the Commission, including stream-lining its agenda and reducing its workload. His other recommendations were more obviously a response to China's own recent experiences and interests. He called for equal attention to be paid to economic, social and cultural, as well as civil and political rights, the standardization of the participation of NGOs, and the elimination of selectivity (i.e. country-specific resolutions) in the Commission's activities. In turning explicitly to the work of the Special Rapporteurs and Working Groups, he argued that some were moving beyond the scope of their mandates and, in their fail-ure to give serious consideration to governmental replies, or to respect sovereign judicial decisions, had cast doubt on their own impartiality. His suggested solution was to formulate a set of rules and procedures to gov-ern their working methods.[105]

Against this background of critical review of its human rights record, at the end of the year the Information Office of China's State Council produced a new White Paper, this one entitled 'The Progress of Human Rights in China'.[106] Although a much shorter document than the 1991 version, there were continuities in certain of the arguments proffered but also developments in other areas. Its foreword emphasized in general terms the progress made in promoting political stability, economic devel-opment and social welfare over the previous four years. As in the 1991 White Paper, however, it noted that 'some human rights situations [were] not so satisfactory because of the limitations of history and level of development', and also as before noted that it would be a long-term task for the people and government to safeguard, promote, and improve the human rights situation for all. Section 1 of the new White Paper was devoted to expounding China's achievements and aspirations in the field of economic development, this time eschewing the temptations of reminding readers of the past crimes committed by Western and Japanese imperialists. The 1991 White Paper had stated that the fundamental demand the Chinese people asked of the new Communist government in 1949 was to 'eat their fill and dress warmly'; in 1995 the White Paper argued that since 1991 the Chinese government had firmly upheld 'eco-nomic construction as the central task' and had pursued the 'basic policy of continually improving the people's right of existence and development on the basis of economic development'. This claim made it difficult to lay direct stress as had been the case in 1991 on the right of subsistence as the

---

[105] E/CN.4/1995/SR.44, 3 Mar. 1995.
[106] BBC Monitoring Reports, *SWB* Asia/Pacific, FE/2497, S2/1-17, 30 Dec. 1995, pro-vides an English translation and indications of where the English version differs from that of the Chinese.

most important of all human rights; thus, the 1995 document was suggesting that the government had satisfied many subsistence requirements;
now it was concerned to ensure that its citizens enjoyed 'various civil and
political rights according to law and that socialist democratic politics be
practised and developed'. It made a direct link between economic development and the enjoyment of civil and political rights in its claim that
China's economy had developed rapidly because these policies had been
proceeding in tandem.

Both documents discussed various legal reforms that had recently been
introduced. However, whereas the 1991 paper emphasized the links
between rights and duties, the 1995 paper made more of citizens'
increased abilities to claim their rights as guaranteed by law, providing
statistics to demonstrate the extent to which this had become a growing
practice in China.[107] Indeed, there was a separate section in the 1995 document outlining those laws that recently had been put into effect with a
direct bearing on human rights, encompassing the police, judges, the public procurator, and the prisons. The new Police Law of 1995, for example,
forbade the police from unlawfully depriving citizens of their freedom of
person and noted that citizens had the right to bring a charge against any
police officer disobeying the law; public procurators and judges as the
result of a series of standardized principles that were being 'specified and
implemented more strictly' were to operate entirely independently of
'administrative organs, social communities and individuals'; the Prison
Law of December 1994 outlined various prisoners' rights, including, as
had been specified in 1991, 'the right of immunity from insult to their
dignity and from infringement on their personal security'. The 1995
document stated more firmly than in 1991 that China opposed 'the
practice of forcing confessions and giving credence to them and strictly
prohibits the use of cruel punishment in every link of the judicial work'
and specified the monitoring mechanisms that had been established in
places of detention.[108]

In accordance with this greater emphasis on citizens' rights in the 1995
paper, section 9 was devoted to a description of actions designed to pop-
ularize knowledge of human rights. China had witnessed the develop-

[107] According to the White Paper, the Administrative Procedural Law (APL), for example, which allows citizens to start legal proceedings against administrative organs in the
event of the infringement of their rights, had led to consideration of 167,882 cases between
Jan. 1990 and Dec. 1994, two-thirds of which had resulted in a change in the original decision (see S2/5).

[108] The 1991 White Paper had stated more simply: 'As a matter of principle and discipline for China's public security and judicial organs in handling cases, it is strictly prohib-
ited to extort confessions by torture' (p. 31). The 1995 White Paper stated that 409 cases of
extortion had been investigated in 1994 (see S2/7).

ment of a 'professional research force consisting of scholars and experts from institutions of higher learning and research institutes all over the country'.[109] Since 1991, China had held 'over a dozen large-scale national theoretical symposiums on human rights and over a hundred discussion meetings, forums and report meetings on human rights', had published nearly a hundred academic books, over a thousand theses in newspapers and magazines, and translated a large number of foreign texts, together with the central international human rights documents. More actively still, 'almost all institutions of higher learning and training organizations' had held either lectures or special courses on human rights, and broadcasting stations, newspapers, and magazines had also been drawn into the promotional exercise. Much as the UN's Special Rapporteur on Religious Intolerance had advocated, and China itself in its statement at the UN Commission had argued was necessary, the White Paper underlined the point that legal reform was not enough on its own and that societal education was an essential part of the process.

As in the 1991 White Paper, the final section of the 1995 document was devoted to international human rights activities. Both White Papers emphasized the Chinese government's active support for UN efforts in the human rights field, the latter in a more detailed way in part because of its participation in the Vienna Conference and role as host for the UN Conference on Women. Both papers also criticized certain countries' attempts to push their values onto others and the prevalence of 'power politics' in the human rights area. However, the 1995 paper was more combative in tone because of its reference to the USA's and other Western countries' ultimately unsuccessful attempts to pass 'five anti-China proposals' at the UN Commission. These were described as wanton interference in China's internal affairs, designed to undermine its stability and thus sabotage its development goals. The failure of these 'plots' was a victory, it averred, 'not only for China but also of the vast number of developing countries and international justice forces in defending the purposes and principles of the Charter of the United Nations.'

Despite the combative nature of this language, it did, however, lack the specificity and certainty of that contained in the 1991 document. There, the authors had argued in that final section that primary attention should be given to the right to subsistence and development. In 1995 this had developed into a statement that, for human rights to be realized fully,

---

[109] The Ford Foundation had been providing some of the financial support for this activity, regularly awarding grants, for example, to the China University of Politics and Law, the Chinese Academy of Social Sciences, (CASS), and Peking University Law School. See Ford Foundation *Annual Reports*.

countries needed to exist in a peaceful international environment and within a 'just and reasonable international economic order'. In 1991 it was also baldly stated that it was contrary to international law and a direct attack on state sovereignty to claim that the 'principle of non-interference in internal affairs does not apply to the issue of human rights', and much play had been made of Article 2 (7) of the UN Charter to bolster this point. This statement was missing from the 1995 document, although, as noted above, China did accuse the West of wanton interference in its internal affairs. These changes could be seen as a masking of 'real' views or a realization and acceptance that its own behaviour and adherence to aspects of the international human rights regime made it difficult if not impossible to retain this strict reading of the UN Charter and of international law on the subject. Its participation and final statements at Vienna may also have made it problematical to put quite the same degree of emphasis on subsistence and development, and may have encouraged it to move towards promoting the argument for the indivisibility of rights. Whatever the underlying reason, the shift in language was an important indication that global factors had brought about some shaping of the discourse, even if much of China's behaviour in the domestic realm still demonstrated a violation of international standards and a continuing failure of implementation.

China also made use of the 1995 White Paper to reiterate what it believed the international community's human rights policy should be in a world where countries had a 'different understanding and practice of human rights owing to various historical, social, economic, and cultural conditions'. In the light of this, China advocated holding 'dialogues and exchanges in the sphere of human rights', and averred that China had had several such constructive meetings in recent years with heads of governments, experts, and human rights delegations. Chinese leaders' reception and reasonable responsiveness to the pleas of American businessman John Kamm on behalf of imprisoned political dissidents were presumably designed to teach others about the value of the dialogic and non-confrontational approach.[110] These statements were clues to China's policy line: to try to take the spotlight away from the UN and the public

---

[110] John Kamm established his own firm in 1975, which specialized in trading with China. He later became chair of Market Access Ltd. (Hong Kong) and President of Asia-Pacific Resources (San Francisco), but more pertinently worked as a monitor of China's human rights and especially of political prisoners. He has described his approach as 'non-confrontational but persistent' and stated that he goes to Beijing in a private capacity as a 'friend of China'. An advocate of MFN renewal, he has been given wide access to ministerial level officials, one of whom told him in 1991 that 'Beijing does not like to be humiliated and told what to do. But "if friends come and treat us with respect, we will consider releasing people".' (quoted in *Washington Post*, 25 Feb. 1992).

discussion of failings in China's human rights record, into a more private sphere that would inevitably result in a less accusatory and more equal exchange of views between individuals or state parties. The Chinese government in its refusal for the time being to allow any further official bilateral dialogues on human rights as a result of the 1995 vote at the UN Commission was making the point that governments had to choose between the two routes they had been seeking to follow in the period to 1995—bilateral dialogue on human rights or condemnatory resolutions through the UN.

CONCLUSION

In the absence of a coordinated economic sanctions strategy among the Western states and Japan, and a declining ability on the part of the US government to convince the Chinese authorities, as well as its allies, of the credibility of US threats that it would deny MFN trading status, it became all but inevitable that bilateral coercive pressures on China to improve its human rights record would be severely reduced. Such pressures had had some effect in the early 1990s as China compromised at certain key moments by releasing a few dissidents, lightening the prison sentences it might otherwise have imposed, and trying to address the thorny question of the exports from prison labour. However, compromise was only a part of China's strategy. In addressing bilateral relations, Beijing adopted a three-pronged approach: first to attempt to equalize the economic relationship and demonstrate through trading missions, and through the timing of particular purchases, that Western economies, and especially the USA, would bear pain if sanctions were applied. Secondly, China reminded the USA and other Western states of its political and strategic weight. Thirdly, in the run-up to the Vienna Conference on Human Rights it attempted to demonstrate that other countries, especially many Asian governments, shared its perspective on human rights, thus raising questions about the acceptability of aspects of the criticisms levelled against China, and more broadly about claims that human rights were widely acknowledged as universal.

Undoubtedly this strategy was effective in removing some of the constraints that had been imposed on the Chinese government, but it was not entirely successful. Moreover, even in the absence of material coercive sanctions, Beijing would still feel obliged to offer some concessions. Several factors ensured continuing perusal of China's human rights record: the voice of the NGO could not be silenced and neither could its points of entry into the political and institutional frameworks be closed off; legislative and bureaucratic changes within the EU and USA, together with Clinton's election promises, and general congressional combativeness over the issue, guaranteed some media and official attention; and the UN Commission provided another important arena in which to expose China's failure to reach international standards. In the light of reduced material pressures, its worth as a substitute venue increased, especially with the break-up of the Soviet voting bloc. Finally, one prize that the USA would not give away at this stage was a full summit meeting between President Jiang and President Clinton in Washington. Although Clinton was to come face to face with Jiang in New York and Seattle, the summit in the nation's capital city continued to elude the Chinese leader.

The effectiveness of many of these factors in inducing positive change in China relied on the degree to which China remained concerned about international image. Multilateral gatherings of various kinds were particularly significant in this period in providing such potential points of leverage. While Beijing could demonstrate its congruence of view with other Asian governments during the Bangkok conference, it could not impose its arguments regarding cultural relativity and developmentalism onto the final document at Vienna. At the annual meetings of the UNCHR it could not prevent the yearly introduction of resolutions mildly critical of its behaviour, resorting unusually for states represented on the Commission to the procedural device of a no-action resolution. China's procedural motion was defeated in 1995, the same year that its human rights record became the subject of every Special Rapporteur's and Working Group's reports. Such individuals and groups were less subject to political pressure and to the changes of membership that affected the Commission and, barring governmental attempts to curtail their mandates, would be continuing their activities into the future. That the Chinese government cared deeply about the criticism contained in the reports and in the Commission's resolutions cannot be denied. It lobbied intensively to build support for its no-action resolutions, tried to attack the legitimacy of working groups, and put forward arguments for the reform but not the strengthening or development of the UN human rights machinery. But it also did not rule out a more conciliatory approach—inviting one Special Rapporteur to visit the country, pointing to its various legal reforms designed to bring its practice more into keeping with international standards, and making some moves towards an argument that stressed the indivisibility of human rights, or that at least played down its previous emphasis on subsistence and development as priorities. Beijing also had come to realize that arguments based on a strict interpretation of Article 2 (7) of the UN Charter were not likely to carry the day. Its 1995 White Paper, in its detailed treatment of Chinese citizens' rights, its discussion of governmental attempts to make these rights known, and provision of statistics to show that Chinese were indeed using the courts to claim these new-found guarantees, clearly demonstrated that Beijing had come to accept that the right to rule depended on a government's willingness to offer such human rights protections. The various forms of experience and pressure between 1992 and 1995, therefore, had proven to be effective in bringing about some discursive change, in wedding Beijing publicly to a series of legal reforms that were related to international standards, and in playing some role in prompting China to introduce those legal changes in the first place.

Those countries that chose to sponsor the China resolutions at the UN Commission had decided to do so primarily because of the removal of the bilateral sanctions policy that had led to renewed criticisms of their failure to offer staunch support to the human rights regime. They no doubt believed too that multilateral mechanisms could help shield them from Chinese retribution. The tough statements by EU member governments, the USA's more active lobbying in 1994 and 1995, and Japan's willingness to co-sponsor resolutions certainly suggested this belief. Thus, China's diplomatic bargaining strategy became to try to demonstrate ways in which multilateral criticism could affect bilateral relationships: hence the decision to cut off bilateral human rights discussions after 1995. Beijing seemed to understand that the break in contact would impose symbolic costs on governments that had made legislative and verbal commitments to a human rights dimension in foreign policies —that these governments still needed something beyond the UN Commission resolution as a way of expressing their commitment to the promotion of human rights in China. Beijing offered instead other, 'less confrontational', ways of addressing the topic—for example, through its preferred mechanism of 'dialogue and mutual exchange of views'. The undermining of the UN route and its replacement with bilateral dialogues became the centre piece of China's diplomatic approach in the next phase.

7

From Public Exposure to Private Dialogue, 1995–1998

Multilateral action in bodies such as the UNCHR has at least two factors in its favour: it helps to legitimize and universalize decisions that might otherwise be seen as reflecting individual interest; it also provides some protection, where necessary, for the individual actors that as a collective arrive at the decision in question. Governments that might be a target of this consensual understanding have three major options at their disposal: they can ignore it, seek to break apart the consensus, or comply with the demand to a greater or lesser degree. Much Chinese effort after the 1995 vote in the UN Commission was directed towards the middle course of action, although it also claimed increasing levels of compliance with the international human rights regime in order to boost the chances for success of its main strategy.

The intensity of China's dislike of the yearly voting ritual at the Commission was plain, even though the body had no ability materially to punish China, only to attempt to shame it. Since Beijing cared about international image for domestic and global reasons, this ruled out either ignoring or dismissing the condemnatory language as irrelevant to its concerns. Instead, it sought to prevent the country's human rights record becoming the focus of attention. Its relative success in weakening the multilateral route over the next few years demonstrated anew the power of language and of China's material attributes. The perceived importance of Beijing's role in the maintenance of the global and regional security order also assisted its attack on multilateralism. China's material and strategic weight influenced the policies of European governments, intent on increasing their economic and political profiles in China relative to the USA and Japan. Security issues were of particular moment to Washington and Tokyo, concerned to ensure there would be no overt military conflict either on the Korean peninsula or between China and Taiwan.

One of the most important linguistic changes, which was promoted persistently by Chinese officials and which became reasonably consolidated after 1995, was the notion that the introduction of country-specific resolutions at the UN Commission's annual meetings was essentially a confrontational approach that was inevitably unproductive. Chinese officials also emphasized that the 'confrontation' played out at the Commission was between the North and South or between a Western and a Chinese (or Asian) conception of human rights, even though the voting coalition comprised countries other than members of the developed West. Moreover, its reiteration of the relativist argument influenced certain governments that, in the most charitable interpretation, might have been acknowledging the long-held and internationally accepted view that universal human rights would necessarily be implemented in ways that reflected local culture;[1] or, alternatively, were simply trying to gain favour with a state that was growing in power by moving towards its cultural relativist language. The effect of this was to undermine the norm of universality and to bolster the idea that individual states had the right to determine for themselves how to interpret core human rights standards.

China also successfully used the more familiar weapons at its disposal: some astute lobbying on Beijing's part pointed up the potential economic costs of its being targeted and the dangers of trying to isolate it politically. Its suspension of the bilateral human rights dialogues after the 1995 vote opened governments to the domestic criticism that their strategies for dealing with the human rights issue in their relationships with China lacked a major component. Finally, China offered governments the prospect of positive change: Beijing would sign the two major international covenants on human rights, and would accept governmental and developmental agency roles in providing technical assistance in the areas of legal reform and training, provided the private bilateral dialogues replaced the public UN route. It would also relax its strict definition of sovereignty in allowing various of the Special Rapporteurs to visit to see for themselves the actual condition of human rights inside the country. This combined effort, with its discursive, power, and bargaining elements, served its purpose in breaking apart the coalition of governments that had been working together at the UN Commission, forcing individual states to find new ways of demonstrating the human rights component in their foreign policies.

---

[1] In R. J. Vincent's oft-quoted and evocative phrase: 'local carriers of a global message'. See his *Human Rights and International Relations* (Cambridge: Cambridge University Press, 1986), 101. The idea behind this is that, 'while the standards are universal, their implementation will be the more successful the closer the attention to local circumstances'.

THE FRACTURING OF THE UN COALITION

The Chinese authorities had made clear in 1995 what they thought the global community's human rights policy towards their country should be: to use Beijing's terminology, it should be based on cooperation and not confrontation, and should involve dialogue and an equal exchange of views on what it purposefully described as the 'Western versus the Chinese' concept of human rights. This phrase represented an obvious attack on the idea that human rights were universal and was designed to elicit sympathy and support from those developing countries that Beijing assumed similarly feared the effects of Western targeting. Beijing tried to convince other governments of the seriousness with which it adhered to a line that rejected UN condemnation of its record by cutting off all bilateral discussions on human rights after the passage of the 1995 UN Commission resolution. However, possibly as an attempt to demonstrate its preferred approach, Chinese officials did continue to receive the US businessman John Kamm, once again accepting from him a list of prisoners on whom he sought information.[2] China was now to embark on something of an offensive to promote this bilateral approach, attempting to divide the European bloc internally as well as from the USA, and wooing the Latin American and African state members of the UN Commission.

Admittedly, the Europeans were something of a soft target, if Sir Leon Brittan's 1995 exposition of China–Europe relations was anything to go by. While claiming that a commitment to human rights was at the heart of EU policy, both for its own intrinsic merit and because of the recognized longer-term benefits to a country's political and social stability, he went on:

The key criterion for pursuing human rights initiatives must be effectiveness, the impact that an initiative would have on the ground. For this reason, there is a danger that relying solely on frequent and strident declarations will dilute the message or lead to knee-jerk reactions from the Chinese government. To make progress, all the EU institutions should pursue human rights issues through a combination of carefully timed statements, formal private discussions and practical cooperation.[3]

---

[2] *Washington Post*, 7 May 1996.

[3] Sir Leon Brittan, Vice-President of the Commission, was responsible for the common commercial policy and for relations with the WTO and with China. His remarks are from European Commission, *A Long-Term Policy for China–Europe Relations* Brussels, 5 July (1995), and quoted in Andrew Clapham, 'Human Rights in the Common Foreign Policy', in Alston (ed.), *The EU and Human Rights*, 646. In 1999 Brittan's post was taken over by China's bête-noire, Chris Patten, former governor of Hong Kong until the handover in July 1997.

That statement came in the context of a new European strategy for strengthening its overall relationship with a rising China, which emphasized China's growing importance in all areas and a Europe-wide sense that its policy to date towards that important country had been ineffectual and undeveloped. Moreover, Lomé IV had marked a more general EU move away from a sanctioning approach towards positive measures designed to address the roots of human rights and other related problems.[4]

Those beliefs in the need for a new strategy towards China were held not only by Sir Leon, but also by the French and German governments. Late in 1995, during Chancellor Kohl's visit to China, the German leader handed over a list of political detainees and called on China to remember that its world image was 'also determined to a large extent by, for example, freedom of religion'. Nevertheless, he also put aside the consensus reached at Vienna in 1993 and agreed on the need to take into account different cultural traditions in the application of international human rights standards.[5] The Minister of Foreign Affairs in the new Chirac government, Hervé de Charette, also indicated his government's movement towards the Chinese approach for dealing with human rights questions. During a trip to Beijing in February 1996, he promised to use 'discretion' rather than a 'belligerent position' in such discussions.[6] At the ASEM summit in Bangkok in March 1996, matters became even more direct, Li Peng in meetings with Chancellor Kohl and President Chirac urging the two leading European statespersons to press for the dropping of the UN resolution. This request allegedly led French, Italian, and German ministers to ask for a number of human rights concessions in exchange, including China's signature of the two international covenants, and a willingness to allow the UN High Commissioner to visit the country. However, de Charette, in an unusually frank statement in April, undermined any pressing need the Chinese leaders might have felt in offering concessions in these areas. He also exposed the secondary importance he attached to human rights matters. As the Minister put it, and in reference to China's somewhat vague and general commitment to satisfying the requests made at the ASEM meeting, 'what [was] important' about Li Peng's visit to Paris were the economic deals struck, including a 'definite sale of 30 Airbuses', an agreement for Citroen to increase its automobile

---

[4] Bruno Simma, Jo Beatrix Aschenbrenner, and Constanze Schulte, 'Human Rights Considerations in the Development Co-operation Activities of the EC', in Alston (ed.), *The EU and Human Rights*, 578–82.

[5] *FBIS*-Chi-95-219, 14 Nov. 1995; *Human Rights Watch World Report 1996* (New York, 1995), p. xx. AI reportedly provided the list of detainees.

[6] *FBIS*-WEU-96-028, 9 Feb. 1996. The trip predominantly had commercial concerns.

production in China, and a new joint venture project worth FF500 million.[7]

These discussions with Chinese leaders in early spring 1996 served to delay European action at the 1996 session of the UN Commission, a failure to prepare that was compounded by US tardiness in beginning its lobbying of the delegates. Indeed, where Washington was concerned, some occasions at which discussions on the resolution could have taken place— in meetings with officials from Angola and Ethiopia, for example—were entirely neglected and stood in marked contrast to Chinese activity, which involved official visits in late 1995 to several African members of the Commission.[8] Nevertheless, tardiness in acting did not mean a complete failure to act. EU members decided that, having raised the matter of an exchange between the resolution and specific Chinese concessions, they had to follow through on this when Beijing declined to respond. Bonn's Foreign Minister, Klaus Kinkel, in his address to the UNCHR, revealed this inability to persuade China when he spoke of 'an exhaustive dialogue' designed to elicit improvements in its human rights situation, and that because of various disappointments the EU and the USA had decided to submit another resolution.[9] When the Italian delegate introduced it on behalf of the EU, USA, Japan, and other sponsors, he stated that it was based on the reports of a number of the Special Rapporteurs, all of whom had indicated there was continuing cause for concern about human rights conditions in China. After China had introduced its usual no-action resolution, Romagnano of the EU, and Ferraro of the USA, among others, spoke against that move, the latter reminding the Commission members: 'No other country, whether the United States, the Russian Federation or the Sudan, for example, [had] tried to prevent all discussion of its human rights record' and that the way for China to prevent such discussion was to 'cease committing human rights violations'. Despite these arguments, the lateness of the decision to sponsor a draft motion, and the general sense that major states were searching for means of deepening their relationship with China, boosted the chances for the success of Beijing's no-action motion. It passed 27–20–6, the Russian Federation abstaining this time, all but one African state voting for it, and the Latin Americans split between voting against and abstention.[10]

---

[7] *FBIS*-WEU-96-072, 12 Apr. 1996; and see Human Rights Watch, *Chinese Diplomacy, Western Hypocrisy*, 4. Hardly surprising, therefore, that such European governments became known derisively (especially in media and NGO circles) as the 'Airbus club'.

[8] Human Rights Watch, *Chinese Diplomacy, Western Hypocrisy*, 7.

[9] E/CN.4/1996/SR.42, 16 Apr. 1996.

[10] E/CN.4/1996/SR.59, 23 Apr. 1996. Russia may well have abstained because it was in the middle of negotiations with Beijing on establishing their 'strategic partnership' and agreeing confidence building measures with respect to the joint border.

Even though the Beijing delegation knew that it was likely to win the vote, this did not prevent it from attempting to weaken the opposition still further. Some delegations had been influenced to vote against or to abstain on the no-action motion because of the publication in January 1996 of a huge and detailed Human Rights Watch report on cases of severe neglect discovered in Chinese orphanages.[11] That report had received enormous worldwide publicity, prompting the European Parliament, for example, to pass a resolution calling on China to open all child welfare institutions to international inspection, and for action at the UN Commission.[12] The EU statement at the UNCHR had referred to the orphanages report in general terms, and Brazil had reportedly been influenced to vote against rather than abstain on the no-action motion in part because the report had made a big impact in the country.[13] Apart from the graphic, specific details of individual cases of neglect, the report damaged severely the Chinese claim that it had an excellent record in the protection of collective social and economic rights. It prompted Beijing to issue a White Paper on child welfare, demonstrating through comparative figures that the conditions for children in China compared very favourably with those in other developing countries.[14] In conjunction with this report, and other commentary on the Human Rights Watch document, Beijing launched a vitriolic attack on that NGO, sometimes using its own GONGO to accuse it of fabricating its evidence and as acting as a tool of the West in the latter's attacks on China.[15]

China's fulminations during 1996, however, went well beyond those against the NGO community. In response to Klaus Kinkel's speech before the UN Commission, the Chinese delegate informed him that, in view of his country's past history, he was not qualified to give lectures to the Chinese people on morals, and that the EU's 'ultimatum' to China that it ratify the international covenants on human rights within a certain period would 'never lead to any result'. He also accused the German minister of

[11] Human Rights Watch, *Death by Default: A Policy of Fatal Neglect in China's State Orphanages,* (Jan. 1996). See too *Chinese Orphanages: A follow-up* (Mar. 1996).

[12] William Korey (*NGO's,* 359) reports that the head of Human Rights Watch's Brussels Office lobbied energetically to get the European Parliament to adopt this resolution.

[13] Human Rights in China, *From Principle to Pragmatism: Can 'Dialogue' Improve China's Human Rights Situation* (June 1998), 21.   [14] *FBIS*-Chi-96-065, 3 Apr. 1996.

[15] According to the head of the China Society for the Study of Human Rights, 'Human Rights Watch was founded in the Cold War era to meet the need of the West to start a cold war, so it has had an ingrained political bias against socialist China from the very beginning. Especially since the end of the Cold War, Human Rights Watch has become the West's daring vanguard amid the latter's attack on China over human rights'. He described the report on orphanages as 'starting an evil wave against China'. See *SWB* FE/2827 G/3, 27 Jan. 1997.

operating a double standard, since the USA had never been given a dead-line for ratifying the ICESCR.[16] As far as the USA itself went, the Chinese pointed once again to the instances of racial discrimination, homelessness, and crime in the country, and recommended that America solve its own problems before 'interfering in the affairs of others'.[17] More broadly, Chinese participants accused Western countries of practising power politics, of trying to impose their views on others, and of operating under double standards. It was evidence that the 'East–West confrontation' had been replaced by a 'North–South' one, in which countries of the North had no compunction in setting themselves up as judges of the human rights situations in the developing world, and in marked opposition to the cooperative spirit that had apparently prevailed at Vienna in 1993.[18] As the head of China's delegation pointed out in response to the EU's 'anti-China draft resolution', that resolution was targeted not just at China but at the whole of the developing world.[19]

Chinese delegates also elaborated arguments that were part of a more generalized attack on the structure and operating principles of the UN Commission, this time using statistics to illustrate points. Since 1992, for example, Chinese officials reported there had been fifty-eight country-specific resolutions, almost all of them against developing countries.[20] If there had to be country-specific resolutions, then these should be based on the 'spirit of consensus' (that is, not majority, roll-call voting); meanwhile, further efforts had to be made to ensure that the Commission paid greater attention to the promotion of economic and social rights and the right to development. As things stood in 1996, Zhang Yishan claimed, of the thirty-three Special Rapporteurs appointed by the Commission, only one dealt with economic and social rights and, of the ninety-three resolutions adopted, only seven referred to such rights. He also argued that the composition of the Commission should be changed better to reflect the principle of 'regional balance', and thus should include more members from developing countries. Once again, Zhang pushed the point that the UN's human rights mechanisms and organs were in 'great need of reform to improve overall efficiency and effectiveness', that the country reporting systems for the treaties, for example, were enormously time-consuming and expensive, and that developing countries in particular found difficulty in meeting deadlines for the submission of their reports. In sum, the problems were, Zhang stated, that their questions were often

---

[16] *FBIS*-WEU-96-077, 19 Apr. 1996.   [17] E/CN.4/1996/SR.50, 18 Apr. 1996.
[18] E/CN.4/1996/SR.48, 18 Apr. 1996 and E/CN.4/1996/SR.2, 19 Mar. 1996.
[19] See report of speech in *FBIS*-Chi-96-080, 24 Apr. 1996.
[20] *Beijing Review*, 13-19 May 1996.

repetitive and the large numbers of reports could not be given prompt consideration. Worse still, some treaty bodies had moved beyond their terms of reference.[21]

China's active diplomacy was to continue in the lead-up to the 1997 UNCHR meeting. Individual governments were to be wooed or warned and ideas regarding the restructuring of UN human rights mechanisms regularly advanced. The Centre for Human Rights was added to the list of those organs requiring an overhaul, again on the grounds of the inequitable distribution of personnel, or, as it was put more baldly at the time of the 1997 UN Commission vote, because there was a ' severe lack of representation of Asian countries in the centre'.[22] Chinese official visits to Latin America in June and November 1996 were all, except in the case of Peru, to imminent or actual Commission members such as Argentina, Brazil, Chile, Cuba, Mexico, and Uruguay. Li Peng's visit to Brazil referred directly to its recent and future voting pattern, the Chinese premier expressing dismay at the government's decision in 1996 to vote against the no-action motion. Li sought at a minimum an abstention at the 1997 session, as he probably did in Chile too, for Santiago had followed Brazil's recent stance. After the close of the 1996 Commission, China received or sent high-ranking officials to all fifteen African members of the UN body, exchanges that may not always have had the UN Commission vote at the top of the agenda—in the case of South Africa, for example, Taiwan and the diplomatic recognition question took pride of place—but that undoubtedly included discussions on the likely voting position.[23] When it came to the 1997 vote, all except for South Africa among African countries voted for China's no-action motion, and Brazil moved once again to an abstention. China's approach to the government to begin a bilateral dialogue on human rights, and then an actual invitation for a delegation to go to Beijing between 18 and 27 February 1997, probably influenced the Brazilian decision to abstain.[24]

However, China's major prize that year, and the one receiving most

[21] E/CN.4/1996/SR.33, 10 Apr. 1996, and E/CN.4/1996/SR.16, 28 Mar. 1996. In 1998, the new UN High Commissioner for Human Rights was also speaking of the need to correct the 'imbalance' in human rights by giving more emphasis to economic, social, and cultural rights. At the 1998 UN Commission meeting, Portugal and France introduced two resolutions, one to create a Special Rapporteur on Economic and Social Rights (starting with the right to education), and the second an independent expert on extreme poverty and human rights. See John Tessitore and Susan Woolfson (eds.), *A Global Agenda: Issues before the 53rd General Assembly of the United Nations* (Lanham, Md.: Rowman & Littlefield, 1998), 168.

[22] *SWB* FE/2888 G/4, 9 Apr. 1997, and see the three Chinese suggestions advanced at the 1997 session of ECOSOC, *SWB* FE/2980 G/1–2, 25 July 1997.

[23] Human Rights Watch/Asia, *Chinese Diplomacy, Western Hypocrisy*, 5–9.

[24] Human Rights in China, *From Principle to Pragmatism*, 21–2.

international publicity, came with the French decision, announced in February, not to support an EU draft resolution, a move that was swiftly supported by other EU members such as Germany, Spain, Greece, and Italy, together with Australia and Canada from the Western group. During Foreign Minister Qian Qichen's visit to Paris in January 1997, President Chirac had already signalled a likely change, stating publicly that he was convinced that a 'strategy of cooperation . . . would go further toward ensuring that progress is made than a strategy of confrontation'.[25] In April, at a meeting between the French Defence Minister, Charles Millon, and President Jiang Zemin in Beijing, Millon was informed that the Chinese intended to sign the ICESCR by the end of the year, and was also studying the ICCPR,[26] the *quid pro quo* that the French government had sought in 1996 but that had then been described by Beijing as an 'unacceptable ultimatum'.

The Beijing leadership gave the French government much praise during this visit, both for its independent action in refusing to support resolutions directed against China at the UN Commission, and for the identical foreign political views it shared with China. Both countries, it was averred, treasured their national independence, and favoured a multipolar over a unipolar world. Jiang promised an even better future for Sino-French economic cooperation and exchanges in the defence field. In case the point had not been brought home strongly enough, Li Peng followed up in a separate visit with Millon, repeating these views, and describing the French move not to support the draft resolution as a 'wise and far-sighted decision'. However, Li also acknowledged that the human rights aspect could not be entirely pushed aside and promised in exchange 'various forms of communication and cooperation with France on the protection and promotion of human rights'.[27] With the stage set for President Chirac's visit to Beijing in May 1997, the two governments signed a declaration for a global partnership, repeating calls for the establishment of a more just multilateral international political and economic order. In a statement open to much debate and interpretation, as well as criticism, Jiang and Chirac also agreed that: 'The two parties emphasize that efforts tending to promote and protect human rights must respect the aims and principles of the United Nations Charter, as well as the universality of human rights, while at the same time taking fully into account particularities of all sides.'[28]

---

[25] Not surprisingly, Qian Qichen endorsed this statement. *FBIS*-WEU-97-008, 11 Jan. 1997.
[26] *Beijing Review*, 28 Apr.–4 May 1997.　　　　[27] *SWB*, FE/2888 G/2, 9 Apr. 1997.
[28] See *Le Monde*, 17 May 1997. In response to a critical editorial in the *Washington Post*, the French Embassy's press and information counselor in Washington wrote: 'France along with some of its European partners, decided this year to put an end to the hypocrit-

The German government had similarly been courting the Chinese.[29] Foreign Minister Kinkel visited in October and President Roman Herzog a month later, during which he signed a number of financial and technological cooperation agreements. In explaining Germany's approach to Beijing to the Bundestag, Kohl stressed the long-standing nature of the German government's one-China policy, his desire for continued cooperation with 'one of the world's oldest cultures', and his determination to ensure that German contacts with the PRC would help support China's process of political reform.[30] With the two key European states advocating a change in UN policy, it was hardly unexpected that the EU Human Rights Working Group would also be affected. At a meeting in December 1996, it was unable to reach a decision on a possible UN Commission resolution, turning the problem over to the Political Affairs Working Group destined to meet the following January. During that later meeting, members discussed a variety of ways of watering down what had become widely described as the confrontational approach, including adopting a resolution by consensus rather than majority voting, or substituting the resolution with investigations by UN thematic rapporteurs. It then referred the issue back to the EU working group.[31] With immaculate timing, the Chinese agreed in mid-February to resume a human rights dialogue with the EU,[32] presumably in the expectation that this would help decide the debate in its favour.

Japan had also been a regular co-sponsor of the UN Commission resolution. Apparently encouraged by Chinese consideration of the two UN covenants and the possibility of its agreeing to a human rights dialogue with Tokyo, in March 1997 Foreign Minister Ikeda told Qian that his

---

ical and unproductive approach of supporting a text that had yielded no results after seven years [*sic*], and whose sole effect was to assuage consciences while enabling all parties to continue trading with China. Instead, France embarked on a path of constructive dialogue with China' (*Washington Post*, 29 May 1997). On the eve of Chirac's visit, he had promised more than fifteen NGOs that he would advocate negotiations with the Dalai Lama, hand his counterpart a list of Chinese prisoners of conscience on whom his government expected to receive information, and sign a political statement that would underline a shared commitment to the universality of human rights. See *FBIS*-WEU-97-134, 14 May 1997.

[29] This policy had slightly come off the rails in the summer of 1996 when a German Foundation, closely connected with Foreign Minister Kinkel, sponsored a conference on Tibet with the assistance of the Dalai Lama's government in exile. Chinese protests, including the decision to close down the Foundation's Beijing office, backfired to the extent that the Bundestag adopted a resolution condemning China's repressive policy in Tibet. The Chinese retaliated and postponed Kinkel's planned visit to the country, together with that of the Parliamentary Subcommittee for Human Rights. *FBIS*-WEU-96-122, 24 June 1996, and WEU-96-123, 25 June 1996.   [30] *FBIS*-WEU-96-126, 28 June 1996.

[31] Human Rights Watch, *Chinese Diplomacy, Western Hypocrisy*, 12.

[32] *Far Eastern Economic Review*, 13 Feb. 1997.

government was considering ending its co-sponsorship. Beijing made a
further appeal to Tokyo during the Commission meeting itself,[33] leading
to Japan's compliance. The Tokyo government later explained that it had
not backed the resolution because the Chinese were making a serious
study of how their domestic laws could be brought into line with the
international covenants on human rights. In October that year the two
sides held their first official talks on human rights questions, the Japanese
side reiterating its request that 'China promote transparency in dealing
with the human rights issue', raising questions about the human rights
situation in Tibet, and the matter of political detainees.[34]

Strategic and economic matters inevitably had been a central feature of
Japan's dealings with China in 1996 and 1997. Tokyo had frozen some of its
grants to China in 1995 in protest at China's continuing nuclear weapons
testing programme. Relations had been further strained by the US–
Japanese negotiations over the defence cooperation guidelines, which
resulted in April 1996 in the US–Japan Joint Declaration. Chinese officials
interpreted this declaration, because of its reference to shared interests in
the peaceful resolution of regional disputes, as an expansion of military
cooperation between the two allies, including in the event of conflict
between China and Taiwan. As a result of this rise in tension in bilateral
relations, a primary Japanese objective in 1997 had been to smooth things
over, and the UN action was one means of signalling this intent. Tokyo was
further encouraged in this path when it became clear that its primary ally,
the USA, similarly was seeking from late 1996 to put its relations with
China on a firmer, and more stable basis. At long last, the administration's
policy of 'comprehensive engagement' seemed destined to be promoted
seriously, a determination that also led Washington to delay taking a decision on the UN draft resolution. The promotion of the engagement policy
was not to be a straightforward enterprise, however, given continuing
difficulties over the trade deficit, intellectual property questions, weapons
proliferation, as well as the human rights issue. The thorny question of
the future of Taiwan also returned to centre stage during this period.

Washington's reversal of its decision, under pressure from Congress,
not to give President Lee Teng-hui a visa to visit his alma mater Cornell
University in 1995 enraged the Chinese, who had taken seriously Warren
Christopher's guarantee that no such visa would be issued.[35] Relations
were further damaged in 1996 when Beijing decided to try and influence

---

[33] *Deutsche Presse-Agentur*, 29 Mar. 1997; *Kyodo News International*, 21 Apr. 1997.
[34] *FBIS*-EAS-97-234, 22 Aug. 1997, and EAS-97-297, 24 Oct. 1997.
[35] To help ensure a favourable outcome, Lee hired a public-relations firm to assist with
the lobbying of Congress. See Nancy Bernkopf Tucker, 'A Precarious Balance: Clinton and
China', *Current History*, Sept. 1998, p. 248.

the resolve of Taiwan's voters on the eve of the island's first direct presidential election by firing live missiles close to Taiwan's shores. The Clinton administration's response was to send two aircraft carrier battle groups into the waters off Taiwan as a strong signal of its intent to stand by its position that it expected a peaceful resolution to the reunification issue between Beijing and Taipei. The effects of this crisis were sobering for both China and the USA. Shortly afterwards the two governments resumed their security discussions, which involved a flurry of high-level contacts. The new US Secretary of State, Madeleine Albright, in testimony before the Senate Finance Committee in June on the MFN issue, made a strong statement in favour of the engagement strategy, listing all the areas in the relationship that required sustained attention. On human rights, she acknowledged, much as President Clinton had done in January 1997, that there had been little progress, but she also implied that the administration had decided to take a more passive stance, arguing that the economic and social integration of China would have a liberalizing effect over the longer term. Clinton had said the same thing in January, 'just as inevitably [as] the Berlin wall fell'.[36]

The timing of these contacts with Beijing held up the decision on whether to sponsor the UN draft resolution, both in Washington and in other Western capitals. In a move designed to try to promote a concerted US–EU approach, the Clinton administration reported on the talks it had held with the Chinese, in the spirit of avoiding 'confrontation in Geneva', and suggested to Brussels that it mirror this approach by asking, for example, for the release of medically sick prisoners, the signing of the two human rights covenants, and a resumption of Beijing's discussion with the International Committee of the Red Cross (ICRC) on prison visits.[37] Albright informed the Dutch Foreign Minister and Leon Brittan,

[36] National Security Adviser Anthony Lake was in Beijing in July 1996, where it was announced that presidential visits would be exchanged in 1997 and 1998. In preparation for these visits and in order to sustain the momentum behind the idea of a new start in bilateral relations, Warren Christopher's replacement as Secretary of State, Madeleine Albright, visited China in Feb. 1997, followed by Vice-President Al Gore in late March. Clinton's speech is reported in the *Far Eastern Economic Review*, 13 Feb. 1997, Albright's in US Deptartment of State, 'Testimony by Secretary of State Madeleine K. Albright before the Senate Finance Committee', 10 June 1997. Al Gore's visit resulted in the signature of contracts for Boeing corporation worth $685 million. On human rights matters, he stated that Chinese leaders had 'a more receptive ear' to such concerns but warned that results could take some time. See *Human Rights Watch World Report 1998*, (New York, 1997), 179.

[37] China had indefinitely postponed its negotiations with the ICRC over access to prisons. The ICRC came to resent being used as a political football in the relationship between China and the USA and wanted to remove itself from this process. Interview in New York, Dec. 1997.

Vice-President of the European Commission, at the end of January that she was still awaiting concessions from China before making a decision about the UN vote. Her visit to Beijing in late February also encouraged a further period of indecision on both Washington's and Brussels' part, and indeed has been claimed to have contributed to the French decision in February to block EU support for a resolution.[38]

The Beijing government did its best to influence the decision-making process, offering hints and half promises that it would be cooperative in granting some of the concessions required of it. In February, just prior to his resignation, the UN High Commissioner for Human Rights, Jose Ayala Lasso, stated that he had been invited to China and had accepted the invitation in principle. Three days after Albright's visit to Beijing, a spokesperson from China's foreign ministry announced that the government was giving 'positive consideration' to signing the two international covenants, and on 1 March Beijing agreed to resume contacts with the ICRC.[39] Nevertheless, Washington did not consider these moves to be enough, especially perhaps in the light of the US State Department's annual human rights report's conclusion that in 1996 'all public dissent against the party and government [had been] effectively silenced by intimidation, exile, the imposition of prison terms, administrative detention, or house arrest'. That statement represented an excellent example of how relatively independent and well entrenched this particular reporting procedure had become, especially when viewed alongside the clear White House desire to improve relations with Beijing.[40] Washington thus determined that it could wait no longer for China to move more concretely on

---

[38] *FBIS*-WEU-97-037, 24 Feb. 1997. The British at EU foreign ministers' meetings and subsequently advanced the argument that their concerns for Hong Kong would make it essential for the London government to continue to support such a resolution at the UN Commission. Ibid. The EU spokesperson at the UN Commission meeting did voice the Union's continuing concern at the 'system of re-education through labour, the excessive use of the death penalty, the imprisonment of dissidents, prison conditions, particularly forced labour, and the human rights in Tibet'. He also called on the Chinese government to ensure that 'open and fair elections' were quickly organized after 1 July in Hong Kong and that Beijing explain how it intended to submit reports on the implementation of the provisions of the two international covenants on human rights, which were to remain in force after the handover. See E/CN.4/1997/SR.48, 8 Apr. 1997. EU joint statements do carry some weight and governments lobby to try to ensure inclusion or exclusion from the list of countries to which reference is made. Clapham, 'Human Rights in the Common Foreign Policy', 645.

[39] Human Rights Watch, *Chinese Diplomacy, Western Hypocrisy* 13–14.

[40] US Department of State, *China Country Report on Human Rights Practices*, (Internet edn., 1997), 2. The administration was also aware of the softness of domestic support for its engagement policy, as witnessed by the uproar that had greeted General Chi Haotian's remark at Fort McNair on 8 Dec. 1996 that 'not a single person lost his life in Tiananmen Square' in June 1989. Further details on the reactions to this statement are contained in Mann, *About Face,* 348–9.

the human rights front and put pressure on Denmark to introduce a resolution that was critical of China's record.[41] Copenhagen quickly agreed to do this, taking the opportunity to criticize Paris openly for blocking the chance of a common move on the question and for undermining EU attempts to forge a common foreign policy.[42] In introducing the resolution, its representative stated that all countries should be 'held accountable for the international human rights standards they had endorsed' and that it was 'high time for the High Commissioner for Human Rights' to enter into his mandated dialogue with the Chinese. The British delegation, with the handover in Hong Kong less than three months away, offered its support as co-sponsor and spoke critically of China's resort once again to the no-action motion. China's three charges of selectivity, subjectivity, and partiality were swept aside. As Mr Steel put it: 'what could be more selective than to argue that the Commission could discuss human rights violations anywhere in the world except China?' In his government's view, 'impartiality would appear to require that the Commission should give no special treatment to any country, whereas China was, in fact, asking it to do so'.[43]

This robust statement did little to mask the real problems that had lain behind the search for co-sponsors and the actual drafting of the resolution, problems that must have influenced a number of governments' responses to the no-action resolution. Washington would not support a Danish clause that condemned the use of the death penalty and wanted to weaken sections dealing with social rights, vividly demonstrating yet again that, even among Western countries, there was disagreement about what constituted human rights.[44] Moreover, Copenhagen had to deal

---

[41] *FBIS*-WEU-97-094, 4 Apr. 1997.

[42] A criticism echoed in a *Netherlands Quarterly of Human Rights* (16/1, Mar. 1998), 90), report on EU activity, which described this as a 'blatant example of the lack of commitment on the part of a number of member states to forge a common human rights strategy *vis-à-vis* important partner countries'.

[43] *FBIS*-WEU-97-101, 11 Apr. 1997; WEU-97-094, 4 Apr. 1997; E/CN.4/1997/SR.65, 15 Apr. 1997. The Canadian representative's speech, however, undercut these British remarks: in reporting that Canada intended to vote against the no-action motion but not to co-sponsor the Danish draft, Mr Hynes explained: 'there was, in fact, a difference between China and other countries; it was the most populous nation on earth, a major political and economic Power, and a permanent member of the Security Council, and its people and Government had a right to be proud of their crucial role in the international community'. (E/CN.4/1997/SR.65, 15 Apr. 1997). To that point Canada had co-sponsored draft resolutions on China some six times. It decided against in 1997 on the grounds of the weakening of consensus on co-sponsorship, and the signature of an MOU with China covering projects in the area of legal and judicial reform. For a fuller discussion of the Canadian position, see Human Rights in China, *From Principle to Pragmatism*, 23–7.

[44] Further evidence of this disagreement occurred at the 1997 UN Commission meeting when Italy and forty-four co-sponsors introduced a resolution on the question of the death

with the timidity of possible co-sponsors and with those potential sup-
porters of the no-action approach who at the time were the subject of
various Chinese threats and blandishments. On the one hand, Beijing
stated quite openly and bluntly that, 'if certain countries insist on
taking the lead in making anti-China motions, their action will
inevitably bring harm to the bilateral relations', while on the other hand
it offered countries bilateral dialogues as a replacement for the annual
resolution.[45]

Among those refusing to co-sponsor this time around, apart from
France, were Japan, Australia, Canada, and Germany. In the event,
Denmark did manage to find other co-sponsors, including its EU partner,
the Netherlands. The Dutch Prime Minister, Kok, complained openly
about EU countries that had allowed concerns about economic gain to
'outweigh criticism of human rights policy in China', and described the
actions as 'definitely not a good thing for the credibility and unity of a
European policy'. However, some domestic critics of the Netherlands
government, notably the head of the Association of Netherlands
Businesses–Netherlands Christian Employers' Association (VNO-
NCW), backed the Chinese stance and complained that the government
should have been more discreet, subtle, and private in its criticism of
China. This argument was more keenly felt still when China moved to
cancel planned exchanges of visits with co-sponsors of the resolution,
including Dutch, Danish, Irish, Austrian, and Luxembourgeois officials,
business leaders, and study groups.[46] Despite a last-minute dash to
Geneva in early April by the US Ambassador to the UN, China's no-
action motion in response to the resolution succeeded by the large
margin of twenty-seven in favour with seventeen against and nine
abstentions, China's best result since this procedural device had first
been used to prevent debate on its record.

Thus, the outcome in 1997 represented a victory of sorts for the
Chinese, a split in the Western bloc, and serious disagreement among
EU members at a time when a common foreign policy had been presented

penalty. This resolution sought to embed the Human Rights Committee's interpretation of
Article 6 of the ICCPR—the right to life. This interpretation read: 'all measures of abolition [of the death penalty] should be considered as progress in the enjoyment of the right
to life.' The resolution as a whole carried 27–11–14, the USA on the opposing side along
with Algeria, Bangladesh, Bhutan, China, Egypt, Indonesia, Japan, Malaysia, Pakistan,
and South Korea. See John Tessitore and Susan Woolfson (eds.), *A Global Agenda: Issues
before the 52nd General Assembly of the United Nations* (Lanham, Md.: Rowman & Littlefield, 1997), 196–7.

[45] *SWB* FE/2889, G/2–3, 10 Apr. 1997; *FBIS*-WEU-97-101, 11 Apr. 1997.
[46] *FBIS*-WEU-97-111, 21 Apr. 1997; *FBIS*-WEU-97-122, 2 May 1997.

as a key goal. Some EU member states tended to blame Paris for striking out on its own so publicly and independently; others were critical of Denmark and the Netherlands for breaking ranks in the opposite direction.[47] The terms of the resolution itself had pointed up differences among Western governments over interpretation of the two core texts of the human rights regime, and whether China was deserving of special treatment. In the domestic realm, there was further evidence of the range of pressures governments faced: for example, in the Dutch and Danish cases, business groups were alarmed that they would lose out on the great prize of the China market; in the French case, the business lobby may have been content, but domestic human rights NGOs needed to be placated.

Chinese delegates inevitably took advantage of this period of indecision in the Western approach, and fiercely attacked the Netherlands and Denmark for leading the charge against their record at the UN Commission. According to a report in *Le Monde*, the Chinese authorities had said that it 'would be for Denmark like holding a stone over its head and letting go'. Beijing also drew attention to the 'cracks' that had appeared among Western countries as evidence that 'confrontation' had become unpopular even among its leading critics.[48] It continued to press for reform of the UN's human rights mechanisms, emphasizing once again the almost total absence of Special Rapporteurs that dealt with economic, social, and cultural rights and that, of the vast bulk of resolutions passed by the Commission, only a handful related to these rights. Wang Guangya also complained that all the talk of democracy for individual states did not seem to prevail in the international system as a whole, where the powerful attacked the weak and imposed sanctions upon them. Chinese diplomats again called for the redress of the 'severe lack of representation of Asian countries' in the Centre for Human Rights, and for the Special Rapporteurs and Working Groups to carry out their work according to established rules and in such a manner that did not 'infringe upon the sovereignty, dignity and interests of host countries'.[49] The latter remarks were particularly directed at such Working Groups as the one dealing with arbitrary detention and had the effect of curtailing its powers in subtle ways: before its mandate was renewed in 1997, for example, the Working Group agreed that, rather than take 'decisions' on whether a case of detention was arbitrary, it would now express its 'views' on such

---

[47] Interview in Brussels, May 1999.

[48] Tessitore and Woolfson (eds.), *Issues before the 52nd General Assembly*, 213; *FBIS-Chi-97-083*, 16 Apr. 1997.

[49] *SWB* FE/2873 G/2, 21 Mar. 1997; FE/2888 G/4–5, 9 Apr. 1997; E/CN.4/1997/SR.43, 7 Apr. 1997.

cases. Governments were invited to 'pay attention to the recommendations of the Working Group concerning persons mentioned in its report'
rather than urged to comply with its recommendations.[50]

The Chinese also offered detailed explanations of their own position
on human rights, in some key venues casting back to the language of the
early 1990s, in others suggesting a more forward-looking China, and one
striving to improve its own record of protection. A long *Renmin Ribao*
article published in mid-March 1997, a week after the opening of the
Geneva meeting, stressed North–South divisions in this area, the need to
recognize that countries of the South placed primary emphasis on the
right to subsistence and development, that Asian countries with their
supposed emphasis on group interests were excellent examples for other
civilizations, and that attempts to universalize the protection of human
rights violated the UN Charter and the central norm of non-interference
in domestic affairs. In support of the various arguments, the author
quoted such Asian leaders as Mahathir Mohamad and Lee Kuan Yew,
resurrecting in many respects the 1993 statements of Bangkok rather than
those of Vienna.[51] However, a month later at Geneva, before a global
audience, the Chinese delegate, Wang Guangya, pointed to actual positive policy changes in his country that indicated a concern for individual
civil and political rights. He noted that rapid sustained economic growth
in China had been accompanied by development of the country's democratic and legal systems, 'with special efforts devoted to promoting and
protecting the rights of individuals'. He drew attention to two particular
developments: the extension of village democracy and the ratification of
the revisions to the CPL. Although Wang did not mention this, of course,
the revised CPL had come on to the statute books as a result of greater
awareness of international practice, sustained criticism of Chinese legal
procedures, especially by the international NGOs, and the argument
among Chinese legal academics that the country needed to incorporate
international human rights standards if it genuinely wished to provide
greater protections for criminal suspects.[52] Wu Jianmin of the Chinese
delegation pointed to his country's 'unprecedented progress' in establishing 'democracy and a legal system' and the 'tremendous efforts' that had

---

[50] Human Rights in China, *From Principle to Pragmatism*, 47; Tessitore and Woolfson
(eds.), *Issues before the 52nd General Assembly*, 195.

[51] *FBIS*-Chi-97-053, 17 Mar. 1997.

[52] See *SWB* FE/2891, G/2, 12 Apr. 1997. For an analysis of China's revised law on criminal procedure, see Lawyers' Committee for Human Rights, *Opening to Reform?* esp.
10–13. It quotes Wang Hanbin, the NPC Vice-Chair, as stating that the legal revision
would help to refute 'Western countries' smears and slanders'. (Ibid. 11, n. 35). See too the
important analysis by Xin, *Chinese Legal System and Current Legal Reform*.

been made to 'promote the civil, political, economic, social and cultural rights of the Chinese people'. Moreover, delegates were aware that, despite Chinese attacks on the Working Group on Arbitrary Detention in 1995, a preparatory visit by the group had been made in the summer of 1996, designed to establish the terms for an official visit in October 1997. Although Beijing imposed certain restraints on the operation of this Working Group, of which more below, the official invitation did seem to indicate China's further acceptance of the need for engagement with the international human rights regime, and a weakening of its strict interpretation of the norm of non-interference and state sovereignty.[53]

The Beijing government also produced a further White Paper on Human Rights at the time of the Commission's gathering in Geneva, which charted the progress that had been made in 1996. As in the 1995 paper, it began with an indication of the country's economic achievements, arguing that statistical evidence demonstrated that, compared with most other developing countries, it was recording genuine successes in alleviating poverty. The paper also noted that efforts to promote a 'socialist democratic and political system' were proceeding in tandem with this positive economic picture, with notable improvement in democratic practices at the grass-roots level. It additionally pointed to the strengthening of the judicial guarantee of human rights as shown by revisions to the Criminal Law (CL) and the CPL, the former of which had included the replacement of the term 'counter-revolutionary crime' with the crime of 'endangering state security'. It recorded the rapid increases in the numbers of Chinese lawyers and the vast increases in the numbers of lawsuits that they were handling.

The CPL was described in considerable detail in the text and depicted as something of a landmark in the development of China's legal system. Generously interpreted, it could be seen this way, with some movement towards the presumption of innocence, its elimination of certain forms of arbitrary detention, and the expansion of the role of defence counsel. However, leaving aside at this point a more careful review of the provisions of the new law, the White Paper itself undermined the sense that the CPL represented a genuine sea change. In the White Paper's discussion of

---

[53] Wu's statement is in E/CN.4/1997/SR.65, 15 Apr. 1997. While Beijing had obviously regarded it as necessary to invite this Working Group, local-level officials were extremely wary. As the Working Group stated in its report of the preparatory 1996 trip, 'there was sometimes undeniable tension during contacts with certain local officials who had difficulty in understanding why United Nations representatives should be looking into their detention facilities'. The Chairman-Rapporteur, Louis Joinet, went on, 'this difficulty was gradually overcome, without the visit itself being compromised, after explanations had been given and the residual misgivings removed' ('Report of the Working Group on Arbitrary Detention', E/CN.4/1997/4, 17 Dec. 1996).

the serious crackdown on crime that had been launched in 1996, a crack-down that had won the 'heartfelt support of the general public', it demonstrated anew the continuing arbitrary use of state power. As AI later recorded, that 'strike-hard' campaign had been marked by 'mass summary trials and executions on a scale unprecedented since 1983'.[54]

The White Paper concluded that, judging by the advancements made, placing 'top priority' on the people's right to subsistence and development had been the correct policy. But it noted too that this had been pro-ceeding under the 'conditions of reform, development and stability, strengthening the democratic and legal systems and giving human rights a comprehensive push'. Its final phrases stressed its developmentalist position, noting room for further improvement, and the restrictions China faced because of its historical and material conditions. However, it also stated that the government and people would 'continue to try every means possible to help the people enjoy human rights in a broader space and at a higher level'.[55]

This document, together with statements at the UN Commission describing legal and other reforms, indicated some changes in China's dis-cursive practices and policy, even if it was clear from NGO reports and other legal analysis that serious problems remained with the new legisla-tion over and above the huge difficulties connected with actual imple-mentation. For those governments that were predisposed to take an optimistic view of these changes, China's developmentalist rhetoric, cou-pled with promises to study or sign the two major international covenants on human rights, could be interpreted generously as heralding a time when China would become a more committed supporter of international human rights standards. Developmentalism fitted well, too, with the orthodoxy current in Western policy circles in an earlier era, rationalized in the arguments of political scientists such as Samuel Huntingdon, which favoured social stability over too zealous political reform, so as not to endanger economic development. Many governments were also watch-ful in the aftermath of the death of China's paramount leader, Deng Xiaoping, in February 1997, concerned that this might foreshadow a period of political uncertainty and instability in the country. Some governments were persuaded that China's demographic and great power status did place it in something of a unique position; others seemed to have seen some merit in the cultural relativist arguments; and some high-lighted, quite baldly, as in the case of the French Minister, Hervé de

---

[54] *Amnesty International Report 1997* (London, 1997), 118 and see more broadly Amnesty's campaign briefing document of Mar. 1996, *No One is Safe*.

[55] An English language version of the White Paper can be found at *SWB* FE/2881 S2/1, 1 Apr. 1997.

Charette, that it was the economic deals that mattered above all else in the relationship with China. There was much, then, that could form the basis of an argument for dropping the use of the UN Commission route for promoting the human rights element in China policy, and why many were willing to adopt China's calls for 'cooperation not confrontation' in this area.

Thus, by mid-1997, if China itself had given some ground, it was also having some considerable success in shifting the discursive and behavioural practices of its major governmental interlocutors. It was also gaining support for its strategy of shifting the emphasis within the Commission and for clipping the wings of the Commission's thematic mechanisms. With regard to the Sub-Commission, as noted earlier, the expert members had already constrained their own ability to introduce country-specific resolutions. However, at its meeting in August 1997, the Chinese delegate, Fan Guoxiang, tabled a resolution—attracting sponsorship from another twenty Sub-Commission members—that further affected its ability to name and shame. Referring to the alleged unfortunate politicization of human rights issues, the resolution called on all those engaged in the work of that body to carry out 'constructive dialogue and consultations on human rights'.[56]

THE RESURGENCE OF BILATERALISM

After the 1997 meeting of the UN Commission, Chinese diplomacy sought two main objectives: the final internment of the UN yearly voting ritual, and an exchange of successful summits between Presidents Jiang Zemin and Bill Clinton. Also of fundamental importance was the smooth handover of Hong Kong, without incident and with all due ceremony. The achievement of these aims required the repeat of some of the methods adopted in the past, with an emphasis on the more consensual among them: fence mending in the Netherlands, Luxembourg, and Denmark through the signature of economic agreements, and more evidence of cooperation with aspects of the international human rights regime. In the case of Hong Kong, for example, China agreed that, since under British rule the territory had been a signatory of the ICCPR, Beijing would now take on the obligation to submit the required information to the Human Rights Committee.[57] China combined this strategy with moves to

[56] *SWB* FE/3011, G/1, 30 Aug. 1997; E/CN.4/Sub.2/1997/L.33, 28 Aug. 1997.
[57] See reports available from ClariNet News, from Agence France-Presse, 20–21 Nov. 1997. The first report after the handover attracted praise but also some criticism from

promote human rights discussions with individual governments and with the EU. Australia, Brazil, Canada, and the EU among others each signed memoranda of understanding on the holding of such dialogues over the course of 1997, even where in a number of cases such exchanges had been taking place intermittently since early in the 1990s. China's own human rights NGO, the China Society for Human Rights Studies, visited Norway, Sweden, Italy, and Spain in June, actually meeting in Oslo with representatives from AI. The terms of the dialogue, at least as reported by the head of China's delegation, Zhu Muzhi, could not have inspired much confidence, however. 'Noteworthy' questions discussed in reference to the condition of human rights in China included: 'Is China's rapid development a blessing or disaster to world peace and stability as well as international human rights? Is it beneficial for a prosperous China to provide a huge market and enormous job opportunities to the world . . . or is it beneficial for a weak and disintegrating China to become the source of millions of refugees?' Not much opportunity for answering in anything other than the affirmative here! This was hardly what was meant by a dialogue on human rights and must have been disappointing to China's dialogue partners. However, of more interest was Zhu's statement that his delegation had 'repeatedly quoted a Western saying, "All roads lead to Rome" ' one optimistic interpretation of which was that China's developmentalist rhetoric should not be taken to imply ineluctable difference of view with other governments or over the core human rights standards, but that China's evolutionary approach to the development of human rights protections would eventually lead it to embrace areas on which there was international consensus.[58]

Other statements in the second half of that year also suggested some forward movement, or at least a position less strident than the one articulated in the *Renmin Ribao* article in March (referred to earlier). The dialogue in Australia in August 1997 resulted in a joint statement reiterating the 'importance of the principle of the universality and indivisibility of human rights' and a recognition that 'respect for human rights is integral to sustainable development'. This statement seemed less of a fudge than the Sino-French one initialled earlier in May and, while it contained a reference to the 'different approaches and perspectives' with regard to human rights, it did not contain any strong cultural relativist or develop-

---

the Human Rights Committee, especially the implications for the independence of the judiciary arising from the Chief Executive's decision to refer an article of the Basic Law concerning right of abode for reinterpretation to the Standing Committee of the Chinese NPC. See *SWB* FE/3686, G/10–12, 8 Nov. 1999.

[58] *FBIS*-Chi-97-207, 26 July 1997.

mentalist rhetoric.[59] The occasion of the visit to Germany of Li Ruihuan (the head of the Chinese People's Political Consultative Conference) also in June 1997 provided a further opportunity for the Chinese government to illustrate the kind of language it would be prepared to use in an era of bilateral dialogues. Outlining 'China's three serious and consistent positions on human rights', Li stated that the country accepted that the 'universally accepted principles on human rights deserved respect and should be applied by all members of the international community'. He pointed to China's active participation in drafting a series of human rights documents and to its signature of seventeen international conventions. Secondly, Li stated that the universal principles had to be 'combined with the particular situations of different countries', a formulation that represented a less harsh way of presenting the relativist argument and one that was more open to interpretation. Finally, Li argued that implementing such principles was a course 'to ever pursue' because these principles were evolving and were being 'promoted to a higher stage'. In a reformulation of the 'all roads lead to Rome' approach, Li claimed that all countries were on this course, 'though their stages [were] different'. He added that, whatever point had been reached, all had the 'responsibility to enhance the level of human rights its people enjoyed.'[60]

THE CLINTON–JIANG SUMMIT

The Beijing government's less strident rhetoric also owed much to a desire to ensure the success of President Jiang Zemin's visit to the USA in October 1997. In order to reinforce the chances for success, on the eve of the visit, and in an unusual appearance before the foreign media, Jiang stated that he had given China's UN permanent representative permission to sign the ICESCR.[61] Human rights questions, of course, were one among many complex topics at this summit and had to compete for time, attention, and place with issues such as Taiwan, the trade imbalance, World Trade Organization (WTO) access, and export controls on weapons sales. There was also a brief to underline the two parties' broader, common

[59] *SWB* FE 3000, G/2, 18 Aug. 1997. However, Ann Kent has rightly criticized other aspects of this dialogue, since it did not contain an expert on China's human rights, had only one China specialist, produced no public report, and displayed little institutional memory, being unable to identify whether any progress had been made since the original human rights delegations of 1991 and 1992. See her *China, the United Nations, and Human Rights*, 200.   [60] *FBIS*-Chi-97-113, 12 June 1997.

[61] As of Feb. 2000, China had still not ratified the covenant.

interests in promoting global and regional security in its new and traditional aspects. However, the human rights angle was ever present, either
in the form of protest demonstrations, or during direct discussions with
the President and members of Congress, or as the focus of media and
NGO attention. Very often such occasions were used to promote particular causes, or were designed to draw attention to the plight of particular
individuals, such as Wei Jingsheng, Wang Dan, and others. But the
broader discursive debate between President Jiang and his interlocutors
was also of significance and acted to condition the visit in many important if less tangible ways. Before Jiang's arrival, Clinton had spelled out
what he saw as the key question for China: 'how to preserve stability, promote growth, and increase its influence in the world, while making room
for the debate and the dissent that are a part of the fabric of all truly free
and vibrant societies.' More specifically, and appealing to the central
goals that Chinese leaders had long sought, the US President argued that
'greater openness [was] profoundly in China's own interest. If welcome, it
will speed economic growth, enhance the world influence of China and
stabilize society.' He went on: 'Without the full freedom to think, question, to create, China will be at a distinct disadvantage, competing with
fully open societies in the Information Age where the greatest source of
national wealth is what resides in the human mind.'[62] This message— that
openness to new ideas was both the source of national wealth and that
membership as a 'full and strong partner in the community of nations'
required not just an increase in power but also an embrace of the democratic values of openness and political tolerance—was deliberately
designed to encourage a particular, Chinese, self-identity. Such language
marked this official meeting off from all previous summits held between
the two states. It was intended to bring home to the Chinese authorities
and people that the definition of a great power had changed by the late
twentieth century. That definition now included the understanding that
the attributes of power involved the acquisition of knowledge-based
skills, and a form of government based not on coercion, but on consent
as measured by an ability to tolerate alternative viewpoints.

As noted earlier, the Chinese government's opening move in this battle
over human rights during the summit had been to sign the ICESCR. In

---

[62] US Office of the Press Secretary, White House, 'Remarks by the President in Address
on China and the National Interest', 24 Oct. 1997. At the end of Dec., however, China
introduced new regulations to try to control the internet entitled 'Administrative Measures
for Ensuring the Security of Computer Information Technology, the Internet' and threatened criminal sanction for use of internet agencies. *Human Rights Watch World Report,
1999* (New York, Dec. 1998), 179.

addition, it adopted its more familiar, indirect tactic of publicizing its primary interest in economic and social rights, releasing a report as Jiang arrived at his first stop in Honolulu detailing China's successes in economic development, literacy levels, and health improvements.[63] As the Tibet question became the focus of discussion and of demonstrations, China's official news agency countered with stories of the 'fine environment' China had provided for the development of Tibetan Buddhism.[64] However, Jiang seemed to be aware that retreading this old ground was not going to satisfy the audiences he met in the USA, and he made use of less formal settings to project a more nuanced discussion of China's position on human rights, and perhaps to remind Americans that through their unwillingness to accede to the ICESCR they too were undermining arguments in favour of universality. In a speech before the Asia Society, while he repeated the official line that the full realization of rights rested on an evolutionary process, he also stated that 'collective and individual human rights, economic, social and cultural rights and civil and political rights are inseparable from one another'.[65] In his address at Harvard University he repeated this formulation in reference to China itself, pointing to the efforts made to build the PRC into a 'prosperous, strong, democratic and culturally advanced modern country'. Jiang's and Clinton's unprecedented press conference at the end of the official part of the visit, when the US President accused the Chinese government of being on the 'wrong side of history' in its approach to political dissent, not surprisingly saw a return to a more formulaic response on Jiang's part, with a stress on the 'specific national situation of different countries' as the main determinant of human rights.[66] Yet their communique, while it acknowledged 'major differences on the question of human rights', made reference to the positive role of the UDHR, and to the need for the two countries to start exchanges of legal experts, the training of judges and lawyers, the strengthening of legal information systems, and the exchange of legal materials.[67] Jiang also agreed that three religious leaders from the USA could visit China, including Tibet, a visit that took place over eighteen days in February 1998. Two weeks after the end of the summit, Wei Jingsheng was released from prison and went into exile in the USA.

The part of the communiqué referring to legal exchanges and training

---

[63] Clari.net news, United Press International (UPI), 27 Oct. 1997.

[64] Clari.net news, Reuters, 29 Oct. 1997.

[65] Excerpts from Jiang's speech to the Asia Society, 30 Oct. 1997, *China News Digest*, Reuters report, 31 Oct. 1997, item 3.   [66] *New York Times*, 30 Oct. 1997.

[67] United States Information Agency, Joint US–China Statement, 29 Oct. 1997. Note, however, that in Aug. 1997 Premier Li Peng had supported his Malaysian counterpart, Mahathir, in calling for a review of the Universal Declaration. *China News Digest*, 3 Aug. 1997.

signalled that the administration had decided that it also needed a long-term strategy designed to effect improvements in China's capacity to implement human rights. This understanding became known as the administration's 'rule of law initiative', an idea that the director of the Lawyers' Committee for Human Rights, Mike Posner, had been early in floating. Posner advised Clinton that his policy of engagement would lack a firm domestic base of support in the absence of a coherent and effective strategy for the promotion of internationally recognized human rights. He also suggested that efforts should be made to reinforce the position of Chinese legal reformers,[68] on the assumption that they either were playing or were likely to play in the future an influential role in bringing about legal change. Professor Paul Gewirtz's appointment as special adviser to the President on rule-of-law questions led to the elaboration of the initiative,[69] and to its prominence at the next Clinton–Jiang summit in Beijing in June 1998 and at the bilateral dialogues on human rights that were to begin shortly after the meeting between the two leaders in Washington. US policy was thus beginning to evolve. In sum, as the Washington director of Human Rights Watch/Asia, Mike Jendrzejczyk, recognized, it would now centre less on releases of individual activists and more on 'quiet diplomacy in regular high-level contacts and a long-term commitment to rule of law training'. Though he was not averse to this approach, his main worry was that, without any real pressure, the forward movement might slow.[70] This approach also favoured the activities of an NGO such as the Lawyers' Committee, which gave more emphasis to promoting knowledge of international human rights standards than to monitoring and publicizing specific cases of abuse.[71]

---

[68] For a discussion of this initiative and for an explanation of the significant role that this NGO plays in this area, see Korey, *NGOs*, Ch. 20 and esp. p. 507.

[69] There are six main elements to it, including commercial and administrative law reform, training of judges and lawyers, and establishing a legal information system. It has had funding difficulties, however, as Congress refused to donate monies towards it. The initiative has relied on such private foundations as Luce to get off the ground. Interview in Washington, Jan. 1999. This lack of official funding may well reinforce the Chinese sense that congressional criticism of its record is purely political in motive and not designed genuinely to bring about improvements in its levels of protection. Some in the US Congress believe they may be contributing to the prolongation of the CCP if they support such reform.   [70] Clari.net news, Agence France-Presse, 24 Nov. 1997.

[71] This perhaps explains the differing reactions to the holding of a bilateral human rights dialogue in Washington in January 1999, a short while after China had arrested and sentenced to prison terms political activists who had attempted to establish a political party. Amnesty and Human Rights Watch recommended that the meeting be called off, whereas the Lawyers' Committee favoured its going ahead.

THE UN'S THEMATIC MECHANISMS

Bilateral dialogues in the spirit of cooperation might have become *de rigueur* by 1997, but China had previously agreed to host a visit by the UN's Working Group on Arbitrary Detention. The formal, official visit took place in October 1997, the group travelling to Beijing, Chengdu, Lhasa, and Shanghai over the course of about ten days. Certainly, Beijing's agreement to host the Working Group might have exacted a higher price than some would have been willing to pay:[72] at its meeting in September 1996, the group had decided to wait until its visit to the country before investigating a number of non-urgent cases that had come before it, promising to renew its deliberations only if the visit did not go ahead as planned.[73] Nevertheless, the fact of its visit and the areas of concern listed in its subsequent report[74] indicated the difficulties for China in trying to sustain the argument that human rights fell into the arena of domestic and not international concern, and its claim that legal reforms had gone a long way to meeting the requirements of international standards.

While acknowledging the Chinese authorities' 'genuine efforts' to make the visit a success, made especially difficult as a result of the inflexibility and suspicion on the part of 'either subordinate or autonomous regions' officials', still the Working Group report pointed to a number of serious lapses in human rights protection. With respect to China's much-vaunted revised CL, for example, it described the concept of 'endangering national security' (the replacement for 'counter-revolutionary crimes') as 'imprecise' and applied 'to a broad range of offences'. It predicted that, without a clear definition, it would be subject to a 'serious risk of misuse'. The report also pointed to a 'crucial' absence of standards that would determine 'the quality of acts that might or could harm national security', a further failure that could result in the abuse of the law. Overall, it

[72] This was certainly the view of the NGO, Human Rights in China; see *From Principle to Pragmatism*, esp. 46–55.

[73] As the Working Group report put it: 'In view of the Working Group's projected visit to China in 1997 and the fact that consultations with the Chinese authorities to finalize the modalities of the visit are at an enhanced stage, the Working Group believes, pending formal confirmation of the projected visit by the Chinese authorities before the end of the fifty-third session of the Commission, that it would be appropriate to defer all deliberations regarding communications received by the Working Group. In the event that the expected formal confirmation is not received, the Working Group will forthwith deliberate on all pending matters. If, however, the formal confirmation is received, all pending matters will be further deferred until after the visit, during which more information could be gathered through contacts and consultations' (E/CN.4/1997/4, 17 Dec. 1996).

[74] This interesting twenty-seven-page 'Report submitted by the Working Group on Arbitrary Detention' can be found at E/CN.4/1998/44/Add.2, 22 Dec. 1997.

saw the new national security provisions as 'even broader than the "counter-revolutionary crimes" which, in name alone, have been abolished'. With regard to the revised CPL, although the Working Group recognized that things were moving in the right direction, it still recommended that the law should 'incorporate expressly' the presumption of innocence. Turning to the administrative sanction of RTL, the Working Group report noted that, in China itself, it was a controversial measure. Jurists, lawyers, and academics in contact with the UN delegation had expressed their concerns that a decision to place a person in administrative detention was taken with no judge present. In consequence, Chinese reformers had unsuccessfully recommended that the measure should be abolished, or, failing that, a 'system of strict judicial supervision . . . for regular monitoring' of the implementation of the measure introduced. Investigation of RTL led the Working Group to conclude that it would be arbitrary in circumstances where it was applied to those 'persons who disturbed the public order by peacefully exercising their fundamental freedoms guaranteed by the Universal Declaration of Human Rights . . . . and who were not prosecuted under the criminal law'. Controversially, it concluded that it would not necessarily be arbitrary in the case of common law offenders, because 'this system was accepted by Chinese society, including those to whom it was applied'. Although several Chinese academics expressed their regret that judges were not involved in the decision to detain offenders, and the group itself agreed that RTL should be decided 'under the a priori supervision of a judge', it was also clearly and probably unduly impressed by the distinction that offenders themselves made between administrative and criminal detention. This was so, 'especially in order to avoid the shameful effects attaching to a criminal sanction, which would appear in the criminal record'.[75]

In its conclusions, the Working Group noted the 'spirit of openness' in which the authorities had approached the visit, as indicated by the fact that interviews with prisoners were conducted 'without witnesses, in locations chosen at the last moment by the delegation, with only the United Nations interpreters present, even, in the case of Drapchi prison [Tibet], with detainees who were not common-law prisoners'.[76] However, the

---

[75] During interviews in the Centre for RTL in Shanghai, two detainees, in response to a query as to the point at which they had seen a judge, replied: 'Why would I see a judge? I am not a delinquent?' (E/CN.4/1998/44/Add.2, 22 Dec. 1997, 23).

[76] Unfortunately, after the visit to Drapchi, three inmates who had shouted slogans in support of the Dalai Lama had suffered beatings and extended prison sentences (despite assurances from Wang Guangya that they would not suffer as a result of their protests). Following up on the reports of these punishments, the Working Group found incredible the Chinese claim that the three had committed new offences, which had led a Chinese

report reiterated in its recommendations that the Chinese government undertake further revisions to its CL and CPL, as noted above, in particular expressing clearly in the latter a presumption of innocence, defining more precisely in the former the crime of endangering national security, and incorporating a statement that any person engaging in peaceful activity in the exercise of those rights guaranteed under the UDHR would not be regarded as a criminal. It also recommended that a judge be associated with the process connected with RTL, 'in order to obviate the possibility of any criticism that the present procedure is not entirely in conformity with international standards for a fair trial'.

These findings, and their exposure of the weaknesses at the heart of a number of Chinese claims with respect to its legal reforms, must have elicited some discomfort. Despite this, Chinese officials continued with policies that attracted far more media attention than the Working Group's report, and that also indicated some willingness to allow its domestic practices to come under UN scrutiny. The invitation, initially offered in February 1997 to the first High Commissioner for Human Rights, was extended to his successor, Mary Robinson, in January 1998. It took place in September and resulted in a Chinese reaffirmation of its pledge to sign the ICCPR with the specific date of 5 October, and the signature of a memorandum of intent to develop technical cooperation activities.[77] The extension of the invitation to Robinson, the delicate fruits of the Clinton–Jiang summit, China's signature of the ICESCR, the meetings in June 1997 and again in February 1998 between an ICRC delegation and Chinese officials, together with the agreement to allow US religious leaders and the UN Working Group on Arbitrary Detention

court to extend their sentences. This case and other instances of reprisals against prisoners (for example, after an EU delegation's visit in May 1998) are covered in the Working Group's report to the 55th session of the UN Commission on Human Rights. E/CN.4/1999/63, 18 Dec. 1998.

[77] *SWB* FE/3131, G/4, 22 Jan. 1998. That this visit was not solely used for establishing initial contacts, but contained some discussions of substance, seems clear from the press conference that Robinson held at the end of the trip. She reported that she had urged President Jiang to meet with the Dalai Lama before the end of this century, and that she had raised specific human rights cases, including the disappearance of the young Tibetan boy named by the Dalai Lama as the reincarnation of the Panchen Lama. She added that 'China has human rights problems, major problems', but that she had found a willingness to admit this among China's leaders. *International Herald Tribune*,16 Sept. 1998, and *China News Digest* reports, 14 Sept. and 17 Sept. 1998. One incident that brought home how much still remained to be done was the arrest and reported later beating of the wife of an imprisoned political prisoner, the arrests occurring in Robinson's hotel as the wife tried to deliver a letter to the High Commissioner. Mrs Robinson apparently called the Chinese Foreign Ministry to demand her release, which happened later that evening. See *International Herald Tribune*, 16 Sept. 1998. A Needs Assessment Mission from the office of the High Commissioner visited China in early spring of 1999.

into the country, formed a record of cooperation that persuaded governments wholeheartedly to implement their growing preference for what they had now invariably begun to call 'dialogue' over 'confrontation'. In the USA, the release in January 1998 of the 1997 annual country report on human rights practices in China reinforced this trend, at least within the executive branch. Unlike in 1996, in 1997 the report depicted China in a more optimistic light. While it acknowledged 'widespread and well-documented human rights abuses . . . stemming from the authorities' very limited tolerance of public dissent, fear of unrest, and the limited scope or inadequate implementation of laws protecting basic freedoms', it also noted 'some limited tolerance of public expressions of opposition to government policies and calls for political reform' and positive steps in the area of legal reform. In areas where China had been the target of particular international disapprobation, including cases of severe neglect in orphanages, the report recorded that China's Civil Affairs Ministry had announced that such institutions would be the government's major welfare priority in 1997 and some US $30 million was reportedly allocated for a programme of improvements.[78]

It was more or less a foregone conclusion, therefore, that there would not be a draft China resolution presented at the 1998 meeting of the UN Commission. Although, during a visit to Washington in early January 1998, Britain's Foreign Secretary—at a time when the UK held the presidency of the EU Council of Ministers—stated that neither the EU nor the USA had yet decided whether they should co-sponsor a draft resolution,[79] shortly afterwards the EU formally announced that it would not. The announcement pointed in particular to the 'encouraging results in

[78] US Deptartment of State, *China Country Report on Human Rights Practices*, (Internet edn., released 30 Jan. 1998). China's NGO, the China Society for Human Rights Studies, produced a lengthy critique of the report, among other matters, attacking the USA for setting itself up as the spokesperson for universality and yet not 'acknowledging economic, social and cultural rights as parts of the human rights in its constitution' (*SWB* FE/3166 S1/1–6, esp. 4).

[79] This seemed to unsettle the Beijing leadership to some extent. Robin Cook went on from Washington to Beijing for his first visit to the country as Foreign Secretary and there had confirmed that the UN High Commissioner for Human Rights would be invited to visit the country. Also in Jan., Chinese officials revealed that in a letter to the UN Secretary General, President Jiang had stated that Beijing 'would seriously consider the question of acceding to the International Covenant on Civil and Political Rights' and would give support to UN activities marking the 50th Anniversary of the UDHR. Economic inducements were also a part of China's strategy, Feb. witnessing the visit of Premier Li Peng to two of the states that had co-sponsored the resolution in 1997, Luxembourg and the Netherlands. While in Holland, Li signed what Chinese sources described as the 'largest ever Sino-foreign joint venture'. *Independent*, 19 Jan. 1998 and 20 Jan. 1998; *SWB* FE/3127, G/1, 17 Jan. 1998; 'Premier Li Peng's Visit to Luxembourg, the Netherlands and Russia: Successful', Chinese Embassy, London, 23 Feb. 1998.

the EU–China human rights dialogue', the invitation to Robinson, and the release of Wei Jingsheng.[80] As Andrew Clapham has noted, it was ironic (or disturbing to use his word) that 'the first time the Council formalized its position with regard to an impending country resolution at the UN, it was to announce that the Union would not be acting, and nor would its Member States'.[81] At the UN Commission meeting itself, the EU representative, Tony Lloyd, outlined the nature of the EU–China dialogue on human rights, stating that it comprised concerns about certain individuals, Chinese authorities' use of the death penalty, and the suppression of religious and cultural freedoms. He noted too the programme of practical cooperation that had been agreed, referring specifically to areas such as the judicial system. Finally, he promised that the EU would keep the situation 'under close review in the light of progress in the Dialogue and developments on the ground, including China's cooperation with the UN human rights system'.[82]

Although gratified at this EU and Japanese agreement not to co-sponsor in 1998,[83] the Chinese realized that it was imperative to get the USA to follow suit. It therefore decided to move from 'seriously considering' signature of the ICCPR, to announcing on 12 March its willingness to sign the covenant. A day later, the Clinton administration reported that it would not pursue the UN Commission resolution, citing this decision, the freeing of Wei, and expectations of the release of other high-profile dissidents such as Wang Dan as the main reasons for the change in tactics. Washington also revealed that at the October 1997 summit the administration had made clear to Chinese officials that they would trade

---

[80] Associated Press report, 23 Feb. 1998; *SWB* FE/3161, G/1, 26 Feb. 1998. Further clues to the basis of EU Commission thinking were contained in European Commission, *Building a Comprehensive Partnership with China* (COM (98)0181, Brussels, 25 Mar. 1998), and adopted by Council on 29 June 1998. Its objectives range from integrating China more fully into international society, including the world economy, to support for China's transition to a more open political system based on the rule of law and respect for human rights. The Commission also announced the development of an ECU13.2million programme of legal and judicial cooperation.

[81] Clapham, 'Human Rights in the Common Foreign Policy', 647. On 23 Feb. 1998 the Council 'agreed that neither the Presidency nor Member States should table or co-sponsor a draft Resolution at the next UN Commission on Human Rights'. Clapham reports that the word 'should' rather than 'would' was deliberately chosen on the insistence of one government, which wished to leave open the possibility of future action (p. 647).

[82] Speech on behalf of the UK Presidency of the EU to the UN Commission on Human Rights, Geneva, 17 Mar. 1998, press release.

[83] Japan's delegate at the UN Commission stated: 'We do not hesitate to evaluate positively, particularly this year, that dialogues on human rights with China have progressed' (Ambassador Nobutoshi Akao, quoted in Nazali Ghanea-Hercock, 'Appendix I: A Review of the 54th Session of the Commission on Human Rights', *Netherlands Quarterly of Human Rights*, 16/3, (1998), 407).

co-sponsorship of the human rights motion if China would release prominent dissidents, sign the two UN covenants, and resume a dialogue with the ICRC on prison visits.[84] By March 1998 all three conditions were close enough to being fulfilled for the US administration to decide to pull back, despite the Senate and House passing non-binding resolutions urging the executive branch not to give up on the UN route. Some ten US human rights organizations also wrote to Clinton arguing that China would not have made even these minimal concessions if there had not been the prospect of a further resolution at the UN Commission.[85] US Ambassador, Bill Richardson made a tough speech at the Commission meeting pointing to repeated violations in China of the rights guaranteed in the ICCPR, but there was no resolution.[86] This form of multilateral pressure, therefore, had finally ended, leaving the bilateral dialogues, bilateral diplomacy, the work of the NGOs, Special Rapporteurs, and Working Groups, together with the intermittent requirements of reporting for those states that had ratified the main international human rights covenants and treaties, as the main international means of promoting human rights norms in China.

CONCLUSION

Over the period 1995–8, China's main objectives in the human rights area had been to shift the venue of the discursive debate on its record away from a public, multilateral forum in which China was placed under critical scrutiny, to a private dialogue that symbolized a more equal exchange of views on such questions. Beijing also attempted to constrain the operations of the UN Commission, its Special Rapporteurs, and Working Groups by stressing their failure to deal with lapses in the protection of economic, social, and cultural rights, and their overweening focus on developing country behaviour. It also alleged that the Commission's approach was unacceptably confrontational and unlikely to reach the targets that it set itself. Possibly in response to this critique, new Special

---

[84] *Washington Post*, 14 Mar. 1998; *International Herald Tribune*, 14–15 Mar. 1998.

[85] Tessitore and Woolfson (eds.), *Issues before the 53rd General Assembly*, 176.

[86] Ibid. 179. Wei Jingsheng spoke at the Commission as a representative of the International League for Human Rights. He said: 'Last year, when the Commission failed to adopt a resolution on China, my prison guards laughed at me and said: "Look at your so-called friends. They betrayed you".' It was precisely at this time, when the Chinese were on their long, non-violent path to human rights and democracy, that 'support from our friends is most needed', he stated. Quoted in ibid.

Rapporteurs were created and the High Commissioner for Human Rights deemed it necessary to give more priority to the right to development,[87] suggesting that others saw merit in Chinese complaints.

In the course of moving towards bilateral dialogues it became apparent that there were areas of softness in some governments' commitment to universalism and that ambiguities inherent in the language surrounding human rights could be exploited. This suggested considerable room for manoeuvre within the international human rights regime when it came to verbal compliance. The slowness of the whole procedure connected with the promotion of human rights—whether that was the arranging of visits, the signing of agreements, the distance between signature of the conventions and their ratification—similarly demonstrated its relatively undemanding nature. Only when the UN Commission was due to deliberate on country resolutions, or when key foreign policy objectives—such as summits with the US President—were at stake, would China make important, visible, and verbal concessions to the regime. Over this period, the Chinese leadership released its most prominent political dissident, signed the two UN covenants, and allowed a UN Working Group and the UN High Commissioner for Human Rights into the country. It also pushed forward with its legal reforms and moved swiftly to address certain areas of particular international concern, including the egregious neglect of children in state orphanages.

Chinese leaders played their hand carefully and with considerable skill, timing statements, agreements, and releases to coincide with debate at the UN Commission especially among the Western group about whether to sponsor a draft condemnatory resolution. On many occasions Beijing promised future adherence to aspects of the international human rights regime and to a number of different interlocutors. Such tactics had the effect of splitting the Western bloc in 1997 and removing completely the threat of a UN draft resolution in 1998. This approach demonstrated the extent to which Chinese leaders saw this process as a bargaining strategy rather than as a series of policy changes that had certain intrinsic merit. However, it also demonstrated indisputably the power of this non-coercive shaming process as well as the utility of the institutions that had provided the platform from which to shame, to effect change in China's behaviour, and to offer compromise in its strict interpretation of state sovereignty.

China's success in persuading some Western leaders to adopt particular features of the cultural relativist–developmentalist rhetoric in joint

---

[87] Robinson 'reminds audiences regularly that she sees the right to development "as a synthesis of civil and political and economic, social and cultural rights" '. Her office, therefore, has expanded its links with the UN's development agencies. See ibid. 168.

statements can be explained by these governments' desire to smooth the path of visits that had several economic and strategic interests to satisfy, together with a more generalized EU belief that it had to raise its profile in China, or risk being left behind the other major industrialized states. Other states found convincing Chinese official arguments that it was deserving of special consideration. Its demographic make-up, economic development objectives, and past traditions were used to support the arguments in favour of its uniqueness.[88] Yet Beijing too, especially in the less-scripted meetings, realized that too great a stress on a cultural relativist position was becoming counter-productive, and thus it moved somewhat closer to acknowledging the universal features of human rights. It became more difficult, therefore, to decide whether its developmentalist rhetoric was being used as a means of promoting the view that China's human rights protections would always and inevitably come into conflict with those outlined in the international covenants, or whether Beijing was striving by means appropriate to its national conditions to reach certain recognized international standards, a commitment that deserved support and recognition that it would be a long-term process.

A number of governments might well have desired to give primary emphasis to areas of their relationship with Beijing other than human rights, but few found they were able to move away from the topic entirely. Those that in the past had been active in promoting the UN route all felt obliged to activate or reactivate bilateral dialogues on human rights. Such dialogues often included practical cooperation and information exchanges in the legal field. The USA chose such a route but coupled this emphasis on promoting long-term change in China with an appeal to Chinese nationalists: if they truly sought a China that would be recognized as a great power, then they had to accept that those attributes included an ability to absorb information and ideas and to find a means of dealing consensually with the unsettling or destabilizing effects such ideas could bring in their wake. It was a theme that was to reappear during Clinton's visit to Beijing in June 1998, and played on Chinese ambivalence about whether it represented the developing world, as it frequently tried to suggest at UN venues dealing with human rights, or was a great power intent on seeking full membership in international society. US potent speeches of that kind, together with NGO actions, represented the main public ways of keeping the attention on China's human rights record. Together with the recommendations of the UN Special Rapporteurs and

---

[88] We have seen how, in the past, US administrations had been willing to accept cultural relativism when it came to China, especially during the Reagan period (see chapter 4 above).

Working Groups, they were probably the best means by which the global community could ensure forward movement in the short to medium term. The dialogues were directed to the long-term prospects, which was their primary weakness in a world where evidence of everyday abuse could no longer be hidden.[89]

[89] Some countries in the EU seemed to recognize this weakness in the dialogue policy, informing China in early 1998 that a 'dialogue without results will soon run out of steam and will not be acceptable to public opinion in Europe' (quoted in *Human Rights Watch World Report 1999* (New York, 1998), 182).

8

Betting on the Long Term, 1998–1999

Concern for reputation and image shaped aspects of the discourse and behaviour of many states involved in the struggle over human rights in China, and pointedly so in the last years of the 1990s. In 1997 and 1998, Japan and the Western governments' decision to eschew the UN route was taken in the realization that they had to have something to replace the annual condemnatory resolutions, or risk being confronted by charges of hypocrisy and a challenge to their self-identity as democracies. States such as Brazil, newly committed to the advancement of human rights in its own country, and mindful of the desire internationally to provide credence to this new stance, also initiated a bilateral dialogue on human rights with China, in exchange for a return to an abstention on the vote at the annual gathering in Geneva. Beijing devoted large-scale diplomatic resources in order to line up allies at the UN, but that strategy also included attempts to project itself as a state that took the international human rights regime seriously. The Chinese leadership's desire to follow the successful summit in Washington in October 1997 with a similar success in Beijing in 1998 also prompted further domestic political loosening and some burnishing of its image, providing welcome political space for Chinese from various strata to test the boundaries of what came to be interpreted as a new period of political liberalization. The external aspects of the human rights issue thus served to empower local human rights activists, and to strengthen their links with the transnational human rights community.[1]

All governments involved in this human rights struggle could claim certain policy successes by 1998: for the democracies, there was the

---

[1] In this sense, therefore, the Chinese case fits reasonably well with the spiral model outlined in Risse *et al.* (eds.) *The Power of Human Rights* esp. 25–6, and the phase they label phase 3, 'tactical concessions'. One rather special external monitoring group, 'Information Centre of Human Rights and Democratic Movement in China' based in Hong Kong has been a vital source of information about human rights abuse in China. That group pays for faxes sent from any part of China that report abuse, information that in turn is then passed onto the international media.

release of a few Chinese dissidents, a visit to China by the UN High Commissioner for Human Rights, some reinforcement of the language of universality of rights and—most gratifying of all—China's signature of the ICCPR. In addition, they could also point to the starting or restarting of dialogues, and their associated training and cooperation activities which showed something tangible was happening—of some value as a shield when NGOs, the media, legislatures and others demanded to know what efforts were being made to improve the Chinese record. On Beijing's part, its efforts to publicize the new legal codes and punish those who failed to observe the legal changes demonstrated a willingness to tackle the mammoth problems associated with implementation. Additionally, it could reassure the more nationalist elements among its domestic public that UN condemnation would now cease,[2] and that it would be engaged in mutual, more respectful, exchanges on human rights with its international counterparts. The Chinese leadership also appeared to have had some success in convincing various international actors of the need to correct the supposed imbalance in attention to civil and political rights, to one that focused more on the right to development and economic, social, and cultural rights.

The fragility of this process was demonstrated far sooner than any had predicted, however, with a distinct chill in the Chinese political climate emerging by the end of 1998. Many Chinese, mostly academics, did continue to publish and debate various aspects of the law and human rights and use international standards as a basis for their arguments.[3] But more organized challenges, including calls for multiparty democracy, or recognition for certain social and religious groups, were swiftly clamped down upon, especially in a year of anniversaries that encouraged reflection on the Party's record.[4] These repressive acts exposed the shallowness of the roots of the new legal codes, the narrow limits of political tolerance, and the relative lack of importance that the state attached to human rights protection when Party control was at stake. They also uncovered the weaknesses in the bilateral dialogue route, and their accompanying

[2] According to an article in the newspaper *Wen Wei Po* a poll among university students in Beijing showed that about four out of five of them greatly resented foreign censure of China over its human rights record, but a nearly equal number (74.1%) believed it essential to point out that certain human rights problems exist in China, relating to corruption, failure to enforce the law, tendency to make use of special privileges, and power for criminal ends. See *SWB* FE/3525 G/7–8, 4 May 1999.

[3] For one among a number of examples see Zhao Jianwen, 'Guoji Renquan Fa de Jishi' [Universal Declaration of Human Rights], *Faxue Yanjiu*, 121 (Mar. 1999), 93–107.

[4] The eightieth anniversary of the 4 May student nationalist uprising; the tenth anniversary of the Tiananmen bloodshed; the fiftieth anniversary of the PRC; and the fortieth anniversary of the rebellion in Tibet.

activities, because these were geared to the idea of promoting long-term change in China, and did not provide much opportunity to register disapproval of sudden instances of enhanced political repression. Moreover, NGO and other evaluations of those dialogues and of the new Chinese legislation in areas that affected human rights protections became more widely disseminated, and probably were taken more notice of at a time of diminishing optimism about the prospects for China's political reform. Thus, calls for tangible results from the dialogues inevitably heightened at the time of China's crackdown, leading to references to the need for benchmarks to mark progress and to the possible negative repercussions from the disappointed expectations of Western public opinion.

Yet any concrete moves to respond directly to the political oppression via a condemnatory resolution at the UN Commission—the obvious point on the human rights timetable at which to do this, and one that could demonstrate a connection between Chinese actions and international disapproval of those actions—provoked a Chinese threat to break off the bilateral dialogues. And indeed China did break off its dialogue with the USA, partly as a result of Washington's decision to co-sponsor (with Poland only) a resolution at the 1999 meeting of the UN Commission and more overtly as a consequence of the accidental NATO bombing of the Chinese embassy in Belgrade. The cooling in relations with the USA for a large part of 1999 occurred as a result of the UN resolution, the failure to resolve the WTO entry issue during the course of Premier Zhu Rongji's visit to Washington in April, and the bypassing of the UN Security Council as a result of China's known disapproval of international intervention in Kosovo.[5] NATO bombing of the province at the time of President Jiang Zemin's tour of Europe, together with the Belgrade embassy incident in May, led to a resurgence of Chinese rhetoric against the hegemonic USA, interfering in the internal affairs of sovereign states on the specious grounds of a norm of humanitarian intervention. The dangers of weakened norms of state sovereignty and territorial integrity in favour of supporting international human rights seemed all too clear to Beijing, and those dangers, together with the nationalist emotions that the NATO bombing evoked among many Chinese, placed new obstacles in the path of those seeking to disseminate human rights ideas in China.[6]

[5] There were, in fact, a seemingly neverending stream of contentious issues between the two states, including USA arms sales to Taiwan, continuing alarms over Theatre Missile Defense, accusations of Chinese stealing of nuclear weapons' production secrets, and so on. China's negotiations with the US over WTO entry were finally successfully concluded in mid-November 1999, prior to consideration by Congress.

[6] Clinton's treatment of Premier Zhu Rongji over the WTO issue during the latter's visit to the USA in Apr. 1999 further stoked this nationalist resentment.

A BEIJING SPRING?

Optimistically interpreted, President Jiang Zemin's report to the 15th Party Congress in September 1997 could be read by those in China committed to political and legal reform as signalling cautious progress in these areas, perhaps heralding a Beijing spring.[7] Jiang described the main tasks of political reform as to 'develop democracy, strengthen the legal system, separate government functions from enterprise management, streamline government organs, improve the democratic supervision system, and maintain stability and unity'. He placed great emphasis on ruling the country by law to allow for China's 'socialist democracy' gradually to be 'institutionalized and codified so that such institutions and laws will not change with changes in the leadership or changes in the views or focus of attention of any leader'. Rule by law was the Party's 'basic strategy . . . in leading the people in running the country', was necessary for the running of a socialist market economy, 'an important hallmark of social and cultural progress, and a vital guarantee for . . . lasting political stability'.[8] There was much additional evidence in 1997 and early 1998 of renewed efforts to promote concepts of legality, including the publication of a series of books comprising statistics on the numbers of people tortured to death while in police custody, in an attempt to improve police practices and promote their knowledge of changes in China's CL and CPL.[9]

The idea of increasing democratic accountability similarly received something of a boost. The newly assertive NPC, which in the 1990s had voted in significant numbers to censure the annual reports of the Supreme Court and Supreme Procurator, further illustrated a modest move towards independence in March 1998, with 10 per cent of delegates voting against or abstaining in the election of former Premier Li Peng as Chair of the NPC. The Procurator-General fared far worse than Li, with only 65 per cent of deputies in support of his nomination, and 40 per cent

[7] I take this heading from the title of an article in the *Far Eastern Economic Review* of 2 Apr. 1998. On 14 Jan. 1999 the magazine published an article entitled 'Beijing Chill', which reported the crackdown on dissidents, but argued there was no wholesale retreat from reform.

[8] Jiang Zemin, 'Report Delivered at the 15th National Congress, 12 Sept. 1997', in *Beijing Review*, 6–12 Oct. 1997, esp. 24–5.

[9] One was entitled 'The Law against Extorting a Confession by Torture'. Information about these books became more widely available in the West through a *Washington Post* report, 29 June 1998, the time of Clinton's visit to China. These books and other instances of Chinese official attempts to disseminate information about its developing legal framework received extensive mention in the US Department of State's Human Rights reports on China in 1997 and 1998.

rejected the report of the Supreme People's Procuratorate.[10] Regional
officials would sometimes seek to take the Party leadership at its word,
one in an article in April, using the language of the Party, and taking
cover under one of the statements Jiang had made at the 15th Party
Congress. The Chinese President had called for an 'atmosphere of democratic discussion' as a way of improving Party policy. The Yunnan official
supported this call and argued that, if the Party made mistakes, 'then
party members should dare to speak the truth'. He warned, 'carrying out
a patriarchal system and suppressing democracy certainly will create a
lifeless atmosphere and create a serious ideological deadlock and
stagnation'.[11]

Scholars in positions of some authority also took advantage of a
period of relative liberalization to advocate the need for enhanced democracy and the protection of human rights, together with a strengthening of
judicial independence. Li Shenzhi, retired head of the American Studies
Institute at the Chinese Academy of Social Sciences (CASS), in *Gaige
(Reform Magazine)* challenged directly the notion that human rights
priorities related mainly to subsistence, calling instead for the adoption of
international standards. In his view, true citizenship required political and
civil rights. Countering the cultural relativist argument, Li stated that
early twentieth-century political discussion in China indicated that the
concept of universal human rights was already a part of the country's
history and culture. Sheng Dewen was particularly adamant about the
need for reforms: 'total political control by a single party is out of step
with modern reality, and it will have to change.' Competition in the
economic area had to be extended to the political field as well, he added.

---

[10] Criticisms voiced included: 'the police bend the law for their own purposes'; 'the legal
authorities think twice when clamping down on high Party Officials ignoring the law'; 'the
courts render severe decisions for minor crimes, but light decisions on serious matters'; and
'the judges and prosecutors close their eyes to injustice to protect local interests' (quoted
in Yoshifumi Nakai (ed)., *China's Roadmap as Seen in the 15th Party Congress* (Tokyo:
Institute of Developing Economies, Mar. 1998), 63). See also Kent, *China, the United
Nations, and Human Rights,* 228, and Minxin Pei, 'Is China Democratizing?', *Foreign
Affairs,* 77/1 (Jan–Feb. 1998), 75.
[11] *Sixiang Zhengzhi Gongzuo Yanjiu* [Research into Thinking on Government Work] is
a centrally sponsored monthly journal. Translation of article in *SWB*, FE/3269 G/6, 3 July
1998. Fang Xue, another provincial reform official who entered into business, distributed a
proposal for political reform in November 1997 that included adoption of a system of
checks and balances and direct elections. Sadly, Fang fell foul of the authorities in July
1998, and was arrested on charges of embezzlement and illegal business activities. He was
eventually given a four-year sentence, but his trial had first been postponed because it was
scheduled to begin the day that Premier Zhu Rongji began his visit to the USA. US intervention probably led to this postponement. See Goldman, 'Politically-Engaged Intellectuals
in the 1990s', 706; *China Rights Forum* (the Journal of Human Rights in China), (Fall
1999), 58. Argument also based on discussions in Beijing, Sept. 1999.

Pointing directly to one of the crucial weaknesses of the post-Deng leadership, he noted: 'The new leaders didn't fight for power the way the revolutionaries did, and people do not believe that they have an automatic right to have it. People ask: "Why do these people deserve all the power?"' Others concentrated on the need for genuine separation of state and judiciary: Liu Hainian in exploring the concept of ruling a country in accordance with law stressed that an independent judiciary and acceptance that the judgment of the court was final were both crucial.[12] Many of those interested in the promotion of human rights and wider political reform knew they had increased political space, at least until the Clinton –Jiang summit in Beijing was over, and possibly longer given the government's intention to sign the ICCPR and to celebrate the fiftieth anniversary of the UDHR in December 1998. Thus, for a time the authorities even tolerated the attempts made in late summer by those outside the intellectual establishment to register an opposition party.[13]

The presidential summit in Beijing was remarkable only for its human rights aspects: the broadcast of Clinton's speech to students at Beijing university—an agreement reached before the visit went ahead—and the unexpected broadcast of a press conference between Jiang and Clinton at the Great Hall of the People, to one side of Tiananmen Square. Jiang's acquiescence to the airing of the speech at China's premier university came in exchange for Clinton's agreement to move his trip forward from November to June 1998. The unexpected decision to be more open still and to broadcast the press conference may well have stemmed from the Chinese President's newfound confidence borne out of his successful weathering of the post-Deng era, the relative smoothness of his trip to the USA in the autumn of 1997, and from a desire to reward the US decision not to sponsor an anti-Chinese resolution at the UN Commission in March 1998.[14] One result was that, overnight, American reportage of the summit, including the controversial welcoming ceremonies at Tiananmen, changed from negative to positive. Prior to that visit, some 160 Republican members of Congress had urged Clinton to postpone the trip or not take part in ceremonies in the Square. To make matters worse, during its early stages in Xian and other cities on the itinerary, several dissidents were detained, leading the National Security Adviser, Sandy Berger, to

---

[12] On Li, see *Far Eastern Economic Review*, 2 Apr. 1998, 21, and Goldman, 'Politically-Engaged Intellectuals in the 1990s', 706. Sheng Dewen's statement was made in Mar. 1998 and was picked up by the *Daily Telegraph* (quoted in Kent, *China, the United Nations, and Human Rights*, 219); Liu Hainian, 'Yi Fa Zhi Guo Yu Jingshen Wenming Jianshe'[Rule of Law and Cultural and Ideological Progress], *Faxue Yanjiu*, 112 (Sept. 1997), 56–66.

[13] *Far Eastern Economic Review* 1 Oct. 1998, 26.

[14] Suggested in discussions with Chinese scholars in Beijing, Sept. 1999. Clinton also answered questions from listeners to a local call-in radio programme in Shanghai.

state, 'people are not debris to be swept up . . . I think China's human rights record is terrible'.[15] The press conference in Beijing gave Clinton an opportunity to regain the initiative and fend off his critics, and for the Chinese leadership to improve its image in the world's media. The US President thus condemned the 1989 events, stating firmly that he believed, as did the American people, 'that the use of force and tragic loss of life was wrong'. Jiang gave the standard reply, arguing that resolute measures in 1989 were necessary to ensure the future stability of the country, and responding robustly to points raised about Tibet, religious freedom, and the like. Although there were no tangible linguistic breakthroughs detectable in Jiang's responses on this occasion, the public debate was still a signal moment, and, as Dai Qing, the Chinese environmental activist, noted, 'something very rare. Nine years after 1989, this is the first time millions of Chinese had heard someone, even though it was a foreigner, say something like this about Tiananmen. It shows that the whole world, not just we Chinese, has not forgotten what happened. It lifted a weight from my heart to hear it.'[16]

The Beijing university speech provided another occasion for Clinton to repeat what had now become standard fare in his administration's discursive approach towards the Chinese: the argument that personal freedom was a necessary element of human and economic development, and that it was profoundly in the interest of all for 'young Chinese minds [to] be free to reach the fullness of their potential'.[17] The trip was also designed to emphasize the US administration's interest in and support for China's law reform, with an agreement to move ahead more quickly on Paul Gewirtz's 'rule-of-law' initiative, to revive the bilateral dialogues on human rights suspended in 1995, and to establish a non-governmental human rights forum.[18] At the end of the year, a legal seminar held at

[15] Mann, *About Face*, 365–6.

[16] Quoted in Kent, *China, the United Nations, and Human Rights*, 201.

[17] *New York Times*, 29 June 1998. Unfortunately, Clinton's remarks might not have had the effect intended on those who heard only the Chinese translation. According to a BBC monitoring report, the simultaneous translation into Chinese (provided by the US embassy) was 'poor with numerous grammatical errors and incomplete sentence structure'. This led the China Central Television Programme to announce at the end of its coverage: 'Perhaps because of their language expression, which is different from ours, some of the translations were not quite comprehensible. It seems that there is a need for the USA to understand China better. And this perhaps should start from the language' *CSWB* FE/3266 G/5–11, 30 June 1998). In a carefully reasoned speech on the eve of Premier Zhu Rongji's visit to Washington in Apr. 1999, Clinton repeated his argument: 'Because wealth is generated by ideas today, China will be less likely to succeed if its people cannot exchange information freely.' The 7 April speech was produced as a North East Asia Peace and Security Network (NAPSNET) special report on 8 Apr. 1999.

[18] See op-ed piece by Anthony Lewis, *New York Times*, 6 July 1998, for further details, and *Beijing Review*'s detailed report of the summit, 20–26 July 1998. Lewis quoted

Airlie House formed the first fruits of the renewed dialogue. There, a gathering of US and Chinese officials, scholars from the CASS Law Institute, and the major Chinese and American university law departments, together with members of US NGOs, such as the Lawyers' Committee, presented in pairs papers that explored the relationship between international and domestic law and the protection of human rights.[19] Harold Hongju Koh, the Assistant Secretary of State at DRL, later characterized the administration's approach overall as an 'outside-inside' human rights strategy: bringing US influence to bear on China from outside the country via the various means Washington had at its disposal, and combining it with activities designed to promote internal reform, such as training of judges and other law-enforcement personnel.[20]

Thus, once again, the human rights dimension at the summit proved to be significant in determining its success, especially in the US media. The human rights statements in Beijing contributed substantially—for a time—to a shift in emphasis in the reporting of China in a more positive direction, depicting it as a country with serious problems but one that was trying to overcome them and already had made some progress. The fact of Mary Robinson's visit in September—if not the actual events that took place during it—and then China's signing of the ICCPR in October further promoted this image. As noted in Chapter 7, dissidents were swept up on the eve of the High Commissioner's visit and she did not achieve her goal of meeting the Panchen Lama, the 9-year-old boy recognized by the Dalai Lama but not by Beijing. However, she at least managed to gain China's signature to a Memorandum of Intent in which

Clinton's reference in his Beijing University speech to the relationship between freedom and stability, noting that it had taken a long time for Americans to understand that the protection of the right to dissent could strengthen societal stability. During the Clinton visit, Hillary Rodman Clinton, Paul Gewirtz, and Secretary of State Albright also visited a women's legal aid centre affiliated with Beijing University's Law School and financed by the Ford Foundation.

[19] 'US–China Symposium on the Legal Protection of Human Rights', 11–13 Dec. 1998. Sessions covered 'The Protection of Human Rights through International Covenants and National Legislation', 'The Reform of Criminal Law and Human Rights Protection', and 'The Legal Protection of Religious Freedom' (agenda in possession of author). The Canadian government held a similar symposium in Mar. 1998 in Vancouver with the theme 'Legal Issues Related to Human Rights in a Civil Society'. One innovation of note is that the Canadians designed this as a 'plurilateral dialogue', as they termed it: it involved some forty mid-level bureaucrats from such Asian countries as Indonesia, Pakistan, Japan, and Mongolia, as well as the Australasians and Norwegians. See Human Rights in China, *From Principle to Pragmatism*, 26.

[20] Koh, US Department of State, 'On-the-Record briefing on US–China Human Rights Dialogue', Washington, 13 Jan. 1999, Internet edn. Or as he put it on a later occasion, combining the 'strategies of internal persuasion with tools of external sanction' ('Promoting Human Rights in the Pursuit of Peace', 12, internet edition.)

Beijing went on record to affirm that: 'As the Chinese Government is committed to the full realization of economic, social, cultural, civil and political rights as well as the right to development, the Government intends to make use of advisory services and technical cooperation and will identify specific cooperation programs.'

Language that gave equal priority to rights specified in both human rights covenants appeared more frequently (although never consistently) in official Chinese statements in 1998. China's deputy UN envoy at the ECOSOC meeting in July, held to conduct a five-year review of the Vienna Declaration, for example, together with the head of China's observer delegation to the UN Sub-Commission meeting in August, both used the phrase that, while 'political and civil rights [were] important . . . the social, economic and cultural rights and the right to development [were] just as important'.[21] At an international symposium to commemorate the fiftieth anniversary of the UDHR (the first time China had hosted an international human rights conference), Vice Premier and former Foreign Minister Qian Qichen described human rights as 'mutually dependent and related' and called on the international community to 'attach equal importance to each and every one of them'.[22] The Chinese government's strong criticism of the Indonesian government for its failure in May 1998 to 'safeguard the personal safety and legitimate rights and interests of the ethnic Chinese and Chinese nationals', and call severely to 'punish those held accountable'[23] appeared to reinforce Beijing's understanding of the value of the internationalist aspects of the

---

[21] *SWB* FE/3287 G/3–4, 24 July 1998; FE/3302 G/2–3, 11 Aug. 1998.

[22] Although referring to interdependence among rights and the universality of rights, Qian did, however, also say that war was responsible for the most gross violations, that poverty was the 'main impediment' to realizing human rights, and that Asian countries 'value collective human rights and the obligations to the family and society'. In these respects, he seemed to be trying to appeal to a variety of domestic and international audiences — a further indication that the human rights discourse was quite unstable. See *Beijing Review*, 16–22 November 1998, and *SWB* FE/3364 G/4–6, 22 Oct. 1998.

[23] See the Chinese Foreign Minister's press statement as outlined in *Beijing Review*, 24–30 Aug. 1998. An article in the same issue by Ren Xin pointed to the valuable role of the world's media and some human rights organizations in exposing the brutality towards the ethnic Chinese. It also argued that effective action by the Indonesian authorities would be 'helpful in regaining [Jakarta's] reputation in the international community' (p. 7). Chinese had been demonstrating outside the Indonesian embassy in Beijing. The extent to which these protests prompted the Chinese government to make public its criticisms directed at Jakarta can only be conjectured. Admittedly, China had issued similar protests against the Thai government in 1958 on behalf of the ethnic Chinese (see Chapter 4 above for details). However, protests then neither received the same level of attention as those forty years later; nor did they gain any reinforcement or particular meaning from either a domestic or an international discourse on human rights.

human rights regime and the inappropriateness of a non-interference approach when such violations took place.

An air of optimism also seemed to pervade the bilateral dialogues on human rights for most of 1998. These had something of the aura of a fresh start in relations between the Chinese government and some of its Western governmental critics.[24] The dialogues were frequently accompanied by the establishment of programmes designed to strengthen the rule of law, provide training courses, and offer study tours and exchanges in the field of human rights. There were also projects that dealt with minority and women's rights. Combined with the high-level diplomatic exchanges and symposia, they both were a means of responding to criticism of governmental failure to sanction China for its record and satisfied a desire among many Western officials to do something concrete in a country where much needed to be done.[25] Such programmes, of course, were directed to bringing about improvements over the long term, as were the dialogues themselves. These involved high-level governmental officials in a process that required time in order for there to be the development of mutual trust, a deepening of the discussion, and then the production of something that could be identified as progress.[26] As such, the dialogues and cooperation programmes were vulnerable to changes in political mood in Beijing and to the impatience of the world's media and human rights NGOs, who were suspicious of the lack of transparency and accountability associated with many of the exchanges, and had a sense that

[24] Many were held in 1997 and 1998, including with Australia, Brazil, Britain, Canada, the EU, Japan, Norway, and Sweden. The one held in London during Britain's holding of the EU Presidency in May 1998 included debate on minority issues, freedom of religion, and the death penalty, together with a visit to a UK prison and a discussion of community policing methods and non-custodial sentencing with the Bristol force. The Chinese delegation also sat through court proceedings. Discussions at Foreign and Commonwealth Office, London, June 1998, and subsequent written communication, Nov. 1999.

[25] The EU training programme, for example, which is separate from the EU–China human rights dialogue, includes training each year for about twenty-five judges, prosecutors, and lawyers in different EU countries, and annual study trips to Europe (for example, to the European Human Rights Commission), for twenty legal and administrative personnel, legislators, and academics. With a budget of ECU 13.2 million ($US15 million) it is the best funded of all the programmes. Individual member states of the EU have also negotiated their own human rights projects with China. For descriptions and evaluations of various programmes, see Mellbourn, and Svensson, *Swedish Human Rights Training in China*; Human Rights in China, *From Principle to Pragmatism*; and 'International Support for Legal Reform, Training and Services', *chinabrief*, 2/1 (Feb. 1999), 7–11.

[26] In these respects, the human rights dialogues show some similarity with cooperative security, the prevailing approach in the multilateral security organization in the Asia-Pacific, the ASEAN Regional Forum, of which China is a member, and in Beijing's bilateral security discussions with such major regional states as India and Japan.

governments perceived that the actual holding of the dialogues was progress enough.[27]

A BEIJING CHILL AND THE GROWTH OF PESSIMISM

As noted earlier, after the 15th Party Congress and in the run-up to the Clinton visit, many politically aware Chinese began to petition and publish calls for political reform. However, amid signs that this political activity was becoming better organized, as with the attempt to establish the CDP, the authorities decided to take action and sanctioned a series of arrests. As the 1998 US State Department's human rights report suggested, November and December were in many respects the worst months for repression for some time, with over thirty members of the CDP being detained, new regulations imposed on the use of the Internet, on the publishing industry, and social organizations, several newspapers closed, and other outspoken editors forced to resign.[28] Both Jiang Zemin and Li Peng made statements that indicated the limits of tolerance, the Chinese President in December placing great stress on the need to maintain political and social stability and unity, and calling on his comrades to be 'vigilant against infiltration, subversive activities and separatist activities' and 'nip [them] in the bud'. For good measure, he added that the 'western mode of political systems must never be copied'. Li's remarks received wider international dissemination because he used an interview with Peter Seidlitz of the German newspaper *Handelsblatt* to underline the Party's approach to those who wanted to form an independent political party or social group:

We will look at the nature of any such organization. If its purposes are against the Constitution or the basic policies of China, against the socialist market economy, national unity, independence and the maintenance of social stability and *if it is designed to go for the multiparty system and try to negate the leadership of the Communist Party, then it will not be allowed to exist* . . . In a word, China promotes democracy and practices the rule of law but our road is not patterned on the Western approach that features the separation of powers, a multiparty system and privatization.[29]

[27] See Human Rights in China, *From Principle to Pragmatism*, for a trenchant criticism of the process.

[28] US Department of State, *China Country Report on Human Rights Practices* (Internet edn., 26 Feb. 1999), 1–2.

[29] Jiang's speech was made in Dec. 1998, at the twentieth anniversary meeting of the pivotal Eleventh Central Committee meeting of the CCP in Dec. 1978, which had introduced China's major reforms. See *SWB* FE/3414 G/5–8, 19 Dec. 1998. 'Li Peng on Press Freedom, Legislation and Political Parties', *Beijing Review*, 4–10 Jan. 1999, 35–42 (emphasis added).

The trials of three central figures in the CDP (Qin Yongmin, Wang Youcai, and Xu Wenli) inevitably attracted much global attention.[30] Tried under the newly revised provisions of the CL, the judicial process demonstrated that those charged with 'endangering state security' were not going to have their newly enshrined legal rights properly protected. Despite Chinese protests that these 'criminals' were dealt with lawfully, and in compliance with the ICCPR,[31] sentences of between eleven and thirteen years were handed down with unseemly haste, in Xu's case within twenty minutes of a three-hour trial. Wang was forced to defend himself during his trial because his lawyer was prevented from travelling to be with him, Qin had no representation at all because in the absence of a guilty plea no lawyer would take his case, and Xu's lawyer met him only once before his trial began.[32]

One consequence was that governments began to evaluate or to look more closely at others' evaluations of the revised CL and CPL. As noted in Chapter 7, the UN Working Group on Arbitrary Detention had recommended after its visit to China in October 1997 greater precision in defining the crime of 'endangering state security' and an explicit reference in the CPL to the presumption of innocence. The US Lawyers' Committee produced its own detailed evaluations of the CPL and the Lawyers' Law. The analysis of the CPL, written by Jonathan Hecht, acknowledged 'some movement toward greater protection of the rights of suspected criminals', and the welcome abolition of the administrative coercive measure 'shelter and investigation'. Nevertheless, provisions on pre-arrest detention had been 'expanded to include the categories of persons to which the shelter and investigation was meant to be applied in the first place'. Although it was welcome news that lawyers would be involved earlier in the judicial proceedings, the exception was cases involving 'state secrets', a category subject to an expansive definition, and with few constraints on the police's ability to invoke it.

Hecht noted that some Chinese and foreign commentators had suggested that the new CPL had incorporated the presumption of innocence. Indeed, Professor Xin Chunying, director of the CASS Law Institute,

---

[30] In addition to extensive media coverage, the chair-rapporteur of the Working Group on Arbitrary Detention and the Special Rapporteur on the Promotion and Protection of the Right to Freedom of Opinion and Expression sent Urgent Action requests to Beijing on 9 Dec. on behalf of the three CDP activists. The UN High Commissioner on 22 Dec. urged China to respect internationally recognized standards on the rights to freedom of expression and association, and to a fair trial.

[31] See several reports in *SWB* FE/3417 G/4–7, 23 Dec. 1998 and *Beijing Review*, 11–17 Jan. 1999.

[32] US Department of State, *China Country Report on Human Rights Practices* (Internet edn., 26 Feb. 1999), 7, 11.

concluded not only that the CPL included this provision but that it had also attracted a wide basis of support.[33] Nevertheless, Hecht recorded that proposals had been made at the drafting stage to include specific language to that effect, but these had been rejected. In addition, he argued there was still no clear commitment to the independence of the judiciary, only to the independent exercise of the power to adjudicate. The CPL did not recognize the right to remain silent, and, while it mandated the police to gather evidence only through legal means, it did not specifically exclude illegally gathered evidence, thus weakening the constraints on the use of torture. Neither did it make any reforms to the administrative measure, RTL 'widely used against political dissidents', where, once again, the police dominate the decision on a case and where suspects 'have no right to counsel or to a hearing, let alone a judicial determination of their obligations'.[34]

The Lawyers' Committee's evaluation of the new Lawyers' Law, by Randall Peerenboom, was similarly cautious in its conclusions, noting with approval sharp breaks with Chinese past practice in the legal area, and acknowledging that the new law did provide a framework for lawyers to represent their clients more effectively and to increase their independence from the state. However, it contained 'enough of the rhetoric of socialism and references to the need to serve society, uphold the Constitution and maintain the confidentiality of broadly defined state secrets to lay the groundwork for a potential conflict between one's duty to one's client and one's duty to the state in certain circumstances'.[35] Clearly, legal reform was not about to go beyond the point where it came into conflict with the Party's preferred means of achieving political and social stability. Moreover, the leadership's statements and actions with regard to

[33] Whereas in the past, and especially between the 1950s and 1980s, some scholars had been 'severely punished' for advocating presumption of innocence, this argument had now been won: 'First they argued that it is a common practice recognized by most all countries, and it is also recognized by international human rights conventions. Secondly, the National People's Congress issued the Basic Law [for Hong Kong and Macao which] clearly stated [that anyone legally detained] has the right for a just trial as early as possible and he is suppose[d] to be innocent before the court judgment . . . Thirdly, the principle of presumption of innocence will be beneficial to the effective protection of human right[s] in the process of the criminal procedure . . . Fourthly, the principle is conducive to the improvement of the professional quality of the police and judicial personnel and to the enhancement of their ability to handle cases according to law.' Xin, *Chinese Legal System and Current Legal Reform*, 681–2.

[34] Lawyers' Committee for Human Rights, *Opening to Reform?* esp. pt. II, and pp. 26, 66. Amnesty International also produced a report entitled *People's Republic of China: Law Reform and Human Rights* (London, Mar. 1997). See also the UN Working Group on Arbitrary Detention's view of RTL, as outlined in Ch. 7 above.

[35] Lawyers' Committee for Human Rights, *Lawyers in China* esp. 94. See also Alford, 'Tasselled Loafers for Barefoot Lawyers'. Lubman (ed.) *China's Legal Reforms*.

this key goal of stability at the end of 1998 sent strong signals to all state organs, and especially to the police, that reinforced a deeply ingrained tendency to put to one side the need to safeguard legally enshrined rights.

Although the 1997 US State Department report had made reference to legal reform, noting some of the strengths and weaknesses of the new legislation, the report's analysis of the CPL in 1998 was far more critical and reflected closely the conclusions in Hecht's study. The nature of the trials of the three Chinese political activists, and China's recent signature of the ICCPR, inevitably prompted re-examination of China's CL reform, and the use that would be made of the new legislation. The bilateral human rights dialogues also began to come under NGO scrutiny, and their conclusions, especially those of Human Rights in China, came to the attention of governments.[36] Its report averred that the dialogues were likely to be ineffective in the absence of more public shaming of China, and that conducting them behind closed doors removed an important aspect of public pressure not only on the Chinese but also on governments that claimed there was a human rights dimension to their policy. Only in a few cases, such as the Canadians and Norwegians, were NGOs regularly consulted about the process, and the dialogues themselves often excluded China specialists. The report also pointed out that many of the cooperation programmes were not in fact new efforts but were a part of the more general development effort that Western countries had been funding in China for some time—these 'new' projects had simply been placed under the human rights umbrella. Moreover, some of the schemes remained in the discussion stage, such as the EU–China Village Governance Programme,[37] despite presentation that suggested they were already functioning. Of great concern to Human Rights in China, and to other NGOs, was that 'Western dialogue partners [had] not set any clear benchmarks for acceptable progress, or indicated any time frame within which certain measures should be taken'.[38] AI concurred with this general conclusion. While prepared in the past to participate in some dialogue sessions itself, on the eve of the EU's bilateral dialogue with China in February 1999, it stated: 'the organization has become progressively

---

[36] Discussions with governmental officials from both Britain and Canada in June 1998 and January 1999 confirmed this, and indeed it was a British foreign office official who first brought the Human Rights in China report to my attention.

[37] As of February 2000, it had still not got off the ground, although EU officials informed me that this was more to do with difficulties at the EU end than at the Chinese.

[38] Human Rights in China, *From Principle to Pragmatism*, 1–16, esp. 13. Ann Kent is also critical of the Australian dialogue, especially its lack of transparency, and accountability, and its failure to draw on expert advice, or to establish benchmarks to monitor progress. See 'Form over Substance: The Australia–China Bilateral Human Rights Dialogue', *China Rights Forum* (Fall 1999).

disenchanted with the process, with the continuing lack of transparency and limits on participation, circular argumentation, indications of a lack of serious intent, and fundamentally the lack of concrete improvements in human rights.'[39]

In late summer 1998, the Swedish International Development Co-operation Agency (SIDA) decided to undertake an evaluation of its legal programme with China, organized by the RWI of Human Rights and Humanitarian Law. That SIDA report, published in early 1999,[40] cautiously endorsed the continuation of the programme, in part because of its focus, which was not to promote a high-level dialogue between diplomats, but was directed towards the training of Chinese civil servants. However, the assessors also drew attention to the absence of any procedures for measuring either the success or the effect of RWI's training activities, and was disturbed that participants primarily saw the courses as ways of increasing their professional skills and obtaining contacts with colleagues overseas. Another finding of real concern was that some interviewees stated they had learned that human rights could be 'interpreted and applied in different ways of equal value'. Repeatedly, Chinese participants had stated to those engaged in the evaluation that at China's present stage of development the country had to focus on the right to subsistence.

The Swedish evaluation also raised the pertinent question of whether the Chinese government was able to set its own agenda in the area of legal training, given the competition among various of its dialogue partners. Certainly, Beijing exhibited a strong desire to retain control over the timing and content of the human rights programmes, as was evident from the experience of the UN High Commissioner for Human Rights. With China having signed the Memorandum of Intent in September 1998, the High Commissioner then found it extremely difficult to advance the process to its next stages—hosting an expert advisers' visit, agreement on specific projects, and the signature of an MOU to underpin these. Eventually, Robinson resorted to reminding China's Assistant Foreign Minister, Wang Guangya, in December 1998 that his country had offered to host the Needs Assessment Mission before the next session of the UNCHR in March 1999. The Needs Assessment Mission finally arrived in China on 7 March with a brief to formulate, in consultation with Chinese officials, specific projects that would strengthen national capacities in the areas of administration of justice, legislative reform, curriculum reform, and

---

[39] Amnesty International, 'Open Letter from Amnesty International to EU Governments on the eve of EU–China Human Rights Dialogue', 4 Feb. 1999.
[40] Melbourn and Svensson, *Swedish Human Rights Training in China,* 1–8, esp. 3.

teacher training, provide help in harmonizing domestic legislation with the requirements of the two international covenants, and give assistance with treaty reporting. Apart from the ratification of the two covenants, the Office of the High Commissioner also hoped to persuade the Chinese government to develop a national human rights plan of action.[41] Despite completion of the Needs Assessment Mission report, the MOU had still not been signed in February 2000, preventing further development of what appears to be a well-designed and essential cooperation programme.

Thus, by early 1999, the credibility of Chinese intentions with respect to the international human rights regime had come under increased suspicion. Some NGOs had more or less washed their hands of the dialogue process, and certain governments displayed unease about the reduced means at their disposal to register disapproval of Chinese actions that included the sentencing of peaceful political activists. Other governments, of course, were less concerned, the Luxembourg Prime Minister arguing that the European media were disproportionately interested in China's human rights failures, compared with other countries that had far worse records. He also suggested that giving up on the dialogues would only help those hardliners in the Party who wanted nothing at all to do with them.[42] However, even Sir Leon Brittan—long seen as especially sympathetic to private diplomacy with the Chinese in this area—began to talk of the need for 'specific and tangible progress to maintain the credibility of this dialogue'. The Chinese had been informed, he said, that the EU would be identifying 'benchmarks by which progress in the dialogue [would] be judged', such as more detailed information on and access to political prisoners, the improvement of prison conditions and reform of the penal system especially with regard to the use of the death penalty, and a reconsideration of the fate of dissidents who had been convicted as counter-revolutionaries. There also had to be progress towards ratification of the two covenants and in the follow-up to Mary Robinson's visit. With respect to Tibet, Sir Leon pointed to the need for greater transparency of demographic information, the free use of the Tibetan language, and information regarding punishments meted out to certain ethnic minority groups, such as had occurred in Drapchi prison after the EU–Troika visit in May 1998.[43]

---

[41] Discussions with UN officials, May 1999.   [42] See *SWB* FE/3432 G/2, 14 Jan. 1999.

[43] Sir Leon Brittan's response to the report of Mr Bernard-Reymond on *Building a Comprehensive Partnership with China*, before the European Parliament, 27 Jan. 1999. See Ch. 7 above for reference to the punishment meted out to certain Tibetan prisoners after the Troika's visit. Sir Leon's replacement at the European Commission, Christopher Patten, is likely to try to be more robust on the human rights issue. Before the European Parliament in Sept. 1999, not unexpectedly perhaps, he promised a harder European stand on human rights in China. *Far Eastern Economic Review*, 16 Sept. 1999, 17.

It was not clear from Sir Leon's statement how the EU would respond if these benchmarks—without any time scales attached—were to be ignored. However, his phrases reinforced the sense that the dialogues were coming under strain, and that some of China's European dialogue partners were reconsidering their decision not to sponsor resolutions at the UN Commission, a path of action that Scandinavian countries were under particular pressure to reconsider.[44] For the time being, the Europeans made do with delivering a *démarche* to the Chinese after the dissident trials, and criticism of China by the President of the EU at the UN Commission meeting in March 1999.[45] The Australians and Canadians also decided not to propose a draft motion at that March meeting. The Clinton administration, on the other hand, was in a particularly difficult position, under great domestic political pressure to introduce a resolution and also to consider postponing or cancelling altogether its first of the renewed official bilateral human rights dialogues, scheduled for 11–13 January 1999.

The NGO community in the USA was divided over whether this dialogue should go ahead, Amnesty and Human Rights Watch advocating postponement, the Lawyers' Committee, led by Michael Posner, recommending in a letter to Harold Koh that the US administration proceed but use the occasion to criticize China for its non-compliance with treaties it had signed, such as the ICCPR. Using that covenant as the framework for the dialogue, he wrote, would allow the US delegation to address concerns with respect to the treatment of members of the CDP, raise the issue of relief for those imprisoned immediately after Tiananmen under the now-defunct classification of counter-revolutionary crimes, and consider the broader problems associated with China's criminal and

---

[44] Discussions with EU officials in the summer of 1999 confirmed this.

[45] The German delegate to the UNCHR spoke on behalf of the EU and the ten East and Central European countries associated with the EU. He stated: 'While applauding the recent improvements in Chinese legislation, especially the incorporation of the principle of the rule of law into the Chinese Constitution, the Union nevertheless encouraged China to ratify and implement the two International Covenants on Human Rights as soon as possible. The widespread and excessive use of administrative detention and the death penalty, restrictions on religious freedom and freedom of speech, and the situation in Tibet were abiding matters of concern' (E/CN.4/1999/SR/13, 1 April 1999, 20). China Radio International described the EU decision not to co-sponsor a resolution as 'wise', noting in passing that the EU, in working to establish a 'comprehensive partnership with China', had 'decided to elevate the political relations between the EU and China to the same level as that between the EU and the United States, Japan, and Russia'; in other words, China was reminding the EU that it had a wide and important agenda with the Beijing government that went beyond the human rights issue, and more particularly that the EU risked being left behind in the development of its relationship with Beijing. *SWB* FE/3494 G/6–7, 27 Mar. 1999.

administrative law.[46] In Koh's extensive briefings after the dialogue, he confirmed (not necessarily at the Lawyers' Committee's urgings) that he had placed US concerns 'in the context of China's decision last October to sign' the ICCPR. More specifically, the talks encompassed all the issues that Posner had raised, and in addition focused on matters that had particularly exercised some members of the US Congress, such as the sale of prison-made goods, the use of organs from executed prisoners, the violation of religious freedom, and coerced abortions. Many aspects of China's policies towards Tibet also came in for criticism, including the lack of progress in initiating negotiations with the Dalai Lama. China's delegation, led by China's Assistant Foreign Minister, Wang Guangya, for its part came with an extensive brief, including information about particular prisoners. It also raised concerns about the racial composition of US prisons, the administration of the death penalty in the USA, and America's poor record of ratification with respect to the two international covenants. One indication that there might also have been less combative aspects to the dialogue, and that the USA could be sensitive to the weaknesses in its own record, came in the discussion of RTL. The US delegation referred to America's own past usage of a juvenile detention system, which had been designed to rehabilitate young people but which—until successfully challenged in the courts— did not have much in the way of due process associated with it. This experience, together with acknowledgement of the problems the two large and diverse countries faced in trying to administer a legal system, were two topics on which there seemed to be some meeting of minds.[47]

The Clinton administration also made efforts to convince the Chinese that human rights issues would not be compartmentalized: that all government officials, from whatever departments they came, would raise human rights matters with their Chinese counterparts. Koh also tried to

---

[46] Letter from Michael Posner, Executive Director of the Lawyers' Committee, to Harold Koh, 24 Dec. 1998, in author's possession. Neither did Posner miss the opportunity to impress on the Clinton administration that its message to China in these areas would be credible only to the extent that officials in all relevant government agencies adhered to it in dealings with Chinese counterparts, and if it was 'accompanied by a meaningful commitment by the United States to live up to these same international commitments in our own enforcement of human rights in this country'. Koh was probably pre disposed towards continuing with the dialogue anyway: as he argued in one of his academic articles, 'repeated participation in the process will help to reconstitute the interests and even the identities of the participants'. ('Why do Nations Obey International Law?', 2646).

[47] Koh, 'On-the-Record Briefing on US–China Human Rights Dialogue'; and discussion with US official in Beijing, Sept. 1999. As noted earlier, as of Feb. 2000 the US had still not ratified the ICESCR, and has entered various reservations with respect to the ICCPR.

appeal to China's image concerns, arguing that what was at stake was Beijing's international reputation for living up to treaty commitments more generally. Those efforts explained the US delegation's reference to Clinton's executive order signed in December 1998, which mandated all Federal Agencies to implement human rights treaties. It also explained the decision to include officials from the NSC as well as the Justice and State Departments in the human rights dialogue. Madeleine Albright's speech at the Chinese embassy in Washington on 12 January, commemorating the twentieth anniversary of the normalization of relations, was similarly designed to emphasize the unified view of the administration. She stressed US dismay at the prison sentences imposed on the CDP activists and urged China to do more than sign, but also to observe the principles of the ICCPR.[48]

Despite Koh's considered approach towards the Chinese, which tried to combine discussion of broad problems with specific demands concerning particular prisoners or practices, and his efforts at openness at the close of the dialogue, the Clinton administration remained under Congressional and NGO pressure to introduce a condemnatory resolution at the next meeting of the UN Commission. In mid March matters came to a head and US officials were dispatched to Brussels, London, and elsewhere to discover whether there would be any support were the USA to co-sponsor a resolution. It was rather late in the day, of course, and Chinese statements on the issue were already in the public record: at the close of the dialogue with Washington in January, Chinese officials had let it be known that the US introduction of such a resolution would put the next such dialogue meeting—to be held in Beijing—in jeopardy.[49] Moreover, it soon became clear that, if Washington went ahead, it would more or less be alone, since its major allies had decided that they were not ready to return to the UN route. Indeed, some officials—even including some Americans—evinced a degree of understanding at the Chinese crackdown on the CDP in the light of its 'frontal assault' on the central leadership's power base, and especially so in this year of critical anniversaries.[50] Some European diplomats were also dismissive of a US position that they—and the Chinese—tended to depict as being forced upon Washington by domestic pressure: signal confirmation that unilateral actions are often

[48] Secretary of State, Madeleine K. Albright, 'Remarks and Toast at Reception at the Embassy of the People's Republic of China', 12 Jan. 1999, US Department of State.

[49] As Assistant Foreign Minister Wang put it: 'Any country which wishes to resume the Geneva scenario would certainly do damage not only to the bilateral relations, but also to the possibility of continuing the human rights dialogue' (*SWB* FE/3433 G/1, 15 Jan. 1999).

[50] *International Herald Tribune*, 13 Jan. 1999; interviews with European officials, May 1999.

perceived as lacking legitimacy and as failing to reflect a common interest.[51] Despite this absence of allied support, the Clinton administration decided that it had to go ahead and introduce a resolution critical of China's record, as the head of its delegation said, in the light of the crackdown against organized political opposition, the detention of dozens of peaceful activists, and the lack of progress in dealing with the problems in Tibet. However, the USA could persuade only Poland to co-sponsor. When China introduced its usual no-action motion, it passed 22–17–14.[52]

CHINA ON THE OFFENSIVE

The disunity in the Western camp over a China resolution was only one reason why the USA had an uncomfortable time in Geneva in 1999. It came under indirect attack when the EU decided that it would introduce a resolution against use of the death penalty. AI targeted the USA directly, putting it in the same company for human rights failures as Algeria, Cambodia, and Turkey, but not China in 1999. Amnesty's secretary general stated that 'human rights violations in the United States are persistent, widespread and appear to disproportionately affect people of racial or ethnic minority backgrounds'; police brutality was also rife. Amnesty also supported the moratorium on executions, pointing to the increasing numbers being executed in the USA and the high numbers on death row.[53]

Amnesty had in fact produced a 150-page report in October 1998 that had provided extensive analysis of many of the same problems it had referred to at Geneva. The Chinese used that publication, together with

---

[51] The head of the Chinese delegation at Geneva stated, among other things, that the US 'anti-China resolution this year is totally out of its internal political needs and is irrelevant to promoting human rights' (*SWB* FE/3518 G/1, 26 Apr. 1999).

[52] See statement by Nancy Rubin, US Ambassador to the UNCHR, 23 Apr. 1999 (US Department of State report); also in E/CN.4/1999/SR.51, 23 Apr. 1999. As Ambassador Rubin put it, 'it is not "confrontation" for this Commission to ask one of its members to obey international standards, it is not interference with internal affairs to ask a member state to respect the right of democratic dissent protected by international law'. In what sounded like a direct reply to Wei Jingsheng who had said at the 1998 meeting of the UN Commission 'this is precisely the time when support from our friends is most needed', she went on: 'When Chinese dissidents have the courage to stand alone, we must have the courage to stand with them. We urge China to engage in genuine dialogue with its dissidents and the Dalai Lama, not just with members of this Commission.' Details of the roll-call vote are also available in *SWB* FE/3518, G/1, 26 Apr. 1999. A similar story can be told about the Commission meeting in 2000.

[53] *International Herald Tribune*, 29 Mar. 1999.

various studies undertaken by US governmental agencies, as sources for criticism of the US record of protection for human rights, and as a way of responding to US attacks on its own record as outlined in the 1998 US State Department report. Although the Chinese had reacted in this way before at the time of the publication of the US annual report, this was the most extensive reference it had yet made to US human rights problems. The Chinese article's final section comprised an examination of US adherence to various international conventions, noting America's failure to sign the CRC and the CEDAW. It also noted that it had taken the USA forty years to ratify the Genocide Convention, fifteen years for the ICCPR, and that it had still not ratified the ICESCR. Yet it was not reluctant to criticize China for its delay in ratifying the two major covenants. The Chinese also recorded that the USA had neither reported to the CAT, nor on its implementation of the International Convention on the Elimination of All Forms of Racial Discrimination, and thus was in breach of its international obligations.[54]

China's retaliation, therefore, took the form of pointing to US double standards. At the UN Commission, Li Baodong listed what he described as Chinese achievements in the protection of human rights, including the constitutional and legal revisions, the freeing of various publications from governmental control, the adoption of practical measures to protect the freedom of religious belief, and increased efforts to ban the use of torture. The USA, on the other hand, had shown its hypocrisy in the field of human rights by attaching many reservations to the ICCPR. He 'urged the United States to cancel these substantive reservations and give the American people real human rights and freedoms'. The Chinese ambassador in Washington later weighed in with similar accusations of hypocrisy: the USA kept urging China immediately to ratify the international covenants, while its own record of ratification was seriously flawed; it stood as one of only two states that had not signed the International Covenant on the Rights of the Child.[55] Chinese officials had certainly learned to home in on the weaknesses in the USA's record, inconsistencies that Koh himself felt keenly, since he referred to the need to address these in a number of his speeches. However, the form of China's discourse surely gave certain hostages to fortune regarding the speed and nature of its own ratification process. It also demonstrated conclusively that the Chinese had become habituated to arguing within the framework of international human rights norms, even while actual

---

[54] Ren Yanshi, 'Human Rights Records of the United States', *Beijing Review*, 22–28 Mar. 1999.   [55] *SWB* FE/3512 G/7, 19 Apr. 1999; FE/3526 G/1, 5 May 1999.

conditions inside China continued to come into serious conflict with those standards.

That continuing disjuncture between discourse, legislation, and actual behaviour on the ground, as detailed in UN, NGO, and media reports, was prominently displayed in 1999, and, if anything, the level of conflict among them was exacerbated by a number of factors peculiar to the last year of the millennium. The broad reasons for the failure successfully to implement fundamental improvements in human rights protections relate to well-entrenched institutional, legal–cultural and political factors. The Party has made it clear on numerous occasions that it does not intend to countenance opposition to its rule. Among other things, this has required it to attempt to place a fence around its international involvement in the human rights regime and certain of the domestic political outcomes that have arisen in response to such involvement. Constant references to the need to sustain political and social stability have lain at the route of the frequent 'strike-hard' campaigns, which have sent a signal to those charged with law enforcement to cut corners and produce results in terms of numbers of arrests and convictions. Given the fragility of the rule of law, this has inevitably meant that implementation of the new legislation has been patchy, and that newly enshrined protections for individual human rights have not had a hospitable climate in which to prosper. Where the requirements of the domestic regime have come into strong contention with the leadership's concern for international image and being in good standing in international regimes, then the latter have been overridden.

In 1999 the authorities were bracing themselves for a year of societal instability arising from the anniversaries and from the economic restructuring and recession. In March 1999, Premier Zhu warned China's NPC of the probable dire consequences of current economic disorder, lax financial discipline, and feeble market demand in China. He also expressed concerns about weaknesses in the chain of command.[56] To continue to deliver policies of growth—the main basis of support for the Party—was going to be a tall order, and the combination of economic lay-offs and recession likely to fuel further social unrest.[57] The actions of

---

[56] This led the Party later to introduce the 'three stresses' campaign, which was to focus on 'study, political awareness and healthy ethics.'. See *Far Eastern Economic Review*, 18 Mar. 1999, 26, for Zhu's statements, *SWB* FE/3486 G/10–11, 18 Mar. 1999 for an early reference to the campaign, and *Far Eastern Economic Review*, 19 Aug. 1999, 16–18, for a description of the three elements of it as study of Marxist-Leninist-Deng Xiaoping thought; support for Jiang and conscientious implementation of Party directives; and the rooting-out of corruption within the Party.

[57] The *China Daily* estimated on 17 Jan. 1999 that some 30 million Chinese would be unemployed that year.

the Falun Gong faith-healing sect, which turned up in its thousands out-side Zhongnanhai in April to protest at the refusal of the authorities to allow its organization to register, compounded this sense of vulnerability. A total ban was imposed on the organization, and several of its members, Party cadres among them, were arrested.[58]

International factors also served to increase the Party's sense of vulnerability. The bypassing of the UN Security Council and the resultant NATO military intervention in Kosovo seriously alarmed the leadership and led to a retreat into the language of state sovereignty as the primary guarantor of human rights. In an authoritative article in *Renmin Ribao* 'US-led NATO' was described as having 'cooked up' the 'absurd theory that "human rights transcend sovereignty"'. What it meant, the editorial averred, was that, 'once the United States believes that an incident of some kind has happened in one of these [developing and socialist] countries that does not fit US-style human rights or suit US interests, the United States can interfere in that country's internal affairs, violate its sovereignty, and even resort to the use of force, under the pretext that "human rights transcend sovereignty"'. Other articles pointed to the neg-ative effect such action would have on the UN's role and status—'Who cares about the UN Charter, norms of international law, UN Security Council's authorization, veto of the five big powers . . . They will all be thrown aside'—and the UN become a talk shop or venue for discussing only such issues as the environment, food, population, and the like. China's human rights NGO inevitably wrote in similar vein on the sub-ject, condemning NATO, but especially the USA, for trampling 'on the norms of international law and brazenly violat[ing] the classical prin-ciples enshrined in the UN Charter'. The launching of air attacks in the cause of the protection of human rights was an 'extremely dangerous signal' and had to be stopped if the concept of state sovereignty was to retain any force.[59] After the bombing of the Chinese embassy in Belgrade

---

[58] Some Chinese legal scholars evinced support for the action against the sect and for the general tenor of Party statements that summer. According to Liu Hainian of the CASS Institute of Law: 'The stability we've had since 1978 has been so hard won' and Falun Gong actions threatened that stability. Quoted in *Far Eastern Economic Review*, 19 Aug. 1999, 18. See also James D. Seymour, 'The Wheel of Law and the rule of law', *China Rights Forum* (Fall 1999), for a valuable discussion of the sect and the leadership's reaction to it. Four of the sect's leaders received harsh prison sentences of between seven and eighteen years on 27 Dec. 1999, a decision that prompted the US government to sponsor another draft resolution at the UNCHR meeting in spring 2000. See Human Rights Watch news reports, 27 Dec. 1999 and 11 Jan. 2000, together with US Office of International Informa-tion Programs statement, on 11 Jan. 2000. US allies failed to support it.

[59] *SWB* FE/3535 G/7–8, 15 May 1999; FE/3512 G/6, 19 Apr. 1999; and FE/3525 G/1, 4 May 1999. At a press conference in Ottawa, Premier Zhu Rongji was reported to have flared up when Kosovo and Tibet were bracketed together. Zhu angrily inquired: 'Do you

in May, the centrality of the human rights issue, the US dominant role in global politics, and China's relationship with the United States became locked together, as reflected in Beijing's decision to make the bilateral human rights dialogue between the two countries a primary casualty. The dialogues with other NATO members seemed not to have been affected; but Beijing decided to call off similar discussions with the United States until further notice.

CONCLUSION

The tenth anniversary of the Tiananmen bloodshed passed off quietly enough, although the authorities had to find a pretext for closing the Square, and also detained a number of activists. Certain brave individuals, such as Bao Tong, former aide to the deposed Zhao Ziyang, decided to exercise his right to free speech as enshrined in the constitution and called for a reassessment of the 4 June 'incident'.[60] Some of the relatives of those who died ten years previously petitioned the government to open a criminal investigation. Their activities encapsulated many of the new developments that had affected the human rights issue in China, with the petitioners drawing support from an internal dissident group, lawyers in Beijing and abroad, and the NGO, Human Rights in China. The relatives of the dead, as well as Bao Tong, framed their appeals in terms of the new criminal code or constitutional guarantees.[61] These actions provided signal evidence that, with the presence of such transnational networks and the publication of the ideas embodied in the new legislation, the human rights movement in China could still garner support and could not be silenced.

The Party's goal in 1999 thus became one of deepening its attempts to delegitimize such activities and to label them unpatriotic. In an appeal to nationalist sentiment already at a fever pitch after the Belgrade embassy bombing, the Beijing government accused the USA of having 'played an inglorious role' in 1989. It had manipulated the demonstrators and inter-

---

want to send troops to Tibet? You only listen to the opinions of so-called dissidents and don't listen to the opinions of the Chinese government. Is this fair?' (*SWB* FE/3514, G/2, 21 Apr. 1999).

[60] In an article discussing his March. letter, Bao Tong wrote: 'Who says divergent views are of no avail? Every bit of progress China has made since the 5th April Tiananmen Movement in 1976 and the third plenary session of the 11th Party Central Committee in 1978 . . . are all attributed to the Chinese common people's efforts to rectify and overcome the mistakes made by Mao Zedong' (*SWB* FE/3525 G/6–7, 4 May 1999).

[61] Details of the petitions are contained in *China Rights Forum*, (Fall 1999), 4 ff.

national opinion in its 'never abandoned scheme to ruin China'. The Party's and Army's 'firm and resolute suppression of the political turmoil in Beijing' thus was essential to the protection of 'national independence, dignity, security and stability and ensured the sustained, healthy development of economic reforms'.[62] Other leadership statements in 1999 similarly stressed that the reform policy was at a critical juncture that required even greater attention to sustaining political stability via strong Party control.

The Chinese leadership's particular focus on the US role and America's intentions with regard to China were hardly new but featured markedly in these remaining years of the 1990s. The summits between Jiang and Clinton were obviously important to Beijing and a certain price had to be paid to make them a success. These two meetings, together with the fierce Chinese desire to stop the introduction of condemnatory resolutions at the UNCHR, were largely responsible for keeping the focus of attention on China's human rights record, and in prompting some forward movement in China's adherence to the regime. The Chinese also seemed to treat the one bilateral dialogue with the Americans in January 1999 with particular seriousness, presumably in the realization that the Clinton administration—of all the democratic states—was under the greatest domestic pressure to show results. Perhaps the US administration had had more success than some of the other dialogue partners in convincing the Chinese that human rights issues had become an integral part of US foreign policy, and that progress on other issues of concern to both parties could be damaged by failure to address the human rights question. Nevertheless, despite these understandings, at the close of the period under review here 'US-led NATO' strategy in Yugoslavia combined with the Beijing government's strong sense of vulnerability to postpone further discussion of the topic. These twin fears possibly also foreshadowed a retreat away from the Chinese verbal acceptance of the indivisibility and universality of human rights, and a return to the emphasis on human rights as the domestic affair of sovereign states.[63]

Constraints on a full return to this position were in place, however, provided by signature of the covenants, the continuation of most of the bilateral dialogues, possible wider support of the UN Commission resolu-

---

[62] See *International Herald Tribune*, 31 May, 1 and 3 June 1999.

[63] China's deputy permanent representative to the third committee of the 54th UN General Assembly reiterated that state sovereignty was 'the prerequisite for the existence and development of human rights' and that interference in other countries' internal affairs through the threat or actual use of force inevitably led to the 'blatant violation of the most fundamental human rights, such as the right to life and the right to existence' (*Xinhua* general news service, 9 Nov. 1999).

tion, and outstanding commitments to the UN High Commissioner for Human Rights. China also had stated its intention in its 1998 White Paper on Human Rights to invite the UN's Special Rapporteur on Torture to visit soon—presented as further evidence that it had 'actively cooperated with the United Nations in the field of human rights'.[64] Earlier in 1998, it had again put itself on public record as arguing not for the priority of economic, social, and cultural rights, but that these rights were just as important as civil and political rights. Chinese criticisms in 1998 and 1999 of the US and Indonesian human rights records were also in the public domain. To attempt a resurrection of Beijing's notion that state sovereignty prevented global attention to a state's human rights record would be a near impossible undertaking, therefore, even for a state that has wielded considerable power over forms of expression.

The legal cooperation and training programmes were also fulfilling a need that had been enshrined in statements at the highest level, including the constitution, which had been revised in March 1999 to read: 'The People's Republic of China shall be governed according to law and shall be built into a socialist country based on the rule of law.'[65] And, although it had been made clear that any threat to the security of the regime would take precedence over concerns for international image or strict adherence to the revised legal codes, strong attempts were made to interpret Chinese actions against CDP activists and other protesters as complying with the ICCPR and these new legal provisions, which themselves had been influenced by international standards. China remained caught, therefore, between wanting to be recognized as a responsible member of the international community, which included participation in the international human rights regime, and a desire to retain the initiative in its own hands as to the extent of its compliance—a formidable task in a world where ideas and information were difficult to contain.

Western governments involved in human rights dialogues with China in these last years of the decade comprised individuals who saw them as a way of reducing NGO and media criticism of their failure to sustain a human rights policy towards China, and those who emphasized they were a practical means of making some small difference inside the country. But most among them were affected by continuing calls to make these dialogues meaningful and to demonstrate that some genuine progress was being made—particularly so in the case of the USA. Those governments that were essentially process-oriented in their approach to the dialogues

[64] China, Information Office of the State Council, 'Progress in China's Human Rights Conditions in 1998', *SWB* FE/3509 S1/1–11, 15 Apr.1999.

[65] For further details of additions and changes to the constitution, see *SWB* FE/3486 G/9–10, 18 Mar. 1999.

and the associated cooperation activities were to find it difficult to argue this line as a consequence of stepped-up levels of repression in China towards the end of 1998. The absence of mechanisms to respond to human rights crises of these kinds, given that none of these governments wanted anything other than full 'engagement' with China, led to a renewal of concern about how to move China closer to ratifying the two major international covenants, and to implementing more fully the legal improvements it had been seeking to introduce. The attractions of combining public shaming with private dialogue, which earlier had led to the great prize of China's signing of the two international covenants, began to revive, holding out the prospect that the struggle over human rights would take another turn in the first years of the new millennium.

Conclusion: Rights beyond Borders?

In late September 1999, two items in the daily newspaper suggested further potential expansion of the human rights agenda. The first, summarizing the UN Secretary General Kofi Annan's speech to the 54th session of the UN General Assembly, reported his argument that the global community had learned that it could not stand idly by watching gross and systematic violations of human rights, that state sovereignty was being redefined to encompass the idea of individual sovereignty, and that in our contemporary reading of the UN Charter we were 'more than ever conscious that its aim is to protect individual human beings, not to protect those who abuse them'. Nothing in that Charter precluded 'recognition that there are rights beyond borders'. The second, two days later, was in the form of an advertisement by Shell International announcing its commitment in support of fundamental human rights as codified in its Statement of General Business Principles. The heading of this advertisement asked rhetorically whether rights were 'none of our business? Or the heart of our business?'[1] Both statements contain ideas that scholars and practitioners will pick over with some scepticism and put to the test in various ways. Even if the sceptics turn out to be correct, the statements nevertheless demonstrate a shift in perception about attitudes that ought to be expressed. They also suggest that, for some, human rights activity neither is solely a state-based activity, nor can any longer be interpreted to mean that the way a government treats its people is nobody's business but its own.

This book has sought to trace the movement towards these principles, to demonstrate via an examination of individual, state, institutional, and advocacy network behaviour that the human rights issue has become a dominant feature of the international system, and that interactions among these actors have led to the erosion of the traditional, Westphalian, concept of state sovereignty. This traditional form has been under challenge since the creation of the UN Charter, the Genocide

[1] *Financial Times*, 21 and 23 Sept. 1999.

Convention, and the UDHR in the 1940s.[2] Following a period of quies-
cence, it has been further weakened after the 1970s with the coming into
force of the two major international covenants, the growing attention to
human rights matters in governmental—especially US—foreign policies
and the widening and deepening of human rights activities within the UN
system. In addition, a vast upsurge in the numbers of NGOs, operating
transnationally, making the most of the information revolution, and able
to put issues on the agenda that in the past would have escaped attention,
has made a crucial difference to the way we respond to abuses of human
rights.

The post-cold-war era has seen further incremental advances, as exem-
plified by the Vienna World Conference on Human Rights, the establishment of a UN Commissioner for Human Rights, the revival of what Jack
Donnelly has aptly described as the 'long-dormant Nuremberg precedent' in the creation of international tribunals for the former
Yugoslavia and Rwanda, and the decision by 120 countries in July 1998
in Rome to adopt the Statute of the International Criminal Court.[3] None
of these changes has come without controversy, disappointment, and
fear: controversy over such matters as definition and interpretation, and
consistency of application; disappointment because of the failure to
move on from standard-setting and promotional activity to real improvements on the ground pushed through in part through enforcement measures; and fear because, as many developing countries' leaders perceive it,
the principles of non-interference and sovereign equality are the 'final
defence against the rules of an unequal world'.[4] Nevertheless, activities
since the late 1980s suggest that the balance has tipped further in favour
of the argument that the global community has the legitimate right to
support those whose human rights are being grossly abused.

In this study, I have concentrated on only some of the actors that make
up this complex picture: parts of the UN system, a few of the major
NGOs, and predominantly among states the Western democracies. It is a
selective range of actors, but it has served to give some indication of the
sources of influence in this issue area, and has also helped to illustrate
how the various parts of the regime have operated in combination.
Among governments, the USA has featured prominently, connected with
its power in the global community, the struggle that the separation of

---

[2] Human rights is only one area that has mounted such a challenge, of course. For one
view that perceives that challenge as less than fundamental, see Krasner, *Sovereignty*.

[3] Donnelly provides a masterly brief summary of the developing regime in 'The Social
Construction of International Human Rights', 71–102.

[4] The last point was made by the head of the OAU, President Abdelaziz Bouteflika, in
response to Kofi Annan's speech of 20 Sept. 1999.

powers sets in train, its susceptibility to NGO and media pressure, and China's fixation on its relationship with America. The primary target of attention has been China, and the way its government has interacted with the various parts of the rights regime, and responded to the pressure that has been exerted. In my explanation of the process of China's involvement with international human rights, I have highlighted its bargaining behaviour, the constraints imposed by use of the language of rights, its concern for international image, and the space that participation has provided to various groups within Chinese society. Attention to process and agency is designed to contribute to an understanding of why there has been an increased global focus on human rights, why there has been some forward movement in China's participation in the rights regime, and why that movement has reached only a certain stage.

Institutions have also played a prominent role in the study. Annual meetings of the UN Commission and Sub-Commission and major gatherings such as that at Vienna in 1993 have served to galvanize all the actors involved and have promoted the review and reappraisal of arguments over priorities, and consideration of the costs of personal, domestic, and international action or inaction. Treaty reporting requirements attached to the various conventions have had similar effects, pitting state evidence against that of the NGO and the expertise and integrity of those who have evaluated Chinese governmental reports. Institutions, then, have been critical in providing openings for individual, governmental, and NGO pressure, opportunities for debate over the interpretation of human rights norms, and occasions for building a public record of verbal and behavioural commitment.

Legislative and bureaucratic changes in individual governments have heightened awareness of the human rights issue. For several years now, Western states, Japan, and other governments committed to democratic practices have had in place domestic legislation or have made statements that pledge attention to the promotion of such rights in their external policies. Indeed, some have claimed human rights to be at the heart of their policies.[5] Having become so identified with the issue, governments—both to the right and the left of the political spectrum—have found it difficult to avoid consideration of its place in the framing of foreign policies, especially in countries with strong advocacy networks. This has led to much preoccupation about the best means to pursue a human rights policy—from private murmurings at one end of the continuum to

---

[5] See, e.g. European Commission, *Building a Comprehensive Partnership with China*, which states: 'A commitment to universally recognized human rights and fundamental freedoms lies at the heart of the EU's policy world-wide' (p. 7, internet edn.).

coercive measures at the other. Their identities as democracies are challenged whenever a government with which they have significant dealings seriously abuses the rights of its people. If they should fail to respond to evidence of transgressions, human rights groups will engage in a process of moral consciousness raising, and mobilization of political forces in order to return them to the path that their own rhetoric and behaviour within their own states demands.

Human rights NGOs have similarly been vital to the regime as forces for empowering the abused, making the voices of the weak heard, and reminding those with more resources and more enviable records of protection of their obligations to common humanity. As we have seen in the China case, however, they are in the end dependent on governments in this state-based regime, and have to remain ever watchful of a state's willingness to propel the regime in directions that they favour. This can be a source of weakness for the NGOs, for it raises dilemmas about whether they should be working cooperatively with the most powerful norm-promoting governments in the system, or should retain fully their separateness and autonomy in order to maintain credibility and leave open the possibility of stringent, public criticism of all governments that are either abusers or failures when it comes to living up to their stated commitments. Moreover, the NGOs' need to concentrate lobbying effort in Washington, New York, Brussels, and Geneva reinforces a perception that promotion of human rights protections is primarily the job of the developed North against activities within the less-developed South,[6] an unwelcome by-product of the need to stick close to state activity.

It is not unusual for governments, individuals, and especially the Beijing leadership itself to question why China's record has been the particular focus of attention since 1989. As noted in earlier chapters, a number of NGOs, from the 1980s, decided to devote more resources to the country than any other in Asia; the Clinton administration's global rule of law initiative when first introduced quickly began to pay primary attention to developments in China; and many states co-sponsored China-specific condemnatory resolutions at the UN Commission from 1990 to 1997.[7] Domestic political pressure explains a lot of this, but that fixation relates also to the concern to maintain a credible human rights regime in the light of the evidence of serious levels of abuse inside a state which has a complex status in the global system. China operates with both a great-power and a developing-country identity, emphasizing one

---

[6] For an argument that has a bearing on this point and extends it into the realm of the international organization, see Ngaire Woods, 'Good Governance in International Organizations', *Global Governance*, 5 (1999), 39–61.   [7] With the exception of 1991.

or the other at particular strategic moments. Membership of the UN Security Council, its operation of an aid programme, growing prominence in the ranks of global traders, a nuclear weapons capability, and involvement in some of the dominant security concerns of East and South Asia give it international status and leverage on a number of fronts. Yet, its search for wealth and power, its problematic drive for higher levels of development, as well as its history as semi-colony resonate with other developing countries, affording it a leadership role here too, particularly noticeable in its statements and actions at the annual meetings of the UNCHR. These characteristics make it complex to operate a human rights policy with respect to China, but they also mean that it matters whether Beijing chooses to support the central norms of the international human rights regime, for it has the potential to bring others in its wake or demonstrate that alternative conceptions exist and can be acted upon.

If these attributes relate in large part to China's material strength, certain of its weaknesses also ensure that human rights conditions within the country remain the focus of attention. The possibility of large-scale social unrest resulting in waves of migration, the total collapse of law and order, and even the break-up of the country fill not only many Chinese with dread, but also several countries, especially the many with which it shares a border. The uncertainty lies in deciding which policies will help most to prevent those outcomes. Many of those committed to the human rights regime and the promotion of democracy believe that Beijing's policies towards its ethnic minorities—in Tibet and Xinjiang predominantly—and reluctance to reform weak state institutions that at present are incapable of resolving conflicts between state and society or between central and local government portend a dismal future and an inevitable worsening of an already lamentable human rights record. Others fear that democratization processes will inevitably bring greater conflict and bloodshed in the short term,[8] which at a minimum suggests that human rights policies need to be designed with considerable care. Additional dilemmas posed relate to clear evidence of a vast increase in personal freedom for those Chinese that do not choose to challenge in an organized way the current political order; however, the reports of UN Special Rapporteurs and Working Groups, as well as those of the NGOs, regularly remind those committed to the advancement of human rights of systemic and enduring problems in the country's record that should not be overlooked.

---

[8] For an academic treatment of this topic, see Edward D. Mansfield and Jack Snyder, 'Democratization and the Danger of War', *International Security*, 20/1 (Summer 1995).

THE PROCESS OF CHINA'S ENMESHMENT

It was the crisis in June 1989, reported so extensively on our TV screens, that brought China's human rights record to the forefront of global attention. Before that time, the advent of the Carter administration had raised the salience of the human rights issue globally but in a non-China-related way. With respect to China's pre-June 1989 record, we were reliant primarily on four main sources of information and activity: an Amnesty report; protests in Tibet and by small numbers of political activists in major cities, news of which began to reach the outside world; a few members of the US Congress concerned about specific issue areas such as population planning that relied on widespread use of abortion; and the Chinese leadership's decision to acknowledge openly the horrors of the Cultural Revolution, and to make some recompense to those who had suffered so egregiously during those terrible years. The last of these, together with China's tentative participation in the early 1980s in the international human rights regime, including membership in the UNCHR and ratification of the Convention against Torture, alongside its commitment to far-reaching economic reforms, seemed enough in the way of progress to some, particularly at a time when developments in the Soviet Union and Eastern Europe were absorbing much energy and attention. The Tiananmen bloodshed, however, brought the struggle to a new, qualitatively, different phase, prompting a reappraisal of the Chinese past and a sense that the sympathy that many had felt when contemplating China's demographic and developmental challenges could no longer excuse condemnation of its record.

In the first months after 4 June, the 'principled-issue networks' were at their most powerful and active.[9] Domestic human rights groups and transnational NGOs, the world's media, international institutions, and national governments fulfilled their mandates or were prodded into action. The US administration took the lead among governments, although with some reluctance and needing to be energized by an outraged US Congress, public, and media. The Western democracies together with Japan coordinated their policies and imposed material and

---

[9] This phrase is used and defined in Risse *et al.* (eds.), *The Power of Human Rights,* 18 (and see, too, references in this text to the authors' earlier related work). This Conclusion demonstrates my indebtedness to the idea of a spiral model of human rights change first introduced in this edited volume. I believe that the Chinese case fits this model reasonably well, although, as noted earlier, the criteria that need to be satisfied in reference to stage 4 of the model, the prescriptive stage, seem overly demanding. My study suggests that there is considerable space between stage 3, 'tactical concessions', and stage 4, 'prescriptive status', the in-between stage that China is at in my view.

symbolic sanctions; the UN Sub-Commission and its parent body introduced condemnatory resolutions; and the Chinese added fuel to the fire
by rounding up activists and forcing others to flee, many of whom joined
human rights campaigning groups overseas or established new organizations of their own. Beijing claimed that sanctions were unjust in circumstances where the Tiananmen protesters were bent on overthrowing the
state; moreover, international condemnation was a violation of the overriding norm of state sovereignty and non-interference in domestic affairs.
Neither of these arguments carried much weight, except perhaps in some
of its Asian neighbours. Instead, the combining of these opposing forces
put the Beijing government decidedly on the defensive.

Despite these Chinese objections to 'external interference', after a time
the leadership felt compelled to respond in two main ways in order to try
to recover some of its position in international society: within seven
months it had offered tactical concessions, such as releasing some
detained demonstrators and removing martial law, and had begun to
engage in public debate with its major critics. But in order to do this with
any degree of sophistication it had to draw on the skills of leading
Chinese academics, encouraging them to study the concept of human
rights, to provide help with the writing of an authoritative statement—the
1991 White Paper—of the Chinese position on rights, and eventually as
the dialogic mode became more prominent to suggest arguments to
counter those of China's major interlocutors.[10] These domestic debates
logically began to feed into those already taking place in the broader
areas of law reform, resulting in reference to international standards as a
way of preventing any return to the highly arbitrary use of power associated with the Cultural Revolution and earlier eras, and tackling legal
problems that the leadership had discovered came in the wake of running
a market economy. Openings had occurred, therefore, opportunities for
those outsiders who stood ready to provide funding to support particular
research projects or training that had a bearing on human rights protections; and space for the elaboration of ideas beyond those officially sanctioned, including for those political activists brave enough to test the real
meaning of the rhetoric of rights. A process had been set in train and
gained momentum, even as the sanctions states had originally imposed
were almost entirely removed. The Chinese leadership moved from the
denial stage, through tactical concessions and argumentation, almost to
prescriptive status where Beijing referred regularly to human rights

---

[10] There were especial ironies here in that a number of the Chinese lawyers that helped
the Beijing government had had their legal and human rights training funded by Western
foundations or governments.

norms in commentary on its own record and that of its major critics. But, as will be shown below, its language on human rights was neither consistent nor linear in development. Although enhanced efforts were made to publicize the new laws, and punish those, for example, who practised torture, or disobeyed other aspects of that revised criminal legislation, it was made apparent that the provisions would be overridden in the event of any threat to the CCP's monopoly on political power, or of widespread social unrest. A heightening of concern over increased reference to the norm of humanitarian intervention also contributed to the unevenness.

Why did the Chinese leadership feel the need to engage in an external debate over its human rights record and to offer compromises? A floor for this had already been built in the pre-Tiananmen era with China's policy decision, connected with its economic reform efforts, to participate more fully in all the central regimes—including human rights—that make up the substance of international society. The aftermath of 4 June forced Beijing to become more attentive to material and symbolic considerations. Foreign trade, investment, and tourism were all affected by the economic sanctions and by evidence that China was not, after all, at the forefront of reform as the cold war was coming to an end. Where once the USA had offered it trading privileges never granted to the Soviet Union, between 1990 and 1994 the renewal of MFN status with the USA came under threat on human rights grounds. Those Chinese committed to the economic reforms were alarmed that the reformist agenda appeared to be in jeopardy. Once Deng Xiaoping had exerted his authority and had called in 1992 for a full-scale return to the open-door policies, this implied unavoidable engagement in the human rights discourse with important trade and investment partners.

Beyond instrumental reasons, however, other aspects of Chinese behaviour showed it cared deeply about its international image, and strongly desired to be able to counter the condemnatory statements made in a variety of venues, whether at the G7, the UNCHR, or at gatherings of the EU Council of Ministers. This required deeper study of the concept of human rights and the development of an authoritative statement to show its domestic élite that it could take on those external critics. Condemnation in the form of UNCHR draft resolutions proved particularly irksome to Beijing, because, despite its politicized nature, this multilateral body still had more legitimacy than individual governments when it came to making critical statements. Year after year Chinese diplomats worked extremely hard to avoid the introduction of a resolution, using the diplomatic tools of promised rewards or retribution, and issuing attacks on the legitimacy of its main critics. China's initial attempts to claim that such resolutions represented interference in internal matters were sternly rebuffed, members of the UNCHR and Chinese scholars—the latter, behind the scenes—pointing to the illogicality, for example, of China's membership of the Commission, or ratification of the Convention against Torture, or—later on—agreement to submit reports on behalf of Hong Kong to the Human Rights Committee, if it were to espouse this view. Better by far to emphasize the improvements China had made in the lives of its citizens, to compare these conditions favourably with those in other developing countries, and to play on those cultural relativist and developmentalist arguments that still commanded a respectful hearing in some parts of the global community. More satisfactory still was the decision to attack the records of major Western critics, especially the USA, harping on about Washington's failure to sign or ratify certain of the major human rights conventions or to recognize the problems in its own society.

Such criticism of the USA could only go so far, however. All Chinese leaders, even Mao Zedong from the mid-1950s, have acted as though they wanted sustained high-level contact with US administrations. Strategic need undoubtedly has always formed a part of the explanation, and in the post-Mao era the strength of the US economic market has also played a major role.[11] Nevertheless, the Beijing leadership has perceived the USA as primarily responsible for denying the country its rightful place in global politics. Sino-American summit meetings and regular diplomatic exchanges, on the other hand, would suggest that China had achieved some equality of status. Concepts such as 'strategic triangle' and 'strategic partnership' were important symbols of that, but so too were public 'mutual exchanges', such as relatively unscripted debates between presidents at press conferences in each country's capital.

In order to secure those meetings, and crucially the summits in Washington and Beijing, Chinese leaders realized that further concessions in the human rights area would be required. The USA and its Western allies, having largely moved away from material sanctions (military sales were still restricted), offered further to temper their verbal criticism if China would deliver on a range of issues. The kinds of changes they were looking for were the release of some of the high-profile dissidents, signature of the covenants, an invitation to the UN High Commissioner for Human Rights to visit, and negotiations with the Dalai Lama. The Chinese decided that staggered adoption of the first three would be enough to offset the pressure, and would allow them to promote their objective of dealing with the human rights issue more

---

[11] Over one-third of Chinese exports go to that important market, for example, boosting China's foreign exchange earnings, and thus having a major effect on other aspects of the economic reform programme.

discreetly, on the basis of mutual exchanges in private bilateral settings. Yet, despite China's success in the promotion of its objective, and the weakening of governmental pressure, the issue still did not go away. Human rights matters continued to cast a shadow over Chinese diplomacy and to contribute to the denial of legitimate statehood as it came to be defined in the late twentieth century. Having extended these invitations, signed such covenants, and engaged more deeply in the international discourse, Beijing found that new expectations regarding compliance came hard on the heels of these commitments: from domestic legal reformers and political activists who pointed to China's signature of international conventions, and the way such standards could solve some of the country's own problems; and from transnational NGOs, UN bodies, and national governments, some of which recognized the value of continuing to play on China's concern for its international reputation and thus the need for it to be seen to live up to its international treaty obligations.

Thus US power, the activities of UN human rights institutions, and NGO lobbying were to prove crucial in drawing China into this normative area, as were Beijing's concerns about image, great power status, and its understanding that the basis of legitimate statehood had undergone change. Having begun to debate the concept of human rights in global and domestic arenas, Chinese officials tended to become locked into particular discursive formulations, not irrevocably, but to a degree sufficient to show that ideas were being shaped and developed. Domestic groups were also to use the political space that was provided by China's international discourse and growing international commitments to push their own arguments for reform, particularly manifest in some of the new or revised legislation that had a bearing on civil rights. Nevertheless, despite these important moves, China's normative enmeshment has only gone so far and has to be distinguished from the deeper task of internalization and domestic implementation.

CONSTRAINTS ON INTERNALIZATION

Academic lawyers, although with different emphases on different parts of the argument, have persuasively argued that legal compliance arrives not as a result of coercion, but from the iterative process of discourse involving justification and persuasion among relevant parties, and from the belief that the rule in question has a high degree of legitimacy.[12] Other

---

[12] See in particular Chayes and Chayes, *The New Sovereignty*, Franck, *Fairness*, and his *The Power of Legitimacy.*

scholars have stated that full compliance comes only with domestic internalization of the rule in question,[13] a much harder test. Many of China's
legal reforms, which have involved the incorporation of international
standards, imply an acceptance of the legitimacy of at least some of the
rules. The Chinese leadership's agreement to dialogues on human rights,
and hosting of visits by a UN Working Group and a Special Rapporteurs,
further help legitimize international standards and practices in this issue
area. These actions also represent an admission that China requires the
help of outsiders to bring those standards to bear in the domestic society.
Movement to the next stage of full implementation, however, is proving
to be an extraordinarily difficult challenge. Those focusing on China's
human rights record want the country to shift to the point where all key
domestic groups accept, either for instrumental or cognitive reasons, the
benefits of adopting international standards. If China moved to the stage
where it became uncontroversial to refer to human rights norms and
where exceptions to the application of the rules were no longer deemed
acceptable, then we could acknowledge that domestic internalization had
indeed taken place.

Neither China's domestic laws and certainly not its practice have
reached that level of compliance, reminders of which came in early 1999
with the continuing use of arbitrary detention, intolerance of peaceful,
organized opposition, and regular reports of torture while in custody.
Moreover, even at the level of discourse, we have seen how unstable
human rights language can be when articulated by Chinese officials, rang-
ing from references that place emphasis on universality and indivisibility
of all rights outlined in the UDHR and two covenants, to those that
stress the need to take full account of a country's culture, history, or level
of development; from direct criticism of Indonesian governmental
failures to protect the rights of ethnic Chinese, to a post-Kosovo re-
emphasis on the norm of state sovereignty strongly linked with non-
interference. At the 1993 Vienna World Conference, for example, Chinese
officials moved from an initial line that there were no rights beyond
borders, no individual rights beyond the needs of state and society, to a
statement in support of the Final Declaration that proclaimed, 'the
protection of human rights was international society's common responsibility'. In the year—1999—that the Chinese government hosted a UN
Needs Assessment Mission and hinted that the Special Rapporteur on
Torture might visit, it also took the lead in voicing strong criticism of Kofi
Annan's speech before the 54th UN General Assembly, China's Foreign

---

[13] Koh, 'Why do Nations Obey International Law?', 2602, makes this point in reference
to Chayes and Chayes, *The New Sovereignty*, and Franck, *Fairness*.

Minister arguing that respect for state sovereignty and non-interference were the 'basic principles governing international relations' and that their absence would lead to a new form of 'gunboat diplomacy' that would 'wreak havoc'.[14]

That instability in rhetoric, ambiguities in revised or new legislation, and failure to follow through to full implementation stem from three main areas: the practical and philosophical underpinnings of the international human rights regime; the concerns and conflicting needs of states operating within it; and domestic factors associated with China, undoubtedly the most crucial level determining full acceptance or otherwise. The size of the implementation task facing China is enormous, deriving from a long-term disrespect and disregard for the law, the inattention to overcoming the fragmentation of laws recently introduced in large numbers and at rapid speed, and what the Beijing leadership has described as weaknesses in the chain of command. But of more significance is the Party's signals to those well attuned to reading them that it is unwilling, finally, to tip the balance towards the rights of the individual and away from the needs of society. The Party defines those needs as the maintenance of political and social stability and the removal of threats to territorial integrity. The means chosen to reach those goals comprise the 'strike-hard' campaigns against supposed criminal elements, the arrest of the leadership of any group that shows evidence of being well organized and capable of promoting alternatives to Party-dominated rule, and—where Tibet is concerned—the attempt to undermine loyalty to the Dalai Lama and the Buddhist religion and culture while treating with extreme harshness any Tibetan who advocates independence.

The Chinese leadership can claim some success in gaining domestic acceptance of these objectives, even though there are 'live volcanoes everywhere' as the result of the lack of institutionalized channels for resolving and channelling grievances.[15] Most Chinese one meets seem to see no real alternative to CCP rule, do not support independence for Tibet, or believe that the Tiananmen demonstrations in retrospect were profitable means of bringing about desired changes within the

---

[14] *International Herald Tribune*, 24 Sept. 1999. A key difference for China is that, in the case of the UN Mission and Special Rapporteur, Beijing had issued the invitations, whereas Annan's speech reinforced the fear that humanitarian intervention could occur in the absence of a government's official invitation. However, given the Beijing government's seeming reluctance to issue its invitations, the distinction risks being overstated.

[15] The phrase was used by a Chinese social scientist in discussion with Andrew Nathan. See his *China's Transition* (New York: Columbia University Press, 1997), 228. See too relevant recent essays by Minxin Pei, 'Is China Unstable?' and 'Will China Become Another Indonesia?', the former distributed via e-mail by the Foreign Policy Research Institute's Asia Program, Philadelphia, 2 July 1999, the latter published in *Foreign Policy*, (Fall 1999).

society.[16] Popular nationalism often bolsters such beliefs and, if survey data are reliable, is reinforced by Western criticisms of China's human rights record. Moreover, the Party has posed serious dilemmas for dissidents in the way in which they articulate their concerns. As Christopher Hughes has put it: more pressing for the political activist than the difficulties of organizing beyond the control of the Party-State is 'how to present dissent as a legitimate activity, rather than as a traitorous movement to derail the process of nation-building',[17] especially so it might be added at a time when the country faces the prospects of low economic growth and the task of massive economic restructuring.[18]

These 'blocking factors'[19] mean that the leadership can appeal to large parts of its domestic audience on the basis of the competing norm of state sovereignty traditionally defined, and with the claim that external criticism of its record is an example of power politics in action. If we accept that external factors are secondary to the domestic realm when it comes to the promotion and protection of human rights, then these arguments are somewhat sobering. When Beijing gives prominence to these points, however, it places the country at the centre of a discourse on human rights that is more frequently found among certain developing countries, and not necessarily among those with whom many Chinese wish to share a common identity. Thus, despite these blocking factors, China's twin identities of great power and developing country introduce particular dilemmas for the leadership in its handling of the human rights question.

The struggle between these nationalist and internationalist aspects in China's foreign policy has led the leadership to seek to demonstrate forward movement with respect to the human rights regime, but only under its full control and at the level of participation that its needs dictate. There is much about the human rights regime that allows for this. Among governments that claim a human rights dimension to their policies, there are still individuals within them, to use Jack Donnelly's threefold distinction, that

---

[16] It hardly needs repeating that the fate of the former Soviet Union resonates strongly in support of this subsequent appraisal of the Tiananmen protests.

[17] Christopher Hughes, 'China and Liberalism Globalised', *Millennium: Journal of International Studies*, 24/3 (1995), 436. And see too his 'Globalisation and Nationalism: Squaring the Circle in Chinese International Relations Theory', *Millennium*, 26/1 (1997), 103–24.

[18] Robert F. Dernberger predicts, for example, that the full impact of the Asian economic crisis is likely to hit China's export trade from late 1999, reducing the vital contribution that such trade has played in sustaining the impressive growth rates of the Chinese economy. See 'The People's Republic of China at 50: The Economy', *China Quarterly*, Special Issue, no. 159, (Sept. 1999), 612–13.

[19] The term is used in Risse *et al.* (eds.), *The Power of Human Rights*, esp. 260–62.

cling to a realist belief that promotion of the national interest mostly does not require a concern for human rights conditions in other states. Others continue to support the statist argument that traditionally defined state sovereignty as the basis for international law has proven a viable means of sustaining some form of world order and should not be jettisoned lightly. Yet others subscribe to the view that we live in a world of diversity and should retain a commitment to international pluralism.[20] Especially where a large and important state such as China is concerned, one or other of these arguments is often not far below the surface, in part because they command some respect, but also because other policy interests are inevitably a part of any relationship with Beijing. In these circumstances, an easy—often wrong—assumption is made that human rights concerns inevitably come into conflict with these other interests. China managed to convince various Western states that it would veto the UN Security Council resolution legitimizing intervention in the Gulf conflict in 1991, that it would exact economic retribution if states persisted in promoting condemnatory resolutions at the UNCHR, that it would withdraw its support from other regimes dear to the hearts of many such governments—involving weapons proliferation, nuclear testing, and the like—and that it would do nothing to help the reduction of tensions on the Korean peninsula, if material and symbolic sanctions connected with the human rights issue remained in place. Yet, in each of these cases, Beijing had interests that were close to those of the Western states, which actually would have placed a restraint on its possibly uncooperative behaviour.

The fear of reverse Chinese economic sanctions has been particularly influential, especially, for example, with EU states, anxious to raise their political and economic profiles in a country (and region of the world) that has until recently posted formidable growth rates and that has retained its allure as the largest potential domestic market. Reaching a common EU foreign policy has proven difficult to effect in a general sense, and especially so in reference to China's human rights record, mainly for economic reasons. Similarly, US business fears that loss of MFN status, or the priority given to human rights issues, would inevitably damage its role as a central Chinese trading and investment partner have regularly been voiced and came to a head in favour of China and US business in 1994. Some governments, such as the French, openly stated that economic deals with China that would improve the economic prospects of French citizens were what truly mattered—by implication, therefore, that democratic

---

[20] Jack Donnelly, *Universal Human Rights in Theory and Practice* (Ithaca, NY: Cornell University Press, 1989), 229–35.

governments do not represent the needs of citizens in another country, but only those within their own borders. The joint statement between Presidents Chirac and Jiang in May 1997 demonstrated a bargaining rather than a principled approach to the human rights issue on the part of the French, with nods in the direction of universality of rights—the French part of the statement—the sanctity of the UN Charter which both parties could interpret in satisfactory ways, and, finally, for China's benefit, the reference to the need to take 'fully into account particularities on all sides'.[21]

Compared with the USA, other governments have operated in more permissive environments when it has come to setting the priorities for their China policies. Foreign policy-making in European capitals, for example, unlike in Washington, tends to be a more élitist affair, and generally less confrontational. The US separation of powers, lack of party discipline, and sense of mission largely account for America's more politicized approach. The growing fragmentation and issue-specific approach to foreign policy provide opportunities for human rights lobbying groups to find support in the US Congress, and increasingly within the administration. These divisions and openings have made it impossible for US administrations to ignore the human rights question in China policy, as we have seen even during the less than receptive Reagan and Bush eras. In the post-cold-war era, and in the absence of the USA–China tacit alliance against the Soviet Union, this avoidance has become more difficult still. Indeed, the loss of this strategic rationale, and the nature of domestic politics, encouraged Clinton when presidential candidate to give emphasis to human rights in relations with Beijing, a stance that proved difficult to slough off when other China issues came to the fore.

Nevertheless, despite the fact that the USA has been crucial to the process as it has unfolded, and has played the leading role among democratic states, Washington has proven controversial as a norm entrepreneur in this field, deriving from its superpower status, which renders it liable to charges of bullying, and an impatience with multilateral approaches to diplomacy, although these remain the best means of avoiding charges of US moral imperialism. Washington has also displayed a lack of consistency in this area, not simply because of strategic structural changes at the systemic level, but also because it perceives itself as operating as the 'custodian of international order', a role that requires attention to a range of global norms beyond those associated with human

---

[21] *Le Monde*, 17 May 1997; see also Ch. 7 above.

rights.[22] The USA's own record of failure to give full protection to certain domestic groups, to ratify all of the central human rights treaties, and especially to eschew reservations at the time of ratification of the ICCPR—some fifteen years after signature—have operated to constrain its role as a spokesperson or model for others. These actions have opened Washington to charges of hypocrisy, and to the claim that international legal rules do not apply to it, only to the weaker states. For these reasons, the US message with respect to China's human rights is made weaker and that weakness reduces the size of the constituency sympathetic to Washington's criticism of Beijing.

Western democratic governments, although they are essential actors in promoting human rights norms, are flawed participants, then, not always able to sustain the human rights element in foreign policies, or to apply it consistently when faced with transgressions by such powerful states as China. The shifting nature of the coalitions at the UNCHR among the Central and East Europeans, Latin American, and African states also points to contingent behaviour rather than consistent support for a strong human rights regime. NGOs, legislatures, and the media thus have had their work cut out. As we have seen, they have played vital roles in providing information, monitoring governmental performance, and casting a sceptical eye over claims that rights issues were still being pursued, especially when human rights dialogues with China came to be organized on a private basis, primarily by foreign ministry officials who had issues in addition to human rights on their agendas. Many of the Western officials and diplomats that I have spoken to some ten years after the Tiananmen bloodshed, when the shock of those events has faded, and especially where their remits have covered political relations rather than solely human rights, acknowledged this conflict among their interests. They have also evinced a sympathy for China's burdens reminiscent of those arguments that had led to the neglect of the country's human rights record prior to June 1989 and that connected with the once fashionable notion that rapid political reform might endanger economic growth rates. Their concern to promote other core foreign policy goals—agreements on controls on weapons of mass destruction or the signature of economic contracts—has inevitably expanded that sympathy. Competing interests, then, have pushed them towards neglect of the inconvenient and difficult human rights issue, a level of neglect contained only by the realization that they cannot abjure it altogether. This governmental realization, coupled with the desire to ensure the issue is handled in a way that mini-

---

[22] See W. Michael Reisman, 'The United States and International Institutions', *Survival*, 41/4 (Winter 1999–2000), for a fuller discussion of this point.

mizes conflict with the Beijing government, underpinned that decision to accept China's call for private dialogue rather than public condemnation.

Conflicts of interest aside, however, by the mid-1990s many Western officials were beginning to demonstrate an impatience with the public, UN, condemnatory route, despite its obvious role in gaining human rights concessions from China. Many focused too directly on the inability to defeat China's no-action motion in the UNCHR, rather than the Chinese concessions that often accompanied the introduction of a draft condemnatory resolution. Others wanted to deal with the problem through positive actions: to offer their expertise in the legal area, for example, in an effort to make some difference on the ground. The liberal principles on which such states are based promoted a sympathy for the size of China's reformist task, a respect for its difference, and a tendency to accept the 'doable' rather than the desirable in terms of policy objectives. Perhaps this explains the obvious dislike of a former British Foreign Minister[23] of some of the analyses contained in NGO reports, which he implied showed a more general lack of understanding of the complexity of decision-making. When out of office, he stated:

The business of government, particularly in face of the unforeseen or the unusual, of disorder or emergency, is immensely difficult. Split second errors of judgement, driven by misunderstanding or fear, peril or inexperience, can often have catastrophic results—from the Boston Tea Party to Bloody Sunday . . . arm-chair verdicts which make no allowance for real difficulties, or which are expressed in terms which are intemperate or absolutist, can be damagingly counter-productive. So too, if they give no credit for improvements in performance, or criticize in terms which are patronising or exaggerated.[24]

One needs to be wary of the 'real' motives of diplomats, and especially arguments justifying human rights abuses that have been in clear violation of international standards; but part of the reason for that generosity of interpretation of the efforts China has made to introduce reforms is a keen sense of past mistakes in one's own country's record and strong attachment to liberal principles of tolerance and diversity. In addition, given the long present aims on the part of the major states to draw China into the international community, another governmental fear is that absolutist criticism will undermine those objectives, fixing China permanently into the status of outsider, and lock it into an opposing block of states.

---

[23] Lord Howe was Foreign Secretary at the time of the Tiananmen massacre and in 1992 led a delegation to China to discuss human rights concerns. The delegation's critical conclusions are in, Howe, *Visit to China by the Delegation led by Lord Howe of Aberavon*, and are outlined in Ch. 6 above.

[24] Geoffrey Howe, Opening Speech to Amnesty International London Seminar on Human Rights in China, 9 Sept. 1996, 5.

Governments, for these kinds of reasons, have provided the Chinese leadership with time, room for manœuvre, and the opportunity to retain a degree of control over its participation in the international human rights regime. Beijing has also found that certain of its descriptions of the regime find resonance with others. One argument it uses to undercut its full acceptance of universality and indivisibility—that human rights improvements are a 'continuously developing process'—are true in a narrow or distorted sense. The list of human rights has evolved and expanded over time in response, for example, to concerns about disappearances, discrimination against women, and other ideas that have emerged as we have considered and reconsidered what contributes to human dignity. This means that some will be reasonably satisfied when Beijing states, as it did in its White Paper of 1996, that 'China, as a developing country, is restricted by its historical and realistic conditions, and the country's human rights conditions still have room for improvement'. Others will be heartened by Chinese statements that 'all roads lead to Rome', suggesting that China shares the same goals as its human rights critics, but has to find its own path to reaching those goals.

Moreover, academics and practitioners in the wider global community still engage in lively debate over what constitutes human rights: whether economic and social rights are really human rights (it remains particularly controversial to claim so in parts of the US political system); whether culture is relevant or irrelevant in testing the validity of a right; and where we draw the line between the idea of human rights being universal and acceptance of the need to allow considerable variation in the ways rights are implemented.[25] The Asian values debate, particularly prominent in the early 1990s, and despite its essentially political and instrumental nature, breathed new life into many of these issues. It reminded China that there was a community of like-minded states that also believed in statist and relativist forms of argument, that saw in the emerging human rights conditionalities new forms of moral and economic imperialism, and that also believed that the growing attention to ideas of humanitarian intervention were likely simply to reinforce the old, familiar international hierarchies. Certain of the Asian values arguments also garnered support among individuals in democratic states, in part because leading proponents, such as officials in Singapore and Malaysia, were governing stable countries and posting enviable growth rates, but also because arguments about the correct balance between rights and

---

[25] See e.g. the debates in Dunne and Wheeler (eds.), *Human Rights in Global Politics.* Where I stand on these matters is beside the point; my argument here is that these key issues remain in some contention.

duties, or between the needs of society and the self, were hardly novel in the developed West either. That Asian values debate seems now to have run its course, at least in the form in which it was articulated in the early 1990s,[26] seen off by the Asian economic crisis, the overthrow of the Suharto regime in Indonesia, the underlying weaknesses in the argument, and the alternative voices that emerged from the region to question its central premisses. However, it served to demonstrate anew that there still exist serious challenges to solidarist conceptions of international society, and that the universality of rights is still under debate even at the philosophical level, thus allowing those who believe in or wish to make use of the belief in relativist conceptions to find sources of legitimation.

Other aspects of the human rights regime also contribute to the delay in full implementation or acceptance. We are familiar with what Chayes and Chayes have referred to as the temporal dimension: the recognition that there is likely to be a considerable time lag before a party can bring itself into full compliance with a treaty.[27] Moreover, in the human rights areas there are important permissible exceptions or reservations that can be entered at the time of treaty adherence. The Chinese government rarely if ever refers to it, for example, but, when it ratified the Convention against Torture, it entered a reservation under Article 28 to denote that it does not recognize the competence of the CAT to examine evidence that indicates that 'torture is being systematically practised in the territory of a State Party' and to undertake a 'confidential inquiry' if the evidence warrants it.[28] States that are party to that convention have to report only every four years. If reports submitted are inadequate or deadlines are missed, there is little the Committee can do beyond issuing admonishments and reminders. Ann Kent has argued persuasively that the Chinese government, in its reports to the CAT, has moved from producing one deemed 'completely inadequate' in 1990, and requiring a supplementary to be submitted,[29] to the point where its second periodic report of December 1995 (two years late) was commended for being in procedural compliance with its reporting obligations. This commendation came even while the Committee recognized that torture was still being carried out on a widespread

---

[26] Even Senior Minister Lee Kuan-yew, a leading spokesperson for Asian values, by 1998 was willing to concede: 'There are certain weaknesses in Confucianism . . . You owe a duty to your family and loyalty to your friends, to help and support them. That's Confucianism. But this value is degraded when you use public resources through your official position to do your duty to your family and be loyal to your friends' (*Time Magazine*, 16 Mar. 1998 and quoted in François Godement, *The Downsizing of Asia* (London: Routledge, 1999), 107).   [27] Chayes and Chayes, *The New Sovereignty*, 15.
[28] It also entered reservations under Articles 22 (acceptance of individual complaints) and 21 (acceptance of complaints of non-compliance by another State Party).
[29] It came in two and half years later.

basis in China, as the Special Rapporteur's annual (though less visible) reports graphically indicated.[30] The CAT is recognized as having one of the strongest monitoring procedures in the human rights treaty area, but even here a state resistant to quickening the pace at which it comes into full behavioural compliance can reduce the effects of shaming by bringing itself into reasonable conformity with the CAT's reporting requirements.[31]

CHINA'S EFFECT ON THE HUMAN RIGHTS REGIME

That China has been brought some way into the international human rights regime, therefore, has been beneficial to the expansion of that regime's claim to universality, but has also exposed the weaknesses within it. Beijing, allying with others on the UNCHR, has worked to restrict the mandates of some of the Working Groups, and has questioned the Commission's impartiality by alleging over-weaning focus on civil and political rights to the neglect of economic and social questions, and on the human rights records of developing countries. These latter moves represent an attempt to undercut the legitimacy of the body and to cast it as a tool of the developed West. A further notable development has been Beijing's success in labelling the UNCHR's attempts to introduce draft resolutions that condemn a state's human rights conduct 'confrontational' and therefore by implication an unproductive route. A similar fate has befallen the Sub-Commission of experts, also persuaded to pass a resolution in 1997 that adopted Chinese language on the benefits of cooperation over confrontation. It has been striking how many of China's dialogue partners have accepted such terminology, initially unaware, perhaps, of the extent to which use of such phrases would act as a constraint on their future options.

Yet, while acknowledging these weaknesses associated with norm promotion in the human rights area, and the linguistic changes that China has been able to introduce, Beijing too has become caught up in the rhetoric. Notwithstanding Beijing's criticisms of Kofi Annan's appeal on behalf of individual sovereignty, it has often adopted the language of universality and indivisibility, particularly in the case of its more regular

---

[30] Kent, *China, the United Nations, and Human Rights*, 93–105.

[31] A valuable discussion of the strengths and weaknesses of international reporting procedures and their effects on implementation is contained in Donnelly, *Universal Human Rights*, 250–58.

communications with the UN Secretary General, with the UN High Commissioner, or at UN meetings. Economic, cultural, and social rights were 'just as important' as civil and political rights, Beijing was to state to more than one international audience in 1998, a formulation on rights that is difficult to keep hidden from other, particularly domestic, arenas. The regular production of human rights White Papers has led to a steadily increasing emphasis on the civil and political rights that Chinese allegedly enjoy and claim, together with more forthright condemnations of unlawful behaviour on the part of those charged with legal enforcement. This provides opportunities for domestic political reformers to explore the implications of those statements when circumstances permit, and avenues for external actors to work with domestic groups in support of those claims. China's discursive enmeshment, thus, can help to promote human rights norms internally and externally.

Some of China's criticisms of the way that human rights questions are dealt with globally have also not been entirely to the detriment of norm diffusion. Achieving a correct balance between the rights contained in the two covenants is a worthwhile ambition for the reasons that underlie the arguments for indivisibility. Also of wider benefit, and as a result of China's dialogue with its critics over human rights, is the contribution these debates have made in making some governments more sensitive to their own records. Some have begun to search for parallels in their past or current experiences to show that countries face many problems in common, although the depth of those problems is plainly much greater in some cases than in others. Harold Hongju Koh's references in discussions with the Chinese to earlier injustices in the USA's juvenile detention system, and in other venues to US failures to ratify certain key conventions, are an indication of that. Before an audience at the US Institute for Peace, and in a speech that made much reference to China, he quoted Martin Luther King in support of an argument that America must recognize the interdependence and interrelatedness of all rights, including the economic, social, and cultural.[32] The EU statement at the 1998 UNCHR, and reference in 1999 in its first ever annual human rights report to actions necessary to combat racism in Europe, though small steps forward, may have been made in part as a result of Chinese promptings and cries of hypocrisy. These developments can only be of benefit to the overall development of the human rights regime, not to mention to the improvement of the lot of individuals at the heart of it.

The level of pressure on China over its human rights record is undoubtedly less in 2000, especially when compared with the period 1989

---

[32] Koh, 'Promoting Human Rights in the Pursuit of Peace', esp. 14 (Internet edn.).

to 1995. The analysis presented here has shown that the movement that has taken place in China's position has come as a result of a combination of public and private pressure, and of material and symbolic sanctions. The discourse of rights with its iterative elements has played its part and has contributed, alongside the political bargaining between China and the West, to the non-linear process of enmeshment that has been set in train. Governments, even under conditions of reduced pressure, do seem to be convinced themselves, and to have had some success in convincing Beijing, that the issue is never going to be laid entirely to rest while China's record invites such concern.

Governmental actions—and especially that of the USA—have been important in extracting concessions from China in the short to medium terms. Over the longer term, however, the work of the UN—the High Commissioner, Special Rapporteurs, and Working Groups—together with the NGOs remains crucial to further forward movement, in drawing attention both to continuing violations, and to failures on the part of governments to take the requisite action in the face of evidence of abuse. They also perform major roles in recommending means of improvement. Gradual acceptance of the idea that legitimate statehood has come to depend on the extent to which governments protect the human rights of their peoples and that others have a right, even a duty, to set and maintain standards has had increasing influence over many areas of behaviour in the international system, and has helped to reinforce the work of these individuals and bodies. Important too is that Chinese society has become more open, and that these ideas regarding legitimate statehood have taken root among some constituencies in China, and could come to the fore with considerable rapidity in changed political circumstances. In the absence of fundamental change, however, this is likely to be a lengthy process of domestic acceptance, with many twists and turns.

Legal and judicial training can play a role in all of this, but that depends on the way those newly trained put their skills to use—whether they service the Party, themselves, or contribute to the collective good. The Chinese government can also undercut the potentially beneficial impact of increased attention to rule of law if its actions do not show consistent disapproval of the arbitrary use of power. Political signals are additionally crucial. Beijing has acted sternly and swiftly from time to time to remove, repress, or constrain the actions and discourse of organized groupings outside the Party's political control. It has also had some considerable success in generating a form of angry nationalism that can similarly stymie engagement with human rights critics.

Many would argue that, at the end of the twentieth-century, the Chinese government's disregard for human rights has substantially increased and would assert that much of what I have designated in this study as progress is a kind of chimera. Certainly the crackdown on Falun Gong members, democracy activists, and on other political reformers leaves no room for complacency. However, it has been my argument that the diffusion of human rights norms is neither linear, nor incapable of being periodically halted. When viewed over the longer term, and despite the recent political chill in China, global criticism of China's human rights record has served to involve Beijing in the international debate over human rights, and drawn it into important aspects of the international human rights regime. It has resulted, too, in legal changes that have shown a partial responsiveness to the requirements of international standards, and has helped to bolster the demands of domestic reformers. Chinese withdrawal from this process or denial that this degree of participation has taken place is no longer a viable option. A type of infrastructure that can help to protect human rights has begun to be built, and it stands ready to be drawn upon in the advent of progressive political reform. Indeed, it may carry within it the capacity to hasten that political change.

China's external critics, as we have seen, have contributed substantially to this process; but—in the absence of specific points of leverage—they are at their most effective when they form credible and united coalitions, supply information that is accurate, operate with some consistency, and firmly base their arguments on international standards. If it is approached in this manner, there is the possibility of undermining the type of Chinese nationalist resentment that reinforces a preference for exclusion from the international society of those in better standing, and for bolstering the position of those in China who regard dissent not as an unpatriotic act but as having played the major role in promoting progress since the opening to reform in 1978.

BIBLIOGRAPHY

SERIES

Amnesty International Reports (annual reports, London)
Beijing Review
British Broadcasting Corporation Monitoring Reports, *Summary of World Broadcasts* (*SWB*), Asia/Pacific
chinabrief (formerly, *China Development Briefing*) (Hong Kong: vols. 1 and 2)
China Daily
China News Digest
China Rights Forum (journal of Human Rights in China, New York)
Clarinet News Service
Far Eastern Economic Review
Faxue Yanjiu
Ford Foundation Annual Reports
Foreign Broadcast Information Service (FBIS), Daily Reports for China, East Asia, former Soviet Bloc, Western Europe
Human Rights Quarterly
Human Rights Watch World Reports (annual reports, New York)
International Herald Tribune
Keesing's: Record of World Events (London: Longmans)
Netherlands Quarterly of Human Rights
Royal Institute of International Affairs, London (press files)
Tessitore, John, and Woolfson, Susan (eds.), *Issues before the xx General Assembly of the United Nations* (annual publication of the United Nations Association of the USA; Lexington, Mass.: Lexington Books, 1988–90).
—— —— (eds.), *A Global Agenda: Issues before the xx General Assembly of the United Nations* (annual publication of the United Nations Association of the USA; Lanham, Md.: Rowman & Littlefield Publishers, 1991–8).
United Nations, ECOSOC, reports of UN Commission, Sub-Commission, Working Groups, and Special Rapporteurs at E/CN.4/.
US Department of State, *Country Reports on Human Rights Practices* (annual reports, Washington: US Government Printing Office) or via Internet as *China Country Report on Human Rights Practices*.
USA, *Public Papers of the President* (Washington: US Government Printing Office).

PUBLISHED MATERIALS

Alford, William P., 'Tasselled Loafers for Barefoot Lawyers: Transformation and Tension in the World of Chinese Legal Workers', in Stanley B. Lubman, B. (ed.), *China's Legal Reforms* (Oxford: Oxford University Press, 1996).

Alston Philip, 'The Commission on Human Rights', in Philip Alston (ed.), *The United Nations and Human Rights: A Critical Appraisal* (Oxford: Oxford University Press, 1992).

—— 'The Committee on Economic, Social and Cultural Rights', in Philip Alston (ed.) *The United Nations and Human Rights: A Critical Appraisal* (Oxford: Oxford University Press, 1992).

—— (ed.), *The United Nations and Human Rights: A Critical Appraisal* (Oxford: Oxford University Press, 1992).

—— 'The UN's Human Rights Record: From San Francisco to Vienna and Beyond', *Human Rights Quarterly*, 16/2 (1994).

—— (ed.), *The EU and Human Rights* (Oxford: Oxford University Press, 1999).

—— 'Leading by Example: A Human Rights Agenda for the European Union for the Year 2000', launched in Vienna, 9–10 Oct. 1998. Annex to Alston (ed.), *The EU and Human Rights* (Oxford: Oxford University Press, 1999).

Amnesty International, *Political Imprisonment in the People's Republic of China* (London, 1978).

—— *China, Violations of Human Rights: Prisoners of Conscience and the Death Penalty in the People's Republic of China* (London, 1984).

—— *China: Torture and Ill-Treatment of Prisoners* (London, 1987).

—— *Peacekeeping and Human Rights* (London, 1994).

—— *No One is Safe: Amnesty International's Report on China* (London, Mar. 1996).

—— 'Torture and Ill-Treatment: Comments on China's Second Periodic Report to the UN Committee against Torture', ASA 17/51/96, Apr. 1996.

—— *People's Republic of China: Law Reform and Human Rights* (London, Mar. 1997).

—— *Gross Violations of Human Rights in the Xinjiang Uighur Autonomous Region* (London, Apr. 1999).

Andreassen, Bard-Anders, and Swinehart, Theresa, *Human Rights in Developing Countries: 1990 Yearbook* (Kehl: N. P. Engel Publisher, 1991).

Apodaca, Claire, and Stohl, Michael, 'United States Human Rights Policy and Foreign Assistance Allocations from Carter to Clinton: Plus ça change, plus c'est la même chose?', Global Studies Program, Purdue University: Research Papers at www.ippu.purdue.edu. (no date and accessed via Internet, 7 Nov. 1997).

Arase, David, 'Japan's Foreign Policy and Asian Democratization', in Edward Friedman (ed.), *The Politics of Democratization: Generalizing East Asian Experiences* (Boulder, Colo.: Westview Press, 1994).

Arrigo, Linda Gail, 'Notes from the Field: A View of the United Nations

Conference on Human Rights, Vienna, June 1993', *Terra Viva*, no. 7, 18 June 1993.

Baehr, Peter R., *The Role of Human Rights in Foreign Policy*, 2nd edn. (Basingstoke: Macmillan, 1996).

Baker, Philip, 'China: Human Rights and the Law', *Pacific Review*, 6/3 (1993).

Barkin, J. Samuel, and Cronin, Bruce, 'The State and the Nation: Changing Norms and the Rules of Sovereignty in International Relations', *International Organization*, 48/1 (Winter 1994).

Bauer, Joanne R., and Bell, Daniel A. (eds.), *The East Asian Challenge for Human Rights* (Cambridge: Cambridge University Press, 1999).

Beck, Robert J., Arend, Anthony Clark, and Van der Lugt, Robert D. (eds.), *International Rules: Approaches from International Law and International Relations* (New York: Oxford University Press, 1996).

Biersteker, Tom, and Weber, Cynthia (eds.), *State Sovereignty as Social Construct* (Cambridge: Cambridge University Press, 1996).

Boekle, Henning, 'Western States, the UN Commission on Human Rights, and the "1235 Procedure": The "Question of Bias" Revisited', *Netherlands Quarterly of Human Rights*, 13/4 (1995).

Booth, Ken, 'Human Wrongs and International Relations', *International Affairs*, 71 (1995).

Boutros-Ghali, Boutros, *An Agenda for Peace: Preventive Diplomacy, Peacemaking and Peacekeeping* (Report of the Secretary General, 1992).

Braithwaite, John B., *Crime, Shame and Reintegration*. (Cambridge: Cambridge University Press, 1989).

Brody, Reed, Convery, Maureen, and Weissbrodt, David, 'The 42nd Session of the Sub-Commission on Prevention of Discrimination and Protection of Minorities', *Human Rights Quarterly*, 13/2 (1991).

—— Parker, Penny, and Weissbrodt, David, 'Major Developments in 1990 at the UN Commission on Human Rights', *Human Rights Quarterly*, 12/4 (1990).

Brown, Chris, *International Relations: New Normative Approaches* (Hemel Hempstead: Harvester/Wheatsheaf, 1992).

Brownlie, Ian (ed.), *Basic Documents on Human Rights*, 3rd edn. (Oxford: Oxford University Press, 1992).

Buergenthal, Thomas, 'The Normative and Institutional Evolution of International Human Rights', *Human Rights Quarterly*, 19/4 (1997).

Bull, Hedley, and Watson, Adam (eds.), *The Expansion of International Society* (Oxford: Oxford University Press, 1984).

Bush, Richard, 'The Role of Congress in Shaping Washington's China Policy', *Heritage Foundation Reports*, 9 July 1991.

Byrnes, Andrew, 'The Committee against Torture', in Philip Alston (ed.), *The United Nations and Human Rights: A Critical Appraisal* (Oxford: Oxford University Press, 1992).

Carleton, David, and Stohl, Michael, 'The Foreign Policy of Human Rights: Rhetoric and Reality from Jimmy Carter to Ronald Reagan', *Human Rights Quarterly*, 7/2 (1985).

Carter, Jimmy, *Keeping Faith: Memoirs of a President* (London: Collins, 1982).

Chan, Anita, 'Labor Standards and Human Rights: The Case of Chinese Workers under Market Socialism', *Human Rights Quarterly*, 20/4 (1998).

Chayes, Abram, and Chayes, Antonia Handler, *The New Sovereignty: Compliance with International Regulatory Agreements* (Cambridge, Mass.: Harvard University Press, 1995).

Chen, Feng, 'Order and Stability in Social Transition: Neoconservative Political Thought in Post-1989 China', *China Quarterly*, 151 (Sept. 1997).

Chen Jie, 'Human Rights: ASEAN's New Importance to China', *Pacific Review*, 6/3 (1993).

China, Information Office of the State Council, *Human Rights in China* (Beijing: Foreign Languages Press, 1991) (see also subsequent Human Rights white papers released by Information Office of State Council).

—— *Historic Sovereignty and the Human Rights Situation in Tibet* (Beijing: Foreign Languages Press, 1992) (see also subsequent reports on Tibet released by Information Office of State Council).

Chow, Gregory C., *Understanding China's Economy* (Singapore: World Scientific Publisher, 1994).

Clapham, Andrew, *Human Rights and the European Community: A Critical Overview* (Baden-Baden: Nomos Verlagsgesellschaft, 1991).

—— 'Human Rights in the Common Foreign Policy', in Philip Alston, (ed.), *The EU and Human Rights* (Oxford: Oxford University Press, 1999).

Clark, Ann Marie, 'Non-Governmental Organizations and their Influence on International Society', *Journal of International Affairs*, 48/2 (Winter 1995).

Cochran, Molly, *Normative Theory in International Relations* (Cambridge: Cambridge University Press, 1999).

Cohen, Roberta, 'People's Republic of China: The Human Rights Exception', *Human Rights Quarterly*, 9/4 (1987).

Cohen, Stanley, 'Government Responses to Human Rights Reports: Claims, Denials, and Counterclaims', *Human Rights Quarterly*, 18/3 (1996).

Copper, John F., 'Peking's Post-Tienanmen Foreign Policy: The Human Rights Factor', *Issues and Studies*, 30/10 (Oct. 1994).

Cortell, Andrew P., and Davis, James W., Jr., 'How do International Institutions Matter? The Domestic Impact of International Rules and Norms', *International Studies Quarterly*, 40 (1996).

Council of the European Union, *EU Annual Report on Human Rights* (Brussels, 1 Oct. 1999).

Davis, Michael C. (ed.), *Human Rights and Chinese Values: Legal, Philosophical, and Political Perspectives* (Hong Kong: Oxford University Press, 1995).

de Neufville, Judith Innes, 'Human Rights Reporting as a Policy Tool: An Examination of the State Department Country Reports', *Human Rights Quarterly*, 8/4 (1986).

Dernberger, Robert F., 'The People's Republic of China at 50: The Economy', *China Quarterly*, Special Issue, no. 159 (Sept. 1999).

Ding Xinghao, 'Managing Sino-American Relations in a Changing World', *Asian Survey*, 31/12 (Dec. 1991).

Dittmer, Lowell, 'China's Search for its Place in the World', in Brantly Womack (ed.), *Contemporary Chinese Politics in Historical Perspective* (New York: Cambridge University Press, 1991).

—— *Sino-Soviet Normalization and its International Implications, 1945–1990* (Seattle: University of Washington Press, 1992).

—— and Kim, Samuel S. (eds.), *China's Quest for National Identity* (Ithaca, NY: Cornell University Press, 1993).

Donnelly, Jack, 'The Impact of International Action', *International Journal*, 43 (Spring 1988).

—— *Universal Human Rights in Theory and Practice* (Ithaca, NY: Cornell University Press, 1989).

—— 'Human Rights: A New Standard of Civilization?' *International Affairs*, 74/1 (Jan. 1998).

—— *International Human Rights* (Boulder, Colo.: Westview Press, 1998).

—— 'The Social Construction of International Human Rights', in Tim Dunne and Nicholas J. Wheeler (eds.), *Human Rights in Global Politics* (Cambridge: Cambridge University Press, 1999).

Drinan, Robert F., and Kuo, Teresa T., 'The 1991 Battle for Human Rights in China', *Human Rights Quarterly*, 14/1 (1992).

Dumbrell, John, *The Carter Presidency: A Re-Evaluation* (Manchester: Manchester University Press, 1993).

—— *American Foreign Policy: Carter to Clinton* (New York: St Martin's Press, 1997).

Dunne, Tim, and Wheeler, Nicholas J. (eds.), *Human Rights in Global Politics* (Cambridge: Cambridge University Press, 1999).

Economy, Elizabeth, and Oksenberg, Michel (eds.), *China Joins the World: Progress and Prospects* (New York: Council on Foreign Relations, 1999).

Edwards, R. Randle, Henkin, Louis, and Nathan, Andrew J., *Human Rights in Contemporary China* (New York: Columbia University Press, 1986).

Egeland, Jan, *Impotent Superpower–Potent Small State: Potentials and Limitations of Human Rights Objectives in the Foreign Policies of the United States and Norway* (Oslo: Norwegian University Press, 1988).

Eide, Asbjorn, 'The Sub-Commission on Prevention of Discrimination and Protection of Minorities', in Philip Alston (ed.), *The United Nations and Human Rights: A Critical Appraisal* (Oxford: Oxford University Press, 1992).

Eiichi, Hoshino, 'Human Rights and Development Aid: Japan after the ODA Charter', in Peter Van Ness (ed.), *Debating Human Rights: Critical Essays from the United States and Asia* (London: Routledge, 1999).

Elster, Jon, *The Cement of Society: A Study of Social Order* (Cambridge: Cambridge University Press, 1989).

European Commission, *Building a Comprehensive Partnership with China* (Brussels, 25 Mar. 1998).

—— *A Long-Term Policy for China–Europe Relations* (Brussels, 5 July 1995).

Evans, Peter B., Jacobson, Harold K., and Putman, Robert D. (eds.), *Double-Edged Diplomacy: International Bargaining and Domestic Politics* (Berkeley and Los Angeles: University of California Press, 1993).

Farer, Tom J., and Gaer, Felice, 'The UN and Human Rights: At the End of the Beginning', in Adam Roberts and Benedict Kingsbury (eds.), *United Nations, Divided World* (Oxford: Oxford University Press, 1993).

Feeney, William R., 'China and the Multilateral Economic Institutions', in Samuel, S. Kim (ed.), *China and the World: Chinese Foreign Relations in the Post-Cold War Era* (Boulder, Colo.: Westview Press, 1994).

Fierke, Karen, *Changing Games, Changing Strategies: Critical Investigations in Security* (Manchester: Manchester University Press, 1998).

Findlay, Christopher, and Watson, Andrew, 'Economic Growth and Trade Dependency in China', in David S. G. Goodman and Gerald Segal (eds.), *China Rising: Nationalism and Interdependence* (London: Routledge), 1997.

Finnemore, Martha, 'International Organizations as Teachers of Norms: The United Nations Educational, Scientific, and Cultural Organization and Science Policy', *International Organization*, 47/4 (1993).

—— 'Constructing Norms of Humanitarian Intervention', in Peter Katzenstein (ed.), *The Culture of National Security: Norms and Identity in World Politics* (New York: Columbia University Press, 1996).

—— *National Interests in International Society* (Ithaca, NY: Cornell University Press, 1996).

—— 'Norms, Culture and World Politics: Insights from Sociology's Institutionalism', *International Organization*, 50/2 (1996).

—— and Sikkink, Kathryn, 'International Norm Dynamics and Political Change', *International Organization*, 52/4 (Autumn 1998).

Foot, Rosemary, *The Practice of Power: US Relations with China since 1949* (Oxford: Oxford University Press, 1995).

—— 'Human Rights, Democracy and Development: The Debate in East Asia', *Democratization*, 4/2 (Summer 1997).

Ford Foundation and China, report no. 488 (New York, Jan. 1991).

Forsythe, David P., 'The United Nations and Human Rights, 1945–1985', *Political Science Quarterly*, 100 (Summer 1985).

—— *Human Rights and U.S Foreign Policy: Congress Reconsidered* (Gainesville, Fl.: University of Florida Press, 1988).

—— (ed.), *Human Rights and Development* (London: Macmillan 1989).

—— *The Internationalization of Human Rights* (Lexington, Mass.: Lexington Books, 1991).

Franck, Thomas, *The Power of Legitimacy among Nations* (New York: Oxford University Press, 1990).

—— *Fairness in International Law and Institutions* (Oxford: Oxford University Press, 1995).

Freeman, Michael, 'Human Rights and Real Cultures: Towards a Dialogue on "Asian Values" ', *Netherlands Quarterly of Human Rights*, 16/1 (1998).

Friedman, Edward (ed.), T*he Politics of Democratization: Generalizing East Asian Experiences* (Boulder, Colo.: Westview Press, 1994).

Frost, Mervyn, *Ethics in International Relations* (Cambridge: Cambridge University Press, 1996).

Garrett, Banning N., and Glaser, Bonnie S., 'Chinese Perspectives on Nuclear Arms Control', *International Security*, 20/3 (Winter 1995/6).

Gelatt, Timothy, 'Law Reform in the PRC after June 4', *Journal of Chinese Law*, 3 (1989).

Ghanea-Hercock, Nazali, 'Appendix I: A Review of the 54th Session of the Commission on Human Rights', *Netherlands Quarterly of Human Rights*, 16/3 (1998).

Gillies, David, *Between Principle and Practice: Human Rights in North–South Relations* (Montreal: McGill–Queen's University Press, 1996).

Godement, François, *The Downsizing of Asia* (London: Routledge, 1999).

Goldman, Merle, 'Human Rights in the People's Republic of China', *Daedalus* (Fall 1983).

—— *Sowing the Seeds of Democracy in China: Political Reform in the Deng Xiaoping Era* (Cambridge, Mass.: Harvard University Press, 1994).

—— 'Politically-Engaged Intellectuals in the Deng-Jiang Era: A Changing Relationship with the Party-State', *China Quarterly*, 145 (Mar. 1996).

—— 'Politically-Engaged Intellectuals in the 1990s', *China Quarterly*, Special Issue, 'The People's Republic of China after 50 Years', 159 (Sept. 1999).

Goldstein, Avery, 'Great Expectations: Interpreting China's Arrival', *International Security*, 22/3 (Winter 1997/8).

Goldstein, Judith, and Keohane, Robert O. (eds.), *Ideas and Foreign Policy: Beliefs, Institutions, and Political Change* (Ithaca, NY: Cornell University Press, 1993).

Gong, Gerrit W., 'China's Entry Into International Society', in Hedley Bull and Adam Watson (eds.), *The Expansion of International Society* (Oxford: Oxford University Press, 1984).

—— *The Standard of 'Civilization' in International Society* (Oxford: Oxford University Press, 1984).

Goodman, David S. G., *Deng Xiaoping and the Chinese Revolution: A Political Biography* (London: Routledge, 1994).

—— and Segal, Gerald (eds.), *China Rising: Nationalism and Interdependence* (London: Routledge, 1997).

Guest, Iain, *Behind the Disappearances: Argentina's Dirty War against Human Rights and the United Nations* (Philadelphia: University of Pennsylvania Press, 1990).

Harding, Harry, *China's Second Revolution: Reform after Mao* (Washington: Brookings Institution, 1987).

—— *A Fragile Relationship: The United States and China since 1972* (Washington: Brookings Institution, 1992).

—— 'China's Cooperative Behaviour', in Thomas W. Robinson and David Shambaugh (eds.), *Chinese Foreign Policy: Theory and Practice* (Oxford: Oxford University Press, 1994).

Hasenclever, Andreas, Mayer, Peter, and Rittberger, Volker, *Theories of International Regimes* (Cambridge: Cambridge University Press, 1997).

He Baogang, *The Democratization of China* (London: Routledge, 1996).

Herman, Robert G., 'Identity, Norms and National Security: The Soviet Foreign Policy Revolution and the End of the Cold War', in Peter Katzenstein (ed.), *The Culture of National Security: Norms and Identity in World Politics* (New York: Columbia University Press, 1996).

Hoffmann, Stanley, *Duties beyond Borders: On the Limits and Possibilities of Ethical International Politics* (Syracuse, NY: Syracuse University Press, 1981).

Honneth, Axel, *The Struggle for Recognition: The Moral Grammar of Social Conflicts* (Cambridge: Polity Press, 1995).

Hooper, Beverley, review article, *Australian Journal of Chinese Affairs*, 10 (1983).

Howe, Geoffrey, *Visit to China by the Delegation led by Lord Howe of Aberavon* (London: HMSO, 1993).

Howell, Jude, *China Opens its Doors* (Hemel Hempstead: Harvester/Wheatsheaf, 1993).

—— 'Post-Beijing Reflections: Creating Ripples but not Waves in China', *Women's Studies International Forum*, 20/2 (1997).

—— 'Prospects for Village Self-Governance in China', *Journal of Peasant Studies*, 25/3 (Apr. 1998).

Hughes, Christopher, 'China and Liberalism Globalised' *Millennium: Journal of International Studies*, 24/3 (1995).

—— 'Globalisation and Nationalism: Squaring the Circle in Chinese International Relations Theory', *Millennium*, 26/1 (1997).

Human Rights in China, *Promoting Three Basic Freedoms* (New York, Sept. 1997).

—— *From Principle to Pragmatism: Can 'Dialogue' Improve China's Human Rights Situation?* (New York, June 1998).

—— *Report on Implementation of CEDAW in the People's Republic of China* (New York, Dec. 1998).

—— *Not Welcome at the Party: Behind the 'Clean-up' of China's Cities* (New York, Sept. 1999).

Human Rights Watch, *Death By Default: A Policy of Fatal Neglect in China's State Orphanages* (New York, Jan. 1996).

—— *Chinese Diplomacy, Western Hypocrisy and the U.N. Human Rights Commission* (New York, Mar. 1997).

—— *China: State Control of Religion* (New York, Oct. 1997).

—— and Tibet Information Network, *Cutting off the Serpent's Head: Tightening Control in Tibet, 1994–1995* (New York, Mar. 1996).

Huntingdon, Samuel P., *Political Order in Changing Societies* (New Haven, Conn.: Yale University Press, 1968).

—— *The Third Wave: Democratization in the Late Twentieth Century* (Norman, Ok.: University of Oklahoma Press, 1991).

—— *The Clash of Civilizations and the Remaking of World Order* (New York: Simon & Schuster, 1996).

Hurrell, Andrew, 'Power, Principles and Prudence: Protecting Human Rights in a Deeply Divided World', in Tim Dunne and Nicholas J. Wheeler (eds.), *Human Rights in Global Politics* (Cambridge: Cambridge University Press, 1999).

Ikenberry, G. John, and Kupchan, Charles A., 'Socialization and Hegemonic Power', *International Organization*, 33/3 (Summer 1990).

Jacobson, Harold K., and Oksenberg, Michel, *China's Participation in the IMF, the World Bank, and GATT: Toward a Global Economic Order* (Ann Arbor, Mich.: University of Michigan Press, 1990).

Johnston, Alastair Iain, 'Learning versus Adaptation: Explaining Change in Chinese Arms Control Policy in the 1980s and 1990s', *China Journal*, 35 (Jan. 1996).

Jones, Sidney, ' "Asian" Human Rights, Economic Growth, and United States Policy', *Current History* (Dec. 1996).

Katzenstein, Peter J. (ed.), *The Culture of National Security: Norms and Identity in World Politics* (New York: Columbia University Press, 1996).

Kaufmann, Chaim D., and Pape, Robert A., 'Explaining Costly International Moral Action', *International Organization*, 53/4 (Autumn 1999).

Keck, Margaret, and Sikkink, Kathryn, *Activists beyond Borders: Advocacy Networks in International Politics* (Ithaca, NY: Cornell University Press, 1998).

Keith, Ronald C., *China's Struggle for the Rule of Law* (New York: St Martin's Press, 1994).

—— 'The New Relevance of "Rights and Interests": China's Changing Human Rights Theories', *China Information*, 10/2 (Autumn 1995).

Kent, Ann, *Human Rights in the People's Republic of China: National and International Dimensions* (Canberra: Peace Research Centre, Australian National University, 1990).

—— 'Waiting for Rights: China's Human Rights and China's Constitutions, 1949–1989', *Human Rights Quarterly*, 13/2 (1991).

—— *Between Freedom and Subsistence: China and Human Rights* (Hong Kong: Oxford University Press, 1995).

—— 'China and the International Human Rights Regime: A Case Study of Multilateral Monitoring, 1989–1994', *Human Rights Quarterly*, 17/1 (1995).

—— 'China, International Organizations and Regimes: The ILO as a Case Study in Organizational Learning', *Pacific Affairs*, 70/4 (Winter 1997–8).

—— *China, the United Nations, and Human Rights: The Limits of Compliance* (Philadelphia: University of Pennsylvania Press, 1999).

—— 'Form over Substance: The Australia–China Bilateral Human Rights Dialogue', *China Rights Forum* (Fall 1999).

Keohane, Robert O., and Milner, Helen V. (eds.), *Internationalization and Domestic Politics* (New York: Cambridge University Press, 1996).

Kesavan, K.V., 'Japan and the Tiananmen Square Incident: Aspects of the Bilateral Relationship', *Asian Survey*, 30/7 (July 1990).

Kim, Samuel S., 'Behavioural Dimensions of Chinese Multilateral Diplomacy', *China Quarterly*, 72 (Dec. 1977).

—— *China, the United Nations and World Order* (Princeton: Princeton University Press, 1979).

—— 'Whither Post-Mao Chinese Global Policy?', *International Organization*, 35/3 (Summer 1981).

—— 'Thinking Globally in Post-Mao China', *Journal of Peace Research*, 27/2 (1990).

—— 'International Organizations in Chinese Foreign Policy', *Annals of the American Academy of Political and Social Science*, 519 (Jan. 1992).

—— (ed.), *China and the World: Chinese Foreign Relations in the Post-Cold War Era* (Boulder, Colo.: Westview Press, 1994).

—— 'China's International Organizational Behaviour', in Thomas W. Robinson and David Shambaugh (eds.), *Chinese Foreign Policy: Theory and Practice* (Oxford: Oxford University Press, 1994).

—— (ed.), *China and the World: Chinese Foreign Policy Faces the New Millennium* (Boulder, Colo.: Westview Press, 1998).

Kissinger, Henry, *Years of Upheaval* (London: Weidenfeld & Nicolson, 1982).

Klaauw, Johnannes van der, 'European Union', *Netherlands Quarterly of Human Rights*, 16/2 (June 1998).

Klotz, Audie, *Norms in International Relations: The Struggle against Apartheid* (Ithaca, NY: Cornell University Press, 1995).

Koh, Harold Hongju, 'Why do Nations Obey International Law?' *Yale Law Journal*, 106 (1997).

—— US Department of State, 'On-the-Record briefing on US-China Human Rights Dialogue', Washington, 13 Jan. 1999, Internet edn.

—— 'Promoting Human Rights in the Pursuit of Peace: Assessing 20 years of US Human Rights Policy', remarks before the US Institute of Peace, Washington, 30 May 1999, Internet edn.

Korey, William, *NGOs and the Universal Declaration of Human Rights* (New York: St Martin's Press, 1998).

Krasner, Stephen D., 'Compromising Westphalia', *International Security*, 20/3 (Winter 1995–6).

—— *Sovereignty: Organized Hypocrisy* (Princeton: Princeton University Press, 1999).

Kratochwil, Friedrich, 'The Embarrassment of Changes: Neo-Realism as the Science of Realpolitik without Politics', *Review of International Studies*, 19 (1993).

Lampton, David, M., 'America's China Policy in the Age of the Finance Minister: Clinton Ends Linkage', *China Quarterly*, 139 (Sept. 1994).

—— 'China Policy in Clinton's First Year', in James R. Lilley and Wendell L. Willkie II (eds.), *Beyond MFN: Trade with China and American Interests* (Washington: American Enterprise Institute, 1994).

Lardy, Nicholas R., *China's Entry into the World Economy: Implications for Northeast Asia and the United States* (London: UPA for the Asia Society, 1987).

—— 'Chinese Foreign Trade', *China Quarterly*, 131 (Sept. 1992).

—— *China in the World Economy* (London: Longman, 1994).

Lauren, Paul Gordon, *The Evolution of International Human Rights: Visions Seen* (Philadelphia: University of Pennsylvania Press, 1998).

Lawyers' Committee for Human Rights, *Criminal Justice with Chinese Characteristics* (New York, 1994).

Lawyers' Committee for Human Rights, *In the National Interest: 1996 Quadrennial Report on Human Rights and U.S. Foreign Policy* (New York, 1996).

—— *Opening to Reform? An Analysis of China's Revised Criminal Procedure Law* (New York, Oct. 1996).

—— *Lawyers in China: Obstacles to Independence and the Defense of Rights* (New York, Mar. 1998).

Legro, Jeffrey W., 'Which Norms Matter? Revisiting the "Failure" of Internationalism', *International Organization*, 51/1 (Winter 1997).

Lilley, James R., and Willkie, Wendell L., II (eds.), *Beyond MFN: Trade with China and American Interests* (Washington: American Enterprise Institute, 1994).

Liu Hainian, 'Yi Fa Zhi Guo Yu Jingshen Wenming Jianshe' [Rule of Law and Cultural and Ideological Progress], *Faxue Yanjiu*, 112 (Sept. 1997).

Lubman, Stanley B. (ed.), *China's Legal Reforms* (Oxford: Oxford University Press, 1996).

Lynch, Daniel C., 'Dilemmas of "Thought Work" in *Fin de siècle* China', *China Quarterly* 157 (Mar. 1999).

Lyons, Gene M., and Mastanduno, Michael (eds.), *Beyond Westphalia? State Sovereignty and International Intervention* (Baltimore, Md.: Johns Hopkins University Press, 1995).

McGoldrick, Dominic, *The Human Rights Committee: Its Role in the Development of the International Covenant on Civil and Political Rights* (Oxford: Oxford University Press, 1994).

Mahbubani, Kishore, 'The Dangers of Decadence: What the Rest can Teach the West', *Foreign Affairs*, 72/4 (1993).

Maher, Robin M., and Weissbrodt, David, 'The 41st Session of the UN Sub-Commission on the Prevention of Discrimination and Protection of Minorities', *Human Rights Quarterly*, 12/2 (1990).

Malik, J. Mohan, 'Peking's Response to the Gulf Crisis', *Issues and Studies*, 27/9 (Sept. 1991).

Mann, James, *About Face: A History of America's Curious Relationship with China, from Nixon to Clinton* (New York: Alfred Knopf, 1999).

Mansfield, Edward, D., and Snyder, Jack, 'Democratization and the Danger of War', *International Security*, 20/1 (Summer 1995).

Martin, Lisa L., *Coercive Cooperation: Explaining Multilateral Economic Sanctions* (Princeton: Princeton University Press, 1992).

Maynard, Edwin S., 'The Bureaucracy and Implementation of US Human Rights Policy', *Human Rights Quarterly*, 11/2 (1989).

Mellbourn, Anders, and Svensson, Marina, *Swedish Human Rights Training in China: An Assessment*, report prepared for the Swedish International Development Cooperation Agency, Feb. 1999.

Moller, Nicholas H., 'The World Bank: Human Rights, Democracy and Governance', *Netherlands Quarterly of Human Rights*, 15/1 (1997).

Moody, Peter R., 'Asian Values', *Journal of International Affairs*, 50/1 (Summer 1996).

Moravcsik, Andrew, 'Taking Preferences Seriously: A Liberal Theory of International Politics', *International Organization*, 51/4 (Autumn 1997).

Mower, A. Glenn, Jr., *Human Rights and American Foreign Policy* (Westport, Conn.: Greenwood Press, 1987).

Mullerson, Rein, *Human Rights Diplomacy* (London: Routledge, 1997).

Nakai, Yoshifumi (ed.), *China's Roadmap as Seen in the 15th Party Congress* (Tokyo: Institute of Developing Economies, Mar. 1998).

Nathan, Andrew J., 'Political Rights in Chinese Constitutions', in R. Randle Edwards, Louis Henkin, and Andrew J. Nathan, *Human Rights in Contemporary China* (New York: Columbia University Press, 1986).

—— 'Human Rights in Chinese Foreign Policy', *China Quarterly*, 139 (Sept. 1994).

—— *China's Transition* (New York: Columbia University Press, 1997).

—— 'Getting Human Rights Right', *Washington Quarterly*, 20/2 (1997).

—— 'China and the International Human Rights Regime', in Elizabeth Economy, and Michel Oksenberg (eds.), *China Joins the World: Progress and Prospects* (New York: Council on Foreign Relations, 1999).

—— and Ross, Robert S., *The Great Wall and the Empty Fortress: China's Search for Security* (New York: W. W. Norton, 1997).

Naughton, Barry, 'The Foreign Policy Implications of China's Economic Development Strategy', in Thomas W. Robinson and David Shambaugh (eds.), *Chinese Foreign Policy: Theory and Practice* (Oxford: Oxford University Press, 1994).

Oberdorfer, Don, *The Two Koreas: A Contemporary History* (Reading, Mass.: Addison-Wesley, 1997).

Orentlicher, Diane F., and Gelatt, Timothy A., 'Public Law, Private Actors: The Impact of Human Rights on Business Investors in China', *Journal of International Law and Business* (Fall 1993).

Oye, Kenneth A., Lieber, Robert J., and Rothchild, Donald (eds.), *Eagle in a New World: American Grand Strategy in the Post-Cold War Era* (New York: Harper Collins, 1992).

Parker, Penny, and Weissbrodt, David, 'Major Developments at the UN Commission on Human Rights', *Human Rights Quarterly*, 13/4 (1991).

Pearson, Margaret M., 'China's Integration into the International Trade and Investment Regime', in Elizabeth Economy and Michel Oksenberg (eds.), *China Joins the World: Progress and Prospects* (New York: Council on Foreign Relations, 1999).

Pei, Minxin, *From Reform to Revolution: The Demise of Communism in China and the Soviet Union* (Cambridge, Mass.: Harvard University Press, 1994).

—— 'Citizens v. Mandarins: Administrative Litigation in China', *China Quarterly*, 152 (Dec. 1997).

—— 'Is China Democratizing?', *Foreign Affairs*, 77/1 (Jan–Feb. 1998).

—— 'Is China Unstable?', e-mail distribution by Foreign Policy Research Institute's Asia Program, Philadelphia, 2 July 1999.

—— 'Will China Become Another Indonesia?', *Foreign Policy* (Fall 1999).

Pfluger, Friedbert, 'Human Rights Unbound: Carter's Human Rights Policy Reassessed', *Presidential Studies Quarterly*, 19/4 (Fall 1989).

Pitts, Joe W. Chip, III, and Weissbrodt, David, 'Major Developments at the UN Commission on Human Rights in 1992', *Human Rights Quarterly*, 15/ 1 (1993).

Rack, Reinhard, and Lausegger, Stefan, 'The Role of the European Parliament: Past and Future', in Philip Alston (ed.), *The EU and Human Rights* (Oxford: Oxford University Press, 1999).

Raymond, Gregory A., 'Problems and Prospects in the Study of International Norms', *Mershon International Studies Review*, 41, supp. 2 (Nov. 1997).

Reierson, Karen, and Weissbrodt, David, 'The Forty-Third Session of the UN Sub-Commission on Prevention of Discrimination and Protection of Minorities: The Sub-Commission under Scrutiny', *Human Rights Quarterly*, 14/2 (1992).

Reisman, W. Michael, 'Sovereignty and Human Rights in Contemporary International Law', *American Journal of International Law*, 84 (Oct. 1990).

—— 'The United States and International Institutions', *Survival*, 41/4 (Winter 1999–2000).

Risse, Thomas, Ropp, Stephen C., and Sikkink, Kathryn (eds.), *The Power of Human Rights: International Norms and Domestic Change* (Cambridge: Cambridge University Press, 1999).

Risse-Kappen, Thomas (ed.), *Bringing Transnational Relations back in: Non-State Actors, Domestic Structures and International Institutions* (Cambridge: Cambridge University Press, 1995).

Roberts, Adam, and Kingsbury, Benedict (eds.), *United Nations, Divided World* (Oxford: Oxford University Press, 1993).

Robinson, Thomas W., and Shambaugh, David (eds.), *Chinese Foreign Policy: Theory and Practice* (Oxford: Oxford University Press, 1994).

Rosen, Stanley, 'Dissent and Tolerance in Chinese Society', *Current History*, 87/530 (Sept. 1988).

Rosenau, James N., *Along the Domestic–Foreign Frontier: Exploring Governance in a Turbulent World* (Cambridge: Cambridge University Press, 1997).

Ross, Robert S., 'The Bush Administration and China: The Development of a Post-Cold War China Policy', in William T. Tow (ed.), *Building Sino-American Relations: An Analysis for the 1990s* (New York: Paragon House, 1991).

—— 'National Security, Human Rights, and Domestic Politics: The Bush Administration and China', in Kenneth Oye, Robert J. Lieber, and Donald Rothchild (eds.), *Eagle in a New World: American Grand Strategy in the Post-Cold War Era* (New York: Harper Collins, 1992).

—— *Negotiating Cooperation: The United States and China, 1969–1989* (Stanford, Calif.: Stanford University Press, 1995).

Rozman, Gilbert, 'China's Quest for Great Power Identity', *Orbis*, 43/3 (Summer 1999).

Ruggie, John G., 'Human Rights and the Future International Community', *Daedalus* (Fall 1983).

—— *Constructing the World Polity* (London: Routledge, 1998).

Sato, Yasunobu, 'New Directions in Japanese Foreign Policy: Promoting Human Rights and Democracy in Asia-ODA Perspective', in Edward Friedman (ed.), *The Politics of Democratization: Generalizing East Asian Experiences* (Boulder, Colo.: Westview Press, 1994).

Schneider, Gerald, and Weitsman, Patricia A., *Enforcing Cooperation: Risky States and Intergovernmental Management of Conflict* (Basingstoke: Macmillan, 1997).

Schoenhals, Michael (guest ed.), 'Selections from Propaganda Trends: Organ of the CCP Central Propaganda Department', *Chinese Law and Government* (Winter 1991–2).

—— *Doing Things with Words in Chinese Politics* (Berkeley, Calif.: Institute of East Asian Studies, University of California Center for Chinese Studies, 1992).

Seymour, James D., 'Human Rights in Chinese Foreign Relations' in Samuel S. Kim (ed.), *China and the World: Chinese Foreign Relations in the Post-Cold War Era* (Boulder, Colo.: Westview Press, 1994).

—— 'The Wheel of Law and the Rule of Law', *China Rights Forum* (Fall 1999).

Shambaugh, David, 'China and Europe', *Annals of the American Academy of Political and Social Science* (Jan. 1992).

Shichor, Yitzhak, 'China and the Role of the United Nations in the Middle East', *Asian Survey*, 31/3 (Mar. 1991).

Shih, Chih-yu, 'Contending Theories of "Human Rights with Chinese Characteristics" ', *Issues and Studies*, 29/11 (Nov. 1993).

Shirk, Susan L., 'Human Rights: What about China?' *Foreign Policy*, 29 (Winter 1977–8).

—— *The Political Logic of Economic Reform in China* (Berkeley and Los Angeles: University of California Press, 1993).

Shue, Henry, *Basic Rights: Subsistence, Affluence and US Foreign Policy* (Princeton: Princeton University Press, 1980).

Sikkink, Kathryn, *Ideas and Institutions: Developmentalism in Brazil and Argentina* (Ithaca, NY: Cornell University Press, 1991).

—— 'The Power of Principled Ideas: Human Rights Policies in the United States and Western Europe', in Judith Goldstein and Robert O. Keohane (eds.), *Ideas and Foreign Policy: Beliefs, Institutions, and Political Change* (Ithaca, NY: Cornell University Press, 1993).

Simma, Bruno, Aschenbrenner, Jo Beatrix, and Schulte, Constanze, 'Human Rights Considerations in the Development Co-operation Activities of the EC', in Philip Alston (ed.), *The EU and Human Rights* (Oxford: Oxford University Press, 1999).

Spence, Jonathan, *The Search for Modern China* (New York: W. W. Norton, 1990).

Steiner, Henry J., and Alston, Philip, *International Human Rights in Context: Law, Politics, Morals* (Oxford: Oxford University Press, 1996).

Stokke, Olav (ed.), *Aid and Political Conditionality* (London: Frank Cass, 1995).

Sullivan, Michael J., 'Development and Political Repression: China's Human Rights Policy since 1989', *Bulletin of Concerned Asian Scholars*, 27/4 (1995).

Swaine, Michael D., and Johnston, Alastair, Iain, 'China and Arms Control

Institutions', in Elizabeth Economy and Michael Oksenberg (eds.), *China Joins the World: Progress and Prospects* (New York: Council on Foreign Relations, 1999).

Tang, James T. H. (ed.), *Human Rights and International Relations in the Asia-Pacific Region* (London: Pinter, 1995).

Thomas, Daniel C., 'The Helsinki Accords and Political Change in Eastern Europe', in Thomas Risse, Stephen C. Ropp and Kathryn Sikkink (eds.), *The Power of Human Rights: International Norms and Domestic Change* (Cambridge: Cambridge University Press, 1999).

Tolley, Howard, Jr., *The U.N. Commission on Human Rights* (Boulder, Colo.: Westview Press, 1987).

Tow, William T. (ed.), *Building Sino-American Relations: An Analysis for the 1990s* (New York: Paragon House, 1991).

Tsang, Steve Y.-S., *Hong Kong: Appointment with China* (London: Tauris, 1997).

Tucker, Nancy Bernkopf, 'A Precarious Balance: Clinton and China', *Current History* (Sept. 1998).

Turack, Daniel C., 'The Clinton Administration's Response to China's Human Rights Record', *Tulsa Journal of Comparative and International Law* (Fall 1995), Internet edn.

US House of Representatives, *Human Rights Conditions in Selected Countries and the U.S. Response* (prepared for the Subcommittee on International Organizations, by Congressional Research Service, Washington: US Government Printing Office, 1978).

US Office of the Press Secretary, White House, Executive Order, 'Implementation of Human Rights Treaties', 10 Dec. 1998.

—— White House, 'Remarks by the President in Address on China and the National Interest', 24 Oct. 1997.

Van Ness, Peter, 'China as a Third World State: Foreign Policy and Official National Identity', in Lowell Dittmer and Samuel S. Kim (eds.), *China's Quest for National Identity* (Ithaca, NY: Cornell University Press, 1993).

—— 'Addressing the Human Rights Issue in Sino-American Relations', *Journal of International Affairs*, 49/2 (Winter 1996).

—— (ed.), *Debating Human Rights: Critical Essays from the United States and Asia* (London: Routledge, 1999).

—— and Raichur, Satish, 'Dilemmas of Socialist Development: An Analysis of Strategic Lines in China, 1949–1981', in The Bulletin of Concerned Asian Scholars (ed.), *China from Mao to Deng* (Armonk, NY: M. E. Sharpe, 1983).

Vincent, R. J., *Human Rights and International Relations* (Cambridge: Cambridge University Press, 1986).

Waller, Peter P., 'Aid and Conditionality: The Case of Germany, with Particular Reference to Kenya', in Olav Stokke (ed.), *Aid and Political Conditionality* (London: Frank Cass, 1995).

Waller, Wynne P., and Ide, Marianne E., 'Trends: China and Human Rights', *Public Opinion Quarterly*, 59/1 (1995).

Wan, Ming, 'Human Rights and Sino-US Relations: Policies and Changing Realities', *Pacific Review*, 10/2 (1997).

Weber, Cynthia, *Simulating Sovereignty: Intervention, the State, and Symbolic Exchange* (Cambridge: Cambridge University Press, 1995).

Wendt, Alexander, 'Constructing International Politics', *International Security*, 20/1 (Summer, 1995).

White, Gordon, *Riding the Tiger: The Politics of Economic Reform in Post-Mao China* (Basingstoke: Macmillan 1993).

Whitehead, Lawrence (ed.), *International Dimensions of Democratization* (Oxford: Oxford University Press, 1996).

Womack, Brantly (ed.), *Contemporary Chinese Politics in Historical Perspective* (New York: Cambridge University Press, 1991).

Woods, Ngaire, 'Good Governance in International Organizations', *Global Governance*, 5 (1999).

World Bank, *Governance and Development* (Washington: 1992).

Xin Chunying, *Chinese Legal System and Current Legal Reform* [in Chinese and in English] (Konrad–Adenauer–Stiftung Occasional Papers, Beijing: Fa Lu Chubanshe, 1999).

Yahuda, Michael B., *Hong Kong: China's Challenge* (London: Routledge, 1997).

Yu Haocheng, 'On Human Rights and their Guarantee by Law', in Michael C. Davis (ed.), *Human Rights and Chinese Values: Legal, Philosophical, and Political Perspectives* (Hong Kong: Oxford University Press, 1995).

Yuan, Jing-dong, 'Sanctions, Domestic Politics, and U.S. China Policy', *Issues and Studies*, 33/10 (Oct. 1997).

Zhang, Yongjin, *China in the International System, 1918–20: The Middle Kingdom at the Periphery* (Basingstoke: Macmillan 1991).

—— 'China and UN Peacekeeping: From Condemnation to Participation', *International Peacekeeping*, 3/3 (Autumn 1996).

—— *China in International Society since 1949: Alienation and Beyond* (Basingstoke: St Antony's/Macmillan, 1998).

Zhao Jianwen, 'Guoji Renquan Fa de Jishi' [Universal Declaration of Human Rights], *Faxue Yanjiu*, 121 (Mar. 1999).

Zhong Wenhui, 'China's Human Rights Development in the 1990s', *Journal of Contemporary China*, 8 (Winter–Spring 1995).

Zhou Wei, 'The Study of Human Rights in the People's Republic of China', in James T. H. Tang (ed.), *Human Rights and International Relations in the Asia-Pacific Region* (London: Pinter, 1995).

Zhu Feng, 'Human Rights Problems and Current Sino-American Relations' in Peter Van Ness (ed.), *Debating Human Rights: Critical Essays from the United States and Asia* (London: Routledge, 1999).

Zweig, David, 'Sino-American Relations and Human Rights: June 4 and the Changing Nature of a Bilateral Relationship', in William T. Tow (ed.), *Building Sino-American Relations: An Analysis for the 1990s* (New York: Paragon House, 1991).

UNPUBLISHED MATERIALS

Alderson, Kai, 'Educating Leviathan: Socialization and the State System', D.Phil. thesis (Oxford, 1998).

Clark, Ann Marie, 'Strong Principles, Strengthening Practices: Amnesty International and Three Cases of Change in International Human Rights Standards', Ph.D. thesis (Minnesota, 1995).

Dicker, Richard, 'The Prospects for Effective Human Rights Monitoring: China, a Case Study', paper presented at a UN 50th Anniversary Conference on 'The Rise of East Asia and the UN', co-sponsored by the ROK Committee for the 50th Anniversary of the UN and the International Institute for Strategic Studies, London, held in Seoul, 12–14 June 1995.

Fung, Daniel R., 'Hong Kong: China's Guide to the 21st Century: The Sherpa Paradigm', paper given at Asian Studies Centre conference, St Antony's College, Oxford, May 1998.

Howe, Geoffrey, The Rt Hon. Lord Howe of Aberavon, Opening Speech at Amnesty International London Seminar on Human Rights in China, 9 Sept. 1996.

Kato, Yuko, 'Determinants of Japanese Responses to Tiananmen: June 1989 to August 1991', M.Phil. thesis (Oxford, 1992).

Keiko, Karube, 'The Influence of Human Rights on International Politics: A Case Study of US Relations with the People's Republic of China, 1977–1992', Ph.D. thesis (Virginia, 1995).

Okubo, Aki, 'The "Asian Values" Debate in Singapore and Malaysia: Motives for Challenging Universal Human Rights in the 1990s', M.Litt. thesis (Oxford, 1998).

Richardson, Munro C., 'From Warmaker to Peacekeeper: China's Role in the Resolution of the Cambodian Conflict', M.Phil. thesis (Oxford, 1996).

Sullivan, Michael J., 'Democracy and Developmentalism: Contending Struggles over Political Change in Dengist China', Ph.D. thesis (Wisconsin, 1995).

Index